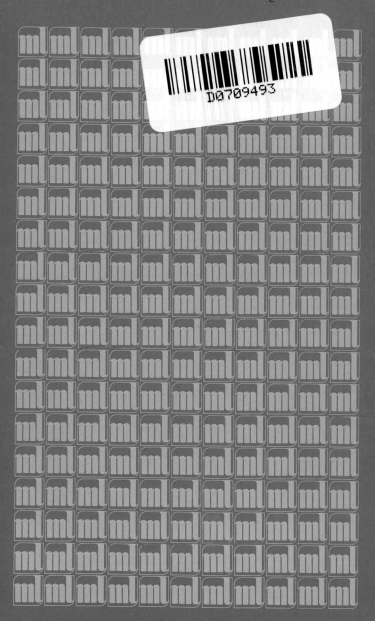

THE BUDDHIST TRADITION

in India, China, & Japan

READINGS IN ORIENTAL THOUGHT

GENERAL EDITOR: WM. THEODORE DE BARY

THE BUDDHIST TRADITION *in*

India, China & Japan

Edited by **WM. THEODORE DE BARY**

*with the collaboration of Yoshito Hakeda
and Philip Yampolsky*

and with contributions by
A. L. Basham, Leon Hurvitz, and Ryusaku Tsunoda

THE MODERN LIBRARY · NEW YORK

The editor wishes to thank the following for permission to reprint material included in this volume:

Bruno Cassirer (Publishers) Ltd., Oxford, and Harper & Row, New York—*Buddhist Texts Through the Ages*, ed. by Edward Conze (1954).

Columbia University Press—*Introduction to Oriental Civilizations: Sources of Japanese Tradition* (1958), *Sources of Indian Tradition* (1958), *Sources of Chinese Tradition* (1960), ed. by W. T. de Bary and others.

Harvard University Press—*Nichiren, The Buddhist Prophet* by Anezaki, Masaharu (1930).

To

RYUSAKU TSUNODA

PREFACE

The idea of this book is not so much to give an account of Buddhism in its historical development as to let Buddhists give an account of themselves. Excerpts are given here from basic scriptures and the major writings of Buddhist thinkers, with necessary background essays and commentary. For the most part these are texts and thinkers recognized by Buddhists themselves as representing the mainstream of Buddhist thought and practice. There is, of course, an enormous diversity within Buddhism and no fixed standard of orthodoxy. Nevertheless, even differing conceptions of the authentic tradition—and each school has some notion of orthodoxy—reveal a common ground of discussion. This is what we have tried to present here.

By extending itself over so many culture areas of South and East Asia, Buddhism has established a greater universality than any other religion in that part of the world. It has behind it a long history and, considering the difficulties of transmission and preservation, a remarkable degree of continuity. Over this great span of time and space, however, discontinuities and discrepancies also appear. To the specialist these differences may sometimes seem more significant than the similarities, and he may even doubt whether one can speak of a single Buddhist tradition. Be this as it may, for the reader making a first approach to Buddhism it will be more useful to follow its growth in areas where the sense of a common tradition is strong and where change takes place in some comprehensible relation to what has gone before. For these purposes the line of development from India through China to Japan may provide a relatively coherent picture.

At the same time these great civilizations of Asia have also served as the major diffusion centers of Buddhism. In other words, the central importance of India, China, and Japan in the development of Buddhism also reflects the very high level of culture which each attained and which each imparted to the further growth and spread of the religion.

It would be wrong to imply, however, that they represent the whole of Buddhism, and one can only regret that in a book of this size the varieties of Buddhism found in Southeast Asia, Tibet and Korea could not be included.

To a considerable extent this book is based on the work done for three volumes of readings, *Sources of Indian Tradition, Sources of Chinese Tradition,* and *Sources of Japanese Tradition,* published by Columbia University Press. We are grateful to the latter for permission to make substantial excerpts from these volumes. The *Sources,* however, were concerned with these civilizations as a whole and Buddhism was dealt with only as one aspect of each. To give a more representative picture of Buddhism itself we have added substantially to the original readings, and in some places have revised and reorganized the earlier materials. The editor wishes to acknowledge the debt owed to three editors of the original *Sources* whose work is still reflected in portions extracted therefrom. They are Wing-tsit Chan, Donald Keene and Burton Watson. The translations from Hsüan-chuang (pages 152–55) and Hui-ssu (pages 160–62) are by Professor Chan. The main contributors to this volume, listed on the title page, have not only translated material in the text; they have brought a great depth of scholarship and acuteness of judgment to their presentation of the material. Their work is identified by their initials alongside the chapter headings in the table of contents.

Wm. Theodore de Bary

New York

EXPLANATORY NOTE

The sources of translations given at the end of each selection are rendered as concisely as possible. Full bibliographical data can be obtained from the list of sources at the end of the book. In the reference at the end of each selection, unless otherwise indicated, the author of the book is the writer whose name precedes the selection. Where excerpts have been taken from existing translations, they have sometimes been adapted or edited in the interests of uniformity with the book as a whole.

Indic words appearing in italics as technical terms or titles of works are rendered in accordance with the standard system of transliteration as found in Louis Renou's *Grammaire Sanskrite* (Paris, 1930), pp. xi–xiii, with the exception that here ś is regularly used for ç. To facilitate pronunciation, other Sanskrit terms and proper names appearing in roman letters are rendered according to the usage of Webster's New International Dictionary, Second Edition, Unabridged, except that here the macron is used to indicate long vowels and the Sanskrit symbols for ś (ç) and ṣ are uniformly transcribed as sh. Similarly, the standard Sanskrit transcription of c is given as ch. In connection with Theravāda Buddhism, the form of technical terms is that of Pali rather than Sanskrit.

The romanization of Chinese terms has been standardized according to the Wade-Giles system; Japanese terms, according to the Hepburn system; and Korean terms, according to the McCune-Reischauer system. In Part Three Chinese philosophical terms appearing in Japanese texts are given in their Japanese readings except where attention is called to the Chinese original.

Chinese and Japanese names are given in their original order, with the family name first and personal name last.

CONTENTS

INTRODUCTION

Buddhism has been known to its followers as both a teaching and a way of deliverance. It has also been a way of life for those so delivered. That is, Buddhism has both freed them from life and freed them for life. In the same way we may speak of Buddhist culture. Though Buddhism has sought to liberate man from the tyranny of culture—from any essential dependence upon it—Buddhism has not failed to manifest its presence in many cultures.

Whether or not Buddhism is also to be considered a religion is a matter of definitions and perhaps of no necessary importance. But many persons do approach it from this standpoint, with a concept of religion based largely on Western experience and yet with genuine eagerness to understand Buddhism in terms of what has been most deeply meaningful in their own spiritual life. To consider, then, the relevance or adequacy of such terms and concepts may not be a useless exercise. Certainly as a way of salvation from oneself and from the world, as an answer to man's finite condition and his longing for transcendence, Buddhism makes claims for itself and claims upon man as final as the other great religions. Yet it also insists on being, in some important ways, different from them.

Since this is a book of readings, it will present Buddhism

primarily as a teaching in the most general sense. Secondarily it will suggest the range of philosophical views and positions which have been developed to explain these basic teachings. To some interpreters the systematic argumentation of Buddhism from well-defined premises has given the impression that it is essentially a metaphysical system, linked to a method of applied psychology. Alfred North Whitehead saw it as "the most colossal example in history of applied metaphysics." He went on to say:

> Christianity took the opposite road. It has always been a religion seeking a metaphysic, in contrast to Buddhism which is a metaphysic generating a religion. The defect of a metaphysic is that it is a neat little system of thought, which oversimplifies its expression of the world. . . .
> Christianity has one advantage. It is difficult to develop Buddhism because Buddhism starts with a clear metaphysical notion and with the doctrines which flow from it. Christianity has retained the easy power of development. It starts with a tremendous notion about the world . . . derived not from a metaphysical doctrine, but . . . from the sayings and actions of certain supreme lives. In the Sermon on the Mount, in the parables, and in their accounts of Christ, the Gospels exhibit a tremendous fact. The doctrine may or may not lie on the surface. But what is primary is the religious fact. The Buddha left a tremendous doctrine. The historical facts about him are subsidiary to the doctrine.[1]

Whitehead's characterization of the two religions is not without some basis: the fact of Christ's appearance in time and the historicity of that event in the context of the Judeo-Christian revelation have a significance for the Christian quite different from Shākyamuni Buddha's appearance in the world. To the Buddhist, history is of little significance compared to the timeless truth manifested by innumerable Buddhas throughout the ages.

There is also a certain plausibility in Whitehead's distinction if taken as applying to what is called the Theravāda or Hīnayāna form of Buddhism, which tends to focus on a clearly stated body of doctrine. But a large segment of Buddhism, including most of the Mahāyāna and Vajrayāna

[1] A. N. Whitehead, *Religion in the Making*, New York: Macmillan, 1926, pp. 49–52.

forms, would insist, along with Whitehead, that a meta-physic is "a neat little system of thought, which oversimplifies its expression of the world," and would reject entirely the notion that such a system could adequately express the truth of Buddhism. Here the focus is on the Buddha, the Awakened One, as the concrete realization of a Truth which cannot be reduced to any precise formula, philosophy, or metaphysic. The Buddha too is primarily a "religious fact," a presence in the world which can like Christ be explained by diverse philosophies but never wholly explained. Were this not the case, Buddhism would indeed have lacked an "easy power of development," and its history in East Asia would have been vastly different, if such it could have had at all.

As the Awakened One, Buddha exemplified to millions of his followers a living Truth, a dynamic wisdom, and an active compassion. It was these qualities which inspired hope and courage in believers who were asked to face the stark reality of man's finitude and his inevitable involvement in suffering. Without the powerful affirmation of his own example, nothing but despair could follow from the pessimistic premises concerning existence which Buddhism takes as its starting point.

In this respect, then, Buddha could accurately be viewed as a kind of savior, and when so conceived he has had for many the attributes of divinity—saving power, omniscience in regard to all essential truth, an all-encompassing compassion, timeless existence, immutable being, unending bliss, etc. But this conception of the Buddha as Supreme Being and Savior has involved difficulties for those reared in Western theological traditions, since both his "being" and his salvific power are understood quite differently from the Judeo-Christian conception of God and the Messiah, and attributes of the latter as Creator, Judge, Redeemer of a chosen people, Father, Son, etc., are largely absent in the Buddha. The multiplicity of the Buddhas and the seeming "polytheistic" character of the religion have only contributed to the confusion.

There are, moreover, other complications. The Buddha himself, according to scripture, took an agnostic position with regard to the existence of God as known in the Indian tradition. He questioned whether the concepts or practices of that tradition offered any fundamental solution to the human predicament. How then can such an agnostic and humanistic teaching become the basis of a devotional cult and an elaborate system of religious worship?

The obvious answer—that theistic notions and superstitious practices attached themselves to Buddhism wherever it went and distorted it beyond recognition—does not wholly dispose of the problem. If we acknowledge that Buddhism was not a set of static truths but had its own power of development, we must beware of the simplistic notion that is so widely held concerning the history of religions: namely, that their original purity and integrity is inevitably lost in the process of historical development. Whether Buddhism's adaptation to another culture, a new mentality or a different religious psychology should be taken as a sign of inner decay or inner strength is a question that must be dealt with in each case according to the evidence. If, for example, the devotees of Amitābha insist that they have abandoned or abrogated none of the traditional doctrines of Buddhism, we are obliged to consider the claim as seriously as we might the fidelity of Christianity to the Old Testament or its claim to have fulfilled rather than abolished the old law. In so doing we may discover a need to go beyond our customary distinctions of "theistic" and "atheistic" in order adequately to represent the living, growing reality of Buddhism.

The Buddha is not God as distinct from man, nor does Buddhism, strictly speaking, have any "theology." It bases itself on neither a revelation from God nor a revelation of God. Its initial orientation is to the human reality rather than a divine reality. Thus there is no possibility of its proceeding from divinely revealed truths and deducing from these authoritative precepts and principles for man through scriptural exegesis or theological reasoning. Buddhism starts rather from an experience of the human condition, an intuition concerning its essential character, and an aspiration to transcend it. Likewise its culmination in the experience of Nirvāna or the realization of Buddhahood, though suggestive of an absolute or transcendent state akin to the divine in other religions, is qualified always, if it can be described at all, by its original premises in regard to the nature of existence. To this extent Whitehead's judgment was certainly right.

We must, however, be equally as guarded in characterizing Buddhism as "humanistic." True, the value of human life is affirmed in that it affords a rare and precious opportunity to attain Nirvāna and Buddhahood. Human virtues such as wisdom, compassion, courage, equanimity, selflessness, etc., are exemplified by the Buddha and his followers, and Buddhist art, especially in painting and sculpture, has inspired peoples of different cultures in the common human ideal of lofty aspiration, contemplative detachment, and compassionate action. Also, according to the Mahāyāna, among all possible existences the human state has a unique potentiality: in man's self-realization the Buddhahood in all things is realized. Man's consciousness is the creative center of the universe.

On the other hand, man's emancipation is achieved at the expense of self, by initially renouncing the claims of his purely human nature. His mortality, his finite being, his incompleteness and therefore his dependence—which he shares with all things—and his liability to suffering and illusion—which he shares with all sentient creatures—are the crucial facts of his existence and the immediate focus of self-reflection. Man's condition is, indeed, hopeless unless he is prepared to accept thorough-going negation of his distinctively human character.

In this respect Confucian humanism offers a useful contrast. Confucius, like Buddha, takes human existence as his starting point. He too sees man in a condition of dependence —of dependence on his parents, family, society and the moral and creative powers of Heaven. Without these, human life cannot come into being. Thus the sustaining of human life inescapably involves relations of dependence and reciprocal obligation. To be human is to fulfill them; to fail them is to cease to be a man. From the Confucian standpoint, there is no room for the renunciation of the ties and obligations through which one is unavoidably involved in the lives of others. Yet from the Buddhist standpoint, self-transcendence cannot be achieved except by first liberating oneself from all that is distinctively human in the Confucian sense and only afterward returning to take up such obligations in a spirit at once detached and compassionate.

In the same way the Buddhist cannot acknowledge either the priority or the ultimacy of human institutions. Political goals, social reform are illusory unless recognized as essentially devoid of substance or value. The precondition of any engagement in achieving them is that one be disengaged from them. No form of human activity has value except insofar as it is based upon or conduces toward self-liberation. To be passionately involved in any political cause is to risk self-delusion: that is, the willful assertion of one's own ideas or desires over those of others. Any violent action, even suicide, only involves one further in bondage to the unreal.

We shall not be surprised, then, to find in these readings so little that can be taken as political or social philosophy in the ordinary sense. Buddhists may be active politically or socially, but their distinctive contribution is not to be seen in any vision of human society, any specific program of social reform, or any definite organization of secular life. It is expressed rather in a spirit or attitude that restrains egotism and self-assertion, rejects political absolutisms and denies the finality of purely human ends.

This does not mean, however, that Buddhism lacks a sense of community. Salvation may be an individual matter, and it is not genuine unless the individual attains essential freedom and autonomy from others. But neither can it be at the expense of others or apart from their salvation. Hence there is a keen sense both of spiritual communion and of fellowship in Buddhism.

Traditionally this sense of community was manifested in the religious orders, consisting of those who had left their homes to follow the way of the Buddha. Many resided in monasteries, and may fairly be called "monks." They underwent an ordination ceremony and undertook to observe disciplinary precepts in a manner somewhat similar to the vows of holy orders in the West. There were, in addition, lay communities or societies whose character and activities varied with time and place. To call the former group "priests," however, would be misleading. The Buddha had set aside the traditional sacrifices of Brahmanism and there is no rem-

nant of the sacerdotal tradition in Buddhism, unless it be
through a process of syncretism by which this traditional
function is reabsorbed even though nonessential.

Likewise there is some question as to how well the term
"church" applies to the religious communities of Buddhism.
Here it may be difficult to generalize or make single com-
parisons; there is a wide range of variation in both Buddhist
and Christian organization from country to country and
period to period. Tibet and China are as different from one
another as are Russia and America. Roughly speaking, however, Buddhist religious organization may be differentiated
from Western churches in the following ways:

There is not the same sense of the church as a corporate
relationship between God and his people, or, until relatively
recent times, of a congregation of members participating in
joint worship. Partly this depends in the West on the conception of God as having entered into a personal relationship with his chosen people, as having vouchsafed them
a special revelation, inspired certain commandments, and
promised them redemption through a Messiah. Partly it reflects the absence in Buddhism of characteristic Roman influences upon ecclesiastical hierarchy and authority, canon
law, and parish organization.

In any case, speaking of the more traditional and orthodox
forms, one may say that the Christian churches consisted of
members subscribing to a stated creed whose places of worship were essentially for the sharing of the sacramental rituals performed there. The Buddhist temple or monastery has
been much more a place for meditation, in its original function, or for practices auxiliary to meditation. The Buddha
seated in quiet contemplation is the typical symbol of this
latter approach to religion, as the crucifix is of Christ's sacrifice on the cross, so central to orthodox Christian worship
and liturgy.

The Buddhist temple, then, corresponds more to the
Christian monastery as a place apart for discipline and meditation, and less to the parish church or diocesan cathedral
with their close involvement in the lay community. But even
as monasteries there is a significant distinction between the
Buddhist and Christian. Buddhist ritual focuses upon the
attainment of a state of mind; the Christian liturgy is a

people's expression of praise and thanksgiving to their Creator and Redeemer. But especially in recent times, with the
decline of the traditional Buddhist meditative disciplines,
the temple has approximated more and more the typical
Christian church as a place of worship.

The Introduction is not the place to continue with a more
detailed comparison of the different types of Buddhism.
That is discussed in the chapters which follow. There the
reader may discover for himself the continuities and discontinuities, the central themes and innumerable variations, the
simple truths and subtle refinements that together have given
Buddhism its universality.

BUDDHISM IN *India*

1

EARLY BUDDHISM

HISTORICAL SETTING

Between the seventh and the fifth centuries B.C. the intellectual life of India was in ferment. It has been pointed out many times that this period was a turning point in the intellectual and spiritual development of the whole world, for it saw the earlier philosophers of Greece, the great Hebrew prophets, Confucius in China, and probably Zarathustra in Persia. In India this crucial period in the world's history was marked on the one hand by the teaching of the Upanishadic sages, who admitted the inspiration of the Vedas and the relative value of Vedic sacrifices, and on the other hand by the appearance of teachers who were less orthodox than they, and who rejected the Vedas entirely. It was at this time that Jainism and Buddhism arose, the most successful of a large number of heterodox systems, each based on a distinctive set of doctrines and each laying down distinctive rules of conduct for winning salvation.

The social background of this great development of heterodoxy cannot be traced as clearly as we would wish from the traditions of Jainism and Buddhism, which have to some extent been worked over by editors of later centuries. But it would appear that heterodoxy flourished most strongly in what is now the state of Bihar and the eastern part of Uttar Pradesh. Here the arrival of Aryan civilization and brahmanical religion seems to have been comparatively recent at the time. The people were probably little affected by the Aryan class system, and the influence of the brāhman was by no means complete. Quite as much attention was devoted to local chthonic gods such as yakshas and nāgas, worshiped at sacred mounds and groves (chaityas), as to the deities of the Aryan pantheon. Cities had arisen, where a class of well-to-do merchants lived in comparative opulence, while the free peasants who made up the majority of the population enjoyed, as far as can be gathered, a somewhat higher standard of living than they do today, when pressure of population and exhaustion of the soil have so gravely impoverished them.

The old tribal structure was disintegrating, and a number of small regional kingdoms had appeared, together with political units of a somewhat different type, which preserved more of the tribal structure, and are generally referred to as "republics" for want of a better word. Most of these republics were of little importance politically, and were dependent on the largest of the kingdoms, Kosala, which controlled most of the eastern part of modern Uttar Pradesh; one such was that of the Shākyas, in the Himalayan foothills, which might well have been forgotten entirely were it not for the fact that the founder of Buddhism was the son of one of its chiefs. The most important of the republics was that generally referred to as the Vajjian Confederacy, of which the largest element was the tribe of the Licchavis; this controlled much of Bihar north of the Ganges, and was apparently governed by a chief who derived his power from a large assembly of tribesmen, and ruled with the aid of a smaller council of lesser chiefs. Much of Bihar south of the Ganges formed the kingdom of Magadha. King Bimbisāra, who ruled Magadha during most of the time in which the Buddha taught, seems to have had more initiative in political organization than his rivals, and managed his little state with more efficiency and closer centralized control than any other chief or king of his time. His son, Ajātasattu, who began to reign some seven years before the Buddha's death, embarked upon a policy of expansion. Magadha soon absorbed the Vajjis and Kosala, and her growth continued until, about two hundred years later, the great emperor Ashoka annexed Kalinga, and Pātaliputra (modern Patna) became the capital of the whole Indian subcontinent except the southern tip.

The development of organized states and the advance of material culture were accompanied by the rapid spread of new religious ideas which were soon to become fundamental to all Indian thought. It is remarkable that in the Vedas and and the earlier Brāhmana literature the doctrine of transmigration[1] is nowhere clearly mentioned, and there is no good reason to believe that the Aryans of Vedic times accepted it. It first appears, in a rather primitive form, in the early Upanishads as a rare and new doctrine, to be imparted as a great mystery by master-hermits to their more promising pupils. In the next stratum of India's religious literature, the Jain and Buddhist scriptures, the doctrine of transmigration is taken for granted, and has evidently become almost universal. With this belief in transmigration came a passionate desire for escape, for union with something which lay beyond the dreary cycle of birth and death and rebirth, for timeless being, in place of transitory and therefore unsatisfactory existence. The rapid spread of belief in transmigration throughout the whole of northern India is hard to account for; it may be that the humbler strata of society had believed in some form of transmigration from time immemorial, but only now did it begin to affect the upper classes. It is equally difficult to explain the growth of a sense of dissatisfaction with the world and of a desire to escape from it. Several reasons have been suggested to account for this great wave of pessimism, occurring as it did in an expanding society, and in a culture which was rapidly developing both intellectually and materially. It has been suggested that the change in outlook was due to the break-up of old tribes and their replacement by kingdoms wherein ethnic ties and the sense of security which they gave were lost or weakened, thus leading to a deep-seated psychological unease affecting all sections of the people. Another suggested cause of the change

---

[1] We use this term, which is the most usual one, with reference to the general Indian doctrine of reincarnation and rebirth; but it must be remembered that it is misleading when applied to Buddhism, which maintains that no entity of any kind migrates from one body to another.

in outlook is the revolt of the most intelligent people of the times against the sterile sacrificial cults of the brāhmans. No explanation is wholly satisfactory, and we must admit our virtual ignorance of the factors which led to this great change in the direction of religious thought which was to have such an effect on the life of India and the world.

Both the sages of the Upanishads and the heresiarchs of the unorthodox schools taught the way of knowledge, as opposed to the way of works. Their primary aim was to achieve salvation from the round of birth and death, and to lead others to achieve it. Most of them maintained that salvation could only be obtained after a long course of physical and mental discipline, often culminating in extreme asceticism, but this was chiefly of value as leading to the full realization of the fundamental truths of the universe, after which the seeker for salvation was emancipated from the cycle of transmigration and reached a state of timeless bliss in which his limited phenomenal personality disintegrated or was absorbed in pure being. The basic truths of the various schools differed widely.

THE RISE OF BUDDHISM

The founder of Buddhism was the son of a chief of the hill-tribe of the Shākyas, who gave up family life to become an ascetic when he was some twenty-nine years old, and, after some years, emerged as the leader of a band of followers who pursued the "Middle Way" between extreme asceticism and worldly life. The legends which were told about him in later times are mostly unreliable, though they may contain a grain of historical truth here and there. Moreover many of the sermons and other pronouncements attributed to the Buddha[1] are not his, but the work of teachers in later times, and there is considerable doubt as to the exact nature of his original message. However, the historicity of the Buddha is

[1] "The Enlightened" or "Awakened," a religious title with which we may compare the Christian "Christ" (i.e., "Anointed") and "Savior." The Buddha's real name was Siddhārtha Gautama (Pali, Siddhattha Gotama).

certain, and we may believe as a minimum that he was originally a member of the Shākya tribe, that he gained enlightenment under a sacred pīpal tree at Gayā, in the modern Bihar, that he spent many years in teaching and organizing his band of followers, and that he died at about the age of eighty in Kusinārā, a small town in the hills. The Sinhalese Buddhists have preserved a tradition that he died in 544 B.C., but most modern authorities believe that this date is some sixty years too early.

The band of yellow-robed *bhikkhus*[2] which the Buddha left behind him to continue his work probably remained for some two hundred years one small group among the many heterodox sects of India, perhaps fewer in numbers and less influential than the rival sects of Jains and Ājīvikas. Though by Western standards its rule was rigid, involving continuous movement from place to place for eight months of the year and the consumption of only one meal a day, which was to be obtained by begging, it was light in comparison with the discipline of most other orders, the members of which were often compelled to take vows of total nudity, were not permitted to wash, and had to undergo painful penances. It is evident that between the death of the Buddha and the advent of Ashoka, the first great Buddhist emperor, over two hundred years later, there was considerable development of doctrine. Some sort of canon of sacred texts appeared, though it was probably not at this time written down, and the Buddhists acquired numerous lay followers. For the latter, and for the less spiritually advanced monks, the sect adapted popular cults to Buddhist purposes—notably the cult of stūpas, or funeral mounds, and that of the sacred pīpal tree. We have seen that these had probably been worshiped in the Ganges valley from time immemorial, and with such cults both Hinduism and Buddhism had to come to terms. Buddhist monks began to overlook the rule that they should travel from place to place except in the rainy season and took to settling permanently in monasteries, which were erected on land given by kings and other wealthy patrons, and were

[2] Literally, "beggars." This is the Pali form, used by the Theravāda Buddhists. The Sanskrit form is *bhikṣu*. Here the word is generally translated "monk."

equipped with pīpal trees and stūpas, theoretically commemorating the Buddha's enlightenment and death respectively.

Quite early in the history of Buddhism sectarian differences appeared. The tradition tells of two great councils of the Buddhist order, the first soon after the Buddha's death, the second a hundred years later. At the latter a schism occurred, and the sect of Mahāsaṅghikas ("members of the Great Order") is said to have broken away, ostensibly on account of differences on points of monastic discipline, but probably on doctrinal grounds also. The main body, which claimed to maintain the true tradition transmitted from the days of the founder, took to calling their system Theravāda³ ("The Teaching of the Elders"). By little over a century after this schism the whole of India except the southern tip had been unified politically by Magadha, after a long and steady process of expansion, which culminated in the rise of the first great Indian imperial dynasty, that of the Mauryas. The third and greatest of the Mauryas, Ashoka, became a Buddhist. According to his own testimony he was so moved by remorse at the carnage caused by an aggressive war which he had waged that he experienced a complete change of heart and embraced Buddhism. His inscriptions, the earliest intelligible written records to have survived in India, testify to his earnestness and benevolence.

Buddhism seems to have received a great impetus from Ashoka's patronage. He erected many stūpas, endowed new monasteries, and enlarged existing Buddhist establishments. In his reign the message of Buddhism was first carried over the whole of India by a number of missionaries, sent out, according to tradition, after a third council which met at Pātaliputra (the modern Patna) in order to purify the doctrine of heresy. It was in Ashoka's reign that Ceylon first became a Buddhist country, after the preaching of the apostle Mahinda, said to have been Ashoka's son, who had become a monk. From that day onwards Ceylon has remained a stronghold of the Buddhism of the Theravāda school; Mahāyāna and other Buddhist sects, though they have at times

³ In Sanskrit Sthaviravāda, but the Pali form is generally used, as Pali was the official language of the sect.

been influential, have never seriously shaken the hold of the form of Buddhism which Ceylon looks on as particularly its own.

It is probable that, by the end of the third century B.C., the doctrines of Theravāda Buddhism were in essentials much as they are now. The monks taught a dynamic phenomenalism, maintaining that everything in the universe, including the gods and the souls of living beings, was in a constant state of flux. Resistance to the cosmic flux of phenomena, and craving for permanence where permanence could not be found, led to inevitable sorrow. Salvation was to be obtained by the progressive abandonment of the sense of individuality, until it was lost completely in the indescribable state known as Nirvāna (Pali, Nibbāna, "blowing out"). The Buddha himself had reached this state, and no longer existed as an individual; nevertheless he was still rather inconsistently revered by his followers, and the less-learned Buddhist layfolk tended to look on him as a sort of high god.

ESSENTIALS OF THERAVĀDA BUDDHISM

The fundamental truths on which Buddhism is founded are not metaphysical or theological, but rather psychological. Basic is the doctrine of the "Four Noble Truths": 1) that all life is inevitably sorrowful; 2) that sorrow is due to craving; 3) that it can only be stopped by the stopping of craving; and 4) that this can only be done by a course of carefully disciplined and moral conduct, culminating in the life of concentration and meditation led by the Buddhist monk. These four truths, which are the common property of all schools of Buddhist thought, are part of the true Doctrine (Pali, dhamma; Skt. dharma), which reflects the fundamental moral law of the universe.[1]

[1] The word dharma is employed in Buddhism a little differently from its use in Hinduism, and is strictly untranslatable in English. One leading authority has translated it as "the Norm"; in our extracts it is translated "the Doctrine," "Righteousness," or "The Law of Righteousness" according to context. The term dharma in Buddhism also has other connotations. Phenomena in general are dharmas, as are the qualities and characteristics of phenomena. Thus

All things are composite. Buddhism would dispute the
Hegelian theory that units may organize themselves into
greater units which are more than the sum of their parts.
As a corollary of the fact that all things are composite they
are transient, for the composition of all aggregates is liable
to change with time. Moreover, being essentially transient,
they have no eternal Self or soul, no abiding individuality.
And, as we have seen, they are inevitably liable to sorrow.
This threefold characterization of the nature of the world
and all that it contains—sorrowful, transient, and soulless—
is frequently repeated in Buddhist literature, and without
fully grasping its truth no being has any chance of salvation.
For until he thoroughly understands the three characteristics
of the world a man will inevitably crave for permanence
in one form or another, and as this cannot, by the nature of
things, be obtained, he will suffer, and probably make others
suffer also.

All things in the universe may also be classified into five
components, or are composed of a mixture of them: form and
matter (*rūpa*), sensations (*vedanā*), perceptions (*saññā*),
psychic dispositions or constructions (*samkhārā*), and consciousness or conscious thought (*viññāna*). The first consists
of the objects of sense and various other elements of less
importance. Sensations are the actual feelings arising as a
result of the exercise of the six senses (mind being the sixth)
upon sense-objects, and perceptions are the cognitions of
such sensations. The psychic constructions include all the
various psychological emotions, propensities, faculties, and
conditions of the individual, while the fifth component, conscious thought, arises from the interplay of the other psychic
constituents. The individual is made up of a combination of
the five components, which are never the same from one
moment to the next, and therefore his whole being is in a
state of constant flux.

The process by which life continues and one thing leads
to another is explained by the Chain of Causation (*Paticca-
samuppāda*, lit. Dependent Origination). The root cause of
the process of birth and death and rebirth is ignorance, the

---

the Buddha's last words might be translated: "Growing old is the
dharma of all composite things."

fundamental illusion that individuality and permanence exist, when in fact they do not. Hence there arise in the organism various psychic phenomena, including desire, followed by an attempt to appropriate things to itself—this is typified especially by sexual craving and sexual intercourse, which are the actual causes of the next links in the chain, which concludes with age and death, only to be repeated again and again indefinitely. Rebirth takes place, therefore, according to laws of karma which do not essentially differ from those of Hinduism, though they are explained rather differently.

As we have seen, no permanent entity transmigrates from body to body, and all things, including the individual, are in a state of constant flux. But each act, word, or thought leaves its traces on the collection of the five constituents which make up the phenomenal individual, and their character alters correspondingly. This process goes on throughout life, and, when the material and immaterial parts of the being are separated in death, the immaterial constituents, which make up what in other systems would be called the soul, carry over the consequential effects of the deeds of the past life, and obtain another body accordingly. Thus there is no permanent soul, but nevertheless room is found for the doctrine of transmigration. Though Buddhism rejects the existence of the soul, this makes little difference in practice, and the more popular literature of Buddhism, such as the *Birth Stories* (*Jātaka*), takes for granted the existence of a quasi-soul at least, which endures indefinitely. One sect of Buddhism, the *Sammitīya*, which admittedly made no great impression on the religious life of India, actually went so far as to admit the existence of an indescribable substratum of personality (*pudgala*), which was carried over from life to life until ultimately it was dissipated in Nirvāna, thus fundamentally agreeing with the pneumatology of most other Indian religions.

The process of rebirth can only be stopped by achieving Nirvāna, first by adopting right views about the nature of existence, then by a carefully controlled system of moral conduct, and finally by concentration and meditation. The state of Nirvāna cannot be described, but it can be hinted at or suggested metaphorically. The word literally means "blowing out," as of a lamp. In Nirvāna all idea of an in-

dividual personality or ego ceases to exist and there is nothing
to be reborn—as far as the individual is concerned Nirvāṇa
is annihilation. But it was certainly not generally thought of
by the early Buddhists in such negative terms. It was rather
conceived of as a transcendent state, beyond the possibility
of full comprehension by the ordinary being enmeshed in
the illusion of selfhood, but not fundamentally different
from the state of supreme bliss as described in other non-
theistic Indian systems.

These are the doctrines of the Theravāda school, and,
with few variations, they would be assented to by all other
schools of Buddhism. But the Mahāyāna[2] and quasi-Mahāyāna sects developed other doctrines, in favor of which they
often gave comparatively little attention to these fundamental
teachings.

Of the Lesser Vehicle only one sect survives, the Theravāda, now prevalent in Ceylon, Burma, Thailand, Cambodia,
and Laos. There were several others in earlier times, some of
which had distinctive metaphysical and psychological systems
which approached more closely to those of the Greater Vehicle than did that of the Theravāda. The most important
of these sects was perhaps that of the Sarvāstivādins, which
stressed the absence of any real entity passing through time
in transmigration, but on the other hand maintained the
ultimate reality of the chain of events which made up the
phenomenal being or object. A sub-sect of the Sarvāstivādins,
the Sautrāntikas, emphasized the atomic nature of the component elements of the chain—every instant a composite
object disappeared, to be replaced by a new one which came
into being as a result of the last. This view of the universe,
which appears in the systems of other Buddhist sects in a
less emphatic form, is akin to the quantum theory of modern
physics.

Another very interesting sect of the Lesser Vehicle was
the Mahāsaṅghika, said to have been the first to break away

[2] With the rise of the Mahāyāna form of Buddhism, Buddhist sects
became divided into two major groups. The newer sects referred to
their doctrine as the "Mahāyāna," the Greater Vehicle (to salvation), and to their rivals' as the "Hīnayāna," the Lesser Vehicle.
We have generally preferred to call the latter group Theravāda
from the name of its major sect.

from the main body of Buddhism. Subdivided into numerous schools, its chief characteristic was the doctrine that the things of the phenomenal world were not wholly real; thus it paved the way for the idealist world-view of Mahāyāna philosophy. Buddhas, on the other hand, according to the fully developed doctrine of the Mahāsaṅghikas, had full reality, as heavenly beings in a state of perpetual mystic trance, and earthly Buddhas such as the historical Gautama were mere docetic manifestations of the Buddhas in their true state. It is possible that gnostic doctrines from the Middle East influenced this form of Buddhism, which came very close to Mahāyānism, differing only in the doctrine of bodhisattvas.

Buddhism also taught an advanced and altruistic system of morality, which was a corollary to its metaphysics, since one of the first steps on the road to Nirvāna was to do good to others, and thereby weaken the illusion of egoity which was the main cause of human sorrow. Buddhism set itself strongly against animal sacrifice and encouraged vegetarianism, though it did not definitely impose it. It tended towards peace, even if Ashoka's successors did not heed his injunctions to avoid aggression. Its attitude to the system of class and caste is not always definite; while passages in the Buddhist scriptures can be found which attack all claims to superiority by right of birth, the four great classes seem to have been recognized as an almost inevitable aspect of Indian society; but the Buddhist classification of these classes varies significantly from that of the Hindus, for in Buddhist sources the warrior is usually mentioned before the brāhman.

The total literature of Buddhism is so large that it is quite impossible for a single individual to master it in his lifetime. Each of the numerous sects of Buddhism had its version of the sacred scriptures written either in a semi-vernacular Prakritic language or in a form of Sanskrit with peculiar syntax and vocabulary, generally known as "Buddhist Sanskrit." Besides these there was a great body of commentarial literature, and much philosophical and devotional writing of all kinds. Much of the literature of the sects other than the Theravāda has been lost, or only survives in Chinese or Tibetan translations, but the complete canon of Theravāda Buddhism has been fully preserved in Ceylon. It is therefore

of fundamental importance in any study of Buddhism. It is
written in Pali, a language related to Sanskrit, and based on
an ancient vernacular, probably spoken in the western part
of India.

The canon is generally known as *Tripiṭaka* (the *Three
Baskets*) after the three sections into which it is divided,
namely *Conduct* (*Vinaya*), *Discourses* (*Sutta*), and *Supplementary Doctrines* (*Abhidhamma*). The first *Piṭaka* contains
the rules of conduct of the Buddhist order of monks and
nuns, usually in connection with narratives which purport
to tell the circumstances in which the Buddha laid down
each rule. The second *Piṭaka* is the most important; it contains discourses, mostly attributed to the Buddha, divided
into five sections: the *Long Group* (*Dīgha Nikāya*) containing long discourses; the *Medium Group* (*Majjhima Nikāya*)
with discourses of shorter length; the *Connected Group*
(*Samyutta Nikāya*), a collection of shorter pronouncements
on connected topics; the *Progressive Group* (*Aṅguttara
Nikāya*), short passages arranged in eleven sections according
to the number of topics dealt with in each—thus the three
types of sin, in act, word and thought, occur in section three,
and so on; and finally the *Minor Group* (*Khuddaka Nikāya*),
a number of works of varying type, including the beautiful
and very ancient Buddhist poems of the *Way of Righteousness* (*Dhammapada*) and a collection of verses which are
filled out by a lengthy prose commentary to form the *Birth
Stories* (*Jātaka*) relating the previous births of the Buddha.

The third *Piṭaka*, the *Supplementary Doctrines*, is a collection of seven works on Buddhist psychology and metaphysics,
which are little more than a systematization of ideas contained in the *Discourses*, and are definitely later than the
main body of the canon.

There is considerable disagreement about the date of the
canon. Some earlier students of Buddhism believed that the
Conduct and *Discourse Baskets* existed in much the same
form as they do now within a hundred years of the Buddha's
death. Later authorities are inclined to believe that the
growth of the canon was considerably slower. On the other
hand many of the discourses may look back to the Buddha
himself, though all have been more or less worked over, and

none can be specified with certainty as being his own words. The orthodox tradition itself admits that the *Basket of Supplementary Doctrines* (*Abhidhamma Piṭaka*) is later than the other two, and was not completed until the time of Ashoka. Sinhalese tradition records that the canon was not committed to writing until the reign of King Vattagāmani (89–77 B.C.), and it may not have finished growing until about this time. Thus it is possible that it is the product of as many as four centuries.

There are numerous other works in Pali which are not generally considered canonical. Perhaps the most important of these works are the standard commentaries on the books of the canon, most of which, it is said, were compiled in Ceylon by the great doctor Buddhaghosa, of the fifth century A.D., from earlier commentaries. As well as passages of explanatory character, the commentaries contain much ancient Buddhist tradition not to be found elsewhere, and the elucidation of the *Jātaka* verses, in plain and vigorous prose, contains some of the finest narrative literature of the ancient world. Buddhaghosa is also the reputed author of a valuable compendium of Buddhist doctrine, *The Way of Purification* (*Visuddhimagga*). Another very important Pali work of early date is *The Questions of King Menander* (*Milindapañha*), from which several passages are translated here. The inscriptions of Emperor Ashoka (c. 273–232 B.C.) must also be included in any survey, since they are inspired by Buddhism and are at least in part intended to inculcate the morality of Buddhism.

The Four Noble Truths

According to Buddhist tradition this was the first sermon preached by the Buddha. After gaining enlightenment under the Tree of Wisdom at Gayā he proceeded to Vārānasī,[1] where, in a park outside the city, he found five ascetics who had formerly been his associates, and who had left him in disgust when he gave up self-mortification and self-starvation as useless in his quest for supreme wisdom. In the presence of these five the Buddha "set in motion

[1] The ancient name of Banaras, now officially revived by the Indian government.

the Wheel [2] *of the Law" by preaching this sermon, which outlines the Four Noble Truths, the Noble Eightfold Path, and the Middle Way, three of the most important concepts of Buddhism.*

Thus I have heard. Once the Lord was at Vārānasī, at the deer park called Iwipatana. There he addressed the five monks:

There are two ends not to be served by a wanderer. What are these two? The pursuit of desires and of the pleasure which springs from desire, which is base, common, leading to rebirth, ignoble, and unprofitable; and the pursuit of pain and hardship, which is grievous, ignoble, and unprofitable. The Middle Way of the Tathāgata[3] avoids both these ends. It is enlightened, it brings clear vision, it makes for wisdom, and leads to peace, insight, enlightenment, and Nirvāna. What is the Middle Way? . . . It is the Noble Eightfold Path—Right Views, Right Resolve, Right Speech, Right Conduct, Right Livelihood, Right Effort, Right Mindfulness,[4] and Right Concentration. This is the Middle Way. . . .

And this is the Noble Truth of Sorrow. Birth is sorrow, age is sorrow, disease is sorrow, death is sorrow; contact with the unpleasant is sorrow, separation from the pleasant is sorrow, every wish unfulfilled is sorrow—in short all the five components of individuality[5] are sorrow.

And this is the Noble Truth of the Arising of Sorrow. It arises from craving, which leads to rebirth, which brings delight and passion, and seeks pleasure now here, now there—the craving for sensual pleasure, the craving for continued life, the craving for power.

And this is the Noble Truth of the Stopping of Sorrow. It is the complete stopping of that craving, so that no passion

[2] The chariot wheel in ancient India symbolized empire and hence this phrase may be paraphrased as: "embarked on his expedition of conquest on behalf of the Kingdom of Righteousness."

[3] "He who has thus attained," one of the titles of the Buddha.

[4] *Sati*, lit. "memory." At all times the monk should as far as possible be fully conscious of his actions, words, and thoughts, and be aware that the agent is not an enduring individual, but a composite and transitory collection of material and psychic factors.

[5] Forms, sensations, perceptions, psychic dispositions, and consciousness.

remains, leaving it, being emancipated from it, being released from it, giving no place to it.

And this is the Noble Truth of the Way which Leads to the Stopping of Sorrow. It is the Noble Eightfold Path—Right Views, Right Resolve, Right Speech, Right Conduct, Right Livelihood, Right Effort, Right Mindfulness, and Right Concentration.

[From Samyutta Nikāya, 5.421 ff.[6]]

The Nature of Consciousness and the Chain of Causation

The following Discourse, though it purports to be a single utterance of the Buddha, is evidently a conflation of separate passages, bearing on the character of consciousness. It contains a short statement of the contingent nature of consciousness or conscious thought, an appeal for an objective and clear realization that everything whatever is dependent on causes outside itself, an enumeration of the elements of the Chain of Causation, given first in reverse order, an exhortation to the monks not to bother unduly about the question of the survival of the personality and to realize the facts of the Doctrine for themselves, not taking them from the lips of the Teacher, and finally an impressive passage comparing the life of the ordinary man with that of the Buddha, which we have not space to give here.

Once a certain monk named Sāti, the son of a fisherman,[1] conceived the pernicious heresy that, as he understood the Lord's teaching, consciousness continued throughout transmigration. When they heard this several monks went and reasoned with him . . . but he would not give in, but held firm to his heresy. . . . So they went to the Lord and put the matter to him, and he sent a monk to fetch Sāti. When Sāti had come the Lord asked him if it was true that he held this heresy . . . and Sāti replied that he did hold it.

[6] In all quotations from the Pali scriptures, except where specified, reference is made to the Pali Text Society's edition of the text.
[1] In theory the origins of a monk, once he had become a full member of the Order, were irrelevant, but the authors of the Pali scriptures often mention the fact that a given monk was of humble birth. It would seem that they were not altogether free from class-consciousness.

"What, then," asked the Lord, "is the nature of consciousness?"

"Sir, it is that which speaks and feels, and experiences the consequences of good and evil deeds."

"Whom do you tell, you foolish fellow, that I have taught such a doctrine? Haven't I said, with many similes, that consciousness is not independent, but comes about through the Chain of Causation, and can never arise without a cause? You misunderstand and misrepresent me, and so you undermine your own position and produce much demerit. You bring upon yourself lasting harm and sorrow!" . . .

Then the Lord addressed the assembled monks:

"Whatever form of consciousness arises from a condition is known by the name of that condition; thus if it arises from the eye and from forms it is known as visual consciousness . . . and so with the senses of hearing, smell, taste, touch, and mind, and their objects. It's just like a fire, which you call by the name of the fuel—a wood fire, a fire of sticks, a grass fire, and cowdung fire, a fire of husks, a rubbish fire, and so on." [2]

"Do you agree, monks, that any given organism is a living being?" "Yes, sir."

"Do you agree that it is produced by food?" "Yes, sir."

"And that when the food is cut off the living being is cut off and dies?" "Yes, sir."

"And that doubt on any of these points will lead to perplexity?" "Yes, sir."

"And that Right Recognition is knowledge of the true facts as they really are?" "Yes, sir."

"Now if you cling to this pure and unvitiated view, if you cherish it, treasure it, and make it your own, will you be able to develop a state of consciousness with which you can cross the stream of transmigration as on a raft, which you use but do not keep?" "No, sir."

"But only if you maintain this pure view, but don't cling to it or cherish it . . . only if you use it but are ready to give it up?" [3] "Yes, sir."

[2] The implication is that just as fire is caused by fuel and varies according to the fuel used, so consciousness is caused by the senses and their objects, and varies accordingly.

[3] Buddhism is a practical system, with one aim only, to free living

"There are four bases which support all organisms and beings, whether now existing or yet to be. They are: first, food coarse or fine, which builds up the body; second, contact; third, cogitation; and fourth, consciousness. All four derive and originate from craving. Craving arises from sensation, sensation from contact,[4] contact from the six senses, the six senses from physical form, physical form from consciousness, consciousness from the psychic constructions, and the psychic constructions from ignorance. . . . To repeat: Ignorance is the cause of the psychic constructions, hence is caused consciousness, hence physical form, hence the six senses, hence contact, hence sensations, hence craving, hence attachment, hence becoming, hence birth, hence old age and death with all the distraction of grief and lamentation, sorrow and despair. This is the arising of the whole body of ill. . . . So we are agreed that by the complete cessation of ignorance the whole body of ill ceases.

"Now would you, knowing and seeing this, go back to your past, wondering whether you existed or didn't exist long ago, or how you existed, or what you were, or from what life you passed to another?" "No, sir."

"Or would you look forward to the future with the same thoughts?" "No, sir."

"Or would you, knowing and seeing this, trouble yourselves at the present time about whether or not you really exist, what and how you are, whence your being came, and whither it will go?" "No, sir."

"Or would you, possessing this knowledge, say, 'We declare it because we revere our teacher'?" "No, sir."

"Or would you say, 'We don't declare it as from ourselves —we were told it by a teacher or ascetic'?" "No, sir."

"Or would you look for another teacher?" "No, sir."

---

beings from suffering. This passage apparently implies that even the most fundamental doctrines of Buddhism are only means to that end, and must not be maintained dogmatically for their own sake. It suggests also that there may be higher truths, which can only be realized as Nirvāna is approached.
[4] Here we are told that craving arises from contact, through sensation, while in the previous sentence contact arises from craving. There is no real paradox, because the chain is circular, and any one link is the cause of any other.

"Or would you support the rituals, shows, or festivals of other ascetics or brāhmans?" "No, sir."

"Do you only declare what you have known and seen?" "Yes, sir."

"Well done, brethren! I have taught you the doctrine which is immediately beneficial, eternal, open to all, leading them onwards, to be mastered for himself by every intelligent man."

[From *Majjhima Nikāya*, 1.256 ff.]

False Doctrines About the Soul

The early Buddhists never ceased to impress upon their hearers the fact that the phenomenal personality was in a constant state of flux, and that there was no eternal soul in the individual in anything like the Hindu sense. On the other hand the perfected being had reached Nirvāna, and nothing could be meaningfully predicated about him. The following passage, attributed to the Buddha himself, criticizes the soul theories of other sects.

It is possible to make four propositions concerning the nature of the soul—"My soul has form and is minute," "My soul has form and is boundless," "My soul is without form and is minute," and "My soul is without form and boundless." Such propositions may refer to this life or the next. . . .

There are as many ways of not making propositions concerning the soul, and those with insight do not make them.

Again the soul may be thought of as sentient or insentient, or as neither one nor the other but having sentience as a property. If someone affirms that his soul is sentient you should ask, "Sentience is of three kinds, happy, sorrowful, and neutral. Which of these is your soul?" For when you feel one sensation you don't feel the others. Moreover these sensations are impermanent, dependent on conditions, resulting from a cause or causes, perishable, transitory, vanishing, ceasing. If one experiences a happy sensation and thinks "This is my soul," when the happy sensation ceases he will think "My soul has departed." One who thinks thus looks on his soul as something impermanent in this life, a blend of happiness and sorrow with a beginning and end, and so this proposition is not acceptable.

If someone affirms that the soul is not sentient, you should ask, "If you have no sensation, can you say that you exist?" He cannot, and so this proposition is not acceptable.

And if someone affirms that the soul has sentience as a property you should ask, "If all sensations of every kind were to cease absolutely there would be no feelings whatever. Could you then say 'I exist'?" He could not, and so this proposition is not acceptable.

When a monk does not look on the soul as coming under any of these three categories . . . he refrains from such views and clings to nothing in the world; and not clinging he does not tremble, and not trembling he attains Nirvāna. He knows that rebirth is at an end, that his goal is reached, that he has accomplished what he set out to do, and that after this present world there is no other for him. It would be absurd to say of such a monk, with his heart set free, that he believes that the perfected being survives after death —or indeed that he does not survive, or that he does and yet does not, or that he neither does nor does not. Because the monk is free his state transcends all expression, predication, communication, and knowledge.

[From Dīgha Nikāya, 2.64 ff.]

The Simile of the Chariot

This passage from the Questions of King Menander is among the best known arguments in favor of the composite nature of the individual. The Greek king Milinda, or Menander, ruled in northwestern India about the middle of the second century B.C. According to the text he was converted to Buddhism by Nāgasena, and the wheel which appears on some of his numerous coins would suggest that he was in fact influenced by the Indian religion. The style of the Questions is in some measure reminiscent of the Upanishads but some authorities have thought to find traces of the influence of Plato and have suggested that the author or authors knew Greek. Though in its present form the work may be some centuries later, its kernel may go back to before the Christian era.

Then King Menander went up to the Venerable Nāgasena, greeted him respectfully, and sat down. Nāgasena replied to the greeting, and the King was pleased at heart. Then King

Menander asked: "How is your reverence known, and what is your name?"

"I'm known as Nāgasena, your Majesty, that's what my fellow monks call me. But though my parents may have given me such a name . . . it's only a generally understood term, a practical designation. There is no question of a permanent individual implied in the use of the word."

"Listen, you five hundred Greeks and eighty thousand monks!" said King Menander. "This Nāgasena has just declared that there's no permanent individuality implied in his name!" Then, turning to Nāgasena, "If, Reverend Nāgasena, there is no permanent individuality, who gives you monks your robes and food, lodging and medicines? And who makes use of them? Who lives a life of righteousness, meditates, and reaches Nirvāna? Who destroys living beings, steals, fornicates, tells lies, or drinks spirits? . . . If what you say is true there's neither merit nor demerit, and no fruit or result of good or evil deeds. If someone were to kill you there would be no question of murder. And there would be no masters or teachers in the [Buddhist] Order and no ordinations. If your fellow monks call you Nāgasena, what then is Nāgasena? Would you say that your hair is Nāgasena?" "No, your Majesty."

"Or your nails, teeth, skin, or other parts of your body, or the outward form, or sensation, or perception, or the psychic constructions, or consciousness?[1] Are any of these Nāgasena?" "No, your Majesty."

"Then are all these taken together Nāgasena?" "No, your Majesty."

"Or anything other than they?" "No, your Majesty."

"Then for all my asking I find no Nāgasena. Nāgasena is a mere sound! Surely what your Reverence has said is false!"

Then the Venerable Nāgasena addressed the King.

"Your Majesty, how did you come here—on foot, or in a vehicle?"

"In a chariot."

"Then tell me what is the chariot? Is the pole the chariot?" "No, your Reverence."

[1] The five components of individuality.

"Or the axle, wheels, frame, reins, yoke, spokes, or goad?"
"None of these things is the chariot."

"Then all these separate parts taken together are the
chariot?" "No, your Reverence."

"Then is the chariot something other than the separate
parts?" "No, your Reverence."

"Then for all my asking, your Majesty, I can find no
chariot. The chariot is a mere sound. What then is the chariot? Surely what your Majesty has said is false! There is no
chariot . . ."

When he had spoken the five hundred Greeks cried "Well
done!" and said to the King, "Now, your Majesty, get out of
that dilemma if you can!"

"What I said was not false," replied the King. "It's on
account of all these various components, the pole, axle,
wheels, and so on, that the vehicle is called a chariot. It's
just a generally understood term, a practical designation."

"Well said, your Majesty! You know what the word
'chariot' means! And it's just the same with me. It's on
account of the various components of my being that I'm
known by the generally understood term, the practical designation Nāgasena."

[From Milindapañha (Trenckner ed.), pp. 25 f.]

Change and Identity

After convincing Menander of the composite nature of the personality by the simile of the chariot, Nāgasena shows him by another
simile how it is continually changing with the passage of time, but
possesses a specious unity through the continuity of the body.

"Reverend Nāgasena," said the King, "when a man is born
does he remain the same [being] or become another?"

"He neither remains the same nor becomes another."

"Give me an example!"

"What do you think, your Majesty? You were once a baby
lying on your back, tender and small and weak. Was that
baby you, who are now grown up?"

"No, your Reverence, the baby was one being and I am
another."

"If that's the case, your Majesty, you had no mother or father, and no teachers in learning, manners, or wisdom. . . . Is the boy who goes to school one [being] and the young man who has finished his education another? Does one person commit a crime and another suffer mutilation for it?"

"Of course not, your Reverence! But what do you say on the question?"

"I am the being I was when I was a baby," said the Elder . . . "for through the continuity of the body all stages of life are included in a pragmatic unity."

"Give me an illustration."

"Suppose a man were to light a lamp, would it burn all through the night?" "Yes, it might."

"Now is the flame which burns in the middle watch the same as that which burned in the first?" "No, your Reverence."

"Or is that which burns in the last watch the same as that which burned in the middle?" "No, your Reverence."

"So is there one lamp in the first watch, another in the middle, and yet another in the last?"

"No. The same lamp gives light all through the night."

"Similarly, your Majesty, the continuity of phenomena is kept up. One person comes into existence, another passes away, and the sequence runs continuously without self-conscious existence, neither the same nor yet another."

"Well said, Reverend Nāgasena!"

[From *Milindapañha* (Trenckner ed.), p. 40]

The Process of Rebirth

In this little passage Nāgasena presses the analogy of the lamp further, and shows Menander how rebirth is possible without any soul, substratum of personality, or other hypothetical entity which passes from the one body to the other.

"Reverend Nāgasena," said the King, "is it true that nothing transmigrates, and yet there is rebirth?"

"Yes, your Majesty."

"How can this be? . . . Give me an illustration."

"Suppose, your Majesty, a man lights one lamp from another—does the one lamp transmigrate to the other?"

"No, your Reverence."

"So there is rebirth without anything transmigrating!"

[From *Milindapañha* (Trenckner ed.), p. 71]

Karma

Buddhism accepted the prevailing doctrine of karma, though it had an original explanation of the process whereby karma operated. In this passage from the Questions of King Menander karma is adduced as the reason for the manifest inequalities of human fate and fortune. Had Nāgasena been disputing with an Indian king instead of with a Greek one the question would not have been asked, for the answer would have been taken for granted.

"Venerable Nāgasena," asked the King, "why are men not all alike, but some short-lived and some long, some sickly and some healthy, some ugly and some handsome, some weak and some strong, some poor and some rich, some base and some noble, some stupid and some clever?"

"Why, your Majesty," replied the Elder, "are not all plants alike, but some astringent, some salty, some pungent, some sour, and some sweet?"

"I suppose, your Reverence, because they come from different seeds."

"And so it is with men! They are not alike because of different karmas. As the Lord said . . . 'Beings each have their own karma. They are . . . born through karma, they become members of tribes and families through karma, each is ruled by karma, it is karma that divides them into high and low.' "

"Very good, your Reverence!"

[From *Milindapañha* (Trenckner ed.), p. 65]

Right Mindfulness

The following passage is of interest as showing the means which the monk should take in order thoroughly to realize the transcience and otherness of all things, and thus draw near to Nirvāna. The bhāvanās, or states of mind, are practiced by Buddhist monks to this day, and are part of "Right Mindfulness," the seventh stage of the Noble Eightfold Path. The translation is considerably abridged.

The Lord was staying at Sāvatthī at the monastery of Anāthapindaka in the Grove of Jeta. One morning he dressed, took his robe and bowl, and went into Sāvatthī for alms, with the Reverend Rāhula[1] following close behind him. As they walked the Lord, . . . without looking round, spoke to him thus:

"All material forms, past, present, or future, within or without, gross or subtle, base or fine, far or near, all should be viewed with full understanding—with the thought 'This is not mine, this is not I, this is not my soul.' "[2]

"Only material forms, Lord?"

"No, not only material forms, Rāhula, but also sensation, perception, the psychic constructions, and consciousness."[3]

"Who would go to the village to collect alms today, when he has been exhorted by the Lord himself?" said Rāhula. And he turned back and sat cross-legged, with body erect, collected in thought.

Then the Venerable Sāriputta,[4] seeing him thus, said to him: "Develop concentration on inhalation and exhalation, for when this is developed and increased it is very productive and helpful."

Towards evening Rāhula rose and went to the Lord, and asked him how he could develop concentration on inhalation and exhalation. And the Lord said:

"Rāhula, whatever is hard and solid in an individual, such as hair, nails, teeth, skin, flesh, and so on, is called the personal element of earth. The personal element of water is composed of bile, phlegm, pus, blood, sweat, and so on. The personal element of fire is that which warms and consumes or burns up, and produces metabolism of food and drink in digestion. The personal element of air is the wind in the body which moves upwards or downwards, the winds

[1] The Buddha's son, who, after his father's enlightenment, became a monk.
[2] Or "self" (*atta*).
[3] The five components of individuality.
[4] One of the Buddha's chief disciples.

in the abdomen and stomach, winds which move from member to member, and the inhalation and exhalation of the breath. And finally the personal element of space comprises the orifices of ears and nose, the door of the mouth, and the channels whereby food and drink enter, remain in, and pass out of the body.[5] These five personal elements, together with the five external elements, make up the total of the five universal elements. They should all be regarded objectively, with right understanding, thinking 'This is not mine, this is not me, this is not my soul.' With this understanding attitude a man turns from the five elements and his mind takes no delight in them.

"Develop a state of mind like the earth, Rāhula. For on the earth men throw clean and unclean things, dung and urine, spittle, pus and blood, and the earth is not troubled or repelled or disgusted. And as you grow like the earth no contacts with pleasant or unpleasant will lay hold of your mind or stick to it.

"Similarly you should develop a state of mind like water, for men throw all manner of clean and unclean things into water and it is not troubled or repelled or disgusted. And similarly with fire, which burns all things, clean and unclean, and with air, which blows upon them all, and with space, which is nowhere established.

"Develop the state of mind of friendliness, Rāhula, for, as you do so, ill-will will grow less; and of compassion, for thus vexation will grow less; and of joy, for thus aversion will grow less; and of equanimity,[6] for thus repugnance will grow less.

"Develop the state of mind of consciousness of the corruption of the body, for thus passion will grow less; and of the consciousness of the fleeting nature of all things, for thus the pride of selfhood will grow less.

"Develop the state of mind of ordering the breath . . .

[5] This interesting passage will give the reader some notion of ancient Indian ideas of anatomy and physics, as it would have been assented to by most schools of thought. In many passages Buddhist texts admit only four elements, rejecting space, which is looked on as an element in orthodox Hindu theory.

[6] Friendliness, compassion, joy, and equanimity are the four cardinal virtues of Buddhism.

in which the monk goes to the forest, or to the root of a tree
or to an empty house, and sits cross-legged with body erect,
collected in thought. Fully mindful he inhales and exhales.
When he inhales or exhales a long breath he knows precisely
that he is doing so, and similarly when inhaling or exhaling
a short breath. While inhaling or exhaling he trains himself
to be conscious of the whole of his body . . . to be fully
conscious of the components of his mind, . . . to realize
the impermanence of all things . . . or to dwell on passionlessness . . . or renunciation. Thus the state of ordered
breathing, when developed and increased, is very productive
and helpful. And when the mind is thus developed a man
breathes his last breath in full consciousness, and not unconsciously." [7]

[From *Majjhima Nikāya*, 1.420 ff.]

The Last Instructions of the Buddha

*The following passage occurs in the Discourse of the Great Passing-
away (Mahāparinibbāna Sutta) which describes the last days and
death of the Buddha. The Master, an old and ailing man, is on the
way to the hills where he was born, and where soon he is to die.
These are among his last recorded instructions to his disciples. Unfortunately we cannot be sure of their authenticity; the fine phrases
concerning "the closed fist of the teacher" are particularly suspect,
for they are just the sort of interpolation which an earnest Theravāda monk would be likely to make, in order to discredit the doctrines of schismatics of a Mahāyānist type, who claimed to possess
the esoteric teachings of the Master. But, whether authentically the
Buddha's words or not, the following passage perhaps gives the
quintessence of Theravāda Buddhism, with its call for self-reliant
striving against all that seems base and evil.*

Soon after this the Lord began to recover, and when he was
quite free from sickness he came out of his lodging and sat
in its shadow on a seat spread out for him. The Venerable

---

[7] The state of mind in the last moments before death was considered extremely important in its effect on the next birth. Some of
the Chinese and Japanese Buddhist sects perform rites at the deathbed similar to the Roman Catholic extreme unction.

Ānanda went up to him, paid his respects, sat down to one side, and spoke to the Lord thus:

"I have seen the Lord in health, and I have seen the Lord in sickness; and when I saw that the Lord was sick my body became as weak as a creeper, my sight dimmed, and all my faculties weakened. But yet I was a little comforted by the thought that the Lord would not pass away until he had left his instructions concerning the Order."

"What, Ānanda! Does the Order expect that of me? I have taught the truth without making any distinction between exoteric and esoteric doctrines; for . . . with the Tathāgata there is no such thing as the closed fist of the teacher who keeps some things back. If anyone thinks 'It is I who will lead the Order,' or 'The Order depends on me,' he is the one who should lay down instructions concerning the Order. But the Tathāgata has no such thought, so why should he leave instructions? I am old now, Ānanda, and full of years; my journey nears its end, and I have reached my sum of days, for I am nearly eighty years old. Just as a worn-out cart can only be kept going if it is tied up with thongs, so the body of the Tathāgata can only be kept going by bandaging it. Only when the Tathāgata no longer attends to any outward object, when all separate sensation stops and he is deep in inner concentration, is his body at ease.

"So, Ānanda, you must be your own lamps, be your own refuges. Take refuge in nothing outside yourselves. Hold firm to the truth as a lamp and a refuge, and do not look for refuge to anything besides yourselves. A monk becomes his own lamp and refuge by continually looking on his body, feelings, perceptions, moods, and ideas in such a manner that he conquers the cravings and depressions of ordinary men and is always strenuous, self-possessed, and collected in mind. Whoever among my monks does this, either now or when I am dead, if he is anxious to learn, will reach the summit." [p. 99 f.]

THE LAST WORDS OF THE BUDDHA

"All composite things must pass away. Strive onward vigilantly." [pp. 155–56]

[From Dīgha Nikāya, 2.99 f., 155–56]

The Buddha in Nirvāna

This brief passage from the Questions of King Menander illustrates the Theravāda conception of Nirvāna. It is not total annihilation, but at the same time it involves the complete disintegration of the phenomenal personality—a paradox which cannot be explained in words.

"Reverend Nāgasena," said the King, "does the Buddha still exist?"

"Yes, your Majesty, he does."

"Then is it possible to point out the Buddha as being here or there?"

"The Lord has passed completely away in Nirvāna, so that nothing is left which could lead to the formation of another being. And so he cannot be pointed out as being here or there."

"Give me an illustration."

"What would your Majesty say—if a great fire were blazing, would it be possible to point to a flame which had gone out and say that it was here or there?"

"No, your Reverence, the flame is extinguished, it can't be detected."

"In just the same way, your Majesty, the Lord has passed away in Nirvāna. . . . He can only be pointed out in the body of his doctrine, for it was he who taught it."

"Very good, Reverend Nāgasena!"

[From *Milindapañha* (Trenckner, ed.), p. 73]

The City of Righteousness

This fine passage, from the latter part of the Questions of King Menander, is probably the work of a hand different from that which composed the dialogues which we have already quoted. In it the Buddha almost takes on the character of a savior god, who, like Amitābha in the developed Mahāyāna mythology, built a heaven for his followers. Nirvāna is not described in negative terms, but in very positive ones, and the metaphor of the busy, populous, and prosperous city hardly suggests the rarified Nirvāna of the previous passage, but a heaven in which personality is by no means lost. It suggests in fact to the Western reader the New Jerusalem of the

Book of Revelation. Clearly this passage is the work of a writer whose attitude approached closely to that of Mahāyāna, but it must be remembered that Theravāda Buddhists look on the text from which it is taken as semi-canonical.

The builder of a city . . . first chooses a pleasant and suitable site; he makes it smooth, and then sets to work to build his city fair and well proportioned, divided into quarters, with ramparts round about it. . . . And when the city is built, and stands complete and perfect, he goes away to another land. And in time the city becomes rich and prosperous, peaceful and happy, free from plague and calamity, and filled with people of all classes and professions and of all lands . . . even with Scythians, Greeks, and Chinese. . . . All these folk coming to live in the new city and finding it so well planned, faultless, perfect, and beautiful exclaim: "Skilled indeed must be the builder who built this city!"

So the Lord . . . in his infinite goodness . . . when he had achieved the highest powers of Buddhahood and had conquered Māra[1] and his hosts, tearing the net of false doctrine, casting aside ignorance, and producing wisdom, . . . built the City of Righteousness.

The Lord's City of Righteousness has virtue for its ramparts, fear of sin for its moat, knowledge for its gates, zeal for its turrets, faith for its pillars, concentration for its watchman, wisdom for its palaces. The *Basket of Discourses* is its marketplace, the *Supplementary Doctrines* its roads, the *Conduct* its court of justice, and earnest self-control is its main street. . . .

The Lord laid down the following subjects for meditation: the ideas of impermanence, of the nonexistence of an enduring self, of the impurity and of the wretchedness of life, of ridding oneself of evil tendencies, of passionlessness, of stopping the influx of evil tendencies, of dissatisfaction with all things in the world, of the impermanence of all conditioned things, of mindful control of breath, of the corpse in disintegration, of the execution of criminals with all its horrors; the ideas of friendliness, of compassion, of joy, of

[1] The spirit of the world and the flesh, the Buddhist Satan.

equanimity,[2] the thought of death, and mindfulness of the
body. . . . Whoever wishes to be free from age and death
takes one of these as a subject for meditation, and thus he
is set free from passion, hatred, and dullness,[3] from pride
and from false views; he crosses the ocean of rebirth, dams
the torrent of his cravings, is washed clean of the threefold
stain [of passion, hatred, and dullness], and destroys all evil
within him. So he enters the glorious city of Nirvāna, stain-
less and undefiled, pure and white, unaging, deathless, secure and calm and happy, and his mind is emancipated as a
perfected being.

[From *Milindapañha* (Trenckner ed.), pp. 330 ff.]

THE PRACTICE OF THERAVĀDA BUDDHISM

In the sphere of personal relations Buddhism inculcated a
morality gentler and more humanitarian than the stern early
Hindu ethic, based chiefly on duty rather than fellowship.
The four cardinal virtues of Buddhism—friendliness, compassion, joy, and equanimity—are extolled in many passages
of the scriptures. The *Birth Stories* teach friendly relations
between man and man and between man and animal, and
encourage the warm virtues of family love, brotherhood, and
honesty (not to speak of shrewdness) in one's dealings with
others. Though the surviving Buddhist religious literature is
chiefly intended for the monastic community Buddhism certainly had, and still has, a message going far beyond the
monastery to the millions of ordinary believers who have no
hope of Nirvāna until after many lives, but who may yet rise
in the scale of being by faith in the teaching of the Buddha,
by service to the Buddhist Order, and by fair dealing with
their fellows.

In this connection we would draw attention to the most
important passage on lay morality in the Pali scriptures—the
Discourse of Admonition to Singāla (Singālovāda Sutta).
It is a solid bourgeois morality that this text encourages.

[2] The four cardinal virtues of Buddhism.
[3] The three "influxes" (*āsava*), the cardinal sins of Buddhism.

Like many older writings of Protestant Christianity it stresses the virtue of thrift—expensive ceremonies and domestic rituals are wasteful as well as useless; fairs and festivals lead men to squander precious time and wealth; from the layman's point of view drink and gambling are evil chiefly for the same reasons; to increase the family estates is a meritorious act. But there is more in the *Discourse* than this. In modern terms the ideal it sets forth is of a society in which each individual respects the other's personality, an intricate network of warm and happy human relationships, where parents and children, teachers and pupils, husbands and wives, masters and servants, and friends and friends look on one another as ends in themselves, and dwell together in mutual respect and affection, each helping the other upward in the scale of being through a cosmos which, though theoretically a vale of tears, yet contains pleasant places and gives many opportunities for real if transient happiness in fellowship with friends and kin. And the inevitable sorrow of all who are born only to grow old and pass away, the lonely anguish of the individual being who finds himself at odds with an unfriendly universe, can only be lessened, at least for the ordinary layman, by brotherhood.

The Morals of the Monk

The following extract is part of a long panegyric of the Buddha, leading up to a description of his perfect wisdom. The moral virtues attributed to him in the earlier part of the passage, which is quoted here, are those after which every monk should strive; and, allowing for their different circumstances, the monk's example should be followed as far as possible by the layman.

The monk Gautama has given up injury to life, he has lost all inclination to it; he has laid aside the cudgel and the sword, and he lives modestly, full of mercy, desiring in compassion the welfare of all things living.

He has given up taking what is not given, he has lost all inclination to it. He accepts what is given to him and waits for it to be given; and he lives in honesty and purity of heart. . . .

He has given up unchastity, he has lost all inclination to

it. He is celibate and aloof, and has lost all desire for sexual intercourse, which is vulgar. . . .

He has given up false speech, he has lost all inclination to it. He speaks the truth, he keeps faith, he is faithful and trustworthy, he does not break his word to the world. . . .

He has given up slander, he has lost all inclination to it. When he hears something in one place he will not repeat it in another in order to cause strife . . . but he unites those who are divided by strife, and encourages those who are friends. His pleasure is in peace, he loves peace and delights in it, and when he speaks he speaks words which make for peace. . . .

He has given up harsh speech, he has lost all inclination to it. He speaks only words that are blameless, pleasing to the ear, touching the heart, cultured, pleasing the people, loved by the people. . . .

He has given up frivolous talk, he has lost all inclination to it. He speaks at the right time, in accordance with the facts, with words full of meaning. His speech is memorable, timely, well illustrated, measured, and to the point.[1]

He does no harm to seeds or plants. He takes only one meal a day, not eating at night, or at the wrong time.[2] He will not watch shows, or attend fairs with song, dance, and music. He will not wear ornaments, or adorn himself with garlands, scents, or cosmetics. He will not use a high or large bed. He will not accept gold or silver, raw grain or raw meat. He will not accept women or girls, bondmen or bondwomen, sheep or goats, fowls or pigs, elephants or cattle, horses or mares, fields or houses. He will not act as go-between or messenger. He will not buy or sell, or falsify with scales, weights, or measures. He is never crooked, will never bribe,

---

[1] The layman in Buddhism is expected to follow the example of Gautama in all the points of morality above, except, of course, that in place of complete celibacy legitimate sexual relations are allowed. Many of the points that follow would be regarded as subjects of supererogation for the layman, though he might adhere to some of them for specified periods. It should be remembered, incidentally, that the vows of the Buddhist monk are not taken in perpetuity, and a Buddhist layman will often take the monk's vows for a short period.

[2] That is, after midday.

or cheat, or defraud. He will not injure, kill, or put in bonds, or steal, or do acts of violence.

[From Dīgha Nikāya, 1.4 ff.]

Care of the Body

The Buddhist Order was very solicitous for the bodily health of its members, and the Buddha is reported to have said, on one occasion: "He who would care for me should care for the sick." [1] Buddhist monasteries often served as dispensaries, and it has been suggested that one of the reasons for the spread of Buddhism in Southeast Asia and elsewhere was the medical lore of the Buddhist monks, which, though of course primitive by modern standards, was superior to anything known to the local inhabitants, and thus added to the reputation of the new religion.

The Questions of King Menander explains the apparent anomaly that a system which stressed so strongly the evils of the things of the flesh should also value physical wellbeing so highly.

The King said: "Reverend Nāgasena, is the body dear to you wanderers?"

"No, your Majesty."

"Then why do you feed it and care for it so well?"

"Have you ever gone to battle, and been wounded by an arrow?"

"Yes, your Reverence, I have."

"And in such a case isn't the wound smeared with ointment, anointed with oil, and bound with a bandage?"

"Yes, that's what is done."

"And is the wound dear to you, your Majesty, that you care for it so well?"

"Certainly not! All those things are done to make the flesh grow together again."

"So, you see, wanderers do not hold the body dear, your Majesty! Without clinging to it they bear the body in continence, for the Lord declared that the body was like a wound. . . .

" 'Covered with clammy skin, with nine openings, a great wound,

[1] Vinaya Piṭaka 1.302 (Mahāvagga 8.26).

" 'The body oozes from every pore, unclean and stinking.' "
"Well spoken, Reverend Nāgasena!"

[From *Milindapañha* (Trenckner ed.), pp. 73–74]

Meritorious Action

In theory "right views" about the nature of the world are the first
step along the Eightfold Path. But the Buddhist literature meant
chiefly for laymen tends to emphasize right actions rather than
right views. Whatever the beliefs of a man may be, his good deeds
and self-discipline are an unfailing source of merit, and lead to a
happier rebirth, which may give him the opportunity for further
spiritual progress. We quote the following little passage partly because it recalls a famous verse of the Sermon on the Mount. "Lay
Not up for Yourselves Treasures upon Earth. . . ." Notice that
the treasure "cannot be given to others." This is the doctrine of the
Theravāda sect. The Mahāyāna teaches that the merit accruing
from good deeds can be transferred by a voluntary act of will, and
men are encouraged, by the example of the compassionate bodhisattvas, to make such transfers of merit.

A man buries a treasure in a deep pit, thinking: "It will be
useful in time of need, or if the king is displeased with me,
or if I am robbed or fall into debt, or if food is scarce, or
bad luck befalls me."

But all this treasure may not profit the owner at all, for
he may forget where he has hidden it, or goblins may steal
it, or his enemies or even his kinsmen may take it when he
is careless.

But by charity, goodness, restraint, and self-control man
and woman alike can store up a well-hidden treasure—a
treasure which cannot be given to others and which robbers
cannot steal. A wise man should do good—that is the treasure
which will not leave him.

[From *Khuddaka Pāṭha*, 8]

The Virtue of Friendliness

The following poem is evidently a conflation from two sources, for
in the middle of the third verse its whole tone changes, and in
place of a rather pedestrian enumeration of the Buddhist virtues we
have an impassioned rhapsody on the theme of friendliness (mettā),
the first of the four cardinal virtues. "Mindfulness of friendliness"

is among the daily exercises of the monk, and can also be practiced by the layman; he detaches himself in imagination from his own body, and, as though looking down on himself, pervades himself with friendliness directed toward himself, for it is impossible to feel true friendliness or love for others unless, in the best sense of the term, one feels it for oneself; then he proceeds in imagination to send waves of friendliness in every direction, to reach every being in every corner of the world. After pervading the world with love he may repeat the process with the three other cardinal virtues—compassion, joy, and equanimity. These forms of the practice of "right mindfulness" are known as Brahma-vihāras, freely translated "sublime moods." They are still practiced by Buddhists throughout the world, and it is believed, especially among the Mahāyānist sects, that the waves of friendliness constantly poured out by many thousands of meditating monks have a very positive effect on the welfare of the world.

This a man should do who knows what is good for him,
Who understands the meaning of the Place of Peace
    [i.e., Nirvāna]—
He should be able, upright, truly straight,
Kindly of speech, mild, and without conceit.

He should be well content, soon satisfied,
Having few wants and simple tastes,
With composed senses, discreet,
Not arrogant or grasping. . . .

In his deeds there should be no meanness
For which the wise might blame him.

May all be happy and safe!
May all beings gain inner joy—
All living beings whatever
Without exception, weak or strong,
Whether long or high
Middling or small, subtle or gross,
Seen or unseen,
Dwelling afar or near,
Born or yet unborn—
May all beings gain inner joy.

May no being deceive another,
Nor in any way scorn another,
Nor, in anger or ill-will,
Desire another's sorrow.

As a mother cares for her son,
Her only son, all her days,
So towards all things living
A man's mind should be all-embracing.
Friendliness for the whole world,
All-embracing, he should raise in his mind,
Above, below, and across,
Unhindered, free from hate and ill-will.

Standing, walking or sitting,
Or lying down, till he falls asleep,
He should remain firm in this mindfulness,
For this is the sublime mood.
Avoiding all false views,
Virtuous, filled with insight,
Let him conquer the lust of the passions,
And he shall never again be born of the womb.

[From *Sutta Nipāta*, p. 143 ff.]

Hatred and Love

*The idea of "turning the other cheek" in one's personal relations is
frequently to be found in Buddhist literature. Nevertheless there are
few condemnations of warfare, as distinct from acts of violence on
the part of individuals, and the Theravāda scriptures contain no
passages on this latter topic as forthright as Ashoka's Thirteenth
Rock Edict (quoted later). The following verses from the Way of
Righteousness exemplify these points.*

"He insulted me, he struck me,
   He defeated me, he robbed me!"
Those who harbor such thoughts
   Are never appeased in their hatred. . . .
But those who do not harbor them
   Are quickly appeased.

Never in this world is hate
   Appeased by hatred;

It is only appeased by love—
This is an eternal law (*sanantana-dhamma*).[1]

Victory breeds hatred
For the defeated lie down in sorrow.
Above victory or defeat
The calm man dwells in peace.

[From *Dhammapada*, 3–5, 201]

Buddhism and Everyday Life

The Admonition to Singāla is the longest single passage in the Pali
scriptures devoted to lay morality. Though put in the mouth of the
Buddha, it is probably not authentically his; parts of it, however,
may be based on a few transmitted recollections of his teaching.
Like many other Discourses it seems to emanate from more than
one source, for the earlier part, enumerating the many sins and
faults to which the layman is liable, and describing the true friend,
is divided by a series of verses from the later and finer passage,
defining the duties of the layman in his sixfold relationship with
his fellows.

The reader should notice the solid, frugal, mercantile virtues
which are inculcated, especially in the first part. This sermon is
evidently not directed chiefly at the very poor or the very rich, but
at the prosperous middle class. Also noteworthy are the paragraphs
on the duties of husbands and wives and masters and servants in
the second part of the sermon—if read in terms of rights rather
than of duties they seem to imply the wife's right to full control
of household affairs and to an adequate dress allowance, and the
employee's right to fair wages and conditions, regular holidays, and
free medical attention.

Once when the Lord was staying in the Bamboo Grove at
Rājagaha, Singāla, a householder's son, got up early, went out
from Rājagaha, and, with his clothes and hair still wet from
his morning ablutions, joined his hands in reverence and
worshiped the several quarters of earth and sky—east, south,
west, north, above, and below. Now early that same morning
the Lord dressed himself, and with bowl and robe went into
Rājagaha to beg his food. He saw Singāla worshiping the
quarters, and asked him why he did so.

[1] Skt. *Sanātana dharma*, a conventional term designating "Hinduism," redefined here in terms of Buddhist ethics.

"When my father lay dying," Singāla replied, "he told me to worship the quarters thus. I honor my father's words, and respect and revere them, and so I always get up early and worship the quarters in this way."

"But to worship the six quarters thus is not in accordance with noble conduct."

"How then, Sir, should they be worshiped in accordance with noble conduct? Will the Lord be so good as to tell me?"

"Listen then," said the Lord, "and I'll tell you. Mark well what I say!"

"I will, Sir," Singāla replied. And the Lord spoke as follows:

"If the noble lay-disciple has given up the four vices of action, if he does no evil deed from any of the four motives, if he doesn't follow the six ways of squandering his wealth, if he avoids all these fourteen evils—then he embraces the six quarters, he is ready for the conquest of both worlds, he is fortunate both in this world and the next, and when his body breaks up on his death he is reborn to bliss in heaven.

"What are the four vices of action that he gives up? They are injury to life, taking what is not given, base conduct in sexual matters, and false speech. . . .

"What are the four motives of evil deeds which he avoids? Evil deeds are committed from partiality, enmity, stupidity, and fear.

"And what are the six ways of squandering wealth? They are addiction to drink, the cause of carelessness; roaming the streets at improper times; frequenting fairs; gambling; keeping bad company; and idleness.

"There are six dangers in addiction to drink: actual loss of wealth; increased liability to quarrels; liability to illness; loss of reputation; indecent exposure; and weakened intelligence.

"There are six dangers in roaming the streets at improper times: the man who does so is unprotected and unguarded; so are his wife and children; and likewise his property; he incurs suspicion of having committed crime; he is the subject of false rumors; in fact he goes out to meet all kinds of trouble.

"There are six dangers in frequenting fairs: the man who does so becomes an insatiable addict of dancing; singing; music; story-telling; jugglers; or acrobats.

"There are six dangers in gambling: the winner incurs hatred; the loser regrets his lost money; there is obvious loss of wealth; a gambler's word is not respected in the law courts; he is scorned by his friends and counselors; and he is not cultivated by people who want to marry their daughters, for the rogue who's always dicing isn't fit to keep a wife.

"There are six dangers in keeping bad company: a man who does so has as his friends and companions rogues; libertines; drunkards; confidence men; swindlers; and toughs.

"And there are six dangers in idleness: A man says, 'it's too cold' and doesn't work; or he says, 'it's too hot'; or 'it's too early'; or 'it's too late'; or 'I'm too hungry'; or 'I'm too full.' And so all the while he won't do what he ought to do, and he earns no new wealth, but fritters away what he has already earned.

"There are four types who should be looked on as enemies in the guise of friends: a grasping man; a smooth-spoken man; a man who only says what you want to hear; and a man who helps you waste your money.

"The grasping man is an enemy on four grounds: he is grasping; when he gives a little he expects a lot in return; what duty he performs he does out of fear; and he only serves his own interests.

"The smooth-spoken man is an enemy on four grounds: he speaks you fair about the past; he speaks you fair about the future; he tries to win you over by empty promises; but when there's something to be done he shows his shortcomings.[1]

"The man who only says what you want to hear is an enemy on four grounds: he consents to an evil deed; he doesn't consent to a good one; he praises you to your face; but he runs you down behind your back.

"The wastrel is an enemy on four grounds: he is your companion when you drink; when you roam the streets at improper times; when you go to fairs; and when you gamble.

"But there are four types who should be looked on as friends true of heart: a man who seeks to help you; a man

[1] The commentator Buddhaghosa gives a quaint example of the conduct of such a false friend—you send a message asking him to lend you his cart, and he replies that the axle is broken.

who is the same in weal and woe; a man who gives good
advice; and a man who is sympathetic. . . .

The friend who is a helper,
    The friend in weal and woe,
The friend who gives good counsel,
    The friend who sympathizes—
These the wise man should know
    As his four true friends,
And should devote himself to them
    As a mother to the child of her body.

The wise and moral man
    Shines like a fire on a hilltop,
Making money like the bee,
    Who does not hurt the flower.
Such a man makes his pile
    As an anthill, gradually.
The man grown wealthy thus
    Can help his family
And firmly bind his friends
    To himself. He should divide
His money in four parts;
    On one part he should live,
With two expand his trade,
    And the fourth he should save
Against a rainy day.[2]

"And how does the noble lay-disciple embrace the six
quarters? He should recognize these as the six quarters:
mother and father as the east; teachers as the south; wife

[2] These verses are undoubtedly popular gnomic poetry, adapted with
little or no alteration to Buddhist purposes. They effectively give
the lie to the picture, still popular in some circles, of ancient India
as a land of "plain living and high thinking." The last three verses
are evidently the product of a society quite as acquisitive as that of
present-day Europe or America. The commentator Buddhaghosa
found them difficult, for the ideal layman is here said to plow half
his income back into his trade, but to devote nothing to religious or
charitable causes. The phenomenal rate of reinvestment advocated
suggests a rapidly expanding economy.

and children as the west; friends and counselors as the north; slaves and servants as below; and ascetics and brāhmans as above.

"A son should serve his mother and father as the eastern quarter in five ways: having been maintained by them in his childhood he should maintain them in their old age; he should perform the duties which formerly devolved on them; he should maintain the honor and the traditions of his family and lineage; he should make himself worthy of his heritage; and he should make offerings to the spirits of the departed. And thus served by their son as the eastern quarter his mother and father should care for him in five ways: they should restrain him from evil; encourage him to do good; have him taught a profession; arrange for his marriage to a suitable wife; and transfer his inheritance to him in due time. Thus he embraces the eastern quarter and makes it safe and propitious.

"A pupil should serve his teacher as the southern quarter in five ways: by rising [to greet him when he enters]; by waiting upon him; by willingness to learn; by attentive service; and by diligently learning his trade. And thus served by his pupil as the southern quarter a teacher should care for him in five ways: he should train him in good conduct; teach him in such a way that he remembers what he has been taught; thoroughly instruct him in the lore of every art [of his trade]; speak well of him to his friends and counselors; and protect him in every quarter. Thus he embraces the southern quarter and makes it safe and propitious.

"A husband should serve his wife as the western quarter in five ways: by honoring her; by respecting her; by remaining faithful to her; by giving her charge of the home; and by duly giving her adornments. And thus served by her husband as the western quarter a wife should care for him in five ways: she should be efficient in her household tasks; she should manage her servants well; she should be chaste; she should take care of the goods which he brings home; and she should be skillful and untiring in all her duties. Thus he embraces the western quarter and makes it safe and propitious.

"A gentleman should serve his friends and counselors as the northern quarter in five ways: by generosity; by courtesy;

by helping them; by treating them as he would treat himself; and by keeping his word to them. And thus served by a gentleman as the northern quarter his friends and counselors should care for him in five ways: they should protect him when he is careless; they should guard his property on such occasions; they should be a refuge for him in trouble; in misfortune they should not leave him; and they should respect other members of his family. Thus he embraces the western quarter and makes it safe and propitious.

"A master should serve his slaves and servants as the lower quarter in five ways: he should assign them work in proportion to their strength; he should give them due food and wages; he should care for them in sickness; he should share especially tasty luxuries with them; and he should give them holidays at due intervals. Thus served by their master as the lower quarter they should care for him in five ways: they should get up before him; they should go to bed after him; they should be content with what he gives them; they should do their work well; and they should spread abroad his praise and good name. Thus he embraces the lower quarter and makes it safe and propitious.

"In five ways a gentleman should serve ascetics and brāhmans as the upper quarter: by affectionate acts; by affectionate words; by affectionate thoughts; by not closing his doors to them; and by duly supplying them with food. Thus served by a gentleman as the upper quarter they should care for him in six ways: they should restrain him from evil; they should encourage him to do good; they should feel for him with a friendly mind; they should teach him what he has not heard before; they should encourage him to follow what he has already learned; and they should show him the way to heaven. Thus he embraces the upper quarter and makes it safe and propitious."

[From Dīgha Nikāya, 3.180 ff.]

THE SOCIAL AND POLITICAL ORDER

Few pages in the massive literature of Buddhism lay down definite instructions on social or political life, and the amount of speculation by Buddhist authors on the problems

of state and society is not large. Indeed Buddhism has sometimes been stigmatized as not a true religion at all, but a
mere system of self-discipline for monks, with no significant
message for the ordinary man except that he should if possible leave the world and take the yellow robe. In fact Buddhists have always realized that not every layman was morally or intellectually capable of becoming a monk, and the
scriptures, as we have seen above, do contain here and there
instructions especially intended for layfolk, together with
occasional passages with a social or political message. Nevertheless it may be that one of the reasons for the disappear-
ance of Buddhism in the land of its birth was that it left the
laymen too dependent on the ministrations of the brāhmans,
and, instead of giving a lead in political and social matters,
was too often willing to compromise with the existing ways
of everyday life.

Though in practice Buddhism seems to have accepted the
existence of a society with sharp class divisions and to have
made no frontal attack on it, there are many passages in
Buddhist literature in which the four classes of Hindu society
are declared to be fundamentally equal, and in which men
are said to be worthy of respect not through birth, but only
through spiritual or moral merit. Though we cannot show
that Buddhism had any definite effect on the Indian system
of class and caste, its teachings obviously tended against the
extremer manifestations of social inequality. In those lands
where Buddhism was implanted upon societies little influenced by Hindu ideas the caste system in its Indian form is
not to be found.

In politics Buddhism definitely discouraged the preten-
sions of kings to divine or semidivine status. While Hindu
teachers often declared that kings were partial incarnations
of the gods and encouraged an attitude of passive obedience
to them, the Buddhist scriptures categorically state that the
first king was merely the chosen leader of the people, appointed by them to restrain crime and protect property, and
that his right to levy taxation depended not on birth or succession but on the efficient fulfillment of his duty. The *Birth
Stories*, among the most influential of the Buddhist scriptures, contain several tales of wicked kings overthrown as a
result of popular rebellion. Thus Buddhism had a rational

attitude to the state. The constitution of the Buddhist order, in which each monastery was virtually a law unto itself, deciding major issues after free discussion among the assembled monks, tended toward democracy, and it has been suggested that it was based on the practices of the tribal republics of the Buddha's day. Though Buddhism never formulated a distinctive system of political ethics it generally tended to mitigate the autocracy of the Indian king.

On the question of war Buddhism said little, though a few passages in the Buddhist scriptures oppose it. Like the historical Ashoka, the ideal emperor of Buddhism gains his victories by moral suasion. This did not prevent many Buddhist kings of India and Ceylon from becoming great conquerors and pursuing their political aims with much the same ruthlessness as their Hindu neighbors. Two of pre-Muslim India's greatest conquerors, Harsha of Kanauj (606–647) and Dharmapāla of Bihar and Bengal (c. 770–810), were Buddhists. In fact Buddhism had little direct effect on the political order, except in the case of Ashoka, and its leaders seem often to have been rather submissive to the temporal power. An Erastian relationship between church and state is indicated in the inscriptions of Ashoka, and in Buddhist Ceylon the same relationship usually existed.

Early travelers have left a number of valuable accounts of conditions in ancient India. Two of these, that of the Greek Megasthenes (c. 300 B.C.) and that of the Chinese pilgrim Fa-hsien (A.D. c. 400), are of special interest for our purposes, for the first was written before Buddhism had become an important factor in Indian life, and the second when it had already passed its most flourishing period and had entered on a state of slow decline. Megasthenes found a very severe judicial system, with many crimes punished by execution or mutilation. The existence of such a harsh system of punishment is confirmed by the famous Hindu text on polity, the *Arthaśāstra*, the kernel of which dates from about the same time. Under Chandragupta Maurya, the grandfather of Ashoka, the state was highly organized and all branches of human activity were hemmed in by many troublesome regulations enforced by a large corps of government officials. Fa-hsien, on the other hand, found a land where the death penalty was not imposed, and mutilation was inflicted only for very serious crime; and he was especially impressed by the fact that human freedom was respected and people were able to move freely from one part of the land to the other without passports or other forms of interference from the government. In Megasthenes' day all classes freely ate meat, while in the time of Fa-hsien only the outcastes did so.[1] It seems certain that Buddhism had something to do with the great change in the direction of mildness and nonviolence which had taken place in the seven hundred years between the two travelers. Certainly Buddhism was not the only factor in the change, for sentiments in favor of tolerance, mildness, and nonviolence are to be found also in Hindu and Jain writings, but it is very probable that Buddhism was the greatest single factor, for it was the most active and vigorous religion in the period in question.

Though Ashoka was practically forgotten by India his message calling for good relations between rulers and ruled was not, and echoes of it may be heard in many non-Buddhist sources of later date. On the other hand his fond hope that aggressive wars would cease forever as a result of his propaganda was unfulfilled, and the successors of Ashoka seem to have been if anything more militant than his predecessors. It would seem that Buddhism had little effect in encouraging peace within the borders of India.

Conditions of the Welfare of Societies

The following passage occurs in the Discourse of the Great Passing-away, which describes the last days and death of the Buddha. Though the words are put into his own mouth, it is quite likely that the passage is based on a series of popular aphorisms current among the Vajjian tribesmen themselves. It is followed by a longer passage in which the Buddha is purported to have adapted the list of the seven conditions of the welfare of republics to the circumstances of the Buddhist Order. According to a tradition preserved by the commentator Buddhaghosa, King Ajātasattu's wily minister Vassakāra, hearing the Buddha's words, set to work by "fifth column" methods to sow dissension among the leaders of the Vajjis, with the result that Magadha was able to annex their lands within a few years.

[1] If we are to believe the pilgrim, who may have exaggerated somewhat.

Notice especially the third condition. No early Indian sect took kindly to innovation, and according to orthodox Hindu thought the purpose of government was not to legislate, but only to administer the eternal law (Sanātanadharma). Though the Buddhists had a somewhat different conception of dharma they shared the conservatism of the Hindus in this respect. Nevertheless new legislation was enacted from time to time, as will be seen later in the edicts of Ashoka.

Once the Lord was staying at Rājagaha on the hill called Vulture's Peak . . . and the Venerable Ānanda was standing behind him and fanning him. And the Lord said: "Have you heard, Ānanda, that the Vajjis call frequent public assemblies of the tribe?" "Yes, Lord," he replied.

"As long as they do so," said the Lord, "they may be expected not to decline, but to flourish."

"As long as they meet in concord, conclude their meetings in concord, and carry out their policies in concord; . . . as long as they make no laws not already promulgated, and set aside nothing enacted in the past, acting in accordance with the ancient institutions of the Vajjis established in olden days; . . . as long as they respect, esteem, reverence, and support the elders of the Vajjis, and look on it as a duty to heed their words; . . . as long as no women or girls of their tribes are held by force or abducted; . . . as long as they respect, esteem, reverence, and support the shrines of the Vajjis, whether in town or country, and do not neglect the proper offerings and rites laid down and practiced in the past; [1] . . . as long as they give due protection, deference, and support to the perfected beings among them so that such perfected beings may come to the land from afar and live comfortably among them, so long may they be expected not to decline, but to flourish."

[From Dīgha Nikāya, 2.72 ff.]

Class and Caste in Buddhism

Though in practice it would seem that Indian Buddhists maintained the system of class and caste, the theoretical attitude of Buddhism

[1] Note the respect paid to popular religion, which Buddhism adapted in the cults of the sacred tree and the stūpa, and later in that of the image.

was equalitarian. We have seen that the division of the four classes was believed to be a functional one, with no divine sanction. The Buddhist view is summed up in the verse of the Discourse Section (Sutta Nipāta, verse 136):

No brāhman is such by birth.
No outcaste is such by birth.
An outcaste is such by his deeds.
A brāhman is such by his deeds.

In the following passage the Buddha puts forward numerous arguments in favor of this view, though many other passages show that lay Buddhists were encouraged to treat worthy brāhmans with respect.

Once when the Lord was staying at Sāvatthī there were five hundred brāhmans from various countries in the city . . . and they thought: "This ascetic Gautama preaches that all four classes are pure. Who can refute him?"

At that time there was a young brāhman named Assalā-yana in the city . . . a youth of sixteen, thoroughly versed in the Vedas . . . and in all brāhmanic learning. "He can do it!" thought the brāhmans, and so they asked him to try; but he answered, "The ascetic Gautama teaches a doctrine of his own,[1] and such teachers are hard to refute. I can't do it!" They asked him a second time . . . and again he refused; and they asked him a third time, pointing out that he ought not to admit defeat without giving battle. This time he agreed, and so, surrounded by a crowd of brāhmans, he went to the Lord, and, after greeting him, sat down and said:

"Brāhmans maintain that only they are the highest class, and the others are below them. They are white, the others black; only they are pure, and not the others. Only they are the true sons of Brahmā, born from his mouth,[2] born of

[1] *Dhammavādī*: Our translation is on the basis of Buddhaghosa's commentary as generally interpreted. Dr. A. K. Warder suggests that the term may here mean "a teacher maintaining that the world is governed by natural law."
[2] According to the *Purusa Sūkta* (*Rig Veda*, 10.90) brāhmans are born from the head of the primeval man, while the other three classes are born from his arms, trunk, and feet, respectively.

Brahmā, creations of Brahmā, heirs of Brahmā. Now what does the worthy Gautama say to that?"

"Do the brāhmans really maintain this, Assalāyana, when they're born of women just like anyone else, of brāhman women who have their periods and conceive, give birth and nurse their children, just like any other women?"

"For all you say, this is what they think. . . ."

"Have you ever heard that in the lands of the Greeks and Kambojas and other peoples on the borders there are only two classes, masters and slaves, and a master can become a slave and vice versa?"

"Yes, I've heard so."

"And what strength or support does that fact give to the brāhmans' claim?"

"Nevertheless, that is what they think."

"Again if a man is a murderer, a thief, or an adulterer, or commits other grave sins, when his body breaks up on death does he pass on to purgatory if he's a kshatriya, vaishya, or shūdra, but not if he's a brāhman?"

"No, Gautama. In such a case the same fate is in store for all men, whatever their class."

"And if he avoids grave sin, will he go to heaven if he's a brāhman, but not if he's a man of the lower classes?"

"No, Gautama. In such a case the same reward awaits all men, whatever their class."

"And is a brāhman capable of developing a mind of love without hate or ill-will, but not a man of the other classes?"

"No, Gautama. All four classes are capable of doing so."

"Can only a brāhman go down to a river and wash away dust and dirt, and not men of the other classes?"

"No, Gautama, all four classes can."

"Now suppose a king were to gather together a hundred men of different classes and to order the brāhmans and kshatriyas to take kindling wood of sāl, pine, lotus or sandal, and light fires, while the low class folk did the same with common wood. What do you think would happen? Would the fires of the high-born men blaze up brightly . . . and those of the humble fail?"

"No, Gautama. It would be alike with high and lowly. . . . Every fire would blaze with the same bright flame." . . .

"Suppose there are two young brāhman brothers, one a

scholar and the other uneducated. Which of them would be served first at memorial feasts, festivals, and sacrifices, or when entertained as guests?"

"The scholar, of course; for what great benefit would accrue from entertaining the uneducated one?"

"But suppose the scholar is ill-behaved and wicked, while the uneducated one is well-behaved and virtuous?"

"Then the uneducated one would be served first, for what great benefit would accrue from entertaining an ill-behaved and wicked man?"

"First, Assalāyana, you based your claim on birth, then you gave up birth for learning, and finally you have come round to my way of thinking, that all four classes are equally pure!"

At this Assalāyana sat silent . . . his shoulders hunched, his eyes cast down, thoughtful in mind, and with no answer at hand.

[From *Majjhima Nikāya*, 2.147 ff.]

Ashoka: The Buddhist Emperor

The great emperor Ashoka (c. 268–233 B.C.), third of the line of the Mauryas, became a Buddhist and attempted to govern India according to the precepts of Buddhism as he understood them. His new policy was promulgated in a series of edicts, which are still to be found, engraved on rocks and pillars in many parts of India. Written in a form of Prakrit, or ancient vernacular, with several local variations, they can claim little literary merit, for their style is crabbed and often ambiguous. In one of these edicts he describes his conversion, and its effects:

When the king, Beloved of the Gods and of Gracious Mien, had been consecrated eight years Kalinga[1] was conquered, 150,000 people were deported, 100,000 were killed, and many times that number died. But after the conquest of Kalinga, the Beloved of the Gods began to follow Righteousness (Dharma), to love Righteousness, and to give instruction in Righteousness. Now the Beloved of the Gods regrets the conquest of Kalinga, for when an independent country is

---

[1] The coastal region comprising the modern Orissa and the northern part of Andhra State.

conquered people are killed, they die, or are deported, and that the Beloved of the Gods finds very painful and grievous. And this he finds even more grievous—that all the inhabitants—brāhmans, ascetics, and other sectarians, and householders who are obedient to superiors, parents, and elders, who treat friends, acquaintances, companions, relatives, slaves, and servants with respect, and are firm in their faith —all suffer violence, murder, and separation from their loved ones. Even those who are fortunate enough not to have lost those near and dear to them are afflicted at the misfortunes of friends, acquaintances, companions, and relatives. The participation of all men in common suffering is grievous to the Beloved of the Gods. Moreover there is no land, except that of the Greeks, where groups of brāhmans and ascetics are not found, or where men are not members of one sect or another. So now, even if the number of those killed and captured in the conquest of Kalinga had been a hundred or a thousand times less, it would be grievous to the Beloved of the Gods. The Beloved of the Gods will forgive as far as he can, and he even conciliates the forest tribes of his dominions; but he warns them that there is power even in the remorse of the Beloved of the Gods, and he tells them to reform, lest they be killed.[2]

For all beings the Beloved of the Gods desires security, self-control, calm of mind, and gentleness. The Beloved of the Gods considers that the greatest victory is the victory of Righteousness; and this he has won here (in India) and even five hundred leagues beyond his frontiers in the realm of the Greek king Antiochus, and beyond Antiochus among the four kings Ptolemy, Antigonus, Magas, and Alexander.[3]

[2] Note that Ashoka has by no means completely abandoned the use of force. This passage probably refers to the wild uncivilized tribesmen of the hills and jungles, who still occasionally cause trouble in Assam and some other parts of India, and in ancient days were a much greater problem.

[3] Antiochus II Theos of Syria, Ptolemy II Philadelphus of Egypt, Antigonus Gonatas of Macedonia, Magas of Cyrene, and Alexander of Epirus. Classical sources tell us nothing about Ashoka's "victories of Righteousness" over these kings. Probably he sent envoys to them, urging them to accept his new policy and his moral leadership. Evidently he never gave up his imperial ambitions, but

Even where the envoys of the Beloved of the Gods have not been sent men hear of the way in which he follows and teaches Righteousness, and they too follow it and will follow it. Thus he achieves a universal conquest, and conquest always gives a feeling of pleasure; yet it is but a slight pleasure, for the Beloved of the Gods only looks on that which concerns the next life as of great importance.

I have had this inscription of Righteousness engraved that all my sons and grandsons may not seek to gain new victories, that in whatever victories they may gain they may prefer forgiveness and light punishment, that they may consider the only [valid] victory the victory of Righteousness, which is of value both in this world and the next, and that all their pleasure may be in Righteousness. . . .

[From the Thirteenth Rock Edict]

This edict of Ashoka is his last important inscription, in which the emperor, eighteen years after his conversion, reviews his reign:

In the past kings sought to make the people progress in Righteousness, but they did not progress. . . . And I asked myself how I might uplift them through progress in Righteousness. . . . Thus I decided to have them instructed in Righteousness, and to issue ordinances of Righteousness, so that by hearing them the people might conform, advance in the progress of Righteousness, and themselves make great progress. . . . For that purpose many officials are employed among the people to instruct them in Righteousness and to explain it to them. . . .

Moreover I have had banyan trees planted on the roads to give shade to man and beast; I have planted mango groves, and I have had ponds dug and shelters erected along the roads at every eight kos.[4] Everywhere I have had wells dug for the benefit of man and beast. But this benefit is but small, for in many ways the kings of olden time have worked for the

---

attempted to further them in a benevolent spirit and without recourse to arms.

[4] There is some uncertainty about the interpretation of this phrase. If that given above is correct, it implies intervals of about sixteen miles, or a day's journey.

welfare of the world; but what I have done has been done that men may conform to Righteousness.

All the good deeds that I have done have been accepted and followed by the people. And so obedience to mother and father, obedience to teachers, respect for the aged, kindliness to brāhmans and ascetics, to the poor and weak, and to slaves and servants, have increased and will continue to increase. . . . And this progress of Righteousness among men has taken place in two manners, by enforcing conformity to Righteousness, and by exhortation. I have enforced the law against killing certain animals and many others, but the greatest progress of Righteousness among men comes from exhortation in favor of noninjury to life and abstention from killing living beings.[5]

I have done this that it may endure . . . as long as the moon and sun, and that my sons and my great-grandsons may support it; for by supporting it they will gain both this world and the next.

[From the Seventh Pillar Edict]

[5] For all his humanitarianism, Ashoka did not abolish the death penalty, as was done by some later Indian kings.

2 ❀

THE LIFE OF BUDDHA AS A WAY

OF SALVATION

INTRODUCTION

One of the great themes of Buddhism is the Buddha himself. As man, as teacher, as savior, and as a being with many
attributes of divinity, he remained a central figure in the
development of the religion and an important link between
the so-called Lesser Vehicle (Hīnayāna) and Greater Vehicle
(Mahāyāna). In the previous chapter our discussion of early
Buddhism focused on the founder's basic teachings concerning the sufferings and illusions of human existence and
the path by which deliverance might be attained. Nirvāna,
not the Buddha, was the ultimate goal of the religious quest.

We have also seen how little can be said about the Buddha's life with historical certainty. That we have so few reliable records, however, does not indicate a lack of interest
in the life and activities of the Buddha. The sense of history
and the practice of historiography may have been relatively
weak in India, but the Buddha as an inspiring example of
his own teachings was much in the minds of his followers.
A process of euhemerization set in very early. Already by the
first century A.D. myths and legends concerning the life and
previous existences of the Buddha abounded. Many of these
reflected popular religious attitudes that had essentially nothing to do with Buddhism itself, but others celebrated and
enhanced what must have been a central core of tradition

concerning the life and teachings of Gotama Buddha himself.

The *Deeds of the Buddha* (*Buddhacarita*), attributed to Ashvaghosha, was written between the first and second centuries A.D. It combines a strong pietistic approach with a concern for preserving the essentials of the traditional faith. Ashvaghosha drew on what he believed to be standard and authoritative accounts of the Buddha's life, rejecting the more extravagant stories that had grown up. At the same time there is here an element of religious awe and devotion expressed through a fertile poetic imagination. The *Buddhacarita* is a masterpiece of Sanskrit poetry, written in the courtly *kāvya* style. Its emotional tone and delight in nature strongly resemble the later poetry of Kālidāsa in the same style. Thus it is not an historical account but religious and poetic truth that Ashvaghosha reveals to us in the *Buddhacarita*.

Worth noting also is Ashvaghosha's concern for the basic moral and spiritual teachings of the Buddha, rather than for any particular philosophical interpretation of them. Although the work was composed in the same religious atmosphere in which the Mahāyāna arose, the characteristic metaphysical doctrines of the Mahāyāna are missing. Ashvaghosha seeks only to convey the established tradition in a popular and appealing form. The explicitly didactic portions confine themselves to such fundamental doctrines as the Four Truths, the Noble Eightfold Path, the Chain of Causation, etc., while the work as a whole stresses devotion to Buddha and the importance of meditation (especially yogic trance) as an essential practice.

In this respect Ashvaghosha presents a kind of common denominator among the various schools and sects. More fundamentally still he is concerned with the common denominator in human experience. The central experiences of the Buddha's life he sees as relevant to every human life, and this is reflected in the structure of the *Buddhacarita*, as we are led along the path of the Buddha's spiritual pilgrimage.

The translation which follows is mainly based on a Sanskrit manuscript of the thirteenth or fourteenth century A.D. from Nepal with missing sections supplied from a Chinese version of the fifth century. Though it is much abridged and lacks the richness of descriptive detail and narrative incident which adorns the original, the reader may still appreciate why this text should have gained such popularity in later times, especially among Mahāyāna Buddhists of the Far East. The Chinese pilgrim I-ching said of it: "The *Buddhacarita* is widely read or sung throughout the five regions of India and the countries of the Southern Sea. Its author clothes manifold meanings and ideas in a few words, which rejoice the heart of the reader, so that he never tires of reading the poem. Besides it may be considered meritorious for one to read this book, inasmuch as it contains the noble doctrine in a concise form."

THE LIFE OF THE BUDDHA

His Birth and the Sages' Prophecies

The Buddha's appearance in the world takes place in splendid surroundings and the most auspicious circumstances. Supernatural elements and fanciful features are freely employed to engage the reader's imagination and heighten his expectations. From many, no doubt, this glorified setting evoked a sense of religious awe, but its deeper meaning becomes apparent with the predictions that the Buddha, heir to so much power and wealth and glory, is destined to renounce all of these for something greater.

The significance of this setting may be appreciated too in the light of the widespread, but shallow, view that Buddhism's preoccupation with suffering must reflect a deep-seated pessimism over the miserable conditions of life in ancient India. Not only is the historical basis for this questionable, but in terms of the traditional Buddhist view there are certainly no grounds for taking poverty or misfortune as the starting point of its inquiry into the nature of human existence. On the contrary the Buddha starts with everything in his favor, and if in spite of this, he must reckon with suffering in this world, then there is no one, no people, no realm and no age, however well-circumstanced, that can avoid this confrontation.

There was a king of the unconquerable Shākya race, descended from Ikshavāku, named Shuddhodana. Endowed with wealth and virtue, he was loved and esteemed by his people, as the moon in autumn.

This king, as powerful as Indra, had a queen comparable to Shachī, Indra's spouse. As steadfast as the earth and as pure in heart as a lotus flower, she was called Māyā. . . .

In her sleep, Māyā saw a white elephant entering her womb and thereby conceived; yet she was free from anxiety and illusion.

She longed however for the peace of a secluded wood, and as the Lumbinī grove, with its fountains, flowers, and fruit trees, was quiet and suitable for contemplation, she asked the king to let her go there.

Knowing her intention, the king, in delight, ordered his followers to accompany the queen to the grove.[1]

In that lovely grove, the queen became aware that the time of her delivery was near; thousands of waiting-girls greeted her as she proceeded to a couch overspread with an awning.

Then, when the constellation Pushya was most clear and serene,[2] from the side of the queen, who was purified by her vows, a son was born for the well-being of the world without causing her any pain or illness. . . .

He shone in splendor and steadfastness, as the morning sun coming down upon the earth; he was exceedingly radiant and drew others' eyes toward him like the moon. . . .

Gazing at the four quarters with the bearing of a lion, he uttered a speech prophesying his auspicious attainment in the future: "I am born to be enlightened for the well-being of the world; this is my last birth." . . .

Present at the grove were dignified and learned brāhmans, experts in reading omens and noted for their eloquence. They were exceedingly delighted on seeing the omens, and revealed the truth to the king who they knew was apprehensive . . .

"Auspicious signs found on his body, such as its golden color and the exquisite radiance of its luster, indicate that

[1] Since the Sanskrit manuscript is missing, the translation thus far has been based on the Chinese text in *Taishō daizōkyō*, IV, 1a.
[2] In Chinese translation, the day is specified as April 8, which has traditionally been celebrated as the date of his birth throughout the Far East.

he is certain to be the perfectly Enlightened One, or a universal monarch if he takes pleasure in worldly affairs.

"Should he be a great, earthly sovereign, he will rule the entire world with courage and righteousness, leading all kings, as the light of the sun leads the lights of the world.

"If he seeks deliverance by living in a forest, he will acquire true wisdom and illumine the entire world, standing aloft like Mt. Meru, the king of mountains.

"As gold is the best of metals; the ocean, of waters; the moon, of planets; the sun, of lights; so is your son the noblest of all men in the world." [3]

The king, pleased, courteously offered gifts to the brāhmans, hoping that his son might become lord of the earth as prophesied and then retire to the forest upon reaching old age.

Then, the great seer Asita, learning by means of signs and ascetic power, of the birth of the prince who would put an end to birth, came to the palace of the Shākya king, thirsting for the true teaching. . . .

When Asita saw the prince on the nurse's lap, as had the son of Agni lain on the lap of Devī (Pārvatī), tears flickered on his eyelashes and he looked up to heaven with a sigh. . . .

Seeing Asita's eyes brimming with tears, the king trembled with affection for his son, and choking with emotion asked him . . .

"Is this young shoot of my family, just born, destined to wither without blooming? Tell me quickly, Venerable One, for I am disturbed; you know the love of a father for his son."

The sage understood the king's agitation, caused by his foreboding of misfortune, and said: "Oh King, be not disturbed. What I have said about the prince admits of no doubt.

"I am distressed not because of anything untoward to befall him, but out of sorrow for myself that I am to be disappointed. It is now time for me to depart this life, just

---

[3] The preceding five verses have been translated from the Chinese, *Taishō IV*, 1c–2a.

when he is born who will attain the Enlightenment so hard to achieve, which brings rebirth to an end.

"He will abandon the kingdom in his indifference to worldly pleasures; he will obtain the Truth (*tattva*) through diligent effort; he will shine forth, like the sun of knowledge, to expel the darkness of delusion in the world." . . .

Then the sage Asita, after telling the prince's true destiny to the king, fearful for his son, went away as he had come by the path of the wind, while all gazed up at him in reverence. . . .

Infancy passed and in due time the young prince received the initiation ceremony. The sciences proper to his family which would ordinarily take many years to learn, he mastered in a few days.

But the king of the Shākya, having heard from the sage Asita that the goal of the prince was to attain supreme bliss, sought to engage the prince in sensual pleasures, lest he should wish to go off to the forest.

Thereupon, the king summoned for his son a famous maiden named Yashodharā, who was endowed with beauty, modesty, and decorum, like the reincarnation of the Goddess of Beauty, from a family of long standing and good character. . . .

And so, in palaces like celestial mansions brought to earth, as white as the clouds of autumn and comfortable in all seasons, the prince spent his time listening to refined music performed by lovely maidens. . . .

In time, the shapely Yashodharā, bearing her own fame, gave in birth to the son of Shuddhodana, a son named Rāhula, whose face resembled the moon.

His Excursions from the Palace

Despite the considerable means at the King's disposal and his strenuous efforts to shield his son from the sufferings of life, the Prince's natural curiosity and the restless search for new pleasures lead him finally to venture forth from the palace. Outside, for the first time, he encounters genuine and irremediable suffering. It is a shocking experience, repeated on three subsequent occasions, as if to emphasize an ever deepening realization of the full implications of suffering. Ashvaghosha, well aware that many men appear insensitive to it, seems to be stressing a point: sooner or later every one must reckon with unmitigated sorrow or loss. The problem ignored does not disappear, but on the other hand a merely passive intellectual recognition avails nothing either. Unless the problem is felt in the core of one's being, there will not be the urgency, the determined motivation, to find a solution.

On one occasion, however, the Prince heard about woods filled with songs, abounding in fresh grass, with trees in which the cuckoos sounded, adorned with many lotus ponds.

And having learned of the attractions of the city's grove, in which the women took delight, the prince like a pent-up elephant, entertained the thought of going out to it.

The king, learning the desire of his dear son, arranged an excursion befitting his affection, majesty, and his son's age.

Yet he ordered that all commoners suffering any affliction should be kept off the royal road lest the tender-hearted prince be distressed at the sight of them.

Thus, those whose limbs were missing or maimed, and those who were old, sick, or wretched, were gently cleared from the royal route. . . .

Whereupon the prince mounted a golden chariot, to which were harnessed four well-trained steeds with golden trappings, driven by a manly, honest and skillful charioteer.

And, as the moon ascending the sky amidst the constellations, he proceeded with fitting retinue on the roads bestrewn with heaps of bright flowers, decorated with garlands and fluttering banners. . . .

When, for the first time, the prince saw the royal way filled with well-behaved citizens wearing clean and simple clothes, he was delighted and felt as if he were a different person.

Seeing that the city was joyful as paradise, however, the Shuddhādhivāsa gods, to incite the prince's renunciation of the world, created an old man.

The prince saw the man overcome with old age, different in form from other people, and his curiosity was aroused. With his eyes fixed on the man, he asked the charioteer:

"Oh, charioteer! Who is this man with gray hair, supported by a staff in his hand, his eyes sunken under his eyebrows, his limbs feeble and bent? Is this transformation a natural state or an accident?"

The charioteer, when he was thus asked, his intelligence being confused by the gods, saw no harm in telling the prince its significance, which should have been discreetly withheld from him:

"Old age, it is called, the destroyer of beauty and vigor, the source of sorrow, the depriver of pleasures, the slayer of memories, the enemy of sense organs. That man has been ruined by old age.

"He, too, in his infancy had taken milk and, in due time, had crawled on the ground; he then became a handsome youth, and now he has reached old age."

The prince, moved, asked the charioteer: "Will this evil come upon me also?" The charioteer then replied:

"Advanced age will certainly come upon you through the inescapable force of time, no matter how long you may live. People in the world are aware of old age, the destroyer of beauty; yet, they seek [pleasures]." . . .

For a long while, the prince kept his gaze on the decrepit man, sighing and shaking his head. Looking at the excited group of people, he said despondently:

"Thus, old age indiscriminately destroys memory, beauty, and strength, yet people in the world are not disturbed at seeing such a sight before them.

"This being so, turn back the horses, charioteer; go home quickly. How can I enjoy myself in the garden when the fear of death is revolving in my mind?"

At the command of the prince, the charioteer turned the chariot back. But when the prince had returned to the palace, struck by anxiety, he felt as if it were empty.

Even there he was unable to find peace of mind; therefore he went out again with the permission of the king, on the same arrangement as before.

Thereupon the gods created a man whose body was afflicted by disease. The son of Shuddhodana fixed his eyes on the man and asked the charioteer:

"Who is this man whose abdomen is swollen and whose body quivers as he breathes? His shoulders and arms are limp, his legs are pale and emaciated. Leaning on another for support, he is crying out, 'Mother!' "

To this the charioteer answered: "Lord, this is the great misfortune called disease, developed from a disorder of elements, by which this man, though he had been strong, has become disabled."

Eyeing him again compassionately, the prince said: "Is this evil peculiar to him or is this [danger of] disease common to all men?"

The charioteer replied: "Prince, this evil is common to all; yet the world filled with suffering seeks enjoyment, however oppressed it is by disease."

On hearing its meaning, the prince became despondent and trembled like the moon reflected on the waves of water. Filled with compassion, he spoke these words in a somewhat subdued tone:

"This is the calamity of disease in all men; yet, people in the world are unconcerned as they watch it. Indeed, vast is the ignorance of people who laugh when they themselves have not been released from the danger of sickness.

"Charioteer, go no farther, but direct the chariot back to the palace. Learning the danger of disease, my mind has been shocked and deflected from pleasures." . . .

[The young prince, however, takes yet another ride out of the palace and again, despite his father's precautions, encounters a distressing sight:]

As the prince rode on, the same gods produced a man's corpse, which the charioteer and the prince could see being carried on the road, though it was visible to no one else.

The prince asked the charioteer: "Who is the man being carried by four others, followed by persons in distress? He is well adorned, yet being mourned."

The charioteer, whose mind was overcome by the Shuddhādhivāsa gods of pure soul, told the Lord what should not have been revealed:

"This is someone bereft of intellect, senses, breath, and powers, lying unconscious like a bundle of grass or a log of wood. He had been raised and guarded with much care and affection, but now he is being abandoned."

Having heard the words of the charioteer, the prince became frightened and asked: "Is this state of being peculiar to this man, or is such the end of all men?"

The charioteer then said to him: "This is the last state

of all men. Death is certain for all, whether they be of low, middle, or high degree."

Though he was a steadfast man, the prince felt faint as soon as he heard about death. Leaning his shoulders against the railing, he said in a sad tone:

"This is the inescapable end for all men; yet, people in the world harbor no fear and seem unconcerned. Men must be hardened indeed to be so at ease as they walk down the road leading to the next life.

"Charioteer, turn back, for this is not the time for the pleasure-ground. How can a man of intelligence, aware of death, enjoy himself in this fateful hour?" . . .

[On his final excursion the prince is overwhelmed by the misery of existence as he watches the pitiful toil of men in the fields. Then:]

Longing for solitude, the prince kept his followers back and approached a lonely spot at the foot of a Jambū-tree, covered all over with beautiful fluttering leaves.

His First Meditation

In contrast to the overwhelming sense of misery which arises from his contacts with suffering, is the immediate reassurance which the prince derives from solitary meditation. Thus the pessimistic view of life is overcome by the mustering of one's own inner resources to deal with it. In the most fundamental sense withdrawal and concentration is a means available to anyone at any time. Here, however, the experience is described in terms of the yogic disciplines which were the common property of the Indian religious traditions.

There he sat on the clean ground where the soft grass glittered like beryl. Contemplating the birth and death of beings, he undertook to steady his mind in meditation.

In no time his mind became firm; he was released from mental distractions, such as the desire for objects of sense, and attained the first trance of calmness, which was characterized by non-defilement and accompanied by distinct cognition and reflection.

Having acquired the concentration of mind which springs from solitude, the prince was filled with extreme joy and bliss; then meditating on the course of the world, he thought that this state was indeed supreme.

Alas, wretched is he who, out of ignorance and the blindness of pride, ignores others who are distressed by old age, sickness, or death, though he himself, being likewise subject to disease, old age, and death, is helpless! . . .

As he thus perceived clearly the evils of disease, old age, and death in the world, the false pride in self, arising from a belief in one's strength, youth, and life, left him instantly.

He became neither excited nor distressed; free from doubt, sloth, and drowsiness, he was unaffected by sensual pleasures; and untouched by hatred or contempt of others.

While this passionless, pure insight of that great-souled one grew, a man in mendicant's clothes approached him without being seen by others.

The prince asked, "Tell me, who are you?" The man replied, "Oh, best of men, I am a mendicant who, in fear of birth and death, has renounced the world for the sake of deliverance.

"In this world which is characterized by destruction, I eagerly search for the blessed and indestructible state. I regard both kinsmen and strangers as equals, and I am free from the evils of passion arising from objects of sense.

"Living wherever I happen to be—at the foot of a tree, in a deserted house, in the mountains, or in the woods—I wander about, living on the alms I receive, without ties to person or place and with no expectation save for the attainment of the ultimate goal."

Saying this, the mendicant flew to the sky as the prince watched. . . . The latter now knew what he should do, and began thinking of a way to leave his home. . . .

His Departure from Home and Family

On returning to the palace, the prince informs his father of his decision to take up the life of a religious mendicant. The king, of course, is determined to prevent this. Significantly, however, he does not contest the validity of the search for religious salvation, but argues from the traditional Brāhmanical standpoint that a man must first fulfill his responsibilities in life; only when these have been discharged will he have the freedom, maturity and self-mastery to engage in the solitary pursuit of religious emancipation. In this crucial dialogue then, the confrontation is not simply between the worldly and spiritual, the secular and religious, but between two opposing views of life recognizing in different ways the ultimacy of the religious claim. The prince, for his part, insists not only on the primacy but also the immediacy of dealing with one's own spiritual problem. His decision to leave home and family thus becomes the prototype of the religious vocation in Buddhism.

"Dear son, give up this idea. The time for you to devote yourself to dharma has not yet come. For, they say the practice of dharma entails much danger when one is young and his mind is unsteady. . . .

"Therefore, give up this resolution. Meanwhile devote yourself to the duties of a householder. Entering the grove of ascetic practice will be agreeable enough after a man has enjoyed the pleasures of youth."

Hearing these words of the king, the prince replied. . . . "Oh king, if I were given a guarantee on four matters, I would not go to the grove of ascetic practice:

"That my life would not be committed to death; that my health would not be overcome by disease; that my youth would not be marred by old age; and that prosperity would not be taken away by disaster."

To his son who had proposed such difficult questions, the Shākya king replied, "Give up this idea which goes too far. Such a fantastic wish is ridiculous and improper."

Then the prince, whose gravity was as imposing as Mt. Meru, said to his father, "If there be no means of solution, I should not be detained; it is not right to hold by force a man who is anxious to escape from a burning house.

"Since for men separation is inescapable, is it not better for me to separate on my own accord for the sake of dharma? Will not death separate me, who am helpless and unsatisfied, without my being able to fulfill my aim?"

Though the king had heard the determined prince, who was anxious to seek deliverance, he said, "The prince must not go." He ordered additional guards around him and provided him with the most pleasurable of entertainments. . . .

Then the loveliest of women waited on him. . . . but even music played on instruments like those of the celestial beings failed to delight him. The ardent desire of that noble prince was to leave the palace in search of the bliss of the highest good.

Whereupon the Akanistha Gods, who excelled in austerities, noting the resolution of the prince, suddenly cast the spell of sleep on the young women, leaving them in distorted postures and shocking poses. . . .

One lay leaning against the side of a window, her slender body bent like a bow, her beautiful necklace dangling. . . .

Another, with loose and disorderly hair, lay like the figure of a woman trampled by an elephant, her ornaments and garments having slipped from her back, her necklace scattered.

And another, of great natural beauty and poise, was shamelessly exposed in an immodest position, snoring out loud, with her limbs tossed about.

Another, with her ornaments and garlands falling off and garments unfastened, lay unconscious like a corpse, with her eyes fixed and their whites showing.

Another with well-developed legs lay as if sprawling in intoxication, exposing what should have been hidden, her mouth gaping wide and slobbering, her gracefulness gone and her body contorted. . . .

Seeing this . . . the prince was disgusted. "Such is the real nature of women in the world of the living—impure and loathsome; but deceived by dress and ornaments, man is stirred to passion for them." . . .

Thus arose in the prince a determination to leave that night. The Gods understood his mind and opened the doors of the palace.

[Unnoticed, the prince goes out of the palace on the white horse Kanthaka, led by the quick-footed groom Chandaka.]

He went out from his father's city with firm determination, leaving behind his father who had been so attached to him, his young son, his joyful people, and his most beautiful princess, suppressing his concerns for all of them.

The prince, whose eyes were long like spotless lotuses, looked back at the city and uttered a lion's roar: "I will not enter the city of Kapila until I have seen the other shore of birth and death." . . .

The Failure of Asceticism

After many wanderings in search of a teacher, overcoming numerous
obstacles and temptations, the prince finally joins some ascetics by
the bank of a river.

Engaged in much difficult fasting, over six years his body
became steadily emaciated. . . . But tormenting his body
through such austerities availed nothing.

"This is not the way to achieve passionlessness, enlightenment, liberation. Better and surer the way I found before beneath the Jambū-tree.

"Nor can that be attained by one who is weak. . . . How
can it be reached by a man who is not calm and at ease,
who is so exhausted by hunger and thirst that his mind is
unbalanced?"

[Just then, on divine inspiration, the daughter of a cowherd appears to offer the prince some milk-rice, which he accepts. So
nourished, he is strengthened for his attainment of Enlightenment, and, as the other mendicants abandon him for having
broken his fast, he goes alone to sit beneath the Tree of Wisdom.
Taking up the immovable, cross-legged posture for sitting in
meditation, he vows: "I shall not rise from this position until I
have achieved my goal." When Māra the Tempter seeks to destroy the prince's resolution by all manner of tempting and terrify-
ing sights, the latter remains steadfast.]

Enlightenment

Having mastered perfectly all the methods of trance, the
prince recalled, in the first watch of the night, the sequence
of his former births. . . .

[He next meditates on the twelve-link chain of causation, leading
from "ignorance" to "old age and death":]

The Rightly-Illumined One perceived all of these things
and thus was decisively awakened: when birth is destroyed,
old age and death ceases; when "becoming" is destroyed,
then birth ceases;[1]

[1] From here on the translation is based on the Chinese text, *Taishō
daizōkyō*, IV, 28a–30c.

When attachment is destroyed, "becoming" ceases; when craving is destroyed, attachment ceases; when sensations are destroyed, craving ceases;

When contact is destroyed, sensation ceases; when the six sense organs are destroyed, contact ceases; when the physical form is destroyed, the six sense organs cease;

When consciousness is destroyed, physical form ceases; when psychic constructions are destroyed, consciousness ceases; when ignorance is destroyed, psychic constructions cease.

Reflecting his right understanding, the great hermit arose before the world as the Buddha, the Enlightened One.

He found self (*ātman*) nowhere, as the fire whose fuel has been exhausted. [Then he conceived] the eightfold path, the straightest and safest path to the attainment of this end. . . .

For seven days, the Buddha with serene mind contemplated [the Truth that he had attained] and gazed at the Bodhi tree without blinking: "Here on this spot I have fulfilled my cherished goal; I now rest at ease in the dharma of selflessness."

His Compassion on the World

At this point a question arises as to whether the Buddha's enlightenment should be shared with others. From the standpoint of ordinary logic, his freedom of all attachments and concerns in the world should mean that he feels no obligation or responsibility to help others, and insofar as they would not be seen to have any true selfhood or individuality, their sufferings would be as transient and illusory as they themselves. There is also the problem of communicating the ineffable truth of Enlightenment or Nirvāna to those whose spiritual receptivity may be limited.

Here the poet implies that the Buddha considers both preaching to others and not preaching to them. In his freedom he can do either and remain at peace with himself; in both cases his transcendent insight would enable him to remain essentially disengaged from their sufferings. As to their ability to comprehend, he teaches others according to their respective levels of receptivity.

Note that the question of "helping" or "saving" others is presented specifically as a question of teaching, i.e. of sharing Enlightenment. Since suffering partakes of illusion, the only way to deal with it is inwardly, not outwardly. External remedies, whether per-

*sonal, social, political, etc., are relevant and of value only to the
extent that they contribute to this inner change. Hence they are all
subordinate to the basic function of "teaching," "preaching," "en-
lightening."*

Observing all sentient beings with the eyes of a Buddha, he
felt deep compassion for them; he wished to purify those
whose minds had been lost in false views arising from hatred,
greed, and folly.

But how could liberation, which is so exquisite and profound, be expressed in words? It may be better not to give
out my thoughts [he said to himself], and so he remained
silent and at peace,

Then remembering his former vow to save others, he again
began to think of preaching. . . .

The god Brahmā, learning of this, came to the Buddha,
radiant with light, asking him to preach for the sake of the
suffering beings. . . .

"I entreat you to save those who have sunk in the ocean
of suffering. As in the world a righteous man distributes the
profit he gains, so must you who have gained the dharma
impart it to people that they may be saved.

"Innumerable are those common men who will be bene-
fited. Difficult though it may be to share this gain with
others, pray have compassion on the world and attempt this
most arduous task."

After begging him earnestly, Brahmā returned to his
heaven, while Buddha, moved by the god's solicitation and
ever more compassionate toward the sentient beings, was
prompted to preach [the dharma].

[*With this intention, slowly and serenely, he proceeds to Vārānasī
and there comes upon the five mendicants who had deserted him
before.*]

With much compassion the Buddha spoke to them, but
out of ignorance they did not believe that he had attained
the perfect enlightenment, saying:

"In vain you devoted yourself to ascetic practices, and then
indulged in the pleasures of body and mouth. How could
it be possible for you to attain Buddhahood?

"Because of such doubts we cannot believe that you have become the Tathāgata, or that you have obtained Buddha-hood by realizing the ultimate Truth, or that you have been endowed with omnipotence." The Buddha, therefore, preached briefly the essentials to them.

"Ignorant people practice austerities; those who seek pleasures gratify their senses. As neither method leads people to liberation, these two extremes are utterly wrong: they are not the right ways.

"Devoting oneself to ascetic practices with an exhausted body only makes one's mind more confused. It produces not even a worldly knowledge, not to speak of transcending the senses. It is like trying to light a lamp with water; there is no chance of dispelling the darkness.

"Just as one cannot start a fire by [rubbing] rotten pieces of wood, so one cannot destroy one's ignorance by trying to light the lamp of wisdom with an emaciated body. It is a vain waste of energy. . . .

"To indulge in pleasures also is not right; this merely increases one's foolishness, which obstructs the light of wisdom. . . .

"It is as if a sick man is eating harmful food. How can a disease as grievous as ignorance be cured by clinging to sensual pleasures? Who can extinguish a blaze in a dry field by stirring up a strong wind? Lust is the same.

"I stand above these two extremes, though my heart is kept in the Middle. Sufferings in me have come to an end; having been freed of all errors and defilements, I have now attained peace."

[The Buddha then preaches to the mendicants the doctrines of the Eightfold Path, the Four Noble Truths, and the Middle Way.]

Among the mendicants, Kaundinya, along with eight-thousand heavenly beings, thoroughly understood the doctrines which the Buddha preached, and, being free from defilements, obtained the pure eyes of the dharma. . . .

He heard the chorus of the earth gods voicing their triumph: "Well done! We have witnessed the revelation of the profound Truth. The Tathāgata has turned the unprecedented wheel of doctrines.

"For gods and men, far and wide, he has opened the gate of immortality. Of the true wheel of dharma the spokes are pure precepts, the axle is well-controlled meditation, the fell, indestructible wisdom, and the hub, wedged with a sense of shame, is right mindfulness. . . ."

Then the gods of the various heavens, up to the highest Brahma heaven, all joined in the eulogy. . . .

"A Buddha has arisen in the world! Far and near we hear that he has turned the wheel of doctrine that gives peace to the world for the sake of all sentient beings."

[From the *Buddhacarita*, Sanskrit text as edited by E. H. Johnson, Calcutta, Baptist Mission Press, 1935, pp. 1–18, 20–29, 46–48, 49–57, 140–142, 157]

3

"THE GREATER VEHICLE" OF
MAHĀYĀNA BUDDHISM

INTRODUCTION

From about the first or second century A.D. onwards, a new and very different kind of Buddhism arose in India. The new school, which claimed to offer salvation for all, styled itself *Mahāyāna*, the Greater Vehicle (to salvation), as opposed to the older Buddhism, which it contemptuously referred to as *Hīnayāna*, or the Lesser Vehicle. The Mahāyāna scriptures also claimed to represent the final doctrines of the Buddha, revealed only to his most spiritually advanced followers, while the earlier doctrines were merely preliminary ones. Though Mahāyāna Buddhism, with its pantheon of heavenly buddhas and bodhisattvas and its idealistic metaphysics, was strikingly different in many respects from the Theravāda, it can be viewed as the development into finished systems of tendencies which had existed long before—a development favored and accelerated by the great historic changes taking place in northwestern India at that time. For over two hundred years, from the beginning of the second century B.C. onwards, this region was the prey of a succession of invaders—Bactrian Greeks, Scythians, Parthians, and a Central Asian people generally known to historians of India as Kushānas. As a result of these invasions Iranian and Western influences were felt much more strongly than before, and new peoples, with backgrounds very different from those of the folk among whom the religion arose, began to take interest in Buddhism.

A tendency to revere the Buddha as a god had probably existed in his own lifetime. In Indian religion, divinity is not something completely transcendent, or far exalted above all mortal things, as it is for the Jew, Christian, or Muslim, neither is it something concentrated in a single unique, omnipotent, and omniscient personality. In Indian religions godhead manifests itself in so many forms as to be almost if not quite ubiquitous, and every great sage or religious teacher is looked on as a special manifestation of divinity, in some sense a god in human form. How much more divine was the Buddha, to whom even the great god Brahmā himself did reverence, and who, in meditation, could far transcend the comparatively tawdry and transient heavens where the great gods dwelt, enter the world of formlessness, and pass thence to the ineffable Nirvāna itself? From the Buddhist point of view even the highest of the gods was liable to error, for Brahmā imagined himself to be the creator when in fact the world came into existence as a result of natural causes. The Buddha, on the other hand, was omniscient.

Yet, according to theory, the Buddha had passed completely away from the universe, had ceased in any sense to be a person, and no longer affected the world in any way. But the formula of the "Three Jewels"—"I take refuge in the Buddha, I take refuge in the Doctrine, I take refuge in the Order"—became the Buddhist profession of faith very early, and was used by monk and layman alike. Taken literally the first clause was virtually meaningless, for it was impossible to take refuge in a being who had ceased to exist as such. Nevertheless the Buddha was worshiped from very early times, and he is said to have himself declared that all who had faith in him and devotion to him would obtain rebirth in heaven. In some of the earliest Buddhist sculpture, such as that of the stūpa of Bharhut (second or first century B.C.), crowds of worshipers are depicted as ecstatically prostrating themselves before the emblems of the Buddha—the wheel, the footprints, the empty throne, or the trident-shaped symbol representing the Three Jewels. At this time it was evidently not thought proper to portray the Buddha or to represent him by an icon; but in the first century A.D., whether from the influence of Greco-Roman ideas and art forms or

from that of indigenous popular cults, the Buddha was represented and worshiped as an image.

A further development which encouraged the tendency to
theism was the growth of interest in the *bodhisattva*. This
term, literally meaning "Being of Wisdom," was first used
in the sense of a previous incarnation of the Buddha. For
many lives before his final birth as Siddhārtha Gautama the
Bodhisattva did mighty deeds of compassion and self-sacrifice,
as he gradually perfected himself in wisdom and virtue.
Stories of the Bodhisattva, known as *Birth Stories* (*Jātaka*)
and often adapted from popular legends and fables, were very
popular with lay Buddhists, and numerous illustrations of
them occur in early Buddhist art.

It is probable that even in the lifetime of the Buddha it
was thought that he was only the last of a series of earlier
Buddhas. Later, perhaps through Zoroastrian influence, it
came to be believed that other Buddhas were yet to come,
and interest developed in *Maitreya*, the future Buddha, whose
coming was said to have been prophesied by the historical
Buddha, and who, in years to come, would purify the world
with his teaching. But if Maitreya was yet to come, the chain
of being which would ultimately lead to his birth (or, in
the terminology of other sects, his soul) must be already in
existence. Somewhere in the universe the being later to become Maitreya Buddha was already active for good. And
if this one, how many more? Logically the world must be full
of bodhisattvas, all striving for the welfare of other beings.

The next step in the development of the new form of
Buddhism was the changing of the goal at which the believer
aimed. According to Buddhist teaching there are three types
of perfected beings—*Buddhas*, who perceived the truth for
themselves and taught it to others, *pratyeka-buddhas*, "private buddhas," who perceived it, but kept it to themselves
and did not teach it, and *arhants*,[1] "Worthies," who learned
it from others, but fully realized it for themselves. According
to earlier schools the earnest believer should aspire to become
an arhant, a perfected being for whom there was no rebirth,
who already enjoyed Nirvāna, and who would finally enter
that state after death, all vestiges of his personality dissolved.

[1] Pali, *arahant*, usually translated "perfect being" in our extracts.

The road to Nirvāna was a hard one, and could only be covered in many lives of virtue and self-sacrifice; but nevertheless the goal began to be looked on as selfish. Surely a bodhisattva, after achieving such exalted compassion and altruism, and after reaching such a degree of perfection that he could render inestimable help to other striving beings, would not pass as quickly as possible to Nirvāna, where he could be of no further use, but would deliberately choose to remain in the world, using his spiritual power to help others, until all had found salvation. Passages of Mahāyāna scriptures describing the self-sacrifice of the bodhisattva for the welfare of all things living are among the most passionately altruistic in the world's religious literature.

The replacement of the ideal of the arhant by that of the bodhisattva is the basic distinction between the old sects and the new, which came to be known as *Mahāyāna*. Faith in the bodhisattvas and the help they afforded was thought to carry many beings along the road to bliss, while the older schools, which did not accept the bodhisattva ideal, could save only a few patient and strenuous souls.

The next stage in the evolution of the theology of the new Buddhism was the doctrine of the "Three Bodies" (*Trikāya*). If the true ideal was that of the bodhisattva, why did not Siddhārtha Gautama remain one, instead of becoming a Buddha and selfishly passing to Nirvāna? This paradox was answered by a theory of docetic type, which again probably had its origin in popular ideas prevalent among lay Buddhists at a very early period. Gautama was not in fact an ordinary man, but the manifestation of a great spiritual being. The Buddha had three bodies—the Body of Essence (*Dharmakāya*), the Body of Bliss (*Sambhogakāya*) and the Transformation Body (*Nirmānakāya*). It was the latter only which lived on earth as Siddhārtha Gautama, an emanation of the Body of Bliss, which dwelled forever in the heavens as a sort of supreme god. But the Body of Bliss was in turn the emanation of the Body of Essence, the ultimate Buddha, who pervaded and underlay the whole universe. Subtle philosophies and metaphysical systems were developed parallel with these theological ideas, and the Body of Essence was identified with Nirvāna. It was in fact the World Soul, the *Brahman* of the Upanishads, in a new form. In the fully developed

Mahāyānist cosmology there were many Bodies of Bliss, all of them emanations of the single Body of Essence, but the heavenly Buddha chiefly concerned with our world was *Amitābha* ("Immeasurable Radiance"), who dwelt in *Sukhā-vatī*, "the Happy Land," the heaven of the West. With him was associated the earthly Gautama Buddha, and a very potent and compassionate Bodhisattva, Avalokiteshvara ("the Lord Who Looks Down").

The older Buddhism and the newer flourished side by side in India during the early centuries of the Christian era, and we read of Buddhist monasteries in which some of the monks were Mahāyānist and some Hīnayānist. But in general the Buddhists of northwestern India were either Mahāyānists or members of Hīnayāna sects much affected by Mahāyānist ideas. The austerer forms of Hīnayāna seem to have been strongest in parts of western and southern India, and in Ceylon. It was from northwestern India, under the rule of the great Kushāna empire (first to third centuries A.D.) that Buddhism spread throughout central Asia to China; since it emanated from the northwest, it was chiefly of the Mahā-yāna or near-Mahāyāna type.

We have already outlined the typical Mahāyāna teaching about the heavenly Buddhas and bodhisattvas, which is a matter of theology rather than of metaphysics. But Mahāyāna also produced philosophical theories which were argued with great ability, and which were influential on the thought of Hinduism, as well as on that of the Far East. The two chief schools of Mahāyāna philosophy were the *Mādhyamika* (Doctrine of the Middle Position) and the *Vijñānavāda* (Doctrine of Consciousness) or *Yogācāra* (The Way of Yoga). The former school, the founder of which was Nāgār-juna (first to second centuries A.D.), taught that the phe-nomenal world had only a qualified reality, thus opposing the doctrine of the Sarvāstivādins. A monk with defective eyesight may imagine that he sees flies in his begging bowl, and they have full reality for the percipient. Though the flies are not real the illusion of flies is. The Mādhyamika philosophers tried to prove that all our experience of the phenomenal world is like that of the short-sighted monk, that all beings labor under the constant illusion of perceiving things where in fact there is only emptiness. This Emptiness or Void (*Śūnyatā*) is all that truly exists, and hence the Mādhyamikas were sometimes also called *Śūnyavādins* ("exponents of the doctrine of emptiness"). But the phenomenal world is true pragmatically, and therefore has qualified reality for practical purposes. Yet the whole chain of existence is only real in this qualified sense, for it is composed of a series of transitory events, and these, being impermanent, cannot have reality in themselves. Emptiness, on the other hand, never changes. It is absolute truth and absolute being—in fact it is the same as Nirvāna and the Body of Essence of the Buddha.

Nāgārjuna's system, however, went farther than this. Nothing in the phenomenal world has full being, and all is ultimately unreal. Therefore every rational theory about the world is a theory about something unreal evolved by an unreal thinker with unreal thoughts. Thus, by the same process of reasoning, even the arguments of the Mādhyamika school in favor of the ultimate reality of Emptiness are unreal, and this argument against the Mādhyamika position is itself unreal, and so on in an infinite regress. Every logical argument can be reduced to absurdity by a process such as this. The ontological nihilism of Mādhyamika dialectic led to the development of a special sub-school devoted to logic, the *Prāsaṅgika*[2] which produced works of great subtlety.

The effect of Mādhyamika nihilism was not what might be expected. Skeptical philosophies in the West, such as that of existentialism, are generally strongly flavored with pessimism. The Mādhyamikas, however, were not pessimists. If the phenomenal world was ultimately unreal, Emptiness was real, for, though every logical proof of its existence was vitiated by the flaw of unreality, it could be experienced in meditation with a directness and certainty which the phenomenal world did not possess. The ultimate Emptiness was here and now, everywhere and all-embracing, and there was in fact no difference between the great Void and the phenomenal world. Thus all beings were already participants of the Emptiness which was Nirvāna, they were already Buddha if only they would realize it. This aspect of

---

[2] So called from its preoccupation with *prasaṅga* the term used in Sanskrit logic for the *reductio ad absurdum*.

Mādhyamika philosophy was specially congenial to Chinese Buddhists, nurtured in the doctrine of the *Tao,* and it had much influence in the development of the special forms of Chinese and Japanese Buddhism, which often show a frank acceptance of the beauty of the world, and especially of the beauty of nature, as a vision of Nirvāna here and now.

The Vijnānavāda school was one of pure idealism, and may be compared to the systems of Berkeley and Hume. The whole universe exists only in the mind of the perceiver. The fact of illusion, as in the case of the flies in the short-sighted monk's bowl, or the experience of dreams, was adduced as evidence to show that all normal human experience was of the same type. It is possible for the monk in meditation to raise before his eyes visions of every kind which have quite as much vividness and semblance of truth as have ordinary perceptions; yet he knows that they have no objective reality. Perception therefore is no proof of the independent existence of any entity, and all perceptions may be explained as projections of the percipient mind. Vijnānavāda, like some Western idealist systems, found its chief logical difficulty in explaining the continuity and apparent regularity of the majority of our sense impressions, and in accounting for the fact that the impressions of most people who are looking at the same time in the same direction seem to cohere in a remarkably consistent manner. Bishop Berkeley, to escape this dilemma, postulated a transcendent mind in which all phenomena were thoughts. The Vijnānavādins explained the regularity and coherence of sense impressions as due to an underlying store of perceptions (*ālayavijñāna*) evolving from the accumulation of traces of earlier sense-impressions. These are active, and produce impressions similar to themselves, according to a regular pattern, as seeds produce plants. Each being possesses one of these stores of perception, and beings which are generically alike will produce similar perceptions from their stores at the same time. By this strange conception, which bristles with logical difficulties and is one of the most difficult of all Indian philosophy, the Vijnānavādins managed to avoid the logical conclusion of idealism in solipsism. Moreover they admitted the existence of at least one entity independent of human thought—a pure and integral being without characteristics, about which nothing could truly be predicated because it was without predicates. This was called "Suchness" (*Tathatā*) and corresponded to the Emptiness or Void of the Mādhyamikas, and to the Brahman of Vedānta. Though the terminology is different the metaphysics of Mahāyāna Buddhism has much in common with the doctrines of some of the Upanishads and of Shankara. The latter probably learned much from Buddhism, and indeed was called by his opponents a crypto-Buddhist.

For the Vijnānavāda school salvation was to be obtained by exhausting the store of consciousness until it became pure being itself, and identical with the Suchness which was the only truly existent entity in the universe. The chief means of doing this, for those who had already reached a certain stage of spiritual development, was yogic praxis. Adepts of this school were taught to conjure up visions, so that, by realizing that visions and pragmatically real perceptions had the same vividness and subjective reality, they might become completely convinced of the total subjectivity of all phenomena. Thus the meditating monk would imagine himself a mighty god, leading an army of lesser gods against Māra, the spirit of the world and the flesh. The chief philosophers of the school were Asanga (fourth century A.D.) and Vasubandhu,[3] of about the same period. According to tradition Dinnāga, the greatest of the Buddhist logicians, was a disciple of Vasubandhu.

The canons of the Mahāyāna sects contain much material which also occurs in Pali, often expanded or adapted, but the interest of the Mahāyānists was largely directed to other scriptures, of which no counterparts exist in the Pali canon, and which, it was claimed, were also the pronouncements of the Buddha. These are the *Vaipulya Sūtras*, or "Expanded Discourses," of greater length than those in the Pali *Basket of Discourses* (*Sutta Piṭaka*), and written in Buddhist Sanskrit; in them the Buddha is supposed to have taught the doctrine of the heavenly Buddhas and bodhisattvas. Of these Mahāyāna sūtras pride of place must be taken by *The Lotus of the Good Law* (*Saddharmapuṇḍarīka*), which pro-

---

[3] There may have been two Vasubandhus, one the approximate contemporary of Asanga and the other about a century later.

pounds all the major doctrines of Mahāyāna Buddhism in
a fairly simple and good literary style with parables and poetic
illustrations. In translation it is the most popular Buddhist
scripture in China and Japan, the Japanese Buddhists of the
Nichiren sect making it their sole canonical text. An important group of Mahāyāna texts is the *Discourses on the
Perfection of Wisdom* (*Prajñāpāramitā Sūtras*), of which
several exist, generally known by the number of verses[4] they
contain, ranging from 700 to 100,000. The primary purpose
of these is to explain and glorify the ten perfections (*pāra-
mitā*) of the bodhisattva, and especially the perfection of
wisdom (prajnā), but they contain much of importance on
other aspects of Buddhism. Other Mahāyāna sūtras are too
numerous to mention.

THE BODHISATTVA

*The essential difference between Mahāyāna and Theravāda Bud-
dhism is in the doctrine of the bodhisattva, who, in Mahāyāna,
becomes a divine savior, and whose example the believer is urged
to follow. It must be remembered that all good Buddhists, from
the Mahāyāna point of view, are bodhisattvas in the making, and
the many descriptions of bodhisattvas in Mahāyāna texts provide
ideals for the guidance of monk and layman alike. One of the chief
qualities of the bodhisattva is his immense compassion for the world
of mortals.*

The bodhisattva is endowed with wisdom of a kind whereby
he looks on all beings as though victims going to the slaugh-
ter. And immense compassion grips him. His divine eye sees
. . . innumerable beings, and he is filled with great distress
at what he sees, for many bear the burden of past deeds
which will be punished in purgatory, others will have unfortunate rebirths which will divide them from the Buddha
and his teachings, others must soon be slain, others are caught
in the net of false doctrine, others cannot find the path [of

[4] Or more correctly the number of verses of thirty-two syllables each
which they would contain if they had been versified. They are actually in prose.

salvation], while others have gained a favorable rebirth only to lose it again.

So he pours out his love and compassion upon all those beings, and attends to them, thinking, "I shall become the savior of all beings, and set them free from their sufferings."

[From Aṣṭasāhasrikā Prajñāpāramitā, 22.402–3]

The Mahāyāna Ideal Is Higher Than That of the Theravāda

Mahāyāna teachers claimed that the ideal of the Theravādins—complete loss of personality as perfected beings in Nirvāna—was fundamentally selfish and trivial. The truly perfected being should devote all his powers to saving suffering mortals. The following passage elucidates this point. It purports to be a dialogue between the Buddha and one of his chief disciples, Shāriputra (Pali Sāriputta).

"What do you think, Shāriputra? Do any of the disciples[1] and private buddhas[2] ever think, 'After we have gained full enlightenment we will bring innumerable beings . . . to complete Nirvāna'?"

"Certainly not, Lord!"

"But," said the Lord, "the bodhisattva [has this resolve]. . . . A firefly . . . doesn't imagine that its glow will light up all India or shine all over it, and so the disciples and private buddhas don't think that they should lead all beings to Nirvāna . . . after they have gained full enlightenment. But the disc of the sun, when it has risen, lights up all India and shines all over it. Similarly the bodhisattva . . . when he has gained full enlightenment, brings countless beings to Nirvāna.

[From Pañcaviṃśatisāhasrikā Prajñāpāramitā, pp. 40–41]

[1] Śrāvaka, literally "hearer," a term often applied by Mahāyāna writers especially to adherents of Theravāda.
[2] Pratyeka-buddha, one who has achieved full enlightenment through his own insight, but does not communicate his saving knowledge to others.

The Suffering Savior

In many passages of the Mahāyāna scriptures is to be found what purports to be the solemn resolve made by a bodhisattva at the beginning of his career. The following fine passage will appear particularly striking to Western readers, for in it the bodhisattva not only resolves to pity and help all mortal beings, but also to share their intensest sufferings. Christians and Jews cannot fail to note resemblances to the concept of the suffering Savior in Christianity and to the "Servant Passages" of Isaiah (53:3–12). It is by no means impossible that there was some Christian influence on Mahāyāna Buddhism, for Christian missionaries were active in Persia very early, and it became a center from which Nestorian Christianity was diffused throughout Asia. From the middle of the third century A.D. Persian influence in Afghanistan and Northwestern India, which had always been felt, was intensified with the rise of the Sāsānian Empire; and it was in these regions that Mahāyāna Buddhism developed and flourished. Thus Christian influence cannot be ruled out. But it is equally possible that the similarities between the concepts of the suffering savior in Buddhism and Christianity are due to the fact that compassionate minds everywhere tend to think alike.

The work from which the following passage is taken, Shāntideva's Compendium of Doctrine, dates from the seventh century. It is extremely valuable because it consists of lengthy quotations from earlier Buddhist literature with brief comments by the compiler, and many of the passages quoted are from works which no longer survive in their original form. The following passages are quoted from two such works, the Instructions of Akshayamati (Akṣayamati Nirdeśa) and the Sūtra of Vajradhvaja (Vajradhvaja Sūtra).

The bodhisattva is lonely, with no . . . companion, and he puts on the armor of supreme wisdom. He acts himself, and leaves nothing to others, working with a will steeled with courage and strength. He is strong in his own strength . . . and he resolves thus:

"Whatever all beings should obtain, I will help them to obtain. . . . The virtue of generosity is not my helper— I am the helper of generosity. Nor do the virtues of morality, patience, courage, meditation and wisdom help me—it is I who help them.[1] The perfections of the bodhisattva do not

[1] These six, generosity (dāna), moral conduct (śīla), patience

support me—it is I who support them. . . . I alone, standing in this round and adamantine world, must subdue Māra,
with all his hosts and chariots, and develop supreme enlightenment with the wisdom of instantaneous insight!" . . .

Just as the rising sun, the child of the gods, is not stopped,
. . . by all the dust rising from the four continents of the
earth . . . or by wreaths of smoke . . . or by rugged mountains, so the bodhisattva, the Great Being, . . . is not de-
terred from bringing to fruition the root of good, whether
by the malice of others, . . . or by their sin or heresy, or by
their agitation of mind. . . . He will not lay down his arms
of enlightenment because of the corrupt generations of men,
nor does he waver in his resolution to save the world because
of their wretched quarrels. . . . He does not lose heart on
account of their faults. . . .

"All creatures are in pain," he resolves, "all suffer from
bad and hindering karma . . . so that they cannot see the
Buddhas or hear the Law of Righteousness or know the
Order. . . . All that mass of pain and evil karma I take in
my own body. . . . I take upon myself the burden of sorrow; I resolve to do so; I endure it all. I do not turn back
or run away, I do not tremble . . . I am not afraid . . .
nor do I despair. Assuredly I must bear the burdens of all
beings . . . for I have resolved to save them all. I must set
them all free, I must save the whole world from the forest
of birth, old age, disease, and rebirth, from misfortune and
sin, from the round of birth and death, from the toils of
heresy. . . . For all beings are caught in the net of craving,
encompassed by ignorance, held by the desire for existence;
they are doomed to destruction, shut in a cage of pain . . . ;

(kṣānti) courage or energy (vīrya), meditation (dhyāna) and wisdom (prajñā) are the Pāramitās, or virtues of the bodhisattva,
which he has developed to perfection. Many sources add four further perfections—"skill in knowing the right means" to take to lead
individual beings to salvation according to their several characters
and circumstances (upāyakauśalya), determination (pranidhāna),
strength (bala), and knowledge (jñāna). Much attention was concentrated on these perfections, especially on the Perfection of Wisdom (Prajñāpāramitā), which was personified as a goddess, and
after which numerous Buddhist texts were named.

they are ignorant, untrustworthy, full of doubts, always at loggerheads one with another, always prone to see evil; they cannot find a refuge in the ocean of existence; they are all on the edge of the gulf of destruction.

"I work to establish the kingdom of perfect wisdom for all beings. I care not at all for my own deliverance. I must save all beings from the torrent of rebirth with the raft of my omniscient mind. I must pull them back from the great precipice. I must free them from all misfortune, ferry them over the stream of rebirth.

"For I have taken upon myself, by my own will, the whole of the pain of all things living. Thus I dare try every abode of pain, in . . . every part of the universe, for I must not defraud the world of the root of good. I resolve to dwell in each state of misfortune through countless ages . . . for the salvation of all beings . . . for it is better that I alone suffer than that all beings sink to the worlds of misfortune. There I shall give myself into bondage, to redeem all the world from the forest of purgatory, from rebirth as beasts, from the realm of death. I shall bear all grief and pain in my own body, for the good of all things living. I venture to stand surety for all beings, speaking the truth, trustworthy, not breaking my word. I shall not forsake them. . . . I must so bring to fruition the root of goodness that all beings find the utmost joy, unheard of joy, the joy of omniscience. I must be their charioteer, I must be their leader, I must be their torchbearer, I must be their guide to safety. . . . I must not wait for the help of another, nor must I lose my resolution and leave my tasks to another. I must not turn back in my efforts to save all beings nor cease to use my merit for the destruction of all pain. And I must not be satisfied with small successes."

[From Śikṣāsamuccaya, pp. 278–83]

The Lost Son

One of the reasons for including this passage is its remarkable resemblance to the famous parable of St. Luke's Gospel (15:11 32). As the Lotus of the Good Law, from which the Buddhist story is taken, was probably in existence well before Christian ideas could have found their way to India via Persia, it is unlikely that this parable owes anything to the Christian one. Similarly it is unlikely that the Christian parable is indebted to the Buddhist. Probably we have here a case of religious minds of two widely separated cultures thinking along similar lines, as a result of similar, though not identical, religious experience. For this reason the resemblances and differences of the two stories are most instructive.[1]

The Prodigal of the Christian story squanders his patrimony in riotous living. The son in the Buddhist story is a wretched creature who can only wander about begging. His fault is not so much in squandering his property as in failing to acquire wealth (i.e., spiritual merit). The Prodigal returns to his father by his own free choice, after repenting his evil ways. In the Buddhist story it is only by chance that the son meets his father again; moreover the son does not recognize the father, though the father recognizes his son—thus the heavenly Buddha knows his children and works for their salvation, though they do not recognize him in his true character, and, if they get a glimpse of him, are afraid and try to avoid him—they feel much more at ease among their own earthbound kind, in "the poor quarter of the town," where their divine father sends his messengers (perhaps representing the bodhisattvas) to find them, bringing them home by force if need be. Here there is no question of a positive act of repentance, as in the Christian parable.

Unlike the Prodigal's father in the Christian story, who kills the fatted calf for his long-lost son, the father in the Buddhist story makes his son undergo a very long period of humble probation before raising him to the position which he merits by his birth. The heavenly Buddha cannot raise beings immediately from the filth and poverty of the earthly gutter to the full glory of his own heavenly palace, for they are so earthbound that, if brought to it at once, they would suffer agonies of fear, embarrassment, and confusion, and might well insist on returning to the gutter again. So they must undergo many years of preparation for their high estate, toiling daily among the material dross of this world, earnestly and loyally striving to make the world a tidier place. Like the father in the story, the heavenly Buddha will cover his glory with earthly dust and appear to his children as a historical Buddha to encourage and instruct them. Thus the Buddha shows the perfection of "skill in means," that is to say, in knowing the best means to take to lead

[1] The text itself purports to give an interpretation of the parable in which the son toiling as a menial in his father's house is compared to the Hīnayāna monk, who is unaware of the true glory of the enlightenment to which he is heir. There is little doubt, however, that the story here turned to purposes of sectarian propaganda was originally meant to have a wider significance, and we believe our interpretation to be that demanded by the spirit of the parable.

each individual to the light according to the circumstances in which he is placed.

Gradually the son grows more and more familiar with the father, and loses his former fear of him, but still he does not know that he is his father's child. So men, even though pious and virtuous, and earnestly carrying out the Buddha's will, do not know that they are already in Heaven; their lives are still to some extent earthbound, and though the Buddha offers them all his wealth of bliss long habit keeps them from enjoying it.

Only when the father is near death does he reveal himself to his son. This seems at first to weaken the analogy, for heavenly Buddhas do not die. But in fact the conclusion of the parable is quite appropriate, for when man has fulfilled his tasks and carried out his stewardship, that is to say when he has reached the highest stage of self-development, he finds that the heavenly Buddha has ceased to exist for him, that nothing is truly real but the great Emptiness which is peace and Nirvāna.

A man parted from his father and went to another city; and he dwelt there many years. . . . The father grew rich and the son poor. While the son wandered in all directions [begging] in order to get food and clothes, the father moved to another land, where he lived in great luxury . . . wealthy from business, money-lending, and trade. In course of time the son, wandering in search of his living through town and country, came to the city in which his father dwelled. Now the poor man's father . . . forever thought of the son whom he had lost . . . years ago, but he told no one of this, though he grieved inwardly, and thought: "I am old, and well advanced in years, and though I have great possessions I have no son. Alas that time should do its work upon me, and that all this wealth should perish unused! . . . It would be bliss indeed if my son might enjoy all my wealth!"

Then the poor man, in search of food and clothing, came to the rich man's home. And the rich man was sitting in great pomp at the gate of his house, surrounded by a large throng of attendants . . . on a splendid throne, with a footstool inlaid with gold and silver, under a wide awning decked with pearls and flowers and adorned with hanging garlands of jewels; and he transacted business to the value of millions of gold pieces, all the while fanned by a fly-whisk.

. . . When he saw him the poor man was terrified . . . and the hair of his body stood on end, for he thought that he had happened on a king or on some high officer of state, and had no business there. "I must go," he thought, "to the poor quarter of the town, where I'll get food and clothing without trouble. If I stop here they'll seize me and set me to do forced labor, or some other disaster will befall me!" So he quickly ran away. . . .

But the rich man . . . recognized his son as soon as he saw him; and he was full of joy . . . and thought: "This is wonderful! I have found him who shall enjoy my riches. He of whom I thought constantly has come back, now that I am old and full of years!" Then, longing for his son, he sent swift messengers, telling them to go and fetch him quickly. They ran at full speed and overtook him; the poor man trembled with fear, the hair of his body stood on end . . . and he uttered a cry of distress and exclaimed, "I've done you no wrong!" But they dragged him along by force . . . until . . . fearful that he would be killed or beaten, he fainted and fell on the ground. His father in dismay said to the men, "Don't drag him along in that way!" and, without saying more, he sprinkled his face with cold water—for though he knew that the poor man was his son, he realized that his estate was very humble, while his own was very high.

So the householder told no one that the poor man was his son. He ordered one of his servants to tell the poor man that he was free to go where he chose. . . . And the poor man was amazed [that he was allowed to go free], and he went off to the poor quarter of the town in search of food and clothing. Now in order to attract him back the rich man made use of the virtue of "skill in means." He called two men of low caste and of no great dignity and told them: "Go to that poor man . . . and hire him in your own names to do work in my house at double the normal daily wage; and if he asks what work he has to do tell him that he has to help clear away the refuse-dump." So these two men and the poor man cleared the refuse every day . . . in the house of the rich man, and lived in a straw hut nearby. . . . And the rich man saw through a window his son clearing refuse, and was again filled with compassion. So he came down, took off his wreath and jewels and rich clothes, put

on dirty garments, covered his body with dust, and, taking
a basket in his hand, went up to his son. And he greeted
him at a distance and said, "Take this basket and clear
away the dust at once!" By this means he managed to speak
to his son. [And as time went on he spoke more often to
him, and thus he gradually encouraged him. First he urged
him to] remain in his service and not take another job,
offering him double wages, together with any small extras
that he might require, such as the price of a cooking-pot
. . . or food and clothes. Then he offered him his own cloak,
if he should want it. . . . And at last he said: "You must be
cheerful, my good fellow, and think of me as a father . . .
for I'm older than you and you've done me good service in
clearing away my refuse. As long as you've worked for me
you've shown no roguery or guile. . . . I've not noticed one
of the vices in you that I've noticed in my other servants!
From now on you are like my own son to me!"

Thenceforward the householder called the poor man "son,"
and the latter felt towards the householder as a son feels
towards his father. So the householder, full of longing and
love for his son, employed him in clearing away refuse for
twenty years. By the end of that time the poor man felt quite
at home in the house, and came and went as he chose,
though he still lived in the straw hut.

Then the householder fell ill, and felt that the hour of his
death was near. So he said to the poor man: "Come, my dear
man! I have great riches . . . and am very sick. I need
someone upon whom I can bestow my wealth as a deposit,
and you must accept it. From now on you are just as much
its owner as I am, but you must not squander it." And the
poor man accepted the rich man's wealth . . . but personally he cared nothing for it, and asked for no share of it,
not even the price of a measure of flour. He still lived in
the straw hut, and thought of himself as just as poor as
before.

Thus the householder proved that his son was frugal, mature, and mentally developed, and that though he knew that
he was now wealthy he still remembered his past poverty,
and was still . . . humble and meek. . . . So he sent for
the poor man again, presented him before a gathering of his
relatives, and, in the presence of the king, his officers, and

the people of town and country, he said: "Listen, gentlemen! This is my son, whom I begot. . . . To him I leave all my family revenues, and my private wealth he shall have as his own."

[From *Saddharmapuṇḍarīka*, 4.101 ff.]

Joy in All Things

Joy is one of the cardinal virtues of Buddhism, and the bodhisattva, who is the example which all Mahāyāna Buddhists are expected to follow as far as their powers allow, has so trained his mind that even in the most painful and unhappy situations it is still full of calm inner joy. The following passage is from the Compendium of Doctrine; *the first paragraph is the work of the author, Shāntideva, while the second is quoted from a lost sūtra, the Meeting of Father and Son (Pitṛputrasamāgama).*

Indeed nothing is difficult after practice. Simple folk, such as porters, fishermen and plowmen, for instance, are not overcome by depression, for their minds are marked by the scars of the many pains with which they earn their humble livings, and which they have learned to bear. How much the more should one be cheerful in a task of which the purpose is to reach the incomparable state where all the joys of all beings, all the joys of the bodhisattvas are to be found. . . . Consciousness of sorrow and joy comes by habit; so, if whenever sorrow arises we make a habit of associating with it a feeling of joy, consciousness of joy will indeed arise. The fruit of this is a contemplative spirit full of joy in all things. . . .

So the bodhisattva . . . is happy even when subjected to the tortures of hell. . . . When he is being beaten with canes or whips, when he is thrown into prison, he still feels happy.[1] . . . For . . . this was the resolve of the Great Being, the bodhisattva: "May those who feed me win the joy of tranquillity and peace, with those who protect me, honor me, respect me, and revere me. And those who revile me, afflict me, beat me, cut me in pieces with their swords, or take my life—may they all obtain the joy of complete enlightenment, may they be awakened to perfect and sublime enlightenment." With such thoughts and actions and resolves

---

[1] Here a long list of the most gruesome tortures is omitted.

he cultivates . . . and develops the consciousness of joy in his relations with all beings, and so he acquires a contemplative spirit filled with joy in all things . . . and becomes imperturbable—not to be shaken by all the deeds of Māra.

[From *Śikṣāsamuccaya*, 181 f.]

The Good Deeds of the Bodhisattva

We have seen that the bodhisattva has ten "Perfections." A further list of good qualities is sometimes attributed to him. Notice that the emphasis is on the positive virtues of altruism, benevolence, and compassion.

There are ten ways by which a bodhisattva gains . . . strength: . . .
He will give up his body and his life . . . but he will not give up the Law of Righteousness.
He bows humbly to all beings, and does not increase in pride.
He has compassion on the weak and does not dislike them.
He gives the best food to those who are hungry.
He protects those who are afraid.
He strives for the healing of those who are sick.
He delights the poor with his riches.
He repairs the shrines of the Buddha with plaster.
He speaks to all beings pleasingly.
He shares his riches with those afflicted by poverty.
He bears the burdens of those who are tired and weary.

[From *Tathāgataguhya Sūtra, Śikṣāsamuccaya*, p. 274]

The Evils of Meat-Eating

According to the scriptures of the Theravāda school the Buddha allowed his followers to eat flesh if they were not responsible for killing the animal providing the meat, and if it was not specially killed to feed them. To this day most Buddhists in Ceylon and other lands where Theravāda prevails eat meat and fish, which are supplied by Muslim or Christian butchers or fishermen. Like the great Ashoka, however, many Buddhists have felt that meat-eating of any kind is out of harmony with the spirit of the Law of Righteousness, and have been vegetarians. The following passage criticizes the Theravāda teaching on meat-eating, and enjoins strict vegetarianism. The words are attributed to the Buddha.

Here in this long journey of birth-and-death there is no living being who . . . has not at some time been your mother or father, brother or sister, son or daughter. . . . So how can the bodhisattva, who wishes to treat all beings as though they were himself . . . eat the flesh of any living being? . . . Therefore, wherever living beings evolve, men should feel toward them as to their own kin, and, looking on all beings as their only child, should refrain from eating meat. . . .

The bodhisattva . . . desirous of cultivating the virtue of love, should not eat meat, lest he cause terror to living beings. Dogs, when they see, even at a distance, an outcaste . . . who likes eating meat, are terrified with fear, and think, "They are the dealers of death, they will kill us!" Even the animalculae in earth and air and water, who have a very keen sense of smell, will detect at a distance the odor of the demons in meat-eaters, and will run away as fast as they can from the death which threatens them. . . .

Moreover the meat-eater sleeps in sorrow and wakes in sorrow. All his dreams are nightmares, and they make his hair stand on end. . . . Things other than human sap his vitality. Often he is struck with terror, and trembles without cause. . . . He knows no measure in his eating, and there is no flavor, digestibility, or nourishment in his food. His bowels are filled with worms and other creatures, which are the cause of leprosy; and he ceases to think of resisting diseases. . . .

It is not true . . . that meat is right and proper for the disciple when the animal was not killed by himself or by his orders, and when it was not killed specially for him. . . . Pressed by a desire for the taste of meat people may string together their sophistries in defense of meat-eating . . . and declare that the Lord permitted meat as legitimate food, that it occurs in the list of permitted foods, and that he himself ate it. But . . . it is nowhere allowed in the sūtras as a . . . legitimate food. . . . All meat-eating in any form or manner and in any circumstances is prohibited, unconditionally and once and for all.

[From *Laṅkāvatāra Sūtra*, pp. 245 ff.]

The Gift of Food

From the Buddhist point of view, as Ashoka said, there is no greater gift than the gift of the Law of Righteousness; but Buddhism never disparaged the value or merit of practical acts of kindness and charity. The Buddhists, as we have seen, set much store on physical well-being. The passage which follows will show that poverty and hunger, unless voluntarily undertaken for a worthy cause, were looked on as unmitigated evils, liable to lead to sin and hence to an unhappy rebirth.

This passage is from the Tamil classic Manimēgalai, perhaps of the sixth century A.D., which is wholly Buddhist in inspiration, and concludes with an exposition of Mahāyāna logic and the doctrine of the Chain of Causation. The poem tells of Manimēgalai, a beautiful girl who, after many adventures, realized the uselessness and sorrow of the world and became a Buddhist nun. Here, led by a demi-goddess, she finds a magic bowl, which gives an inexhaustible supply of food.

The bowl rose in the water and . . . moved toward her hand. She was glad beyond measure, and sang a hymn in praise of the Buddha:

"Hail the feet of the hero, the victor over Māra!
Hail the feet of him who destroyed the path of evil!
Hail the feet of the Great One, setting men on the road of
    Righteousness!
Hail the feet of the All Wise One, who gives others the eye
    of wisdom!
Hail the feet of him whose ears are deaf to evil!
Hail the feet of him whose tongue never uttered untruth!
Hail the feet of him who went down to purgatory to put an
    end to suffering. . . .
My tongue cannot praise you duly—All I can do is to bend
    my body at your feet!"

While she was praying thus Tīvatilagai told her of the pains of hunger and of the virtue of those who help living beings to satisfy it. "Hunger," she said to Manimēgalai, "ruins good birth, and destroys all nobility; it destroys the love of learned men for their learning, even though they previously thought it the most valuable thing in life; hunger takes away all sense of shame, and ruins the beauty of the features; and it even forces men to stand with their wives at the doors of others. This is the nature of hunger, the source of evil craving, and those who relieve it the tongue cannot praise too highly! Food given to those who can afford it is charity wasted,[1] but food given to relieve the hunger of those who cannot satisfy it otherwise is charity indeed, and those who give it will prosper in this world, for those who give food give life. So go on and give food to allay the hunger of those who are hungry."

"In a past life," said Manimēgalai, "my husband died . . . and I mounted the pyre with him. As I burned I remembered that I had once given food to a Buddhist monk named Sādusakkāra; and I believe it is because of this virtuous thought at the moment of death that this bowl of plenty has come into my hands. Just as a mother's breast begins to give milk at the mere sight of her hungry baby, so may this bowl in my hand always give food . . . at the sight of those who suffer hunger and wander even in pouring rain or scorching sun in search of food to relieve it."

[From Maṇimēgalai, 11.55–122]

The Three Bodies of the Buddha

The following passage expounds the doctrine of the Three Bodies (Trikāya). It is taken from Asaṅga's Ornament of Mahāyāna Sūtras, a versified compendium of Mahāyāna doctrine, with a prose commentary. The latter is quoted where it throws light on the difficult and elliptical verses.

The Body of Essence, the Body of Bliss,[1] the Transformation
    Body—these are the bodies of the Buddhas.
The first is the basis of the two others.
The Body of Bliss varies in all the planes of the Universe,
    according to region,

---

[1] This may be a criticism of the Hindu virtue of *dāna*, which is usually translated "charity," but includes feasts given to brāhmans who may be much richer than the donor.
[1] *Sambhoga*, more literally "enjoyment"; in some contexts it implies little more than "experience."

In name, in form, and in experience of phenomena.
But the Body of Essence, uniform and subtle, is inherent in
the Body of Bliss,
And through the one the other controls its experience, when
it manifests itself at will.

Commentary: The Body of Essence is uniform for all the
Buddhas, because there is no real difference between them.
. . .

The Transformation Body displays with skill birth, enlighten-
ment, and Nirvāna,
For it possesses much magic power to lead men to enlighten-
ment.
The Body of the Buddhas is wholly comprised in these three
bodies. . . .
In basis, tendency, and act they are uniform.
They are stable by nature, by persistence, and by connection.

Commentary: The Three Bodies are one and the same for all
the Buddhas for three reasons: *basis*, for the basis of phenomena[2] is indivisible; *tendency*, because there is no tendency particular to one Buddha and not to another; and *act*,
because their actions are common to all. And the Three
Bodies have a threefold stability: by *nature*, for the Body
of Essence is essentially stable; by *persistence*, for the Body
of Bliss experiences phenomena unceasingly; and by *connection*, for the Transformation Body, once it has passed away,
shows its metamorphoses again and again.

[From *Mahāyānasūtrālaṅkāra*, 9.60–66]

Emptiness

The doctrine of Śūnyatā, "Emptiness" or "the Void," is aptly expressed in these fine verses from the Multitude of Graceful Actions,
a life of the Buddha in mixed verse and prose, replete with marvels
and miracles of all kinds, which formed the basis of Sir Edwin
Arnold's famous poem, The Light of Asia.

[2] *Dharmadhātu*, the Absolute.

All things conditioned are instable, impermanent,
    Fragile in essence, as an unbaked pot,
Like something borrowed, or a city founded on sand,
    They last a short while only.

They are inevitably destroyed,
    Like plaster washed off in the rains,
Like the sandy bank of a river—
    They are conditioned, and their true nature is frail.

They are like the flame of a lamp,
    Which rises suddenly and as soon goes out.
They have no power of endurance, like the wind
    Or like foam, unsubstantial, essentially feeble.

They have no inner power, being essentially empty,
    Like the stem of a plantain, if one thinks clearly,
Like conjuring tricks deluding the mind,
    Or a fist closed on nothing to tease a child. . . .

From wisps of grass the rope is spun
    By dint of exertion.
By turns of the wheel the buckets are raised from the well,
    Yet each turn of itself is futile.

So the turning of all the components of becoming
    Arises from the interaction of one with another.
In the unit the turning cannot be traced
    Either at the beginning or end.

Where the seed is, there is the young plant,
    But the seed has not the nature of the plant,
Nor is it something other than the plant, nor is it the plant—
    So is the nature of the Law of Righteousness, neither
      transient nor eternal.

All things conditioned are conditioned by ignorance,
    And on final analysis they do not exist,
For they and the conditioning ignorance alike are Emptiness
    In their essential nature, without power of action. . . .

The mystic knows the beginning and end
  Of consciousness, its production and passing away—
He knows that it came from nowhere and returns to no-
    where,
  And is empty [of reality], like a conjuring trick.

Through the concomitance of three factors—
  Firesticks, fuel, and the work of the hand—
Fire is kindled. It serves its purpose
  And quickly goes out again.

A wise man may seek here, there, and everywhere
  Whence it has come, and whither it has gone,
Through every region in all directions,
  But he cannot find it in its essential nature. . . .

Thus all things in this world of contingence
  Are dependent on causes and conditions.
The mystic knows what is true reality,
  And sees all conditioned things as empty and powerless.

                              [From *Lalitavistara*, 13.175–77]

Faith in Emptiness

*The following passage needs little comment. Belief in Śūnyavāda,
the doctrine of Emptiness, encourages a stoical and noble equanimity.*

He who maintains the doctrine of Emptiness is not allured
by the things of the world, because they have no basis. He
is not excited by gain or dejected by loss. Fame does not
dazzle him and infamy does not shame him. Scorn does not
repel him, praise does not attract him. Pleasure does not
please him, pain does not trouble him. He who is not allured
by the things of the world knows Emptiness, and one who
maintains the doctrine of Emptiness has neither likes nor
dislikes. What he likes he knows to be only Emptiness and
sees it as such.

        [From *Dharmasaṅgīti Sūtra*, Sikṣāsamuccaya, p. 264]

Karma and Rebirth

In an illusory world, rebirth is also illusory. The things a man craves for have no more reality than a dream, but he craves nevertheless, and hence his illusory ego is reborn in a new but equally illusory body. Notice the importance of the last conscious thought before death, which plays a very decisive part in the nature of the rebirth. The chief speaker in the following dialogue is said to be the Buddha.

"The senses are as though illusions and their objects as dreams. For instance a sleeping man might dream that he had made love to a beautiful country girl, and he might remember her when he awoke. What do you think— . . . does the beautiful girl he dreamed of really exist?"

"No, Lord."

"And would the man be wise to remember the girl of his dreams, or to believe that he had really made love to her?"

"No, Lord, because she doesn't really exist at all, so how could he have made love to her—though of course he might think he did under the influence of weakness or fatigue."

"In just the same way a foolish and ignorant man of the world sees pleasant forms and believes in their existence. Hence he is pleased, and so he feels passion and acts accordingly. . . . But from the very beginning his actions are feeble, impeded, wasted, and changed in their course by circumstances. . . . And when he ends his days, as the time of death approaches, his vitality is obstructed with the exhaustion of his allotted span of years, the karma that fell to his lot dwindles, and hence his previous actions form the object of the last thought of his mind as it disappears. Then, just as the man on first waking from sleep thinks of the country girl about whom he dreamed, the first thought on rebirth arises from two causes—the last thought of the previous life as its governing principle, and the actions of the previous life as its basis. Thus a man is reborn in the purgatories, or as an animal, a spirit, a demon, a human being, or a god. . . . The stopping of the last thought is known as decease, the appearance of the first thought as rebirth. Nothing passes from life to life, but decease and rebirth take place nevertheless. . . . But the last thought, the actions (karma), and the first thought, when they arise come from nowhere and when they cease go nowhere, for all are essentially defective, of themselves empty. . . . In the whole process no one acts and no one experiences the results of action, except by verbal convention.

[From *Pitṛputrasamāgama*, *Śikṣāsamuccaya*, pp. 251–52]

Suchness

The Vijñānavādin school called their conception of the Absolute Tathatā or "Suchness," in which all phenomenal appearances are lost in the one ultimate being.

The following passage is taken from a text which was translated into Chinese in the seventh century from a recension more interesting than the extant Sanskrit form. The whole passage considers the "Suchness" of the five components of being in turn. Here we give only the passage relating to the first of these.[1]

What is meant by . . . knowing in accordance with truth the marks of form? It means that a bodhisattva . . . knows that form is nothing but holes and cracks and is indeed a mass of bubbles, with a nature that has no hardness or solidity. . . .

What is meant by . . . knowing in accordance with truth the origin and extinction of form? It means that a bodhisattva . . . knows . . . that when form originates it comes from nowhere and when it is extinguished it goes nowhere, but that though it neither comes nor goes yet its origination and extinction do jointly exist. . . .

What is meant by . . . knowing in accordance with truth about the Suchness of form? It means that a bodhisattva . . . knows . . . that Suchness of form is not subject to origination or extinction, that it neither comes nor goes, is neither foul nor clean, neither increases nor diminishes, is constant in its own nature, is never empty, false or changeful, and is therefore called Suchness.

[From *Mahāprajñāpāramitā*, ch. 29, 1]

[1] Translated by Dr. Arthur Waley from the Chinese version of Hsüan-tsang. Reprinted by permission of Messrs. Bruno Cassirer, Oxford, from *Buddhist Texts through the Ages*, ed. by Edward Conze, Oxford, 1954, p. 154 f.

All Depends on the Mind

The following passage expresses the idealism of Mahāyāna thought.

All phenomena originate in the mind, and when the mind is fully known all phenomena are fully known. For by the mind the world is led . . . and through the mind karma is piled up, whether good or evil. The mind swings like a fire-brand,[1] the mind rears up like a wave, the mind burns like a forest fire, like a great flood the mind bears all things away. The bodhisattva, thoroughly examining the nature of things, dwells in everpresent mindfulness of the activity of the mind, and so he does not fall into the mind's power, but the mind comes under his control. And with the mind under his control all phenomena are under his control.

[From *Ratnamegha Sūtra*, Śikṣāsamuccaya, pp. 121–22]

Nirvāna Is Here and Now

The two following passages, the first Mādhyamika, and the second Vijnānavādin in tendency, illustrate the Mahāyāna doctrine that Nirvāna, the highest state, Pure Being, the Absolute, the Buddha's Body of Essence, is present at all times and everywhere, and needs only to be recognized. Thus the older pessimism of Buddhism is replaced by what is almost optimism. With this change of outlook comes an impatience with the learned philosophers and moralists who repeat their long and dreary sermons on the woes of samsāra, the round of birth-and-death. Though this attitude may have contributed to the antinomian tendencies of tantric Buddhism, it will probably stir an answering chord in many Western minds. Most people are like the man in the parable of the Lost Son, who year after year cleared away the refuse of his father's house without knowing that he was the son and heir.

That which the Lord revealed in his perfect enlightenment was not form or sensation or perception or psychic constructions or thought; for none of these five components come into being, neither does supreme wisdom come into being . . . and how can that which does not come into being know

---

[1] An allusion to a famous simile. The world is like a firebrand which, when swung round in the hand, resembles a solid wheel of flame.

that which also does not come into being? Since nothing can be grasped, what is the Buddha, what is wisdom, what is the bodhisattva, what is revelation? All the components are by nature empty—just convention, just names, agreed tokens, coverings. . . .

Thus all things are the perfection of being, infinite perfection, unobscured perfection, unconditioned perfection. All things are enlightenment, for they must be recognized as without essential nature—even the five greatest sins[1] are enlightenment, for enlightenment has no essential nature and neither have the five greatest sins. Thus those who seek for Nirvāna are to be laughed at, for the man in the midst of birth-and-death is also seeking Nirvāna.

[From Śikṣāsamuccaya, p. 257]

Those who are afraid of the sorrow which arises from . . . the round of birth-and-death seek for Nirvāna; they do not realize that between birth-and-death and Nirvāna there is really no difference at all. They see Nirvāna as the absence of all . . . becoming, and the cessation of all contact of sense-organ and sense-object, and they will not understand that it is really only the inner realization of the store of impressions.[2] . . . Hence they teach the three Vehicles,[3] but not the doctrine that nothing truly exists but the mind, in which are no images. Therefore . . . they do not know the extent of what has been perceived by the minds of past, present, and future Buddhas, and continue in the conviction that the world extends beyond the range of the mind's eye. . . . And so they keep on rolling . . . on the wheel of birth-and-death.

[From Laṅkāvatāra Sūtra, pp. 61–62]

[1] Murdering one's mother, murdering one's father, murdering a perfected being (arhant), trying to destroy the Buddhist Order, and maliciously injuring a Buddha.
[2] Ālayavijñāna.
[3] The two "Lesser Vehicles" (to salvation) of the older Buddhism —namely, those of the disciples and of private buddhas—and the vehicle of the bodhisattva.

Praise of Dharma

Dharma, the cosmic Law of Righteousness proclaimed by the Buddha, was revered quite as highly by the Mahāyānists as by the Theravādins. The ultimate body of the Buddha, which was roughly equivalent to the World-Soul of the Hindus, was called the Dharma-body, and the basic element of the universe was also often known as Dharmadhātu, "the Raw-material of the Law," especially by the Vijnānavāda.[1] The following passage, perhaps originally intended for liturgical purposes, exemplifies the mystical attitude toward Dharma, which was widespread in later Buddhism. Here Dharma seems to have much in common with the Tao of Lao Tzu. Notice that it is prior to the heavenly Buddhas themselves.

The blessed Buddhas, of virtues endless and limitless, are born of the Law of Righteousness; they dwell in the Law, are fashioned by the Law; they have the Law as their master, the Law as their light, the Law as their field of action, the Law as their refuge. They are produced by the Law . . . and all the joys in this world and the next are born of the Law and produced by the Law. . . .

The Law is equal, equal for all beings. For low or middle or
    high the Law cares nothing.
    So must I make my thought like the Law.
The Law has no regard for the pleasant. Impartial is the Law.
    So must I make my thought like the law.
The Law is not dependent upon time. Timeless is the
    Law. . . .
    So must I make my thought like the Law.
The Law is not in the lofty without being in the low.
    Neither up nor down will the Law bend.
    So must I make my thought like the Law.
The Law is not in that which is whole without being in that
    which is broken. Devoid of all superiority or inferiority
    is the Law.
    So must I make my thought like the Law.

---

[1] Or, as many philosophers of this school would have interpreted it, "the Raw-material of Phenomena," since dharma in Buddhism had also a special philosophical connotation.

The Law is not in the noble without being in the humble.
   No care for fields of activity has the Law.
So must I make my thought like the Law.
The Law is not in the day without being in the night. . . .
   Ever firm is the Law.
So must I make my thought like the Law.
The Law does not lose the occasion of conversion. There is
   never delay with the Law.
So must I make my thought like the Law.
The Law has neither shortage nor abundance. Immeasurable,
   innumerable is the Law. Like space it never lessens or
   grows.
So must I make my thought like the Law.
The Law is not guarded by beings. Beings are protected by
   the Law.
So must I make my thought like the Law.
The Law does not seek refuge. The refuge of all the world
   is the Law.
So must I make my thought like the Law.
The Law has none who can resist it. Irresistible is the Law.
So must I make my thought like the Law.
The Law has no preferences. Without preference is the Law.
So must I make my thought like the Law.
The Law has no fear of the terrors of birth-and-death, nor is
   it lured by Nirvāna. Ever without misgiving is the Law.
So must I make my thought like the Law.

[From *Dharmasaṅgīti Sūtra, Śikṣāsamuccaya,* pp. 322–23]

Perfect Wisdom Personified

Prajñāpāramitā, *the Perfection of Wisdom, is praised in many passages of Mahāyāna literature. As with the early Jews, the divine Wisdom was personified,*[1] *but the process went much further with the Buddhists than with the Jews, for in India Prajñāpāramitā became a goddess worshiped in the form of an icon. She was especially cultivated in the Vajrayāna, but by no means neglected in Mahāyānist sects.*

Perfect Wisdom spreads her radiance . . . and is worthy of worship. Spotless, the whole world cannot stain her. . . . In

[1] Compare especially Proverbs 8 and 9:1–6.

her we may find refuge; her works are most excellent; she
brings us to safety under the sheltering wings of enlightenment. She brings light to the blind, that all fears and calamities may be dispelled . . . and she scatters the gloom and
darkness of delusion. She leads those who have gone astray
to the right path. She is omniscience; without beginning or
end is Perfect Wisdom, who has Emptiness as her characteristic mark; she is the mother of the bodhisattvas. . . . She
cannot be struck down, the protector of the unprotected,
. . . the Perfect Wisdom of the Buddhas, she turns the
Wheel of the Law.

[From Aṣṭasāhasrikā Prajñāpāramitā, 7.170–71]

The Blessings of Peace

The following passage is one of the few in the literature of early
India which call upon the many kings of the land to forget their
quarrels and live together in peace. It seems to contain an implicit
criticism of the Hindu ideals of kingship, which encouraged kings
to aim at territorial aggrandizement, and to attack their neighbors
without good reason, in order to gain homage and tribute.

In the sixth section of the Sūtra of the Excellent Golden Light,
the four great kings Vaishravana, Dhritarāshtra, Virūdhaka, and Virū-
pāksha, who are the gods guarding the four quarters of the earth
and correspond to the Lokapālas or world-protectors of Hindu
mythology, approach the Buddha and declare that they will give
their special protection to those earthly kings who patronize monks
who recite the sūtra, and encourage its propagation in their domains.
The Buddha replies with the words which follow. The sūtra probably belongs to the third or fourth century A.D., before the full expansion of the Gupta empire, when warfare was widespread. The
reference to the title devaputra, "Son of the Gods," in the passage
quoted after the following suggests that it emanated from northwestern India, where devaputra was a royal title of the Kushāna
kings.

Protect all those royal families, cities, lands, and provinces,
save them, cherish them, guard them, ward off invasion from
them, give them peace and prosperity. Keep them free from
all fear, calamity, and evil portent. Turn back the troops of
their enemies and create in all the earthly kings of India a
desire to avoid fighting, attacking, quarreling, or disputing
with their neighbors. . . . When the eighty-four thousand

kings of the eighty-four thousand cities of India are contented with their own territories and with their own kingly
state and their own hoards of treasure they will not attack
one another or raise mutual strife. They will gain their
thrones by the due accumulation of the merit of former
deeds; they will be satisfied with their own kingly state, and
will not destroy one another, nor show their mettle by laying
waste whole provinces. When all the eighty-four thousand
kings of the eighty-four thousand capital cities of India think
of their mutual welfare and feel mutual affection and joy,
. . . contented in their own domains . . . India will be
prosperous, well-fed, pleasant, and populous. The earth will
be fertile, and the months and seasons and years will all occur
at the proper time.[1] Planets and stars, moon and sun, will
duly bring on the days and nights. Rain will fall upon earth
at the proper time. And all living beings in India will be rich
with all manner of riches and corn, very prosperous but not
greedy.

[From *Suvarṇaprabhāsottama Sūtra*, 6, pp. 73–75]

The Divine Right (and Duty) of Kings

As we have seen, the early Buddhists evolved the story of the first
king Mahāsammata, which implies a doctrine of social contract. In
Hinduism, however, ideas of a different kind developed, and from
early in the Christian era it was widely proclaimed in Hindu religious literature that the king was "a great god in human form,"
made of eternal particles of the chief gods of the Hindu pantheon.
It became usual to address the king as Deva or "god," and the
older ideas of Buddhism on kingship were, at least in Mahāyāna circles, modified in consequence.

The Sūtra of the Excellent Golden Light, as well as the striking
call for peace previously quoted, contains one of the few passages
in the Mahāyāna scriptures in which problems of government are
discussed. It is not admitted that the king is a god in his own right,
but he holds his high estate by the authority of the gods, and

---

[1] Note that, as we have seen elsewhere, the welfare of the whole
land, and even the regularity of the calendar and of heavenly phenomena generally, were believed to be dependent on the morality
of men, and more especially on the morality of ruling kings. This
idea, which is also found in Hinduism, was well known in China,
where it developed independently.

therefore is entitled to be addressed as Deva, and as "Son of the
Gods." This doctrine of divine appointment may be compared with
that widely proclaimed in England during the Stuart period, and it
is also closely akin to the Chinese doctrine of the "mandate of
Heaven." Like the Son of Heaven in imperial China, the Indian
"Son of the Gods" held his title on condition of fulfilling his function properly, and might incur the anger of his divine parents. The
verses quoted implicitly admit the moral right of revolt against a
wicked or negligent king, for in conspiring against him his subjects
are serving the heavenly purpose, and plotting the overthrow of
one who no longer enjoys the divine blessing on which his right to
govern depends. This too is a doctrine well known in China.

This poem on government, in Buddhist Sanskrit, purports to be
a speech of the high god Brahmā, delivered to the four Great Kings,
whom we have met in the previous extract.

How does a king, who is born of men, come to be called
    divine?
Why is a king called the Son of the Gods?
If a king is born in this world of mortals,
How can it be that a god rules over men?

I will tell you of the origin of kings, who are born in the
    world of mortals,
And for what reason kings exist, and rule over every province.
By the authority of the great gods a king enters his mother's
    womb.
First he is ordained by the gods—only then does he find an
    embryo.

What though he is born or dies in the world of mortals—
Arising from the gods he is called the Son of the Gods.

The thirty-three great gods assign the fortune of the king.
The ruler of men is created as son of all the gods,
To put a stop to unrighteousness, to prevent evil deeds,
To establish all beings in well-doing, and to show them the
    way to heaven.
Whether man, or god, or fairy, or demon,
Or outcaste, he is a true king who prevents evil deeds.
Such a king is mother and father to those who do good.

He was appointed by the gods to show the results of
   karma. . . .

But when a king disregards the evil done in his kingdom,
And does not inflict just punishment on the criminal,
From his neglect of evil, unrighteousness grows apace,
And fraud and strife increase in the land.

The thirty-three great gods grow angry in their palaces
When the king disregards the evil done in his kingdom.

Then the land is afflicted with fierce and terrible crime,
And it perishes and falls into the power of the enemy.
Then property, families, and hoarded wealth all vanish,
And with varied deeds of deceit men ruin one another.

Whatever his reasons, if a king does not do his duty
He ruins his kingdom, as a great elephant a bed of lotuses.

Harsh winds blow, and rain falls out of season,
Planets and stars are unpropitious, as are the moon and sun,
Corn, flowers, and fruit and seed do not ripen properly,
And there is famine, when the king is negligent. . . .

Then all the kings of the gods say one to another,
"This king is unrighteous, he has taken the side of unright-
   eousness!"
Such a king will not for long anger the gods;
From the wrath of the gods his kingdom will perish. . . .

He will be bereft of all that he values, whether by brother or
   son,
He will be parted from his beloved wife, his daughter will die.
Fire will fall from heaven, and mock-suns also.
Fear of the enemy and hunger will grow apace.
His beloved counselor will die, and his favorite elephant;
His favorite horses will die one by one, and his camels. . . .

There will be strife and violence and fraud in all the provinces;
Calamity will afflict the land, and terrible plague.

The brāhmans will then be unrighteous,
The ministers and the judges unrighteous.

The unrighteous will be revered,
And the righteous man will be chastised. . . .
Where the wicked are honored and the good are scorned
There will be famine, thunderbolts, and death . . .
All living beings will be ugly, having little vigor, very weak;
They will eat much, but they will not be filled.
They will have no strength, and no virility—
All beings in the land will be lacking in vigor. . . .

Many ills such as these befall the land
Whose king is partial [in justice] and disregards evil
      deeds. . . .

But he who distinguishes good deeds from evil,
Who shows the results of karma—he is called a king.
Ordained by the host of gods, the gods delight in him.
For the sake of himself or others, to preserve the righteous-
      ness of his land,
And to put down the rogues and criminals in his domains,
Such a king would give up [if need be] his life and his king-
      dom. . . .

Therefore a king should abandon his own precious life,
But not the jewel of Righteousness, whereby the world is
      gladdened.

                    [From Suvarṇaprabhāsottama Sūtra, 12 (cento)]

Magical Utterances

It would be wrong to depict Mahāyāna Buddhism as simply a system of idealist philosophy, with a pantheon of benevolent and compassionate deities and an exalted and altruistic ethical system. It
contained many elements from a lower stratum of belief, as will be
made clear from the following extract from the Laṅkāvatāra Sūtra,
one of the most important sacred texts of Mahāyāna Buddhism,
from which we have already given two quotations.

Belief in the magical efficacy of certain syllables, phrases, and
verses is as old as the Rig Veda. The Pali scriptures, however, pay
little attention to this aspect of popular religion, and it would seem

that the early Buddhists who were responsible for the compilation of these texts took a comparatively rationalistic view of the world. The criticism of vain and useless rituals contained in the Pali texts and in Ashoka's edicts was probably intended to cover the vain repetition of mantras or magical utterances. But from early in the Christian era onwards, such things became more and more closely associated with Buddhism, especially with the Mahāyāna sects. Hinduism and Buddhism alike developed schools which taught that the constant repetition of mantras was a sure means of salvation. The following passage is not strictly Tantric, for it does not attribute to the mantras it quotes any efficiency other than in the dispelling of evil spirits; but the importance given to the mantras, and the fact that they are attributed to the Buddha himself, show that Mahāyāna Buddhism was, by the fourth or fifth century A.D., permeated with the ideas which were to lead to fully developed Tantricism.

Then the Lord addressed the Great Being, the Bodhisattva Mahāmati thus:

Mahāmati, hold to these magic syllables of the *Laṅkā-vatāra*, recited . . . by all the Buddhas, past, present, and future. Now I will repeat them, that those who proclaim the Law of Righteousness may keep them in mind:

Tuṭṭe tuṭṭe vuṭṭe vuṭṭe paṭṭe paṭṭe kaṭṭe kaṭṭe amale amale vimale vimale nime nime hime hime vame vame kale kale kale kale aṭṭe maṭṭe vaṭṭe tuṭṭe jñeṭṭe spuṭṭe kaṭṭe kaṭṭe laṭṭe paṭṭe dime dime cale cale pace pace bandhe bandhe añce mañce dutāre dutāre patāre patāre arkke arkke sarkke sarkke cakre cakre dime dime hime hime ḍu ḍu ḍu ḍu ḍu ḍu ḍu ḍu ru ru ru ru phu phu phu phu svāhā. . . .

If men and women of good birth hold, retain, recite, and realize these magical syllables, nothing harmful shall come upon them—whether a god, a goddess, a serpent-spirit, a fairy, or a demon.[1] . . . If anyone should be in the grip of misfortune, let him recite these one hundred and eight times, and the evil spirits, weeping and wailing, will go off in another direction.

[From *Laṅkāvatāra Sūtra*, pp. 260–61]

[1] The names of many other supernatural beings follow.

4

TANTRICISM AND THE DECLINE OF
BUDDHISM IN INDIA

INTRODUCTION

The early centuries after Christ were very prosperous ones
for Buddhism. In the Northwest it seems to have been the
major religion, for hardly any specifically Hindu remains of
this period are to be found there. Elsewhere the influence of
Buddhism can be measured by the numerous remains of
stūpas and monasteries to be found in many parts of India,
which are among the finest and most beautiful relics of
ancient Indian civilization. From India Buddhism spread not
only to Central Asia and China but also to many parts of
Southeast Asia. It is certain that it had some effect on the
religious thought of the Middle East, and Buddhist influence
has been traced in Neo-Platonism, Gnosticism, and Mani-
chaeism. Many authorities believe that early Christianity
was influenced, directly or indirectly, by Buddhist ideas. In
the Eastern churches the story of Buddha's abandonment of
his home for a life of asceticism, "the Great Going-forth,"
has been adapted as a Christian legend, the name of its
protagonist, St. Josaphat, being evidently a corruption of the
word *bodhisattva*.

But never in any part of India did Buddhism wholly sup-
plant the other cults and systems. Theistic Hinduism continued to develop even during the period when Buddhism
was strongest, as did the six orthodox philosophical systems.

Layfolk, though they might support Buddhist monks and worship at Buddhist shrines, would usually patronize brāhmans also, and call on their services for the domestic rites such as birth ceremonies, initiations, marriages, and funerals, which played and still play so big a part in Indian life. Outside the monastic order those who looked on themselves as exclusively Buddhist were at all times probably comparatively few, and Ashoka, when he called on his subjects to respect the members of all sects and patronized Buddhists and Ājīvikas and probably other sects also, merely followed the practice of most religiously minded Indians down to the present day. It must be remembered that Indian religion is not exclusive. The most fanatical sectarian would probably agree that all the other sects had some qualified truth and validity. Hence Buddhism was never wholly cut off from the main stream of Indian religion.

The fourth century A.D. saw the rise of a second great empire, which at its zenith controlled the whole of northern India from Saurashtra to Bengal. This was the empire of the Guptas, whose greatest emperors were Hindus and gave their chief patronage to Vaishnavism.[1] From this period Buddhism began to lose ground in India. Its decline was at first almost imperceptible. The Chinese traveler Fa-hsien, who was in India at the very beginning of the fifth century, testified to the numerous well-populated Buddhist monasteries in all parts of the land. He noted, however, that Buddhists and Hindus joined in the same religious processions, as though Buddhism was looked on as a branch of Hinduism, rather than as an independent religion. In the seventh century the later Chinese travelers such as Hsüan-tsang and I-Ching reported a considerable decline in Buddhism. Numerous monasteries, even in the sacred Buddhist sites, were deserted and in ruins, and many monks were said to be corrupt, and given to superstitious and un-Buddhist practices. Some access of strength no doubt resulted from the support of Harsha (606–647), one of the last Hindu emperors to control the major part of northern India, who is said by Hsüan-tsang to have ended his life as a devotee of Buddhism. The chief stronghold of Buddhism from this time onward was Bihar

[1] The cult of Vishnu.

and Bengal. In Bihar the great Buddhist monastery of Nālandā, probably founded in the fifth century A.D., was one of the chief centers of learning in the whole of India, to which students came from as far afield as China and Java. In eastern India Buddhism continued to flourish until the twelfth century, with the support of the Pāla dynasty, which ruled Bihar and Bengal, and the kings of which, though by no means exclusive in their religious allegiance, gave their chief support to Buddhism. It was from this region that Buddhism was carried in the eighth century to Nepal and Tibet, to be revived and strengthened by later missions in the eleventh century.

The Buddhism which prevailed in India at this time was of a type very different from that known to the pious emperor Ashoka. The Hīnayāna schools had almost disappeared in eastern India, and allegiance was divided between the Mahāyāna and a new branch of Buddhism, often referred to as a separate vehicle, "the Vehicle of the Thunderbolt" (*Vajrayāna*). From the middle of the fifth century onwards, with the decline of the Gupta empire, Indians began to take more and more interest in the cults of feminine divinities and in the practice of magico-religious rites, which were believed to lead to salvation or to superhuman power, and which often contained licentious or repulsive features. There is no reason to believe that such practices were new—they can be traced in one form or another right back to the Vedas. But until this time they are little in evidence either in literature or in art, and we must assume that they had not much support among the educated, but were practiced chiefly by the lower social orders. As with many other features of Hinduism, they gradually influenced the upper classes, until in the Middle Ages groups of initiates, both Hindu and Buddhist, were to be found all over India, who practiced strange secret ceremonies in order to gain the magic power which, it was believed, would lead to salvation.

Earlier Buddhism had never been so rationalistic as to reject the supernatural. Thus it was taken for granted that the monk who was highly advanced in his spiritual training was capable of supranormal cognition and of marvelous feats such as levitation. The Buddha himself is said to have made a mango tree grow from a stone in a single night and to have multiplied himself a thousandfold; but these miracles were only performed on a single occasion to show the superiority of Buddhism over other sects, and the Master gave explicit instructions to his followers that they were not to make use of their magical powers, the exercise of which might lead them astray from the straight path to Nirvāna. There were, however, at all times hermit monks, living apart from the monasteries in solitude or semi-solitude, and it was probably among such monks that the practice of magic grew.

The new magical Buddhism, like the magical Hinduism which arose at about the same time, is often known as *Tantricism*, from the *Tantras*, or scriptures of the sects, describing the spells, formulas, and rites which the systems advocated. Probably Tantricism did not appear in organized Buddhism until the seventh century, when Hsüan-tsang reported that certain monastic communities were given to magical practices. Tantric Buddhism was of two main branches, known as Right and Left Hand, as in Tantric Hinduism. The Right Hand, though it became very influential in China and Japan, has left little surviving literature in Sanskrit; it was distinguished by devotion to masculine divinities. The Left Hand sects, to which the name Vajrayāna ("Vehicle of the Thunderbolt") was chiefly applied, postulated feminine counterparts or wives to the Buddhas, bodhisattvas, and other divinities of the mythology of later Buddhism, and devoted their chief attention to these *Tārās*, or "Savioresses." As in Hinduism they were thought of as the personified active aspects of the deities in question. The lore of this form of Buddhism was not generally given to the ordinary believer, but was imparted only to the initiate, who need not be a monk, but might be a layman. Adepts who had learned the secrets of Vajrayāna at the feet of a spiritual preceptor (guru) would meet together, usually at night, in small groups to perform their secret ceremonies.

Among the chief features of the ritual of Vajrayāna was the repetition of mystical syllables and phrases (mantra), such as the famous *Oṃ maṇi padme hūṃ.*[2] Yoga postures

---

[2] "Ah! The jewel is indeed in the lotus!" Though there are other interpretations this seems the most probable significance of the mysterious and elliptical phrase, which is specially connected with

and meditation were practiced. But the Tantric groups also followed more questionable methods of gaining salvation. It was believed that once the adept had reached a certain degree of spiritual attainment the normal rules of moral behavior were no longer valid for him, and that their deliberate breach, if committed in an odor of sanctity, would actually help him on the upward path. Thus drunkenness, meat-eating, and sexual promiscuity were often indulged in, as well as such repulsive psychopathic practices as eating ordure, and sometimes even ritual murder. Such antinomianism was perhaps the logical corollary of one of the doctrines which Tantric Buddhism took over from the Yogāchāra school of Mahāyāna, that all things in the universe were on ultimate analysis the illusory products of mind.

We must not believe that the whole of Tantric Buddhism is included in the practice of unpleasant secret rites. Many Tantric circles practiced such rites only symbolically, and their teachers often produced works of considerable philosophical subtlety, while the ethical tone of some passages in the Tantricist Saraha's *Treasury of Couplets* (*Dohākośa*), one of the last Buddhist works produced in India, is of the highest.

The Vajrayāna developed its own system of philosophy by adapting the doctrines of the Vijnānavādins and Mādhyamikas to its own world view. It admitted the emptiness of all things, but maintained that, once the emptiness was fully recognized, the phenomenal world was not to be disparaged, for it was fundamentally identical with the universal Emptiness itself. Thus the adept was encouraged to utilize the phenomenal world for his psychic progress to supreme wisdom. The world was a Means (*upāya*, a masculine noun in Sanskrit), and full consciousness of the Emptiness of all things was the Supreme Wisdom (prajnā, a feminine noun), often personified both in Mahāyāna and Vajrayāna circles as a goddess. Final bliss was to be obtained by the union of the phenomenal Means with the noumenal Wisdom, and the most vivid symbol of such union was sexual intercourse. Thus

―――――――――――――

the Bodhisattva Avalokiteshvara, and is still believed in Tibet to have immense potency. Its significance may be sexual, implying that the Bodhisattva has united with his Tārā.

a philosophical basis was found for the erotic practices of Tantric Buddhism. The Vajrayāna position was rather like that of certain deviationist Christian sects, the morals of which were completely antinomian, because their members were the Elect, and thus above the law.

The end of Buddhism in India is still not completely elucidated. Buddhist monasteries survived in many parts of the land until the time of the Muslim invasions at the very end of the twelfth century. Though there had been some loss of ground to Hinduism, it is clear that the great monasteries of Bihar and Bengal were inhabited down to this time. Fine illustrated manuscripts of Mahāyāna and Tantric scriptures were produced in Eastern India, some of which found their way to Nepal, where they have survived to this day. Inscriptions and archaeological evidence show that there were still fairly prosperous Buddhist monasteries at the sacred sites of Sarnath, near Vārānasī, where the Buddha preached his first sermon, and Shrāvastī, in northern Uttar Pradesh, where he spent much of his actual life. In the Deccan and the Dravidian south there are few evidences of Buddhism after the tenth century, though here and there it survived. It would seem that the life of the monasteries became gradually more and more estranged from that of the people, and that the activities of the monks, grown wealthy from long-standing endowments, became increasingly confined to small circles of initiates. This, however, is not the whole story, for Buddhists were among the earliest writers of Bengali, and this would indicate an attempt to make contact with a popular audience. Thus the end of Buddhism was not wholly due to the divorce of Buddhism and everyday life, or to corruption and decay, as some have suggested.

By the time of the Guptas we find the Buddha worshiped in his shrines as a Hindu god, with all the ritual of pūjā,[3] and Buddhist monks and Hindu priests joined in the same processions. The Pāla kings, who claimed to be "supreme worshipers of the Buddha," were also proud of the fact that they maintained all the rules of Hindu dharma,[4] and many of their ministers were orthodox brāhmans. We can perhaps

[3] Worship of an idol with offerings of lights, flowers, food, etc.
[4] The Sacred Law.

imagine the attitude of the layman to Buddhism from this analogy. For ordinary folk living near a Buddhist monastery, Buddha would be one god among many; they might pay him special homage and worship because their ancestors had done so and because his temple was nearby, but they would not look upon his worship as in any way excluding them from the Hindu fold. Medieval Hinduism knew many sects, each specially devoted to one or other of the gods, who was looked upon as supreme, the lesser gods being mere emanations or secondary forms of the great one. From the point of view of the layman this would be the position of Buddhism—a sect of Hinduism with its own special order of devotees, the monks, pledged to the service of their god. It cannot be too strongly emphasized that Hinduism has always tended to assimilate rather than to exclude.

At this time anti-Buddhist activity was not completely unknown. There are traditions, most of them preserved only in Buddhist sources and therefore suspect of exaggeration, of occasional fierce persecution by anti-Buddhist kings, chiefly Shaivites,[5] some of whom are said even to have gone as far as to place a price on the head of every Buddhist monk. Allowing for all exaggerations, it is clear that some kings were strongly anti-Buddhist and took active steps to discourage Buddhism. More serious opposition came from certain medieval Hindu philosophers and their disciples. Teachers such as Kumārila and Shankara are said to have traveled far and wide throughout India preaching their own doctrines and attacking those of their rivals, and Buddhism seems to have been singled out for special attention by those reformers. Anti-Buddhist propaganda of one kind or another may have had a significant influence in the decline of Buddhism.

By the time of the Muslim invasion (1192 A.D.) Buddhism was rapidly merging in the body of Hinduism. The process is exemplified in the doctrine of the incarnations of Vishnu, which does not appear in its final form until just before the Muslim invasion. Here the Buddha figures as an incarnation of the Supreme God, who took human form in order either to put a stop to the sacrifice of living animals, or, according to some formulations, to destroy the wicked by leading them

[5] Worshipers of Shiva.

to deny the Vedas and so accomplish their own perdition. Thus the Buddha was placed, in theory at least, on the same exalted level as the great popular divinities Krishna and Rāma, and his devotees might worship him as a full member of the orthodox pantheon. There is no reason to believe that the cult of Buddha as a Hindu god was ever widespread, but certainly in the great temple of Gayā, the scene of the Master's enlightenment, he was adored by simple Hindu pilgrims with all the rites of Hinduism as a Hindu god until very recent times, when the ancient temple was transferred back to Buddhist hands. Other traces of Buddhism survive in parts of eastern India. Thus it is said that the peasants of Bengal and Orissa still worship a divinity called Dharma, who seems to be a faint folk recollection of the ancient religion of the land.

When the Turkish horsemen occupied Bihar and Bengal, slew or expelled the "shaven-headed brāhmans," as they called the Buddhist monks, and destroyed their monasteries and libraries, Buddhism was dead in India. The *purohitas* (chaplains) of Hinduism, who performed the domestic rites for the layfolk, and the Hindu ascetics who wandered from place to place, were in need of no organization and could survive the disruption of the Muslim invasion and the aggressive propaganda of the alien faith. Buddhism, dependent on the monasteries for its survival and without the same lay support as Hinduism received, was destroyed by the invader. It is noteworthy that Islam had its greatest success in those parts of India where Buddhism had been strongest, in the Northwest, and in Bengal. Only in the Himalayan regions, especially Nepal, did Buddhism survive, kept alive largely by contact with Tibet. Though in many parts of Asia it has flourished, and indeed spread and developed in the last seven hundred years, in the land of its birth it has died. Only in the last few decades have intelligent Indians begun once more to take an interest in the religion founded by India's greatest son. Thanks largely to the work of the Mahābodhi Society the sacred sites of Buddhism are once more cared for, and Buddhist monasteries again exist in many parts of India. Though the number of professing Buddhists in India and Pakistan is still very small, there is no doubt that the doctrines of Buddhism are beginning to influence more and

more Indians, and Buddhism may well become a force to be
reckoned with in the India of the future.

PASSION AS A MEANS OF SALVATION

*The doctrine that the round of birth-and-death was really the same
as Nirvāna, the cult of feminine divinities, and the growing interest
in magic, especially magical utterances, led to the appearance of
Vajrayāna, or Tantric Buddhism. The rather dangerous view that
all things are legitimate to those who fully know the truth is already to be found in specifically Mahāyāna texts. In the texts of
Vajrayāna it is developed further, for it is declared that, at a certain
stage of self-development, to give way to the passions, especially
the sexual passions, is a positive help along the upward path. This
passage is taken from a Tantric poem, Disquisition on the Purification of the Intellect, composed by Āryadeva[1] toward the end of the
seventh century.*

They who do not see the truth
  Think of birth-and-death as distinct from Nirvāna,
But they who do see the truth
  Think of neither. . . .

This discrimination is the demon
  Who produces the ocean of transmigration.
Freed from it the great ones are released
  From the bonds of becoming.

Plain folk are afflicted
  With the poison of doubt. . . .
He who is all compassion . . .
  Should uproot it completely.

As a clear crystal assumes
  The color of another object,
So the jewel of the mind is colored
  With the hue of what it imagines.

[1] Not the same as an earlier Āryadeva, disciple of Nāgārjuna and
author of the *Four-hundred Stanzas* (*Catuḥśataka*).

The jewel of the mind is naturally devoid
   Of the color of these ideas,
Originally pure, unoriginated,
   Impersonal, and immaculate.

So, with all one's might, one should do
   Whatever fools condemn,
And, since one's mind is pure,
   Dwell in union with one's divinity.[2]

The mystics, pure of mind,
   Dally with lovely girls,
Infatuated with the poisonous flame of passion,
   That they may be set free from desire.

By his meditations the sage is his own Garuda,[3]
   Who draws out the venom [of snakebite] and drinks it.
He makes his deity innocuous,
   And is not affected by the poison. . . .

When he has developed a mind of wisdom
   And has set his heart on enlightenment
There is nothing he may not do
   To uproot the world [from his mind].

He is not Buddha, he is not set free,
   If he does not see the world
As originally pure, unoriginated,
   Impersonal, and immaculate.

The mystic duly dwells
   On the manifold merits of his divinity,
He delights in thoughts of passion,
   And by the enjoyment of passion is set free.

What must we do? Where are to be found
   The manifold potencies of being?

[2] That is, the woman with whom the Tantricist practices his rites.
[3] A mythical, divine bird, the enemy and slayer of snakes.

A man who is poisoned may be cured
  By another poison, the antidote.

Water in the ear is removed by more water,
  A thorn [in the skin] by another thorn.
So wise men rid themselves of passion
  By yet more passion.

As a washerman uses dirt
  To wash clean a garment,
So, with impurity,
  The wise man makes himself pure.

                          [From *Cittaviśuddhiprakaraṇa*, pp. 24–38]

Everything Is Buddha

The last phase of Buddhism in India was the school of Tantricism
sometimes known as Sahajayāna or Sahajīya, "the Vehicle of the
Innate," which stressed the doctrine that Ultimate Being was ever
present in all things living, a view not strange to Buddhism, and
very well known in Hinduism. The Sahajayāna teachers, like other
Tantricists, strongly supported the view that sexual activity and
other forms of worldly pleasure were positive helps to salvation for
those who made use of them in the proper spirit, but their teaching was distinguished by its emphasis on simplicity—it was possible
for the ordinary layman, living a normal life in every respect, to
achieve salvation, simply by recognizing the Buddha within himself
and all things.

The teachers of this school began to write in the vernaculars, and
a number of their poems and series of verses, composed either in
Apabhramsha[1] or Old Bengali, survive from among the many which
must now be lost. All these works date from the tenth to the
twelfth centuries. Unlike Sanskrit poetry their verses are rhymed
and they employ meters which are still widely used in the vernaculars. For these reasons they give an impression very different from
that of earlier Buddhist poetry. In their simplicity of style, and in
the simplicity of their doctrines, they seem to look forward rather
than back—towards the simple mystical verse of Kabīr, who also
taught that the Ultimate Being was to be found in one's own home,
as one went about one's daily work. Like Kabīr's verses again they

[1] The early medieval vernaculars, which had moved much further
from Sanskrit than had Pali or the Prakrits, and were much closer
to the modern languages of India.

sometimes have a strong ethical content; for all their emphasis on the value of sex as a means of salvation, the Sahajayāna teachers, like all Buddhists, taught the virtues of compassion, kindliness, and helpfulness.

The following verses are taken from the Treasury of Couplets ascribed to Saraha, and written in Apabhramsha in the eleventh or twelfth century.

As is Nirvāna so is Samsāra.[2]
  Do not think there is any distinction.
Yet it possesses no single nature,
  For I know it as quite pure.

Do not sit at home, do not go to the forest,
  But recognize mind wherever you are.
When one abides in complete and perfect enlightenment,
  Where is Samsāra and where is Nirvāna?

Oh know this truth,
  That neither at home nor in the forest does enlightenment
    dwell.
Be free from prevarication
  In the self-nature of immaculate thought!

"This is my self and this is another."
  Be free of this bond which encompasses you about,
And your own self is thereby released.

Do not err in this matter of self and other.
  Everything is Buddha without exception.
Here is that immaculate and final stage,
  Where thought is pure in its true nature.

The fair tree of thought that knows no duality,
  Spreads through the triple world.
It bears the flower and fruit of compassion,
  And its name is service of others.

The fair tree of the Void abounds with flowers,
  Acts of compassion of many kinds,

[2] Transmigration, i.e., this world.

And fruit for others appearing spontaneously,
  For this joy has no actual thought of another.

So the fair tree of the Void also lacks compassion,
  Without shoots or flowers or foliage,
And whoever imagines them there, falls down,
  For branches there are none.[3]

The two trees spring from one seed,
  And for that reason there is but one fruit.
He who thinks of them thus indistinguishable,
  Is released from Nirvāna and Samsāra.

If a man in need approaches and goes away hopes unfulfilled,
  It is better he should abandon that house
Than take the bowl that has been thrown from the door.

Not to be helpful to others,
  Not to give to those in need,
This is the fruit of Samsāra.
  Better than this is to renounce the idea of a self.

He who clings to the Void
  And neglects Compassion,
Does not reach the highest stage.

But he who practices only Compassion,
  Does not gain release from toils of existence.
He, however, who is strong in practice of both,
  Remains neither in Samsāra nor in Nirvāna.

> [From Saraha, *Dohākośa*, v. 102–end; as translated by
> D. S. Snellgrove in Conze, *Buddhist Texts*, pp. 238–
> 39]

[3] All things are ultimately one in the eternal and infinite Emptiness
which is the body of the Buddha; therefore there is no real distinction between self and others, and on analysis the "fair tree" is
nonexistent. But, as we shall see in the following verse, on a still
higher plane of thought it shares the reality of the Ultimate Being,
and therefore, to the man who sees the world with complete clarity,
acts of mercy and kindness are still valid.

BUDDHISM IN *China*

THE COMING OF BUDDHISM
TO CHINA

INTRODUCTION

The coming of Buddhism to China was an event with far-reaching results in the development of Chinese thought and culture and of Buddhism itself. After a long and difficult period of assimilation, this new teaching managed to establish itself as a major system of thought, contributing greatly to the enrichment of Chinese philosophy, and also as a major system of religious practice which had an enduring influence on Chinese popular religion. Indeed, it came to be spoken of along with the native traditions, Confucianism and Taoism, as one of the Three Teachings or Three Religions, thus achieving a status of virtual equality with these beliefs.

As Buddhism spread from its homeland, it became the harbinger of civilization in many of the areas which it penetrated. Many of them had no system of writing before the advent of the new religion. One of the most notable exceptions to this statement, however, was China. By the time Buddhism was introduced, China boasted a civilization already very old, a classic canon, time-hallowed traditions, and the conviction that its society was the only truly civilized society in the world. Thus, while Buddhism was the vehicle for the introduction into such a country as Tibet of religion, art, script, literature, philosophy, etc., the Buddhist missionaries found in China a country that possessed these things in an already highly developed state. Buddhism was obliged to compete with indigenous philosophical and religious systems to win the hearts of the Chinese, and the Chinese, for their own part, were hindered in their understanding of Buddhist philosophy by preconceptions based on indigenous philosophical systems.

BUDDHISM AND THE CHINESE TRADITION

It is commonly said that the Chinese are this-worldly and extremely practical in their outlook. Confucianism, the dominant ethical and intellectual tradition, seems to have a strong secular orientation. Buddhism, on the other hand, has often been regarded as quite other-worldly. On what basis could it appeal to the Chinese? Could Buddhism really coexist with Confucianism and Taoism? In what sort of relationship could these Three Teachings stand to one another?

According to one opinion, Buddhism was able to gain a foothold in China, and later a large following, precisely because it offered solutions to religious problems which Confucianism did not deal with. There is some truth in this, as our subsequent readings will show, but there is more to the problem. Confucianism is not wholly "this-worldly" a teaching nor is Buddhism wholly "other-worldly." There were important points both of convergence and conflict between them.

It is true that the ultimate destiny of the individual, for Confucius, is inseparable from the personal fulfillment attained through facing the immediate needs and responsibilities of human life. It is "this" life—man in his concrete situation, in his normal relations—that Confucius' thought centers around. Yet such an attitude does not make him irreligious, because it is precisely in the human order that Confucius recognizes the workings of Heaven and man's obligation to serve Heaven. His lofty moral idealism is based not on a supernatural revelation, but rather on the natural revelation of the Heavenly order in man's moral sense and reason.

Thus, Confucius' affirmation of life can be considered

"this-worldly," but only if we recognize that for him "this world" was not opposed to Heaven. Indeed, the common term for this world was "All-under-Heaven," reflecting both man's dependence on the physical heavens and the supremacy of the Heavenly order in the affairs of men. For Confucius, however, if this order were recognized and followed, it should be possible to achieve good government and world peace. The perfecting of the individual in society, and of society through the cultivation of the individual, would bring about something very much like Heaven-on-Earth.

Of the more common religious view, which sees an afterlife in Heaven as the end of personal salvation, Confucius would have little reason to speak. Heaven for him is not an after-life, a separate sphere or state of being; it is the moral order, the ruling power in *this* world. And it is in this life that salvation, personal or social, comes about.

The other major strain of native Chinese thought, Taoism, departed from the man-centeredness of Confucianism, insofar as it defined man so largely in ethical and social terms, and viewed human life in relation to a transcendent, all-pervading Way (or *Tao*) which was the ultimate principle of all life. Thus Taoism, no less than Confucianism, was fundamentally life-affirming. It might differ on the proper methods of self-cultivation and the governing of society, and it might even dispute the high place Confucianists gave man in the universe, but it did not question that life was worth living. A more spontaneous enjoyment of life, drawing on the inexhaustible riches of the Tao; a looser form of government, permitting greater freedom of human activity; a serene life, extending to the utmost a man's natural span of years—these are the ideals which Taoism opposed to the human cares and concerns of the Confucianist. Mystical and religious though it was in spirit, Taoism manifested the same this-worldliness and practicality in combination with its nature-mysticism that Confucianism had with its ethical idealism.

It was its love of life that led Taoism, whether in its more sophisticated philosophic or its cruder religious forms, to the aspiration for immortality. In this case, immortality meant either the indefinite extension of *this* life or a higher form of existence after one had undergone the transformation of death. Transcendence of the world was of course implied in the desire to rise in some sense above change, but there is no suggestion of contempt for the world, disgust with life.

As we turn to Buddhism, certain contrasts to the native Chinese tradition immediately appear in such a basic formulation as the Four Noble Truths. Taken together, these Truths express succinctly both Buddhism's initial pessimism about life and its final optimism. What could be more starkly in contrast to the Chinese attitude than the initial premise that existence is suffering, that to be born into this world involves inevitable pain, and that even death brings no cessation since rebirth involves one again in the endless cycle of transmigration? Surely, if pessimism be thought a characteristic of Indian religions, Buddhism manifests it most uncompromisingly here. There is no avoiding or mitigating the harsh confrontation with pain which Buddhism insists upon. Whether in its philosophical analyses, its meditations on human corruptibility, or its religious legendry dramatizing the young prince Siddhartha's own shocking experience of suffering as he came out of his palace—in all of these ways Buddhism compels its followers to face the inherent suffering of life without any illusions or sentimentality. And nowhere in the early Chinese experience is there any parallel to this radical confrontation of human suffering.

Nevertheless, if Buddhism focuses sharply on the painfulness of life at the outset, it more than balances this pessimism by its optimistic assertion that deliverance may be had through the extinguishing of desire and the attainment of the peace of Nirvāna. In the Mahāyāna form of Buddhism which was to have the greatest influence in China, this positive aspect of Buddhism is most emphasized. In the Theravāda or Hīnayāna the goal of Nirvāna seemed to some too negative or lifeless, and was easily mistaken for annihilation; in the Mahāyāna the resplendent attributes of Buddhahood as the ultimate end of religious aspiration are brought into the foreground. Technically, Buddhahood was a state transcending "existence" in the ordinary sense. To the believer, however, it could easily be understood as a higher form of life, a flowering out of the seed nourished in this existence.

A third-century Chinese Buddhist meditation text, vividly illustrates the initial pessimistic thesis of Buddhism as it was

conveyed to China. The aspirant is asked to meditate on the
corrupt and painful character of human life:

The ascetic engages in contemplation of himself and observes
that all the noxious seepage of his internal body is impure. Hair,
skin, skull and flesh; tears from the blinking of the eyes and spittle;
veins, arteries, sinew and marrow; liver, lungs, intestines and stomach; feces, urine, mucus and blood: such a mass of filth when combined produces a man. It is as if a sack were filled with a leaky
bag. Carefully observing it one distinguishes each of the various
items. When one understands that a man is such as this, contemplating internally one's body, one perceives that each item of the
four elements (mahābhūta) are nominal, and all of them taken
together do not constitute a (real) person (pudgala). Because he
contemplates without desire he perceives the basic emptiness of all
things (śūnyatā), and thus concentrating his mind, he gains
dhyāna.

And again:

Or internally contemplating [his body], he deeply ponders on
how below it is constrained by excrement and urine, and above it
is oppressed by cold and heat, and awakened to the detestability of
the body, concentrating his mind, he gains dhyāna.[1]

There seems to be no precedent in earlier Chinese literature for the morbid picture of man's bodily existence which
is fixed as the starting point of this meditation. And it is not
surprising that in the early dialogues which reveal the doubts
and difficulties of the Chinese in accepting Buddhism there
should be resistance to Buddhism's deprecation of the body.
The common Chinese approximation of immortality had been
bound up with biological reproduction and survival. A prime
filial duty of the Confucianist was to keep his body intact
and unscarred and to assure the continuity of the family line
through successive generations. Chinese conditioned by this
kind of thinking had to be re-educated to a far more spiritual
view of life before they could believe that conformity to the
Buddhist way of celibacy and ritual acts of bodily mortifica-

---

[1] Liu-tu chi ching 7 in Taishō daizōkyō, III, 39ab, from manuscript
translation by Arthur E. Link.

tion rendered a higher service to their parents than preservation of the body and perpetuation of the family.

How did Buddhism succeed in overcoming these natural reservations of the Chinese? It was in part, perhaps, because it offered a new explanation for the sorrow of life, which Confucianism and Taoism dealt with less squarely. But even more than this, it was because the positive aspect of Buddhism, its faith in ultimate deliverance, exerted a powerful attraction in terms more familiar to them. For this development we now turn to the early history of Buddhism in China.

THE INTRODUCTION OF BUDDHISM

No one can say when or in what fashion the Chinese first came into contact with Buddhism. It is to be presumed, from conjecture and from what sparse documentation there is, that this contact was with Buddhist icons worshiped by Central Asians coming into China. The Chinese of the time adopted the Buddha into their scheme of things as a demigod on the order of their own mythical Yellow Emperor and the philosopher Lao Tzu, who was believed to have attained immortality. But the dawn of history for Chinese Buddhism comes with the rendition of Buddhist sacred texts into the Chinese language.

The Chinese were particularly desirous of knowing whether Buddhism could add to their knowledge of elixirs and practices that would contribute to longevity, levitation, and other superhuman achievements. As it happened, Buddhism (like many other Indian religions) prescribed a precise set of practices, varying from school to school, which was believed to enhance the intuitive faculties. The early Buddhist missionaries found that the scriptures containing these prescriptions were what the Chinese wanted most to read and proceeded to translate them. This is the beginning of Buddhist literature in China.

As time went on, and as the interest of China's intellectuals veered toward metaphysical speculation, it became fashionable to seek in Buddhism those sublime truths that persons so inclined were seeking in some of China's own canonized classics. When, in 317 A.D., non-Chinese nations forced the Chinese court to abandon North China for what was to be a period of nearly three hundred years, the South Chinese intelligentsia became more and more effete, and the dominant trend in the Buddhism of the time was toward abstruse philosophic discussion in salons that brought together the cream of secular society and the best wits in the great metropolitan monasteries. A facile interpretation of Buddhism in Neo-Taoist terms prevailed and Buddhism's Indian origins were all but forgotten.

There were contrary trends, however. In the first place, not a few monks, in both North and South China, were earnestly concerned with the true meaning of Buddhism and of Buddhist salvation. The Chinese aversion to foreign languages being what it was, these persons showed their zeal principally in seeking out capable translators or in participating in translation projects themselves. Also, simultaneously with the philosophical salons and the great translation projects there was a trend, more pronounced in the north than in the south, toward a practical and devotional Buddhism. This consisted of an emphasis on contemplative practices as well as on adoration, good works, etc. The erection of temples and statuary soon spread all over China.

The selections which follow are intended to illustrate the general character of Buddhism in this early period and some of the problems encountered in gaining acceptance for it among the Chinese.

IS BUDDHISM UN-CHINESE?

The date and authorship of the Disposition of Error *are not known. The surname of the alleged author, Mou, led many persons to identify him with a Latter Han personality named Mou Jung, but subsequent scholarship has demonstrated beyond any reasonable doubt that this cannot be.*

As for the date, the general tone of the composition leads one to suspect that the work was written at a time when Buddhism had gained a sufficient foothold to cause many Chinese to fear its influence and to attempt to strike back. While the counterattack against Buddhism in the north took the form of an official persecution or curtailment, under the Southern Dynasties (420–589 A.D.) it usually took the form of polemics. The Disposition of Error *or Li-*

huo lun, as it is known in Chinese, appears to be an apologia for Buddhism, written in answer to such polemical writings.

The author takes the stand that it is possible to be a good Chinese and a good Buddhist at the same time, that there is no fundamental conflict between the two ways of life, and that the great truths preached by Buddhism are preached, if in somewhat different language, by Confucianism and Taoism as well.

Why Is Buddhism Not Mentioned in the Chinese Classics?

The questioner said: If the way of the Buddha is the greatest and most venerable of ways, why did Yao, Shun, the Duke of Chou, and Confucius not practice it? In the seven Classics one sees no mention of it. You, sir, are fond of the *Book of Odes* and the *Book of History*, and you take pleasure in rites and music. Why, then, do you love the way of the Buddha and rejoice in outlandish arts? Can they exceed the Classics and commentaries and beautify the accomplishments of the sages? Permit me the liberty, sir, of advising you to reject them.

Mou Tzu said: All written works need not necessarily be the words of Confucius, and all medicine does not necessarily consist of the formulae of [the famous physician] P'ien-ch'üeh. What accords with principle is to be followed, what heals the sick is good. The gentleman-scholar draws widely on all forms of good, and thereby benefits his character. Tzu-kung [a disciple of Confucius] said, "Did the Master have a permanent teacher?" Yao served Yin Shou, Shun served Wu-ch'eng, the Duke of Chou learned from Lü Wang, and Confucius learned from Lao Tzu. And none of these teachers is mentioned in the seven Classics. Although these four teachers were sages, to compare them to the Buddha would be like comparing a white deer to a unicorn,[1] or a swallow to a phoenix. Yao, Shun, the Duke of Chou, and Confucius learned even from such teachers as these. How much less, then, may one reject the Buddha, whose distinguishing marks are extraordinary and whose superhuman powers know no bounds! How may one reject him and refuse to learn from

[1] *Ch'i-lin*, a mythical beast like the unicorn, but not actually one-horned.

him? The records and teachings of the Five Classics do not contain everything. Even if the Buddha is not mentioned in them, what occasion is there for suspicion?

Why Do Buddhist Monks Do Injury to Their Bodies?

One of the greatest obstacles confronting the early Chinese Buddhist church was the aversion of Chinese society to the shaving of the head, which was required of all members of the Buddhist clergy. The Confucianists held that the body is the gift of one's parents, and that to harm it is to be disrespectful toward them.

The questioner said: The *Classic of Filial Piety* says, "Our torso, limbs, hair, and skin we receive from our fathers and mothers. We dare not do them injury." When Tseng Tzu was about to die, he bared his hands and feet.[1] But now the monks shave their heads. How this violates the sayings of the sages and is out of keeping with the way of the filially pious! . . .

   Mou Tzu said: . . . Confucius has said, "He with whom one may follow a course is not necessarily he with whom one may weigh its merits." This is what is meant by doing what is best at the time. Furthermore, the *Classic of Filial Piety* says, "The kings of yore possessed the ultimate virtue and the essential Way." T'ai-po cut his hair short and tattooed his body, thus following of his own accord the customs of Wu and Yüeh and going against the spirit of the "torso, limbs, hair, and skin" passage.[2] And yet Confucius praised him, saying that his might well be called the ultimate virtue.

Why Do Monks Not Marry?

Another of the great obstacles confronting the early Chinese Buddhist church was clerical celibacy. One of the most important features of indigenous Chinese religion is ancestor worship. If there are no descendants to make the offerings, then there will be no

---

[1] To show he had preserved them intact from all harm.
[2] Uncle of King Wen of the Chou who retired to the barbarian land of Wu and cut his hair and tattooed his body in barbarian fashion, thus yielding his claim to the throne to King Wen.

sacrifices. To this is added the natural desire for progeny. For a Chinese traditionally there could be no greater calamity than child-lessness.

The questioner said: Now of felicities there is none greater than the continuation of one's line, of unfilial conduct there is none worse than childlessness. The monks forsake wife and children, reject property and wealth. Some do not marry all their lives. How opposed this conduct is to felicity and filial piety! . . .

Mou Tzu said: . . . Wives, children, and property are the luxuries of the world, but simple living and inaction are the wonders of the Way. Lao Tzu has said, "Of reputation and life, which is dearer? Of life and property, which is worth more?" . . . Hsü Yu and Ch'ao-fu dwelt in a tree. Po I and Shu Ch'i starved in Shou-yang, but Confucius praised their worth, saying, "They sought to act in accordance with humanity and they succeeded in acting so." One does not hear of their being ill-spoken of because they were childless and propertyless. The monk practices the way and substitutes that for the pleasures of disporting himself in the world. He accumulates goodness and wisdom in exchange for the joys of wife and children.

Death and Rebirth

Chinese ancestor worship was premised on the belief that the souls of the deceased, if not fed, would suffer. Rationalistic Confucian-ism, while taking over and canonizing much of Chinese tradition, including the ancestral sacrifices, questioned the existence of spirits and hence the immortality of the soul.

The Buddhists, though likewise denying the existence of a soul, ac-cepted transmigration, and the early Chinese understood this to imply a belief in an individual soul which passed from one body to another until the attainment of enlightenment. The following passage must be understood in the light of these conflicting and confusing interpretations.

The questioner said: The Buddhists say that after a man dies he will be reborn. I do not believe in the truth of these words. . . .

Mou Tzu said: . . . The spirit never perishes. Only the

body decays. The body is like the roots and leaves of the five grains, the spirit is like the seeds and kernels of the five grains. When the roots and leaves come forth they inevitably die. But do the seeds and kernels perish? Only the body of one who has achieved the Way perishes. . . .

Someone said: If one follows the Way one dies. If one does not follow the Way one dies. What difference is there?

Mou Tzu said: You are the sort of person who, having not a single day of goodness, yet seeks a lifetime of fame. If one has the Way, even if one dies one's soul goes to an abode of happiness. If one does not have the Way, when one is dead one's soul suffers misfortune.

Why Should a Chinese Allow Himself to Be Influenced by Indian Ways?

This was one of the objections most frequently raised by Confucianists and Taoists once Buddhism had acquired a firm foothold on Chinese soil. The Chinese apologists for Buddhism answered this objection in a variety of ways. Below we see one of the arguments used by them.

The questioner said: Confucius said, "The barbarians with a ruler are not so good as the Chinese without one." Mencius criticized Ch'en Hsiang for rejecting his own education to adopt the ways of [the foreign teacher] Hsü Hsing, saying, "I have heard of using what is Chinese to change what is barbarian, but I have never heard of using what is barbarian to change what is Chinese." You, sir, at the age of twenty learned the way of Yao, Shun, Confucius, and the Duke of Chou. But now you have rejected them, and instead have taken up the arts of the barbarians. Is this not a great error?

Mou Tzu said: . . . What Confucius said was meant to rectify the way of the world, and what Mencius said was meant to deplore one-sidedness. Of old, when Confucius was thinking of taking residence among the nine barbarian nations, he said, "If a gentleman-scholar dwells in their midst, what baseness can there be among them?" . . . The Commentary says, "The north polar star is in the center of heaven and to the north of man." From this one can see that the land of China is not necessarily situated under the center

of heaven. According to the Buddhist scriptures, above, below, and all around, all beings containing blood belong to
the Buddha-clan. Therefore I revere and study these scriptures. Why should I reject the Way of Yao, Shun, Confucius, and the Duke of Chou? Gold and jade do not harm
each other, crystal and amber do not cheapen each other.
You say that another is in error when it is you yourself
who err.

Why Must a Monk Renounce Worldly Pleasures?

The questioner said: Of those who live in the world, there
is none who does not love wealth and position and hate poverty and baseness, none who does not enjoy pleasure and
idleness and shrink from labor and fatigue. . . . But now
the monks wear red cloth, they eat one meal a day, they
bottle up the six emotions, and thus they live out their lives.
What value is there in such an existence?

Mou Tzu said: "Wealth and rank are what man desires,
but if he cannot obtain them in a moral way, he should not
enjoy them. Poverty and meanness are what man hates, but
if he can only avoid them by departing from the Way, he
should not avoid them." [1] Lao Tzu has said, "The five colors
make men's eyes blind, the five sounds make men's ears deaf,
the five flavors dull the palate, chasing about and hunting
make men's minds mad, possessions difficult to acquire bring
men's conduct to an impasse. The sage acts for his belly, not
for his eyes." Can these words possibly be vain? Liu-hsia Hui
would not exchange his way of life for the rank of the three
highest princes of the realm. Tuan-kan Mu would not exchange his for the wealth of Prince Wen of Wei. . . . All
of them followed their ideals, and cared for nothing more.
Is there no value in such an existence?

Why Does Mou Tzu Support His Contentions from Secular Rather Than Buddhist Literature?

The questioner said: You, sir, say that the scriptures are like
the rivers and the sea, their phrases like brocade and em-

[1] *Analects* IV, 5.

broidery. Why, then, do you not draw on the Buddhist scriptures to answer my question? Why instead do you refer to the books of *Odes* and *History*, joining together things that are different to make them appear the same?

Mou Tzu said: . . . I have quoted those things, sir, which I knew you would understand. Had I preached the words of the Buddhist scriptures or discussed the essence of non-action, it would have been like speaking to a blind man of the five colors or playing the five sounds to a deaf man.

Does Buddhism Have No Recipe for Immortality?

Within the movement broadly known as "Taoism" there were several tendencies, one the quest for immortality, another an attitude of superiority to questions of life and death. The first Chinese who took to Buddhism did so out of a desire to achieve superhuman qualities, among them immortality. The questioner is disappointed to learn that Buddhism does not provide this after all. Mou Tzu counters by saying that even in Taoism, if properly understood, there is no seeking after immortality.

The questioner said: The Taoists say that Yao, Shun, the Duke of Chou, and Confucius and his seventy-two disciples did not die, but became immortals. The Buddhists say that men must all die, and that none can escape. What does this mean?

Mou Tzu said: Talk of immortality is superstitious and unfounded; it is not the word of the sages. Lao Tzu says, "Even Heaven and earth cannot be eternal. How much the less can man!" Confucius says, "The wise man leaves the world, but humanity and filial piety last forever." I have observed the six arts and examined the commentaries and records. According to them, Yao died, Shun had his [death place at] Mount Ts'ang-wu, Yü has his tomb on K'uai-chi, Po I and Shu Ch'i have their grave in Shou-yang. King Wen died before he could chastise Chou, King Wu died without waiting for King Ch'eng to grow up. We read of the Duke of Chou that he was reburied, and of Confucius that [shortly before his death] he dreamed of two pillars. [As for the disciples of Confucius], Po-yü died before his father, of Tzu Lu it is said that his flesh was chopped up and pickled. Of [the fatal illness of] Po-niu the Master said, "It must be fate," while of Tseng Shen we read that he bared his feet before death. And of Yen Yüan the Master said, "Unfortunately, he was short-lived," and likened him to a bud that never bloomed. All of these things are clearly recorded in the Classics: they are the absolute words of the sages. I make the Classics and the Commentaries my authority and find my proof in the world of men. To speak of immortality, is this not a great error?

[From *Hung-ming chi*, in *Taishō daizōkyō*, LII, 1–7]

6

THE SCHOOLS OF CHINESE

BUDDHISM I

INTRODUCTION

Sectarian Buddhism developed in China at least three hundred years after Buddhism's presence was first noted there in the first century. It arose, not as a result of schisms, protestant revolts, or individual claims to some new religious revelation, but as a natural outgrowth of tendencies already manifest in the earlier period of indigenous Buddhist thought.

The division of Chinese Buddhism into discrete sects had its origins in the tendency to concentrate on the study of one particular scripture or group of scriptures, as containing the most essential truths of the religion. The Chinese knew almost nothing of the splintering of Buddhism into sects in India and Central Asia. They did not know to what extent the scriptures themselves were sectarian writings, nor did they properly understand the sectarian motivation that lay behind the selection by the various missionaries of the scriptural texts they translated. For them, any Buddhist text translated into Chinese was the word of the Buddha. And since all of the Buddha's pronouncements had to be true, it was necessary to find some way to reconcile the frequently glaring inconsistencies found in the scriptures. A suggestion on how to deal with this problem was furnished to them by the Mahāyāna scriptures themselves.

By the time of the emergence of the Mahāyāna, the Hīna-

yāna scriptures had already been canonized, and anyone calling himself a Buddhist regarded them as the word of the
Buddha. The Mahāyānists composed their own scriptures
as they went along, and they found themselves obliged to
justify their scriptures as the good coin of Buddhism to a
religious community accustomed to reading religious writings
of a vastly different tone. To deny the validity of the firmly
entrenched Hīnayāna canon was impossible, and the Mahāyānists resorted to a more subtle device. They said that the
Hīnayāna was not untrue, but was merely a preparatory doctrine, preached by the Buddha to disciples whose minds were
not yet receptive to the ultimate truth. When he had prepared them with the tentative doctrine, he then revealed to
them his final truth. Thus the Mahāyāna and the Hīnayāna
were both alike the word of the Buddha, and the contradiction between them was only apparent.

The difficulty here, as far as the Chinese were concerned,
was the fact that while the Hīnayāna scriptures, having been
canonized by a series of ecclesiastical councils, were more or
less homogeneous, the Mahāyāna scriptures had never been
canonized or coordinated, and frequently contradicted not
only the Hīnayāna sacred writings but one another as well.
Nevertheless, the scriptures themselves had given them a
valuable hint, and some of them proceeded to act on it. The
first distinct sects in Chinese Buddhism were, in short, of
two kinds: 1) those that concentrated on one scripture or
set of scriptures in preference to all others, and 2) those that
catalogued the entire canon in such a way as to make one
particular scripture appear to contain the Buddha's ultimate
teaching. The great T'ien-t'ai and Hua-yen schools are examples of the latter type.

But the sects exemplified by the T'ien-t'ai and the Hua-
yen were of a kind that could never have any popular appeal.
Their philosophic ideas were of a high-flown variety that the
bulk of China's illiterate populace could not hope to understand. In addition, the religious practices prescribed by them
for the attainment of salvation could be performed only by
monks whose whole lives were devoted to religion. On both
accounts these sects tended to be limited to the upper classes,
for only they had the leisure and education that was required
for the study and understanding of such sophisticated teach-

ings. Among the great masses of people, therefore, it was not doctrine of this type but rather salvationism of the type represented by the Pure Land sect which prevailed.

Furthermore, the attitude that all scriptures represented the word of the Buddha tended to blur, even for the educated specialist, the doctrinal differences which distinguished one sect from another. In the latter half of the T'ang dynasty, from about 750 to about 900, one frequently encounters an eminent Chinese monk going about from one sectarian center to another studying the teachings of all the sects, as if anything short of mastery of all of them was an imperfect knowledge of Buddhism. Some Chinese monks are claimed as patriarchs by as many as three or four different sects. Thus was confirmed in Chinese Buddhism a strong tendency toward syncretism which had long been a marked feature of Chinese thought.

Buddhist philosophy, it will be recalled, first began to flourish in the fourth century A.D. It was interpreted then largely in Taoist terms, on the basis of which "six schools and seven branches" were formed, including Tao-an's theory of Original Nonbeing or the Originally Undifferentiated; the same theory as modified by Fa-shen; Chih Tao-lin's theory of Matter-as-Such; and Fa-wen's theory of No Mind or the Emptiness of Mind. These men were simply individual thinkers, not sectarian leaders. As important Indian texts were introduced and translated, as Indian masters arrived, and as Chinese Buddhist scholars finally developed their own systems, differences in opinion appeared and sects came into being. In their zeal to defend their ideas, certain schools of thought denounced others as heretical and established a lineage to earlier masters in order to claim for themselves the authority of tradition. As far as the ordinary Buddhist was concerned, these differences were academic. Thus the sects were essentially different systems of thought rather than contending denominations of religious practice.

Altogether there were ten principal schools, traditionally divided into two main categories, schools of Being and schools of Nonbeing, depending on whether they assumed or denied the self-nature of the dharmas (here "elements of existence") and the ego. Three of these, the Ch'eng-shih (*Satyasiddhi*, "Establishment of Truth"), the Chü-she

(*Abhidharmakośa*), and the Disciplinary (Lü, *Vinaya*), were regarded in China as Hīnayāna schools. The Ch'eng-shih, based on the Satyasiddhi treatise by Harivarman (A.D. c. 250–350), maintained that both dharmas and the ego are unreal. It is not certain whether the school ever existed in India. The treatise was translated into Chinese by Kumā-rajīva (A.D. 344–413) and was very popular in the fifth and sixth centuries. However, during the eighth century it was absorbed into the Middle Doctrine school.

Another Hīnayāna school, the Chü-she, grew up around the study of Vasubandhu's *Abhidharmakośa,* after it had been translated into Chinese. This school held that "both dharmas and the ego exist." It was active in the sixth and seventh centuries, having replaced the earlier P'i-t'an school which had promulgated the "All Exists" doctrine.

The third Hīnayāna school, the Disciplinary, was based on the Vinaya section of the Buddhist canon. Its doctrine was elaborated and completed by Tao-hsüan (596–667) in the South Mountain. The discipline for which it was known included 250 "prohibitive precepts" for monks and 348 for nuns. Nevertheless, this school hardly existed as an independent sect in China.

None of these three schools exerted much influence or lasted very long. The same may be said of two Mahāyāna schools, the Three-Treatise school and the Consciousness-Only school. They, like the Hīnayāna schools, taught one-sided philosophies, the former reducing everything to Emptiness and the latter reducing everything to Consciousness. Representing such extreme positions, they did not suit the temper of the Chinese. Both the concepts of Emptiness and of the Mind, however, were accepted as basic tenets of the remaining schools, and in this way they have been of great importance in Chinese Buddhist history.

The schools that have formed the spirit and substance of Chinese Buddhism have been the T'ien-t'ai, Hua-yen, Meditation, and Pure Land schools. The common Chinese saying, "The T'ien-t'ai and Hua-yen schools for doctrine and the Meditation and Pure Land schools for practice," accurately describes both the strong influence of these schools in particular and the syncretic nature of Chinese Buddhism in general.

These are essentially Chinese schools because the T'ien-t'ai did not exist in India and while the Pure Land, Hua-yen, and Meditation schools can be traced to India, they developed along characteristically Chinese lines. For this reason they came to overshadow the others and persisted throughout Chinese history.

The remaining Mahāyāna school, the Esoteric school (Chen-yen, "True Word"), believes that the universe consists of the "three mysteries" of action, speech, and thought. All phenomena represented by these categories of action, speech, and thought are manifestations of the Great Sun Buddha, which is the universe itself. Through secret language, "mystical verse," "true words," etc., the quintessential truth of the Buddha can be communicated to human beings. This doctrine was transmitted to China by several Indian monks and attained a considerable vogue in the eighth century, but rapidly declined thereafter. Its influence was felt mostly in Tibet and Japan, rather than in China.

THE THREE-TREATISE SCHOOL

The Three-Treatise (San-lun) school is the Chinese representative of the Indian Mādhyamika (Middle Doctrine) school of Nāgārjuna (A.D. c. 100 to 200). It was introduced into China by a half-Indian missionary named Kumārajīva (344–413) who translated into Chinese the three Indian works systematizing the Middle Doctrine, two by Nāgārjuna, and the other by his disciple Deva. Hence the name Three-Treatise school.

For an understanding of this doctrine as it is discussed in Chinese texts familiarity with certain technical terms is necessary. One is the concept of "common truth" and "higher truth." It is from the standpoint of common or worldly truth, i.e., relatively or pragmatically, that dharmas are said to exist. From the standpoint of "higher truth" they are seen to be transitory and lacking in any reality or self-nature. Emptiness or the Void alone represents the changeless Reality. The dialectical process by which this ultimate truth is reached is known as the "Middle Path of Eightfold Negations," which systematically denies all antithetical assertions regarding things: "there is no production, no extinction, no annihilation, no permanence, no unity, no diversity, no coming in, no going out." Production, extinction, etc. are proved by the school to be unreal by the use of the "Four Points of Argument": that is, by refuting an idea as being, as nonbeing, as both being and nonbeing, and as neither being nor nonbeing. The belief in any of the four is an extreme and must be transcended by a higher synthesis through the dialectic method until the Ultimate Void is arrived at, which is the Absolute Middle.

The Middle Doctrine was greatly elaborated and systematized by Chi-tsang (549–623), who had a Parthian father and a Chinese mother. Kumārajīva's introduction of the three treatises had been an effective blow against the metaphysical salons which flourished in the South during the fourth and fifth centuries, interpreting Buddhism in largely Taoist terms. Chi-tsang made the treatises the center of his system of thought and his influence extended to the eighth century. However, the school rapidly declined after the ninth century and soon disappeared.

A large number of Chi-tsang's writings survive, consisting principally of commentaries on Mahāyāna scriptures and treatises, and containing one of the earliest overall attempts at a systematization of Mahāyāna teaching.

The Twofold Truth

Having set forth his interpretation of the three treatises in detailed commentaries to each of them, Chi-tsang in The Profound Meaning of the Three Treatises *arranges topically what he considers to be the essential doctrine of the treatises as a whole. The stated purpose of his treatise is the "refutation of wrong and demonstration of right." First, he attacks the errors of "outside" or non-Buddhist doctrines among the philosophical schools of India, and then takes up errors within Buddhism.*

Of those who misunderstand the Twofold Truth there are, in all, three kinds of men. First are the Abhidharmists, who insist upon the existence of a definite substance, who err in [taking as ultimate what is in fact no more than] dependent existence [that is, a thing coming into existence depending on causes and conditions], and who therefore lose [the true meaning of] Common Truth. They also do not know that dependent existence, just as it is, has no existence, and thus they also lose [the true meaning] of the One True Emptiness. Second are those who learn the Great Vehicle and who are called the Men of the Extensive and Broad Way. They adhere to a belief in Emptiness and fail to know dependent existence, hence they lose the [true meaning of] Common Truth. Having adhered to the misunderstood Emptiness, they err with regard to the true Emptiness, and thus also lose the [true meaning of] Higher Truth. Third are those in this very age who, though knowing of the Twofold Truth, in some cases say that it is one substance, in some cases say that it is two substances. The theories are both untenable, hence they lose the [true meaning of both] Higher and Common Truth.

Question: "Higher and Common Truths are one substance." What error is there in this?

Answer: If Higher and Common Truths are one and the same in being true, then Higher Truth is true and Common Truth is also true. If Higher Truth and Common Truth are one and the same in being common, then Common Truth is common and Higher Truth is also common. If Higher Truth is true and Common Truth is not true, then Common Truth and Higher Truth are different. If Common Truth is common and Higher Truth is not common, then Higher Truth and Common Truth are different. Therefore both ways are blocked, and the two cannot be one.

Question: If it is an error to regard the two as one substance, then it should be blameless to regard them as different.

Answer: The scriptures say, "Matter in and of itself is void, void in and of itself is matter." If you say that each has its own substance, then their mutual identity is destroyed. If they have mutual identity, then duality of substance cannot be established. Therefore there is no latitude [for argument] in any direction, and conflicting theories are all exhausted.

Mahāyāna Truth is beyond all predication. It is neither one nor many, neither permanent nor impermanent. In other words, it is above all forms of differentiation or, as its adherents might say, it transcends both difference and identity. In order to make this point clear, San-lun doctrine teaches that each thesis that may be proposed concerning the nature of Truth must be negated by its antithesis, the whole process advancing step by step until total negation has been achieved. Thus the idea of being, representing Common Truth, is negated by that of nonbeing, representing Higher Truth. In turn the idea of nonbeing, now become the Common Truth of a new pair, is negated by the idea of neither being nor nonbeing, and so forth until everything that may be predicated about Truth has been negated.

Question: If the inner [Buddhist schools] and the outer [Heretics] are both refuted, if the Great [Vehicle] and the Small [Vehicle] are both rejected, then this is the heresy of annihilation. Why call it "true principle"?

Answer: Once the inner and the outer are both obliterated, [the heresies of] annihilation and eternity are thereupon silenced. Once the two extremes are rejected, how can it be other than true principle?

Objection: Now there is [the heresy of] annihilation and there is [the heresy of] eternity; therefore one says that they "are." If there is no [heresy of] annihilation and no [heresy of] eternity, one designates them by saying that they "are not." If they truly "are not," how does [this assertion of their nonexistence] escape [identity with the heresy of] annihilation?

Answer: Once [the heresies of] annihilation and eternity have been silenced, then existence and nonexistence have been equally avoided, and one may no longer charge that [this doctrine] is contaminated by [adherence to the notion of positive] nonexistence.

Objection: Though you have this way out, still you cannot escape rebuttal. Now when there is existence or there is nonexistence, one says that it "is." If there is neither existence nor nonexistence, this itself is "great nonexistence." [1] But once one has fallen into [the idea of] nonexistence, how can [this assertion of nonexistence] escape [identity with the heresy of] annihilation?

Answer: Originally, it was to counter the disease of [belief

---

[1] That is, a sort of super-negative, which even negates negation.

in] existence that we preached nonexistence. If the disease of [belief in] existence vanishes, the medicine of Emptiness is also useless. Thus we know that the Way of the sage has never held to either existence or nonexistence. What obstacle can there be, then?

Objection: "It *is* existence, it *is* nonexistence,"—one may call this twofold affirmation. "It is *not* existence, it is *not* nonexistence,"—one may call this twofold negation. But once one has fallen into affirmation and negation, one has reverted to [the teachings of] Confucius and Mo [Tzu].

Answer: At bottom, it is because it repudiates twofold affirmation that it has twofold negation. But once twofold affirmation has been banished from the mind, twofold negation also ceases. Hence one knows that it is not affirmation, but also that it is not negation.

Objection: "It is *not* affirmation and it is *not* negation." Once again you have fallen into twofold negation. How can you escape negation?

Answer: Twofold affirmation begets a tiger in a dream, twofold negation conjures up a flower in the air.[2] Thus we know that originally there is nothing to affirm, and consequently there is nothing to negate.

Objection: If there is neither affirmation nor negation, then there is also no wrong and no right. Why, then, in the beginning section do you call it "The Refutation of Wrong and the Demonstration of Right"?

Answer: [The idea that] there is affirmation and negation, we consider "wrong." [The idea that] there is neither affirmation nor negation, we call "right." It is for this reason that we have thus called the section explaining the refutation of wrong and the demonstration of right.

Objection: Once there is a wrong to be refuted and a right to be demonstrated, then the mind is exercising a choice. How can one say then that it "leans on nothing"?

Answer: In order to put an end to wrong, we force ourselves to speak of "right." Once wrong has been ended, then neither does right remain. Therefore the mind has nothing to which it adheres [or on which it leans].

[2] That is, they are both figments of the imagination.

Objection: If wrong and right are both obliterated, is this not surely a [positive] view of Emptiness?

Answer: The *Treatise on Right Views* says:

The Great Sage preached the Law of Emptiness
In order to separate [men] from all [positive] views.
If one still has the view that there "is" Emptiness,
Such a person even the Buddhas cannot transform.

If water could extinguish fire and then again produce fire, what can be used to extinguish it? [The heresies of] annihilation and eternity are a fire, and Emptiness can extinguish it. But if one clings to Emptiness, then there is no medicine that can extinguish [that disease].[3]

Objection: Once a person is attached to the disease of Emptiness, why, instead of giving him the medicine of existence, do you say that he cannot be converted?

Answer: If one teaches in terms of existence, then one becomes bogged down in existence. At the other extreme, if one banishes words, one becomes attached to annihilation. How can one convert such persons as these?

Question: If the mind has an attachment, what error is there in that?

Answer: If there is an attachment, then there is a fetter, and one cannot obtain release from birth and old age, sickness and death, care and sorrow, pain and suffering. Therefore the *Lotus of the Wonderful Law* says: "I, by means of numberless devices, attract the multitudinous beings, causing them to be separated from all attachments." The *Vimalakīrti* says: "To be unattached to the world is to be like the lotus flower. One is never skilled at entering into empty and quiescent action, one attains to the essence of the dharmas without ensnarement or impediment. I bow my head to that which, like space itself, is without any base." The Buddhas of the three ages, because the minds of the beings in the six stages of existence have their attachments, came into the world to preach the scriptures. The Guides of the Fourth

[3] That is, the view that Emptiness (the absence of all predication) is a positive attribute, a cardinal heresy from the Mahāyāna point of view.

Refuge,[4] because the minds of the great and small learners
had their props,[5] came into the world to compose their discourses. Hence, when there is a leaning or an obtaining, this
is the source of birth and death. To be without any dwelling
or attachment is the great principle of the scriptures and
treatises.

Question: Why does the scripture set up the Twofold Truth?
Answer: There are two reasons. First it wishes to demonstrate that the Law of Buddha is the Middle Way. Since
there is a Common Truth, there is no [heresy of] annihilation [that is, that things have no existence whatever]. Because
of the Supreme Truth there is no [heresy of] eternity [that
is, that things have eternal existence]. This is why it establishes the Twofold Truth. Further, the two wisdoms are the
father and mother of the Dharma-Body of the Buddhas of
the three ages [past, present, and future]. Because there is
the Supreme Truth, true wisdom is produced. Because there
is Common Truth therefore [the use of] expedient devices
[to save all sentient beings] comes into being. When true
wisdom and expedient wisdom are both present, then one
has the Buddhas of the ten directions and the three ages.
For this reason it establishes the Twofold Truth.

Again, to know the Supreme Truth is to benefit oneself; to
know the Common Truth is to be able to benefit others; to
know both truths simultaneously is to be able to benefit
all equally. Therefore it establishes the Twofold Truth. Also,
it is because there is Twofold Truth that the Buddha's words
are all true. By virtue of the Common Truth, when he
preaches the doctrine of existence, that is true. By virtue of
the Supreme Truth, when he preaches the doctrine of Emptiness, that is true. In addition, the Law of Buddha becomes
gradually more profound. First he preaches the Common
Truth of cause and effect to convert people. Then he
preaches the Supreme Truth for them. Also, for the purpose of achieving perfection and achieving the Way he

---

[4] Those in the final stage of bodhisattvahood who open the way of
salvation for others.
[5] What we have rendered "refuge," "prop," and, below, "leaning,"
all go back to Chinese *i*, the basic meaning of which is "to lean."
The truth, according to the Mahāyāna, is supposed to have no substance, nothing on which one can lay hold or lean.

preaches the Supreme Truth to those who possess wisdom and the Common Truth to those who do not. Furthermore, had he not first preached the Common Truth of cause and effect, but preached right away the Supreme Truth, he would have given rise to the heresy of annihilation. For these reasons he preaches both aspects of the Twofold Truth.

[From San-lun hsüan-i, in Taishō daizōkyō, XLV, 1–11]

THE SCHOOL OF CONSCIOUSNESS-ONLY

The school of Consciousness-Only (Wei-shih) corresponds to the Vijñānavāda or Yogāchāra school of Indian Buddhism, which, together with the Middle Doctrine school, represented one of the two main branches of Mahāyāna philosophy. Its great teachers in India were Asanga (fourth century A.D.) and Vasubandhu, of about the same period. When Asanga's works were translated into Chinese in the sixth century A.D., the school was first known as the She-lun, but eventually it was absorbed into the school of the great Chinese monk, translator and philosopher, Hsüan-chuang or Hsüan-tsang (596–664). The latter's school was also known as the Dharma-Character (Fa-hsiang) school after one of the characteristic features of its teaching, as explained below.

The pilgrimage of Hsüan-tsang to the Western regions, in search of the true teachings of Buddhism, is one of the great sagas of Chinese history and literature. After a long and arduous journey he reached the great centers of Buddhist learning in India and Central Asia, where he studied for many years and engaged in debate with the great philosophers of the time. Upon returning home he devoted himself to the monumental task of translating no less than seventy-five basic Buddhist texts into Chinese. Among his most significant accomplishments was the selecting, summarizing, translating, and systematizing of the works of ten great idealists, especially Dharmapāla, in his Ch'eng-wei-shih lun (Vijñapti-mātratāsiddhi or Establishment of the Consciousness-Only System).

In its more technical formulation, as expounded in China, this doctrine reduces all existence to one hundred dharmas in five divisions, namely, Mind, Mental Functions, Form, Things Not Associated with Mind, and Non-created Elements. Whereas the other schools treated the mind as one dharma, here it is divided into eight consciousnesses. According to this doctrine, the external world is produced when the ālaya (storehouse) consciousness, which is in constant flux, is influenced ("perfumed") by "seeds" or effects of good and evil deeds. As such the phenomenal world is one of appearance or specific characters. It is from this that the school is called Fa-hsiang or Dharma-Character school. But in the final analysis everything is consciousness only, whence comes the other common name for this school.

With regard to the nature of dharmas, the school classifies them into three species. Those of the "character of sole imagination" have only "false existence." Those of the "character of dependence" have "temporary existence," for things produced through causation enjoy neither self-nature nor permanent reality. Only those of the "character of ultimate reality" have "true existence." This ultimate reality is Suchness, or the true noumenon transcending all appearance and specific characters. It is Nirvāna. It is the True State of the Tathāgata, the Thus-Come-One.

In order to reach this state, it is necessary to go through various stages of spiritual development leading to Perfect Wisdom or the Fourfold Wisdom of the Buddha. This is achieved when the first five consciousnesses have become the "wisdom of action," the sense-center consciousness has become the "wisdom of insight," the mind consciousness has become the "wisdom of equanimity," and the ālaya consciousness has become the "wisdom of magnificent mirror."

The school began to decline in China in the ninth century and disappeared several hundred years afterward. This was probably because, like the Three Treatise school, its philosophy was too subtle, too abstract, and too extreme for most Chinese. Moreover, unlike the Three Treatise school, it seems to have resisted the tendency to synthesize with other schools. In the twentieth century a new interest was shown in this philosophy by Chinese scholars, and a few Buddhists even made a serious effort to revive it.

Confirmation of the Consciousness-Only System

The following selection is made from the Ch'eng-wei-shih lun, the most important philosophical work of Hsüan-chuang (or Hsüan-tsang), to give an idea of its central concept of consciousness as the only reality.

The verse [by Vasubandhu] says:

First of all, the storehouse [ālaya] consciousness,
Which brings into fruition the seeds [effects of good and evil deeds].
[In its state of pure consciousness] it is not conscious of its clinging and impressions.
In both its objective and subjective functions it is always associated with touch,
Volition, feeling, sensation, thought, and cognition.
But it is always indifferent to its associations. . . .

The Treatise says:
    The first transformation of consciousness is called ālaya in both the Mahāyāna and Hīnayāna. . . . Why are the seeds so called? It means that in consciousness itself fruitions, functions, and differentiations spontaneously arise. These are neither the same nor different from the consciousness or from what they produce. . . .
    In this way the other consciousnesses which "perfume" [affect] it and the consciousness which is perfumed arise and perish together, and the concept of perfuming is thus established. To enable the seeds that lie within what is perfumed [storehouse consciousness] to grow, as the hemp plant is perfumed, is called perfuming. As soon as the seeds are produced, the consciousnesses which can perfume become in their turn causes which perfume and produce seeds. The three dharmas [the seeds, the manifestations, and perfuming] turn on and on, simultaneously acting as cause and effect. . . .
The verse says:

The second transformation
Is called the mind-consciousness
Which, while it depends on that transformation, in turn
    conditions it.
It has the nature and character of intellection.
It is always accompanied by the four evil defilements,
Namely, self-delusion, self-view,
Self-conceit, and self-love,
And by touch, etc. [volition, feeling, sensation, thought, and
    cognition]. . . .

The Treatise says:
    "That transformation" refers to the first transformation,
because according to the sacred teaching, this consciousness
depends on the storehouse consciousness. . . . "It" refers
to the consciousness on which this transformation depends,
because according to the sacred teaching, this consciousness
conditions the storehouse consciousness.
    Spontaneously this mind perpetually conditions the store-
house consciousness and corresponds to the four basic defilements. What are the four? They are self-delusion, self-view,
and also self-conceit and self-love. These are the four different names. Self-delusion means ignorance, lack of understanding of the character of the self, and being unenlightened about the principle of the non-self. Therefore it is called
self-delusion. Self-view means clinging to the view that the
self exists, erroneously imagining to be the self certain
dharmas that are not the self. Therefore it is called self-
view. Self-conceit means pride. On the strength of what is
clung to as the self, it causes the mind to feel superior and
lofty. It is therefore called self-conceit.
The verse says:

Next comes the third transformation
Which consists of the last categories of discrimination
With subject and object as the nature and character.
They are neither good nor evil.

The Treatise says:
    This consciousness is divided into six categories, in accord-
ance with the six different sense organs and the six sense

objects. They refer to the consciousness of sight and so on [hearing, smell, taste] in the sense-center consciousness. . . . The verse says:

Based on the root-consciousness [ālaya]
The five consciousnesses [of the senses] manifest themselves
    in accordance with the conditioning factors.
Sometimes [the senses manifest themselves] together and
    sometimes not,
Just as waves [manifest themselves] depending on water con-
    ditions.
The sense-center consciousness always arises and manifests
    itself,
Except when born in the realm of the absence of thought,
In the state of unconsciousness, in the two forms of concen-
    tration,
In sleep, and in that state where the spirit is depressed or
    absent.

The Treatise says:
    The root consciousness is the storehouse consciousness because it is the root from which all pure and impure consciousnesses grow. . . . By "conditioning factors" are meant the mental activities, the sense organs, and sense objects. It means that the five consciousnesses are dependent internally upon the root consciousness and externally follow the combination of the conditions of the mental activities, the five sense organs, and sense objects. They [the senses] manifest themselves together and sometimes separately. This is so because the external conditions may come to be combined suddenly or gradually. . . .
The verse says:

Thus the various consciousnesses are but transformations.
That which discriminates and that which is discriminated
Are, because of this, both unreal.
For this reason, everything is mind only.

The Treatise says:
    "The various consciousnesses" refer to the three transformations of consciousness previously discussed and their men-

tal qualities. They are all capable of transforming into two seeming portions, the perceiving portion and the perceived portion. The term "transformation" is thus employed. The perceiving portion that has been transformed is called "discrimination" because it can apprehend the perceived portion [as the object of perception]. The perceived portion that has been transformed is called the "object of discrimination" because it is apprehended by the perceiving portion. According to this correct principle, aside from what is transformed in consciousness, the self and dharmas are both definitely nonexistent, because apart from what apprehends and what is apprehended, there is nothing else, and because there are no real things apart from the two portions.

Therefore everything created [by conditions] and noncreated, everything seemingly real or unreal, is all inseparable from consciousness.

[From the Ch'eng-wei-shih lun, in Taishō daizōkyō, XXXI, 7, 10, 22, 25, 37, 38]

THE LOTUS SCHOOL: T'IEN-T'AI SYNCRETISM

From the philosophical standpoint, and in terms of its influence on other schools in China and Japan, the Lotus or T'ien-t'ai teaching is of major importance. Moreover, it is distinctively Chinese. Though its basic scripture is the Lotus of the Wonderful Law (Saddharmapuṇḍarīka Sūtra), a work from North India or Central Asia, the school is founded upon the interpretation given this text by the great Chinese monk, Chih-k'ai (or Chih-i, 538–597), and its alternate name indicates its place of geographical origin, the T'ien-t'ai (Heavenly Terrace) Mountain of Chekiang Province, where Chih-k'ai taught.

For this Grand Master of the T'ien-t'ai, the Lotus, one of the most popular of Mahāyāna sūtras, was not merely a theological document but also a guide to religious salvation through practice. He lectured for years on its written text, minutely examining every detail of language and subtlety of meaning, and giving special attention to the methods of religious practice embodied in the Lotus. His deliberations were recorded by his pupil Kuan-ting and have come down to us as the "Three Great Works" of the school, namely, the *Words and Phrases of the Lotus* (*Fa-hua wen-chü*), *Profound Meaning of the Lotus* (*Fa-hua hsüan-i*), and *Great Concentration and Insight* (*Mo-ho chih-kuan*).

At Chih-k'ai's time, Buddhist thought in South China was distinctly intellectual in character, while in the north Buddhists were developing a religion of faith and discipline. Himself a product of the South Chinese gentry, but with a northerner, Hui-ssu (514–577), as his teacher, Chih-k'ai came to the conclusion that the contemplative and intellectual approaches to religion were like the two wings of a bird. Consequently, the T'ien-t'ai school is characterized by a strong philosophical content and at the same time a strong emphasis on meditative practice.

The T'ien-t'ai doctrine centers around the principle of the Perfectly Harmonious Threefold Truth. This means that 1) all things or dharmas are empty because they are produced through causation and therefore have no self-nature; but that 2) they do have temporary existence; and that 3) being both Empty and Temporary is the nature of dharmas and is the Mean. These three—Emptiness, Temporariness, and the Mean—involve one another so that one is three and three is one, the relative thus being identified with the absolute.

Furthermore, in the world of Temporariness, there are ten realms of existence—those of the Buddhas, bodhisattvas, private buddhas, direct disciples of the Buddha, heavenly beings, fighting demons, human beings, hungry ghosts, beasts, and beings in hell. Each of these shares the characteristics of the others, thus making one hundred realms. Each of these in turn is characterized by ten suchnesses or suchlikenesses through which the true state is manifested in phenomena, namely, such-like character, such-like nature, such-like substance, such-like power, such-like activity, such-like causes, such-like conditions, such-like effects, such-like retributions, and such-like beginning-and-end-ultimate. This makes one thousand realms of existence. In turn, each realm consists of the three divisions of living beings, of space, and of the aggregates which constitute dharmas, thus making a total of three thousand realms of existence or aspects of reality.

These realms are so interwoven and interpenetrated that

they may be considered "immanent in a single instant of thought." This does not mean that they are produced by the thought of man or Buddha, as taught in some Mahāyāna schools, but rather that in every thought-moment, all the possible worlds are involved. Accordingly the great emphasis in this school is on concentration and insight as a means of perceiving the ultimate truth embodied in such a thought-moment. In short, this is a philosophy of One-in-All and All-in-One, which is crystallized in the celebrated saying that "Every color or fragrance is none other than the Middle Path." Every dharma is thus an embodiment of the real essence of the Ultimate Emptiness, or True Suchness. It follows that all beings have the Buddha-nature in them and can be saved. This is the great message of the *Lotus*.

The school claims that the *Lotus* is the most complete doctrine among all the Buddhist teachings. It classifies the teachings of the Buddha into five periods. The first four, represented by the literature of various schools, are regarded as exploratory or temporary, whereas the teaching contained in the *Lotus* is considered final. Thus a measure of truth is seen in the teachings of other schools, which in certain respects are mutually contradictory, while the *Lotus* is seen as fulfilling and reconciling them in a final synthesis. It is an attempt to replace the Three Vehicles[1] by One Vehicle. In its all-inclusiveness, then, the T'ien-t'ai points again to the doctrine of universal salvation, the outstanding characteristic of the Mahāyāna movement.

The *Words and Phrases*, being a phrase by phrase commentary, does not yield excerpts of a summary character. Those given below are taken from the other two of the "Three Great Works." They are preceded by a short selection from the *Lotus* to give an idea of its message of salvation for all, and a selection from *The Method of Concentration and Insight in the Mahāyāna* (*Ta-ch'eng chih-kuan fa-men*) attributed to Chih-k'ai's teacher Hui-ssu.

---

[1] Those of the direct disciples who attain to their own salvation by hearing the Buddha's teaching, the private buddhas who attain to their personal enlightenment by their own exertions, and the bodhisattvas who postpone their own Buddhahood for the sake of helping all beings to be saved.

All Things Have the Buddha-Nature

The following passages are taken from the Lotus Sūtra ("The Scripture of the Lotus of the Wonderful Law") ascribed to the Buddha.

The Buddha appears in the world
Only for this One Reality.
Both the Vehicle of the Direct Disciples and the Vehicle of
    the Private Buddhas[1] are not real.
For never by the Small Vehicle
Would the Buddhas save all beings.
The Buddha himself abides in the Great Vehicle,
And in accordance with the Law he has attained,
By meditation and wisdom and the effort and ornament of
    virtue,
He saves all beings.
I have realized the Supreme Way.
The Law of the Great Vehicle applies to all beings.
If I converted by the Small Vehicle
Even one single human being,
I should fall into stinginess and greed.
Such a thing cannot be done.
If men turn in faith to the Buddha,
The Tathāgata[2] will not deceive them.
O, Shāriputra! you should know that
From the very start I made a vow,
With the desire to enable all beings
To be the same as we are,

To convert all beings
And enable them all to enter the Path of the Buddha.
Although I preach Nirvāna,
It is not real extinction.
All dharmas from the beginning
Are always tranquil in themselves and are devoid of appear-
    ance.
When the Buddha-son fulfills his course,
He becomes a Buddha in his next life.

[1] See the preceding note.
[2] The Thus-Come-One, a name for the Buddha.

Because of my adaptability [to use every suitable means for
    salvation]
I reveal the Law of Three Vehicles.
Any among the living beings,
Who have come into contact with former Buddhas,
Have learned the Law and practiced charity,
Or have undergone discipline and endured forbearance and
    humiliation,
Or have made serious efforts at concentration and under-
    standing, etc.,
And cultivated various kinds of blessing and wisdom—
All of these people,
Have reached the level of Buddhahood.

Those people who, for the sake of the Buddha,
Installed images,
Or have had them carved,
Have reached the level of Buddhahood.

Those who with a happy frame of mind
Have sung the glory of the Buddha,
Even with a very small sound,

Or have worshiped,
Or have merely folded their hands,

Or have uttered one "Namo" [Praise be . . .],
All have reached the level of Buddhahood.
About the Buddhas of the past—
After they passed away from this world,
They heard the Law,
And all reached the level of Buddhahood.
As to the Buddhas of the future,
Their number will be infinite.
All these Tathāgatas
Will preach the Law by all suitable means.
All these Buddhas,
With an infinite number of suitable means,
Will save all living beings,
And enable them to dwell in the Pure Wisdom of the
    Buddha.
Among those who have heard the Law,

None will fail to become Buddha.
All Buddhas have taken the vow:
"The Buddha-way which I walk,
I desire to enable all living beings
To attain the same way with me."
Although Buddhas in future ages
Preach hundreds and thousands and tens of thousands
Of methods, beyond number,
In reality there is only the One Vehicle.
All the Buddhas, past and future,
Know that dharmas have no [self-] nature,
And Buddha-seeds [all beings and defilements] are produced
    by causation.
Therefore they preach the One Vehicle.
All the direct disciples
And private buddhas
Cannot by their powers
Penetrate this scripture.
You, Shāriputra,
Can, into this scripture,
Enter only by faith.

[From *Taishō daizōkyō*, IX, 8–9, 15]

The Method of Concentration and Insight in the Mahāyāna

Selections from writings attributed to Chih-k'ai's teacher, Hui-ssu.

The Mind is the same as the Mind of Pure Self, Nature, True Suchness, Buddha-Nature, Dharma-Body, Tathāgata-Store, Realm of Law, and Dharma-Nature.
Question: Why is [the Mind] called True Suchness?
Answer: All dharmas depend on this Mind for their being and take Mind as their substance. Viewed in this way, all dharmas are illusory and imaginary and their being is really nonbeing. Contrasted with these unreal dharmas, the Mind is called True.

Furthermore, although the dharmas have no real being because they are caused by illusion and imagination, they have the appearance[1] of being created and annihilated. When

[1] The Chinese word *hsiang* is a key term in Buddhist philosophy

unreal dharmas are created, this Mind is not created, and when the dharmas are annihilated, the Mind is not annihilated. Not being created, it is therefore not augmented, and not being annihilated, it is therefore not diminished. Because it is neither augmented nor diminished, it is called Suchness.

By concentration is meant to know that all dharmas, originally having no self-nature of their own, are never created nor annihilated by themselves, but come into being because they are caused by illusions and imagination, and exist without real existence. In those created dharmas, their existence is really nonexistence. They are only the One Mind, whose substance admits of no differentiation. Those who hold this view can stop the flow of false ideas. This is called concentration.[2]

By insight is meant that although we know that [things] are originally not created and at present not annihilated, nevertheless they were caused to arise out of the Mind's nature and hence are not without a worldly function of an illusory and imaginative nature. They are like illusions and dreams; they [seem to] exist but really do not. This is therefore insight.

As to the function of concentration and insight: It means that because of the accomplishment of concentration, the Pure Mind is merged through Principle with the Nature which is without duality and is harmoniously united with all beings as a body of one single character. Thereupon the Three Treasures [The Buddha, the Law, and the Order] are combined without being three, and the Two Levels of Truth are fused without being two. How calm, still, and pure! How deep, stable, and quiet! How pure and clear the inner silence! It functions without the appearance of functioning, and acts without the appearance of acting. It is so because all dharmas are originally the same everywhere without differ-

---

with a wide range of meanings, including specific character or characteristic, appearance, phenomenon, etc. In general here it is translated as "character[istic]" when contrasted with a universal nature, and as "appearance" or "phenomenon" when contrasted with the ultimate reality.

[2] *Chih* in Chinese, literally "to stop," used as a translation for the Sanskrit *śamatha*, which represents a mental calm that shuts out all distractions.

entiation and the nature of the Mind is but dharma. This
is the substance of the most profound Dharma-Nature.

It also means that because of the accomplishment of insight, the substance of the Pure Mind and the functioning
of the objective world are manifested without obstacle, spontaneously producing the capabilities of all pure and impure
things. . . . Again, owing to the accomplishment of concentration, one's mind is the same everywhere and one no
longer dwells within the cycle of birth and death; yet owing
to the accomplishment of insight, one's attitudes and functions are results of causation and one does not enter Nirvāna.
Moreover, owing to the accomplishment of concentration
one dwells in the great Nirvāna, and yet owing to the attainment of insight, one remains in the realm of birth and death.
Further, owing to the accomplishment of concentration one
is not defiled by the world, but owing to the attainment of
insight one is not confined to the realm of silence. Further,
owing to the accomplishment of concentration, one achieves
eternal silence in the process of functioning, and owing to
the attainment of insight, one achieves eternal function in
the state of silence. Further, owing to the accomplishment
of concentration one knows that the cycle of birth and death
is the same as Nirvāna, and owing to the attainment of
insight, one knows that Nirvāna is the same as the cycle of
birth and death. Further, owing to the accomplishment of
concentration, one knows that the cycle of birth and death
and Nirvāna cannot be attained at the same time, but owing
to the attainment of insight, one knows that transmigration
is the cycle of birth and death and the absence of transmigration is Nirvāna.

[From Ta-ch'eng chih-kuan fa-men, in Taishō daizōkyō, XLVI, 642–61]

Emptiness, Temporariness and the Mean

FROM THE PROFOUND MEANING OF THE
SCRIPTURE OF THE LOTUS OF THE
WONDERFUL LAW BY CHIH-K'AI

This text, being in the form of a commentary, proceeds by way of
an analysis of specific passages in which key concepts are set forth,
here, for instance, the term "dharmas."

To detail the dharma of the beings is to discuss the whole range of cause and effect, as well as all the dharmas. To detail the Buddha-dharma is to take the standpoint of effect. To detail the Mind-dharma is to take the standpoint of cause.

The dharma of the beings consists of two parts, the former a statement of the number of dharmas, the latter an interpretation of the appearance of these dharmas.

As for the number, the scriptures sometimes declare that one dharma comprises all dharmas, meaning that the Mind is the three worlds and that there is no dharma apart from it, everything else being merely the creation of the single Mind. They sometimes declare that two dharmas comprise all dharmas, to wit, name and form. In all the worlds there are only name and form. They sometimes declare that three dharmas comprise all dharmas, namely, life, consciousness, and warmth.[1] In this way the number is increased by one at a time until it reaches a hundred thousand. The present scripture uses ten dharmas to comprise all dharmas, namely, the such-like character, such-like nature, such-like substance, such-like power, such-like activity, such-like causes, such-like conditions, such-like effects, such-like retributions, such-like beginning-and-end-ultimate, and the like of the dharmas. The Master of Nan-yüeh reads these phrases with the word "like" at the end of each, calling them the "ten likes." The Master of T'ien-t'ai says that, if they are to be read for meaning, there are in all three different ways of reading them. The first is "this character's suchness, this nature's suchness . . . this retribution's suchness." The second is "such-like character, such-like nature . . . such-like retribution." The third is "their character is like this, their nature is like this . . . their retribution is like this." Since all readings contain the word "like," the word "like" is common to all of them.

The first reading gives the passage the meaning of Emptiness. If one reads "such-like character, such-like nature, etc.," enumerating the character, nature, etc., of Emptiness, assigning names and titles in a differentiated series, such a reading

---

[1] The Sarvāstivāda school posits the existence of a life-element which transmits the consciousness and bodily warmth of each being from incarnation to incarnation.

gives the passage the meaning of Temporariness. If one reads "character is like this, etc.," then one is equating the ten dharmas to the "this" of the reality of the Middle Way. Such a reading gives the passage the meaning of the Mean [of Emptiness and Temporariness]. Distinction makes it easier to understand, hence we specify Emptiness, Temporariness, and the Mean. But if one is to speak from the standpoint of meaning, Emptiness is identical with Temporariness and the Mean. If one explains Emptiness in terms of suchness, then one Emptiness equals all Emptiness. If one details the aspects of suchness into character, etc., then one Temporariness equals all Temporariness. If one discusses the Mean in terms of "this," then one Mean equals all Means. They are not one, two, three, and yet they are one, two, three. They are neither horizontal nor vertical. This is called the true character. Only the Buddhas can exhaust these dharmas. These ten dharmas comprise all dharmas. If one is depending upon meaning, then one may interpret the passage in three senses. If one is depending upon rhythm, then one must read according to the verses, "The meaning of such-like great effect and retribution and of sundry natures and characters."

All "dharma-spheres" are so called in three senses. The number ten depends entirely on the dharma-spheres. Outside of the dharma-spheres there is no other dharma. That which depends and that upon which it depends are joined together in the appellation, hence we speak of the "ten dharma-spheres." Secondly, of these ten kinds of dharmas, each has a different lot. Their several causes and effects are separate from one another, and the common and saintly states have their differences. Therefore the word "sphere" is added to their name. Thirdly, of these ten, each and every dharma-sphere in and of itself comprises all dharma-spheres. For example, all dharmas are contained in hell. This state, without exceeding itself, is substantially identical with Truth, and requires no other point of reliance. Therefore the name "dharma-sphere." The same is true of all the other dharma-spheres, up to and including that of the Buddha. If the number ten depends on the dharma-spheres, then that which depends, accompanying that upon which it depends, enters directly into the sphere of Emptiness. To say that the ten spheres are delimited one from another refers to the sphere of the temporary. To say that the number ten is all the dharma-spheres refers to the sphere of the Mean. Wishing to make this easy to understand we distinguish in this way. If we were to speak from the standpoint of meaning, then Emptiness is identical with Temporariness and the Mean. There is no one, two, three, as we have said before.

This one dharma-sphere contains the ten "such-likes." Ten dharma-spheres contain one hundred "such-likes." Also, since one dharma-sphere contains the other nine dharma-spheres as well, there are thus a hundred dharma-spheres and a thousand "such-likes." One may unite them under five distinctions, the first being evil, the second good, the third the Two Vehicles, the fourth the bodhisattva, and the fifth the Buddha. One may then divide these into two dharmas, the first four being the tentative dharma, the last one being the ultimate dharma. To treat them in detail, each of them comprises both the tentative and the ultimate. We observe this dichotomy only as a practical expedient. But this tentative-and-ultimate, this inconceivable, is the object of the two-fold wisdom of the Buddhas of the three periods [past, present, and future]. If one takes this as an object, what dharma is not contained therein? If this object impels wisdom, what wisdom is not impelled thereby? Therefore the scripture says "dharmas." "Dharmas" means that the object understood is broad. "Only the Buddhas can exhaust [them]" means that the wisdom that understands it is deep, reaching its limit, and scouring its bottom.

[From *Fa-hua hsüan-i*, in *Taishō daizōkyō*, XXXIII, 693]

One Mind Comprises All Dharmas

The Great Concentration and Insight (Mo-ho chih-kuan), from which this portion is quoted, was written by Chih-k'ai as a manual of religious practice, specifically of the methods of gaining religious intuition.

Now one Mind comprises ten dharma-spheres, but each dharma-sphere also comprises ten dharma-spheres, giving a hundred dharma-spheres. One sphere comprises thirty kinds of worlds, hence a hundred dharma-spheres comprise three thousand kinds of worlds. These three thousand are contained in a fleeting moment of thought. Where there is no Mind, that is the end of the matter; if Mind comes into being to the slightest degree whatsoever, it immediately contains the three thousand. One may say neither that the one Mind is prior and all dharmas posterior nor that all dharmas are prior and the one Mind posterior. For example, the eight characters [of matter] [1] change things. If the thing were prior to the characters, the thing would undergo no change. If the characters were prior to the thing, it would also undergo no change. Thus neither priority nor posteriority is possible. One can only discuss the thing in terms of its changing characters or the characters in terms of the changing thing. Now the Mind is also thus. If one derives all dharmas from the one Mind, this is a vertical relationship. If the Mind all at once contains all dharmas, this is a horizontal relationship. Neither vertical nor horizontal will do. All one can say is that the Mind is all dharmas and that all dharmas are the Mind. Therefore the relationship is neither vertical nor horizontal, neither the same nor different. It is obscure, subtle, and profound in the extreme. Knowledge cannot know it, nor can words speak it. Herein lies the reason for its being called "the realm of the inconceivable."

[From Mo-ho chih-kuan, ch. 5a, in Taishō daizōkyō, XLVI, 48–59]

THE FLOWER GARLAND SCHOOL

The name Flower Garland comes from the Avataṁsaka Scripture, an Indian work purporting to give the teaching of Shākyamuni as a manifestation of the Buddha Vairochana. In Chinese the name is rendered "Hua-yen." This school as such never existed in India. Its nominal founder in China was Tu-shun (557–640), but Fa-tsang, the Great Master of

---

[1] The primary and secondary characteristics of coming into being, abiding, changing, and perishing (an Abhidharma doctrine).

Hsien-shou (643–712), is considered the real founder. Consequently the school is also known as the Hsien-shou school.

The main tenet of the school is the Universal Causation of the Realm of Law (*Dharmadhātu*). This means that the entire universe arises simultaneously. All dharmas have the characteristics of universality, speciality, similarity, diversity, integration, and differentiation, and also the Ten States of Suchness, or such-like-ness as given in the selection which follows. In other words, all dharmas are in the state of Suchness. In its static aspect, Suchness is the Void, the noumenon, the realm of Principle. In its dynamic aspect, it is manifestation, the phenomenon, the realm of Facts. The two realms are so interpenetrated and interdependent that the entire universe arises through reciprocal causation. As can readily be seen, this concept resembles the T'ien-t'ai idea of "all three thousand realms immanent in an instant of thought," so much so that the teachings of the two schools are often indistinguishable.

In a manner similar to that of the T'ien-t'ai, the Hua-yen school classifies Buddhist sects into five Vehicles. These are: 1) the Small Vehicle, or Hīnayāna, which includes the Chü-she school and advocates individual salvation; 2) the Elementary Great Vehicle, embracing the Three-Treatise and Consciousness-Only schools, which teach universal salvation, assuring human beings that, with some exceptions, all will cross the sea of suffering in a Great Vehicle to the Other Shore; 3) the Final Great Vehicle, that of T'ien-t'ai, which teaches that without any exception all beings, including the depraved, will be saved; 4) the Sudden Doctrine of the Great Vehicle, identified with the Meditation school, which teaches that salvation can be achieved through abrupt enlightenment; and 5) the Perfect Doctrine of the Great Vehicle, that of Hua-yen, which combines all the other Vehicles. The underlying spirit here, as in the case of T'ien-t'ai, is syncretic. Because of this, the two schools have been able to serve as the philosophical foundation of Chinese Buddhism in general.

Principle and Fact

The following treatise by Fa-tsang is called the Golden Lion because it was based on a sermon Fa-tsang preached to the empress
in the palace in 699, using the golden lion figure in the imperial
hall to illustrate his metaphysical ideas.

1. *Clarification of Dependent Origination*
Gold has no self-nature. Through the agency of a skilled
craftsman there is at length the coming-into-being of this
phenomenon of the lion. But since this coming-into-being is
dependent, therefore it is called "dependent origination."

2. *Distinction of Matter and Emptiness*
The character [phenomenon] of the lion is empty [of substantial reality]; there is nothing but gold. The lion is not
existent, but the substance of gold is not nonexistent. Therefore they are called separately Emptiness. Also, Emptiness,
having no self-character and manifesting itself through matter, does not prevent illusory existence. Therefore they are
separately called matter and Emptiness.

3. *Relation to Three Natures*

The Yogāchāra school, whose philosophy influenced the Hua-yen,
posited a triad of natures. The first of these is the world of phenomena, that which is "ubiquitously construed and clung to." The
second nature is "dependent on something else," that is, the product of causes and conditions. The third nature is "perfect." It refers
to the identity of everything with the Absolute.

The lion comes into existence because of our senses. This
is called "ubiquitously construed." The golden lion has apparent existence. This is called "dependent on something
else." The nature of the gold [of which the lion is made] is
unaltered. This is called "roundly perfected."

4. *Manifestation of Characterlessness*
Since the gold comprises the whole lion, and since there is
no lion-character to be found apart from the gold, therefore
it is called "characterlessness."

5. *Explanation of Not-Coming-into-Being*

If one rightly looks at the lion at the time of its coming into being, it is only gold that comes into being. Apart from the gold there is nothing. Although the lion has [the characteristics of] coming into being and extinction, the gold-substance at bottom neither increases nor decreases. Therefore we say that there is no coming-into-being.

6. *Treatment of the Five Doctrines*

This golden lion is nothing but dharmas of cause and condition, coming into being and perishing every moment. There is in reality no lion-character to be found. This is called the Doctrine of the Shrāvaka Ignorant of the Dharmas. Secondly, these dharmas, born of conditions, are each without self-nature. It is absolutely only Emptiness. This is called the Initial Doctrine of the Great Vehicle. Thirdly, although there is absolutely only Emptiness, this does not prevent the illusory dharmas from remaining as they are. The two phenomena of conditioned origination and temporary or transitory existence subsist side by side. This is called the Final Doctrine of the Great Vehicle. Fourthly, since these two aspects cancel each other out, they both perish, and neither [the result of] our senses nor false existence exists. Neither of the two aspects has any potential power and both Emptiness and existence perish. Then the way of names and words [which gives rise to phenomena] is terminated, and the mind [that contemplates them] has nought to attach itself to. This is called the Sudden Doctrine of the Great Vehicle. Fifthly, when the erroneous consciousness has been annihilated and true substance revealed, all becomes a single mass. Vigorously then does function arise, and on each occasion perfect reality obtains. The myriad forms, in disarray, mix and yet are not confused. The all is the one, both alike having no "nature." [At the same time] the one is the all, for cause and effect clearly follow each other. The [potential] power and the [actual] function involve each other, the folding and unfolding are unhampered. This is called the Rounded Doctrine of the Single Vehicle.

7. *Mastering the Ten Profound Theories*

The gold and the lion come into being at the same time, full and complete. This is called the Theory of Simultaneous

Completeness and Mutual Correspondence. Secondly, the gold and the lion come into being each being compatible with the other, the one and the many each having no obstruction for the other. In this situation the principle [one] and fact [many] are different. Whether the one or the many, each occupies its own position. This is called the Theory of the Mutual Compatibility and Difference of the One and the Many. Thirdly, if one contemplates the lion, then it is only a lion, and there is no gold about it. In this case the gold is hidden and the lion manifested. If one contemplates the gold, then it is only gold, and there is no lion about it. In this case the gold is manifested and the lion is hidden. If one contemplates both, then both are manifested and both hidden. Being hidden, they are concealed and secret. Being manifested, they are evident and revealed. This is called the Theory of the Mutual Completion of the Hidden and the Manifested. Fourthly, the lion's eyes, ears, limbs, joints, and every single pore completely contain the golden lion. In each pore the lion simultaneously and all at once enters into a single strand of hair. Each and every strand of hair contains unlimited lions. Each [of these lions] in turn has hairs each and every one of which contains unlimited lions, all of which in turn enter into a single strand of hair. In this way the progression is infinite, like the celestial jewels on the net of Indra. This is called the Theory of the Realm of Indra's Net. Fifthly, since this lion's eye completely contains the lion, the whole lion is pure eye. If the ear completely contains the lion, then the whole lion is pure ear. If all the sense organs simultaneously contain it, then all are complete, each of them pure and each of them mixed [with the others]. Also, each one of them is a full storehouse. This we call the Theory of the Full Possession by the Storehouses of the Faculties of Purity and Mixture. Sixthly, since the lion's several organs and each and every hair involve the whole lion, each of them pervading the whole, the lion's ear is its eye, its eye is its ear, its ear is its nose, its nose is its tongue, its tongue is its body. Each freely maintains its existence without conflict or obstruction. This is called the Theory of the Dharmas Mutually Identified While Self-existent. Seventhly, the gold and lion may be hidden or manifest, one or many, definitely pure or definitely mixed, powerful or powerless, this or that. The principle and the comparison illuminate each other. Fact and principle are both revealed. They are completely compatible with each other, and do not obstruct each other's peaceful existence. When the most minute are thus established and distinguished this is called the Theory of the Small and Minute Being Compatible Along with Peaceful Existence. Eighthly, this lion is a created dharma, coming into being and perishing every instant, dividing into three periods of time, past, present, and future, without a moment's interval. Of these three periods of time each contains within itself past, present, and future. By uniting the three triads of degrees one has nine periods, which again in turn may be united to form a single dharma. Although they are nine periods, they each have their differences of coalescence and separation. Yet they exist in mutual dependence, fading one into the other without obstruction, and all together constituting a single moment of thought. This is called the Theory of the Distinct Existence of Separate Dharmas in the Ten Periods.[1] Ninthly, this lion and this gold may be hidden or manifested, one or many, thus having no self-nature, being evolved out of the Mind. Yet whether spoken of as fact or principle, they are completed and they have existence. This is called the Theory of the Skillful Completion Through the Evolution of the Mind-Only. Tenthly, this lion is spoken of in order to demonstrate ignorance, while the reality of the gold is spoken of in order to manifest the True Nature. These two, principle and fact, explained in conjunction and likened to storehouse consciousness, cause right understanding to be born. This is called the Theory of the Manifestation of the Doctrine with Reference to Facts and the Fostering of Understanding Thereby.

BINDING TOGETHER THE SIX CHARACTERS

The lion is the character of universality. The five sense-organs, being various and different, are the characters of speciality. Since they arise out of a single condition, they are the characters of similarity. The fact that its eyes, ears, etc. do not overlap is the character of diversity. Since the

---

[1] The nine periods separately, plus all of them as one period.

lion is made of the combination of these sense organs, this
is the character of integration. The several organs each occu-
pying its own position is the character of disintegration.

ACHIEVEMENT OF BODHI

"Bodhi" means the Way, it means enlightenment. When
the eye beholds the lion, it sees that all created dharmas,
even before disintegration, are from the very beginning
quiescent and extinct. By avoiding both attachment and
renunciation, one, along this very road, flows into the sea
of perfect knowledge. Therefore it is called "the Way." One
understands that all of the misconstructions perpetrated since
time without beginning have not a single real substance to
them. Therefore one calls this "enlightenment." Ultimately,
it contains within itself the wisdom that comprises all kinds.
This is called "the achievement of bodhi."

ENTRY INTO NIRVĀNA

When one sees this lion and this gold, the two characters
are both annihilated, the passions do not come into being,
and although beauty and ugliness are displayed before the
eye, the mind is as calm as the sea. False thoughts vanish
completely, there are no pressures. One issues forth from
one's bonds and separates oneself from hindrances, and cuts
off forever the foundations of suffering. This is called "entering Nirvāna."

[From Chin-shih-tzu chang, in Taishō daizōkyō, XLV, 663–67]

The Vow to Live the Life of Samanta-bhadra

This devotional hymn has long been revered by the Mahāyāna Buddhists of China, Korea, and Japan regardless of sect, and is perhaps
one of the most popular pieces of Buddhist literature. As there is
repeated mention of Amitābha's Pure Land in the hymn, it has also
won special favor with the followers of that sect. Thus in the beginning it was not exclusively identified with the Hua-yen school
but later became incorporated in the last section of the Hua-yen
Sūtra, with characteristic overtones of its philosophy and abundant
use of its symbolism.
    Samanta-bhadra, often abbreviated to Bhadra, is the embodiment
of the Mahāyāna ideal in action and devotion, as Avalokiteshvara is

the symbol of compassion, and Manjushrī of wisdom. He is repre-
sented in painting and sculpture as riding on a white elephant.

ASPIRATIONS TO LIVE THE LIFE OF
SAMANTA-BHADRA

1. I sincerely salute with body, speech and mind all Lions of Mankind (Buddhas) residing in the past, present, and future in the ten quarters of the Universe.

2. I reverently prostrate myself before all the Victorious Ones (Buddhas), multiplying my obeisances as if with bodies as numerous as the dust particles in the earth, with my heart devoted to them on the strength of the vows that I live the life of Bhadra.

3. I rejoice in the belief that the entire Universe is filled with the Victorious Ones; even on the tip of a grain of sand, Buddhas as numerous as particles of dust exist, each of them sitting in the center surrounded by bod-hisattvas.

4. I glorify all those who have attained bliss, and in unison with the eulogies offered by the ocean of all sounds, exalt the Victorious Ones' virtues, as inexhaustible as the sounds of the oceans.

5. And I make offerings to the Buddhas with the best of flowers, wreaths, musical instruments, ointments, umbrellas, lamps, and incense.

6. And I make offerings to the Buddhas, adorning them with the best of garments, perfumes, and containers of powdered incense like Mt. Meru.

7. And I earnestly devote myself to the acts of offering to the Buddhas, offerings exquisite and noble; I salute and make offerings by virtue of my earnest application to live the life of Bhadra.

8. And I confess whatever evil deeds I might have committed with my body, speech, and mind due to passion, anger, and delusion.

9. I feel sympathetic joy for all the meritorious deeds performed by people, disciples still to be trained, accomplished disciples, private buddhas, bodhisattvas, and all the Victorious Ones in the ten quarters.

10. And I entreat all the Lords, who are the Lights of the world in the ten quarters, who have awakened in En-

lightenment and obtained non-attachment—to revolve the unsurpassed Wheel of the Law.

11. And also with clasped hands, I entreat those who expect to manifest Nirvāna that they should remain in the world for ages yet to come, as many as the particles of dust in the earth, for the benefit and welfare of all beings.

12. I apply toward Enlightenment whatever good I have accumulated through the practice of adoration, offering, confession, sympathetic joy, asking for instruction, and begging.

13. May all the Buddhas in the past be revered; may the Buddhas residing in the ten quarters of the world be honored; may those who are yet to come be at ease and awaken to Enlightenment fulfilling their wishes.

14. May all the lands in the ten quarters be pure and extensive and filled with bodhisattvas and the Victorious Ones who have stayed under the Tree of Wisdom.

15. May all beings in the ten quarters always be happy and healthy; may they be endowed with the benefits of piety, may they be successful and their wishes be fulfilled.

16. And may I be able to remember my previous births in all paths of existence while practicing the way to Enlightenment; may I always remain a mendicant in the course of coming and going through all forms of life.

17. May I always practice a spotless life of morality, without defect and without interruption, imitating all the Victorious Ones and realizing the life of Bhadra.

18. May I be able to disclose the teachings of the Buddhas with all the kinds of voices that exist in the world—the voices of gods, Nāgas, Yakshas, Kumbhāndas, and mankind.

19. Let him, who applies himself steadfastly to the excellent virtues (pāramitās), never be confused in mind as to Enlightenment; let him be wholly free from evils that might obstruct his way.

20. Let him walk in the paths of the world, free from karma, defilement and the course of the Tempter, like the lotus floating free on the water, or like the sun and moon not fixed in the sky.

21. Allow me to work for the welfare of all creatures, as long

as the lands and roads exist in the ten quarters, relieving anxieties, extinguishing pain, and assisting all beings in the Six Paths of transmigratory existence.

22. Allow me to work till the end of time, adjusting myself to the lives of beings, fulfilling the life of Enlightenment, and cherishing the life of Bhadra.

23. Allow me always to be associated with those who would be companions in living the life of Bhadra; and let me practice the same vows with my body, speech, and mind.

24. May I always be associated with those well-wishing friends who advocate the life of Bhadra and may I never be estranged from them.

25. May I always be in the presence of the Victorious Ones, the Lords surrounded by bodhisattvas; allow me to make extensive offerings to the end of time without wearying.

26. May I discipline myself to the end of time, upholding the Truth of the Victorious Ones, manifesting the life of Enlightenment, and living the life of Bhadra with purity.

27. May I be an inexhaustible storehouse of all excellences —wisdom, skillful devices, concentration, emancipation —transmigrating all paths of existence and becoming an indefatigable one because of my merits and wisdom.

28. May I see the Buddhas while practicing the course to Enlightenment; on the tip of a particle of dust there are fields as numerous as particles of dust, and in each of these fields there are innumerable Buddhas, each sitting in the midst of bodhisattvas.

29. Allow me to go deep into the oceans of Buddhas, of lands, and of aeons of devotional life, throughout time and everywhere without exception, even on paths as narrow as a hair.

30. Allow me always to comprehend the voices of the Buddhas and their speeches responding to the aspirations of all beings, pure in the quality of their sound, with an ocean of meanings in even one sound.

31. And allow me, while I turn the Wheel of the Law, to penetrate, on the strength of my understanding, into those everlasting utterances of the Victorious Ones residing in the past, present, and future.

32. May I instantly advance into all aeons of time to come,

and may I instantly place myself in aeons of time past as long as the times of future, present, and past combined.

33. May I see at once the Lions of Mankind, staying in the three divisions of time, and may I always enter their realms on the strength of being emancipated from the course of Illusion (*māyā*).

34. May I produce on the tip of a particle of dust supernal arrangements of the lands in the past, present, and future, and may I enter the Victorious Ones' lands supernally arranged in the whole of ten quarters.

35. And may I reverently approach all the future Lords, the Lamps of the world, who would revolve the Wheel of the Law when enlightened, and who would reveal perfect peace in manifestation of Nirvāna.

36. By supernatural powers swiftly moving everywhere, by the power of vehicles turning to all directions, by the power of conduct, of perfect virtues, and of all-pervading goodwill;

37. By the power of the merits of complete purity, of wisdom free from attachment, of insight, clever devices, concentration, and of acquiring the force of Enlightenment;

38. Purifying the power of influences from past evil actions, crushing the forces of defilement, and rendering impotent the Tempter, may I utilize to the fullest all of my energy toward living the life of Bhadra.

39. Purifying the ocean of lands, releasing the ocean of beings, observing the ocean of phenomena, plunging into the ocean of wisdom.

40. Purifying the ocean of conduct, fulfilling the ocean of vows, and honoring the ocean of Buddhas, may I discipline myself without growing weary throughout the ocean of aeons.

41. And may I awaken to Enlightenment by living the life of Bhadra, fulfilling completely in the course of Enlightenment all the vows of the Victorious Ones in the past, present, and future.

42. May I extend all my merits to those who walk on the same path as the Wise One whose name is Samantabhadra, the most cherished son of all the Buddhas.

43. May I be like him, the Wise One, whose name Bhadra signifies purity of body, speech, mind, life, and the land [where he resides].

44. May I practice the vows of Manjushrī to consummate the living of the life of Bhadra; and may I perfect all disciplines without exception throughout aeons to come.

45. May I discipline myself through and through, and may I accumulate immeasurable merits; and making myself firm in countless disciplines, may I know all the supernatural powers of the Buddhas and bodhisattvas.

46. When space reaches non-existence, when all beings cease, and when karma and defilements are exhausted, only then should my vows come to an end.

47. May I offer the Buddhas the innumerable lands in the ten quarters adorned with gems; and may I give them excellences conducive to the happiness of gods and men, for aeons countless as the particles of dust in the earth.

48. By listening to this [hymn which may be called], "the king of merit-extending," one should be inspired at once to apply it earnestly; the merits acquired by seeking superb Enlightenment are the highest and most excellent.

49. Those who devote themselves to living the life of Bhadra will be kept away from evil states and bad friends, and be enabled instantly to perceive the Buddha Amitābha.

50. With ease will they obtain whatever is profitable and live most happily; they will be welcome when born among men; and before long they will be like Samanta-bhadra.

51. Should one commit any of the five deadly sins[1] out of ignorance, if he recites this hymn of living the life of Bhadra, his sins will quickly be extinguished;

52. He will be endowed with wisdom, beauty, and auspicious marks, he will be born in a high caste, in a noble family; he will not be attacked by the host of heretics and the Tempter, but will be honored in all the three worlds;

53. He will go directly under the Tree of Wisdom, the king of trees, and there he will meditate for the sake of the

---

[1] The killing of a mother, father, or an arhant, causing dissension in the order of monks, and deliberately causing a Buddha's blood to flow.

welfare of mankind; overcoming the Tempter and his followers, he will awaken in Enlightenment and revolve the Wheel of the Law.

54. When one recites, preaches, and adheres to this "vow of living the life of Bhadra," the Buddha will know its consequences; have no doubt about [attaining] peerless Enlightenment.

55. The powerful Manjushrī knows, as does Samanta-bhadra; following them I will extend what is meritorious [toward Enlightenment].

56. I wish to extend all that is meritorious to the matchless living of the life of Bhadra; that "merit-extending" comes foremost has been preached, is being preached, and will be preached by the Buddhas of the past, present, and future.

57. When the time comes for me to die, may I come into the presence of Amitābha and, clearing away all hindrances, go to the land of bliss.

58. Having gone there, may all the vows be equally present in my mind; and fulfilling them completely, may I endeavor to work for the welfare of beings in the world as far as the world extends.

59. Being born in the glorious assembly of Buddhas, graceful and beaming with beautiful lotus flowers, may I be given the assurance [that I shall attain Enlightenment] in the presence of the Buddha Amitābha.

60. Having obtained that assurance, may I change myself into numberless forms and benefit the beings in the ten quarters by virtue of my wisdom.

61. By whatever merits I have accumulated reciting the vows of living the life of Bhadra, may all the pure vows of the world be fulfilled in a moment.

62. By the infinite and most excellent merit acquired through perfecting the living of the life of Bhadra, may those people drowned in the flood of calamities go to the most excellent city of Amitābha.

[From *Gandhavyūha Sūtra*, new revised edition of the Sanskrit text, edited by D. T. Suzuki and Hokei Idzumi, Kyoto 1949, 543–548]

On the Original Nature of Man

Both this treatise and its author Tsung-mi (780–841 A.D.) occupy a rare position in the history of Buddhism in the Far East. Tsung-mi has been revered as the fifth and last patriarch of both the Hua-yen school and the Ho-tse (Kataku) branch of the Southern School of Ch'an (Zen) Buddhism. His early training was in classical Chinese studies, preparatory to taking the civil service examinations, but in his late twenties he was converted to Ch'an Buddhism and gave up thought of an official career. Then in his early thirties he met Ch'eng-kuan, fourth patriarch of the Hua-yen school, who opened up Hua-yen philosophy to him. Although Tsung-mi succeeded Ch'eng-kuan in the Hua-yen school, he did not abandon the practice of Ch'an, but wrote many works which advocate combining Ch'an meditation with the philosophical Buddhism represented by the doctrinal schools. The abstruse metaphysical system of Hua-yen, formulated by the third patriarch Fa-tsang, was presented in much more understandable form by Tsung-mi, who also left many commentaries on the scriptures and on Ch'an writings. They, and especially the Treatise on the Original Nature of Man (Yüan jen lun), are standard works for the training of Buddhist monks in Japan today.

The importance of the present work lies in its systematic discussion and critical evaluation of the principal schools of thought in his day. Here Tsung-mi's own spiritual development and his consideration of alternative philosophies are clearly reflected, as is his awareness of the need to defend his new faith against critics upholding Chinese tradition against Buddhism. It has been said that Tsung-mi wrote this treatise as an answer to the famous essays On the Original Nature of Man (Yüan jen) and On the Tao (Yüan tao) by his contemporary Han Yü (768–824), leader of the Confucian resurgence against Buddhism.

Less polemical in tone than Han Yü, and more eclectic in spirit, Tsung-mi recognizes Confucianism as having a certain value but in the end accords it no very high standing. His choice of title suggests, however, that he is meeting the Confucian on his own ground: the nature of man. The original Chinese title, Yüan jen, has the sense of going to the source or root of the matter, of establishing its fundamental basis. Tsung-mi contends that the Confucian conception of man, which he understands exclusively in ethical and social terms, does not provide an answer to more ultimate questions. He criticizes Confucianism and Taoism for having no adequate theory of causation, citing the impossibility of man, an intelligent being, having a non-intelligent cause, primordial matter (or the

primal force, yüan ch'i). He also finds in these teachings no explanation for the existence of evil and injustice in the world.

The Indian ethical system based on the theory of karma is superior to Confucianism in that it does not attempt to see the human sphere as morally self-contained, but allows for past and future
existence in the scheme of moral retribution. Nevertheless, even
the karmic system is inadequate without some theory of the self
or soul as the subject of action. This Buddhism provides. Tsung-mi
then takes up in turn the Buddhist doctrines, showing how each
progresses toward a more comprehensive view of the self. Finally
he offers a summary statement, combining the insights of the various teachings. Here his thinking is much influenced by the Awakening of Faith in the Mahāyāna. This critique was accepted as authoritative among later Buddhists and often reasserted, in its essentials, as the basic Buddhist standpoint with regard to other
philosophies.

PREFACE

All sentient beings that are in motion have their origins;
all non-sentient beings that abound have their roots. It has
never been that what had stems and branches had no origin
or root. How then could man, the most excellent sentient
being of all, not have them?

[The Tao-te ching XXVIII says:] "To understand others,
wisdom is needed; to know oneself, insight is needed." I was
given a human body, yet I did not know whence I came, how
much less could I know whither I would go after death? How
was I to know about human affairs in the world, past, and
present? Searching for my original nature, I studied for many
years under no fixed teacher, giving serious and extensive
thought to both Buddhist and non-Buddhist teachings, and
finally I came to understand the original nature.

Students of Confucianism and Taoism only know that, in
the immediate past, their bodies have come down from their
grandparents through their own parents; and that in the
distant past, there was an undifferentiated "primal force
(ch'i)" which divided into two, the yin and the yang. These
then created the triad—Heaven, earth, and man—which in
turn created the myriad creatures.

The myriad creatures and men, therefore, have their origin
in the primal force. Some students of Buddhism say that, in

the immediate past (i.e. directly) they obtained their bodies as the fruit of their karma in previous lives; that, in the distant past, their karma developed over successive periods in proportion to the degree of their delusions, and that the storehouse-consciousness [in which these karmic influences accumulate] is the origin of their existence. All claim to have exhausted the matter and reached the final principle; in reality, they have not.

Confucius, Lao Tzu, and Shākya Buddha were perfect sages. They established their teachings according to the demands of the age and the needs of the various beings. They differ, therefore, in their approach. Buddhist teachings and non-Buddhist teachings, however, complement each other: they benefit people, encourage them to perfect all good deeds, clarify the beginning and end of causal relationship, penetrate all phenomena (dharma), and throw light on [the relationship] between root and branch by which all things come into being. Although the teachings reflect the intentions of the sages, differences exist in that there are real and provisional doctrines. Confucianism and Taoism are provisional doctrines; Buddhism consists of both real and provisional doctrines. In that they encourage the perfection of good deeds, punish wicked ones, and reward good ones, all three teachings lead to the creation of an orderly society; for this they must be observed with respect. In going to the root of things, Buddhism—since it examines all phenomena and, using every means, investigates their principles in an attempt to reveal their nature—decisively leads the other schools.

Scholars of the present day cling each to his own school so that they, and students of Buddhism as well, are perplexed as to what is the truth. Consequently, they fail to inquire into the ultimate source of Heaven, earth, man and things. Here, I would like to examine all phenomena according to both Buddhist and non-Buddhist doctrines, starting from the superficial and ending with the profound, so that those who study the provisional doctrines may without obstruction eventually get to the root of things. Later I shall reveal the significance of the development and coming into being of things, in order to perfect the imperfect understanding of students, who will then be able to reach a correct understanding of the end products (Heaven, earth, man and things). This treatise, divided into four sections, is entitled *On the Original Nature of Man* (*Yüan jen*).

I. REFUTATION OF CLINGING TO DELUSIONS—CONFUCIANISM AND TAOISM

In Confucianism and Taoism it is explained that all species —such as human beings, beasts, and others—are generated from and nourished by the Great Way of Nothingness. The principle of Tao gave rise spontaneously to the primal force, the primal force created Heaven and earth, and Heaven and earth produced the myriad creatures. The intelligent and the stupid, the high-born and the low-born, the rich and the poor, those who have ease and those who suffer—their lots are all bestowed by Heaven. They are dependent on time and destiny, and when death comes they return to Heaven and earth, and revert to Nothing. The purport of teachings other than Buddhism lies in establishing [proper] conduct for oneself, not in inquiring into the origin of oneself. In their discussion of the myriad creatures, they exclude that which lies beyond the phenomenal world. Although they point to the Great Way as their source, they do not clarify in detail the order of the causes and conditions of their defilements and purifications, of their coming into existence and going out of existence. Unaware that their teachings are provisional, students hold to these doctrines as final. Let us briefly criticize these doctrines.

If, as they say, the myriad creatures were generated from the Great Way of Nothingness, the Great Way then is the basis of birth and death, of wisdom and foolishness, of good luck and bad, of fortune and misfortune. The basis of their existence being constantly fixed [in the Great Way], there can be no removing of misfortune, disorder, bad luck, or foolishness; nor can there be any increase of good fortune, happiness, intelligence, or goodness. Then why resort to the teachings of Lao Tzu and Chuang Tzu? It is the Way that also sustains tigers and wolves, that carried in its womb the wicked kings Chieh and Chou; that took away the lives of [Confucius' disciples] Yen and Jan while they were still young, and brought misfortune to such ancient worthies as Po I and Shu Ch'i. How then can the Way be called Noble?

If, as they say, myriad creatures were generated spontaneously without causes or conditions, then even where there are no causes or conditions creatures could be generated. Stones could grow grass, grass could perhaps give birth to men, men to beasts, and so on. There could be no priority or posteriority in generation; no time sequence in production. Immortals would not need to rely on elixirs nor a peaceful country on the help of the capable and wise; benevolence and righteousness could be had without instruction or learning. Why then was it necessary for Lao Tzu, Chuang Tzu, the Duke of Chou and Confucius to establish their teachings, framing them into rules and regulations?

If all things are created out of the primal force, a soul, for instance, created all of a sudden, would have no habits or thoughts. How is an infant able to show its affection or aversion, or to behave willfully? If the person who came into existence all at once could follow his own thinking and spontaneously show affection and aversion and the like, he should be able also to understand the Five Cardinal Virtues and the Six Disciplines simply by following his own thoughts. Why should he have to wait until the causes and conditions of learning were suitable for him to study and perfect them?

If life suddenly comes into existence out of the primal force, and death suddenly reduces life to Nothing through the dispersion of the primal force, then what are the spirits of the dead (*kuei-shen*)? In this world, there are cases in which people have seen and recollected their past lives as if they were reflected in a mirror. It is well known that life today is but a continuation of a previous life, and not something that suddenly came into existence out of the primal force. Since it has been verified that there is no cessation of the consciousness of spirits, man is not suddenly reduced to Nothing because of the dispersion of the primal force. Religious rites and prayers are therefore offered to the spirits; reference to this can be found in the Classics and other books. We read of dead persons who have revived and told about happenings in the world of the dead; of a dead man coming back to the delight of his wife and children; of spirits who take revenge on their enemies, or repay a favor received while alive. Such events have been recorded both in the past and in recent times.

Someone might say in criticism: if man becomes a spirit after death, then the spirits from the ancient past to the present must crowd the roads and surely be noticed by others; why then do we not see them? I would reply that there are six transmigratory states for the dead, and not all the dead turn into spirits. Some spirits at death become men again, and so on. So why should there be a great number of spirits accumulated from olden times?

The primal force of Heaven and earth is originally and essentially devoid of intelligence. How is it possible for a man endowed with primal force, which is devoid of intelligence, suddenly to come into being and possess intelligence? Grass and stones are endowed with the primal force; yet why do they lack intelligence? To be rich or poor, noble or base, wise or foolish, good or bad, lucky or unlucky, fortunate or unfortunate—all this depends on the Will of Heaven. Why does Heaven decree that there should be so many poor and so few rich, so many base and so few high-born, so many unfortunate beings and so few fortunate ones, and so on? If the allotment lies in [the Will of] Heaven, why is it not equitable?

Moreover, how can we explain that there are some of high status who have done no good deeds; that some are rich yet without virtue, while others are virtuous and yet poor; that some rebels meet with good fortune and some righteous men with bad; that some benevolent men die early in life, while tyrants live to a ripe old age; that some who conform to the proper way decline, while those who violate it prosper, and so on? If these are based on [the Will] of Heaven, then Heaven gives prosperity to those who offend and destroys those who conform to the Way. How can there be any reward from Heaven that blesses the good and profits the humble, or punishment that brings misfortune to the wicked or suffering to the arrogant? If calamities, disorders, and rebellions are dependent on the Will of Heaven, then for the sages to have established teachings which blame man and not Heaven, or find fault not with Heaven but with its creatures, was wrong indeed! Nevertheless, in the Book of Odes, there is criticism of the disorder in the world; and in the *Book of History*, we find praise for the Kingly Way [of old]. The claim is made that nothing is superior to the Rites for relieving the anxieties [of the ruler and his people], nor to Music for improving customs. Do all these statements reflect the Will of Heaven, or are they in accordance with the mind of Heaven and earth? It is evident that the followers of these teachings will be unable to get to the origin of man.

II. REFUTATION OF IMPERFECT AND SUPERFICIAL DOCTRINES

In Buddhism there are, in short, five types of doctrines, ranging from the most superficial to the most profound: 1) the doctrine concerning man and Heaven; 2) the doctrine of the lesser Vehicle (Hīnayāna); 3) the Dharma-Character (Consciousness-Only) School of Mahāyāna; 4) the Mahāyāna School of Dialectical Negation; and 5) the One and Ultimate Vehicle (Ekayāna).

(1) For beginners the Buddha preached the provisional [doctrine of] retribution which operates throughout the past, present, and future, and [the doctrine of] cause and effect of good and evil. The Buddha said that if a man of high grade commits the ten evils, at death he falls into hell; if a man of medium grade commits the ten evils he becomes a hungry ghost; and if a man of low grade commits the ten evils, he becomes a beast. Therefore, the Buddha prescribed for them five precepts analogous to the Five Cardinal Virtues, so that they might avoid falling into the three states and be born among men. If a man of high grade practices the ten good deeds, charity, and the other precepts, he will be reborn in one of the six heavens of desire; if he practices the four kinds of meditation and the eight kinds of concentration, he will be reborn in the heavens of form or non-form. It is therefore called the doctrine concerning Man and Heaven. [The law of] karma is the basis of one's existence according to this doctrine.

Criticism: One is given existence in the five transmigratory states as a consequence of one's deeds; but the question remains, who creates the karma and who receives the consequences?

If eyes, ears, hands, and feet can create karma, why cannot the eyes, ears, hands, and feet of a man who has just died, see, hear or move, for they are the same as when he was alive? If one says that it is the mind that creates karma, then what is mind? If one says that it is the mind in one's own body [that creates karma], then, because that mind is endowed with physical substance and is linked somewhere inside of one's body, how can it be possible for the mind to run swiftly into the ears and eyes and to discriminate between good and bad which exist externally? And if the mind knows neither good nor bad, by what can it discriminate and choose?

Furthermore, the mind, the eyes, ears, hands and feet are separated by physical substances; how can they communicate with each other internally and externally, correspond in their functions, and in the same manner create karma? Can it be said that joy, anger, affection and aversion arise in body and in speech and that these emotions create karma? Emotions such as joy, anger, etc., however, disappear no sooner than they arise and they have no entity of their own. Then what agent can be identified as creating karma? One might say that our body and mind as a whole create karma and that they should not be considered separately. But then, after the death of the body, who receives the fruit of suffering or joy? Or, one might say that after death a body different from the present one exists; but then how can the present body and mind, having committed sins or having practiced good to gain blessings, cause the body and mind [after death] to receive the fruit of suffering or joy? According to this theory, the one who practices good deeds to gain blessings, contrary to expectation, may suffer extremely, and the one who commits sins may enjoy great happiness. [If so], how unjust must the divine principle be! Thus we know that those who follow only this doctrine, even if they believe in the law of karma, will not reach to their origin.

(2) In Hīnayāna Buddhism it is explained that since the beginningless beginning, because of the power of causes and conditions, both physical matter and the thinking mind have been arising and perishing continuously every moment, like a stream of water flowing drop by drop, or like a burning candle, its flame incessantly flickering. Body and mind, united temporarily, give this appearance of being a single constant thing; the ignorant man fails to see through this

and clings to that which appears single and constant, believing it to be self.[1]

By treasuring this self, he develops three passions: greed,
hate, and foolishness. The three poisons stimulate thinking
and manifest themselves in speech and behavior, thus creating all manner of karma. Once these karma are formed,
there is no way to escape them. As a result, according to his
karma, the ignorant man receives an appropriate form of
existence in the five transmigratory states, one either of suffering or of joy, and either a superior or inferior place in
the three realms (of desire, form, and non-form). He again
will cling to the form of existence which he receives, believing it to be his self; thus repeating the development of greed
and so forth, he creates new karma and bears its fruits. His
form of existence repeats the cycle of birth, old age, sickness, and death; after death, again it resumes with birth.
Meanwhile the realms in which he is found undergo the
process of the four cycles to which they are subject: formation, existence, destruction, and complete annihilation. After
the period of annihilation there will come again a period of
formation. Aeon after aeon, birth after birth, transmigration
continues without a beginning and without an end like the
wheel of a well. All this develops from the failure to understand that the form of existence in its essence is not the self.
That [the form of existence] is not the self means that this
form of existence, in its essence, has been formed by means of
the union of physical elements and mental components. Let
us then examine and analyze [these elements and com-
ponents].

There are four material elements—earth, water, fire, and
air—and four mental components—sensation, conception,
inclination, and discrimination—which relate to perception
and cognition. If each of these exists as a self, then there
are eight selves. Moreover, even the earthly elements [in our
body] are numerous: there are 360 bones, each separate;
skin, hair, muscles, liver, heart, spleen, kidneys, each of
them distinct from the other; the various functions of mind,
each different from the other; seeing, which differs from
hearing; joy in contrast to anger. There will be as many as

---

[1] Understood as an absolutely independent, enduring entity.

84,000 defilements. There are so many things that we cannot single out any as the self. If each of these is self, there might be a hundred or even a thousand selves. There would be so many subjects (selves) within a body that the body would be in complete disorder.

Apart from these [attributes of earthly elements], they are not distinct dharmas [i.e. they have no independent identity]. No matter how one examines them in an attempt to identify self, it cannot be found. Consequently, we realize that this body is merely [a concatenation of] various conditions with a semblance of unity. There is originally no "I" or "you." Then to whom are greed and hatred directed? For whom are killing and stealing, charity and observation of precepts performed? Finally, not being obstructed in mind either by the defilements in the three realms or by good and evil, the common man should merely make an effort to gain insight into non-self; by uprooting greed and the like, he should put a stop to karma in its various forms and realize selflessness and Suchness (tathatā). In the end he will obtain the fruit of arhantship; by reducing his body and intellect to nil, he will extinguish suffering.

According to this doctrine, the physical elements, the mental components, greed, hatred, and folly are the origins of our body and mind and also of objects in the external world; no other elements in the future or in the past can be the origin.

Criticism: The basis of our form of existence which has passed through births generation after generation should itself have no interruption. Now, the five senses do not operate when the necessary conditions are absent; consciousness sometimes does not continue in a stream; in the realm of non-form the four physical elements are lacking; how is it possible [without some perduring substrate] to retain this form of existence in successive existences and not perish? Thus we know that those who hold this doctrine do not get to the bottom of our form of existence.

(3) In the Dharma-Character (Consciousness-Only or Yogahāra) School of Mayhāyāna it is explained that all sentient beings, from their beginningless beginning, are spontaneously endowed with an eightfold consciousness, of which the eighth, Storehouse Consciousness, is the basis. This con-

sciousness abruptly produces the organs of sense, the external world, and the karmic seeds which in turn give rise to the seven consciousnesses [of eyes, ears, nose, tongue, body, mind, and ego consciousness]. The seven consciousnesses project corresponding objects [e.g., eye-consciousness projects the objects of sight]; however, there is no real existence (dharma) in all [that is produced or projected].

How are they produced? Because the Storehouse Consciousness is imbued with the false notion that the self and external objects are real, when the various consciousnesses are at work there appear semblances of self and external objects. Because the sixth [the mind] and the seventh consciousness [ego-consciousness] are veiled by ignorance, being conditioned by these two consciousnesses one develops an attachment [to the notion of existence of self and external objects] and comes to regard them as real as in the hallucinations of a man seriously sick or as in a dream. Because of the illness or dream, the mind produces things that are similar to the objects which exist in the external world. While dreaming, one clings to these objects as if they were real existences in the external world. Once awakened, one knows that these objects were only created in the dream. Our form of existence is the same: our form of existence is only what appears in the [Storehouse] Consciousness. Confused, one clings to [the notion of] the existence of self and external objects, giving rise to illusions and karma. Thus, the cycle of birth and death never ceases. If one realizes this principle [that both self and external world are products of the Storehouse Consciousness] one immediately understands that one's form of existence is nothing but the creation of the Storehouse Consciousness. The Storehouse Consciousness then is the origin of our form of existence.

(4) The Mahāyāna Doctrine of Dialectical Negation (Mādhyamika) refutes attachment to dharma (categorical notions of phenomena) and *lakṣanas* (characteristic marks of phenomena) as taught in the Hīnayāna and Mahāyāna doctrines mentioned before, but in a profound way, reveals the principles of Reality and Emptiness (*śūnyatā*), which will be discussed later.

Its refutation of the foregoing doctrine: If the world of objects created out of the Storehouse Consciousness is unreal, then can the Consciousness, the creating subject, be real? If one is real but the other is not, then the consciousness [the subject] while dreaming is different from what one sees in one's dream [the objects]. If they are different [independent existences], then, because the dreaming subject is not the objects [seen in the dream] and the objects cannot be [identical to the subject of] the dream, after one awakens from the dream, the objects which appeared in the dream should remain as real existences. Also, if the objects appearing in the dream are independent of the dreaming subject, then they both should be real existences. If the dreaming subject is independent of the objects in the dream, what are the things that appear in the dream? Thus, it is known that while one is dreaming, the dreaming subject and the objects in the dream seem to be distinct; however, logically speaking, both are unreal and devoid of real existence. [Therefore, the claim that the subject is real and the objects are unreal cannot be verified.]

The various consciousnesses are the same: they are not independent entities, as they are related and dependent on conditions. Therefore, in the *Mādhyamaka-kārikā* it is said: "As there has never been a dharma [state of existence] which was produced without causes or conditions, so there has never been a dharma which was not empty." Elsewhere it says: "Dharmas produced by causes and conditions, these I call empty." In the *Awakening of Faith* it is said, "All dharmas, because of our deluded thinking, are differentiated; apart from our deluded thinking, there are no distinguishing marks in the entire world of objects." It is said in the [*Vajracchedikā*] *Sūtra* that all marks are unreal and that those who are free of all marks are called the Buddhas. That both mind [subject] and world [object] are empty is the real principle of Mahāyāna. If we seek for the original nature of our existence on the basis of this principle, our existence is empty. Emptiness is then the origin.

Criticism: If the subject and object are both unreal, who is he that knows they are unreal? If there is no real state of being (dharma), on what basis do the unreal images appear? In fact, the unreal images that we actually see in the world could never come into existence without having a real state of existence. Therefore, if no water subsisted, how could

there be the illusion of waves? If there were no clear and un-
distorted mirror, how could there be ephemeral reflections?
Similarly, with regard to the assertion before that the subject
of the dream and the objects in the dream are unreal; the
dream itself, which is unreal, depends necessarily on the
existence of the man who is sleeping. If both the subject and
object are empty, I wonder whence the illusion appears? I
know, therefore, that this doctrine merely serves the destruction of attachments and still does not reveal the true nature.
This is why the *Mahābherīhāraka Sūtra* says: "All the sūtras
that speak of Emptiness are yet to be explained." The *Mahāprajñāpāramitā Sūtra* says: "[The doctrine of] Emptiness is
the first step to the Mahāyāna."

If we examine in succession the four doctrines already
discussed, we find that the earlier doctrines are superficial
and the later ones profound. If one studies these doctrines
and comes to the understanding that they are not complete
doctrines, one may consider them as "superficial." [On the
other hand] if one clings to any of them as final, then one's
mentality is called "one-sided." Here the terms, "one-sided"
or "superficial" are used in view of [the types of mentality
of] those who study them [and not used in an attempt to
evaluate the doctrines, since they are all preached by the
Buddha, accommodating himself to the capacity of his lis-
teners].

III. DIRECT REVELATION OF THE TRUE ORIGIN

(5) The School of the One Vehicle (Ekayāna), which reveals the real Nature, explains that all sentient beings have
been endowed with the true mind of original enlightenment.
From the beginningless beginning this mind has been constant, pure, luminous, and unobscured; it has always been
characterized by bright cognition; it is also called the Buddha
Nature or the Womb of Tathāgata. From the beginningless
beginning, man's delusions have obscured it so that he has
not been aware of it. Because he recognizes in himself only
the ordinary man's characteristics, he indulges in a life of
attachment, increases the bond of karmic power and receives
the suffering of repeated births and deaths. The great Enlightened One pitied him and preached that everything is
empty; then he revealed to him that his true Mind of spirit-

ual enlightment is pure and is identical with that of the Buddhas. Therefore, in the *Avataṁsaka Sūtra* it is said: "O son of Buddha, there is not even a single sentient being who is not endowed with the Tathāgata's wisdom, but, because of his illusions, he is unable to realize it. Once freed from his illusions, his all-knowing wisdom, his natural wisdom, and his unobstructed wisdom shall instantly emerge." Furthermore, the *Sūtra* states that a particle of dust contains within itself one thousand volumes of the sūtras. "A particle of dust" is compared to a sentient being, and the "*Sūtra*" to the wisdom of Buddha. Still further in the *Sūtra* we read: "At that time the Tathāgata observed all the sentient beings in the phenomenal world and uttered these words: 'Strange, strange, that these sentient beings, who are endowed with the wisdom of Tathāgatas, not realizing this wisdom are being misled. I must teach them the Noble Paths and free them forever from their delusions so that they can see in themselves the boundless great wisdom of the Tathāgatas, so that they may be no different from the Buddhas.' "

Evaluation: For a long time we have not met with the true doctrine and have been unable to understand how to reflect upon ourselves and seek for [the origin of] ourselves. We have been deeply attached to the characteristics which appear through our illusions, being content with our baseness and unconcerned over being born sometimes as human beings and sometimes as beasts. But now on the basis of this last doctrine, we have traced our origin and realized finally that we are from the outset Buddhas. Therefore, we should carry out our deeds in accordance with those of the Buddha, and identify our mind with that of the Buddha. Returning to and reinstating ourselves in the root and source, we should sever the habits we had as ordinary men. We must give up [these habits] and further give up [even the attempt at] abandonment until in the end we reach [the state of] "non-action (*wu-wei*)" [2] wherein we can be spontaneously active, accommodating ourselves to as many situations as there are grains of sand in the Ganges. Then we will be called Buddhas. It should be known that both non-enlightenment and enlightenment are aspects of the same True Mind. How

_____
[2] I.e., no conscious striving.

great is this mysterious gate [to the source]! Here ends the search for the original nature of man.

IV. SYNTHESIS

Though the True Nature is the basis of our existence, our coming into existence must have a cause, since nothing takes form all at once without any seed. Since this matter has not been dealt with in the first four doctrines, I have criticized each in turn. Now I shall synthesize everything, root and branch, including Confucianism and Taoism.

In the beginning there was a single, true, spiritual Nature, uncreated and imperishable, subject neither to increase nor decrease, changeless and immutable. Sentient beings from the beginningless beginning, suffering delusions, have been unaware of it. Since it is hidden, it is called the "Womb of Tathāgata." Because of the "Womb of Tathāgata" [remaining unrealized] there are the mental characters of birth and death. The so-called True Mind, which is unborn and imperishable, and our delusions of birth and death coexist. They are neither the same nor different! This is called the Storehouse Consciousness. This Consciousness has two aspects: the enlightened and the unenlightened. On account of its unenlightened aspect, when a deluded thought first arises, it is called a sign of karma [deluded activity]. And since this thought is not recognized as essentially unreal, it activates the subjective consciousness and further projects the unreal world of objects. One does not recognize, however, that this world of objects has made its appearance from the delusions of one's own mind. One clings to this world of objects, considering it to have definitive existence. This we call "attachment to phenomena [dharma]."

Because of attachment to phenomena, man finally sees a distinction between himself and others, increasing his attachment to himself. Because of this attachment to himself, he cherishes with deep-rooted greed objects which are agreeable to his feelings and of benefit to himself. He feels anger and disgust at objects which are not agreeable to his feelings, fearing that the former objects might be missed and the latter objects might cause him pain. These feelings, derived from stupidity, increase gradually and grow in intensity. Carried by their bad karma, therefore, the spirits of murderers and thieves are reborn in hell, among ghosts and beasts, and so on. Then there are those who are afraid of suffering or those whose nature is good, who practice charity, observe the precepts, and the like; their spirits, carried by their good karma to the intermediate state,[3] later enter a human womb. [Here the spirit] is endowed with "primal-force" and physical substance. The "primal-force" is suddenly supplied with the four great elements (earth, water, fire, and air), and gradually forms the various sense organs; the mind is suddenly supplied with the four components (*skandhas*: sensations, perceptions, predispositions, and consciousness) and gradually produces various consciousnesses. After ten [lunar] months have passed, a being is born and is called man; this is all that there is to us, in our present mind and body. Thus we know that our body and mind have their origin: that a man comes into existence out of the coalescence of these two things, as do the heavenly beings, fighting demons (*asuras*), etc.

Although we have received our present form of existence because of primary karma, secondary karma gives rise to different states of existences: high-born or low-born, rich or poor, long-lived or short-lived, healthy or ill, thriving or declining, suffering pain or enjoying pleasure. It has been said that one's humility or arrogance in the previous life bears the fruit of high or low status in the present; benevolence brings longevity; murder, a short life; greed causes poverty; these various consequences cannot be described in detail. A man may suffer calamity without doing evil; he may enjoy prosperity without performing good deeds, a man may be blessed with longevity despite his lack of benevolence; or he may die young even though he has not committed murder. All these are predetermined by the secondary karma in the previous life.

Thus, to some who do not recognize that the present state is determined by previous actions, these things are the result of [the random operation] of natural spontaneity, and non-Buddhists, ignorant of previous existences, simply affirm, on

[3] The intermediate state is the period between death and reincarnation ranging from one to seven weeks.

the basis of what they see, that the differences are due to this natural spontaneity.

Also there are men who in their previous lives performed good deeds while young but committed evil when old; or who did evil while young but good deeds when old. Accordingly, these men are rich and honorable and enjoy pleasures while young, but are poor and base and suffer bitterly when old; or they are poor and filled with misery while young, but are rich and honorable in their old age. Non-Buddhists, ignorant of this, merely affirm that men are in trouble or at peace in accordance with fate.

Man's physical endowment, when traced to its origin, can be reduced to the "Primal Spirit of Undifferentiated Oneness." The mind which arises with it, if traced back to its source, is the "Spiritual Mind of True Oneness." In the final analysis, there are no phenomena (dharmas) outside the Mind. The "Primal spirit" also follows the transformations of the Mind and belongs to the dimension of the world of objects projected by the evolving subjective consciousness discussed in the foregoing. It belongs to the objective aspect of the Storehouse Consciousness. The deluded activity in a moment of thought has split the original undifferentiated unity into two—the mind and the world of objects. The mind develops in succession from subtle to coarse with an increase in deluded thinking, thus creating karma. The world of objects also, moving successively from fine objects to large, develops and extends to heaven and earth. When one's karma matures and ripens, one receives the two "forces" of one's father and mother, which are joined with the activating consciousness to form a man.

According to this doctrine the world of objects, created by mind and consciousness, develops into two parts—one joins with mind and consciousness to become man; the other which does not join with mind and consciousness turns into heaven and earth, rivers and mountains, countries and villages. Among heaven, earth, and man, man is the most spiritual, because of his being joined to the spirit of mind. The Buddha meant this when he preached that the external great elements differed from the four internal great elements.

What a pity that, having incomplete knowledge, people

cling to [their respective narrow views] and remain confused. I should like to present this treatise to students who seek the way so that those who wish to attain enlightenment will have a clear insight into the distinction between coarse and subtle [doctrines], between what is essential and what is non-essential. Giving up the non-essential, they should return to the essential and reflect upon the source of Mind. When their petty errors are exhausted and their major misconceptions removed, their spiritual Nature will be manifested. There will be nothing which they cannot master. This state is called the Body of Essence or the Body of Bliss. Its spontaneous manifestation in accordance with the needs of sentient beings will be limitless; we call this the Buddha's Body of Transformation.

[From *Taishō daizōkyō* XLV, 707–710]

7

SCHOOLS OF CHINESE BUDDHISM II

In the preceding chapter, four of the major schools of Buddhist doctrine have been presented. Here we shall introduce two of the most important schools of Buddhist religious practice. The first of them, the Pure Land sect, emphasized salvation by faith and became the most popular form of Buddhism in China. The second, the Meditation sect, though appealing to a more limited following, became the most influential form of Buddhism among artists and intellectuals as well as monks. Together they may be taken to represent a general reaction against the scriptural and doctrinal approach to religion, but their growing ascendancy in later centuries should not be regarded as the superseding of older schools by newer ones. In fact, both the Pure Land and Meditation schools existed along with the others, even antedating some like the T'ien-t'ai, and it was only a matter of their surviving better the vicissitudes of religious and social change.

PURE LAND BUDDHISM

The "Pure Land" (Chinese, *Ching-t'u*; Sanskrit, *Sukhāvatī*) is the sphere believed by Mahāyāna Buddhists to be ruled over by the Buddha Amitābha (also known as Amitāyus and Amita). Indian Mahāyānists conceived of the universe as consisting of an infinite number of spheres and as going through an infinite number of cosmic periods. In the present period there is, according to this belief, a sphere called Suk-hāvatī, the beauties and excellences of which are described in the most extravagant terms by certain of the Mahāyāna scriptures. Among its advantages is the fact that it is free of the temptations and defilements which characterize the world inhabited by mortals (for example, the presence of women).

A common belief among Mahāyāna Buddhists, and one supported by scripture, was that the earthly reign of each Buddha, terminating in his attainment of Nirvāna, is followed by a period of gradual degeneration in his teaching. The period immediately following the Buddha's demise, known as the era of the True Law, is characterized by the continued vigor of the Faith in spite of his absence. It is followed in turn by the era of Reflected Law in which the outward forms of the religion are maintained but the inner content perishes. Finally comes the era of the Final Degenerate Law in which both form and substance come to nought. The scriptures dealing with the reign of Shākyamuni differ considerably as to the relative length of the periods of the three eras following his entry into Nirvāna. But it was possible for certain Chinese clerics during the Six Dynasties to find scriptural justification for their feeling that the period in which they themselves were living was the very era of Final Degenerate Law which the sacred writings had predicted. The confused state of Buddhist doctrine and the difficulty of any but a few to master it, either in the pursuit of scriptural studies or the practice of monastic disciplines, helped to convince many clerics and untold numbers of laymen that their only hope of salvaton lay in faith—faith in the saving power of the Buddhas.

In the *Pure Land Scripture* (*Sukhāvatīvyūha*), one of the principal scriptural bases of Pure Land salvationism, Amitābha, while yet a bodhisattva under the name Dharmākara, took forty-eight vows which were instrumental in his attainment of buddhahood. The eighteenth of these, which came to be considered the most important of them, was: "If, O

Blessed One, when I have attained enlightenment, whatever beings in other worlds, having conceived a desire for right, perfect enlightenment, and having heard my name, with favorable intent think upon me, if when the time and the moment of death are upon them, I, surrounded by and at the head of my community of mendicants, do not stand before them to keep them from frustration, may I not, on that account, attain to unexcelled, right, perfect enlightenment." Since, according to believers in this scripture, the bodhisattva Dharmākara did in fact become a Buddha (Amitābha), the efficacy of his vows is proved, and anyone who meditates or calls upon his name in good faith will be reborn in his Buddha-world.

Hence the simple invocation or ejaculation of Amitābha's name (A-mi-t'o-fo in Chinese) became the most common of all religious practices in China and the means by which millions sought release from the sufferings of this world. Nor was it simply a sectarian devotion. The meditation upon Amitābha and his Pure Land became a widespread practice in the temples and monasteries of other sects as well. In religious painting and sculpture too, Amitābha, seated on a lotus throne in his Western paradise, and flanked by his attendant bodhisattvas (e.g., Kuan-yin, the so-called "Goddess of Mercy") was a favorite theme.

Rebirth in the Pure Land

The work by T'an-luan from which portions are presented below is a commentary on the Chinese translation of a short essay, partly in prose and partly in verse, ascribed to Vasubandhu and purporting to set forth the essence of the Pure Land Scripture (Sukhāvatīvyūha). The author of the commentary is T'an-luan (476–542), a famous patriarch of the Pure Land school. Note how the meditation on Amitābha is explained in the same terms used for T'ien-t'ai meditative practice, reflecting a close association between this type of devotion and the T'ien-t'ai school.

Behold the phenomena of yon sphere,
How they surpass the paths of the three worlds!

The reason that the [Amitābha] Buddha brings forth the pure merit of these adornments of his sphere is that He sees

the phenomena of the three worlds as false, ceaselessly changing in a cycle, and without end, going round like a canker-
worm, imprisoned like a silkworm in its own cocoon. Alas
for the sentient beings, bound to these three worlds, perverse
and impure! He wishes to put the beings in a place that is
not false, not ceaselessly changing in a cycle, not without
end, that they may find a great, pure place supremely happy.
For this reason He brings forth the pure merit of these
adornments. What is meant by "perfection"? The meaning
is that this purity is incorruptible, that it is incontaminable.
It is not like the phenomena of the three worlds, which are
both contaminable and corruptible.

Question: Vasubandhu . . . says: "All together with the
sentient beings shall go to be reborn in the Happy Land."
To which "beings" does this refer?

Answer: If we examine the *Scripture of the Buddha of Limitless Life,* preached at Rājagriha city, we see that the Buddha
announced to Ānanda: "The Buddhas, the Thus-Come-Ones
of the ten directions, as numerous as the sands of the Ganges, shall all together praise the incalculable awesome divinity and merit of the Buddha of Limitless Life. Then all of
the beings that are, if, hearing his name, they shall with a
believing heart rejoice for but a single moment of consciousness and with minds intent on being reborn in His land,
shall be immediately enabled to go there and be reborn and
stay there without return. There shall be excepted only those
who commit the Five Violations[1] and malign the True Law."
From this we see that even the commonest of men may go
thither to be reborn. . . .

How does one give rise to a prayerful heart? One always
prays, with the whole heart single-mindedly thinking of being ultimately reborn in the Happy Land, because one wishes
truly to practice *śamatha* [concentration]. . . .

Śamatha is rendered *chih* [stop] in three senses. First, one
thinks single-mindedly of Amitābha Buddha and prays for
rebirth in His Land. This Buddha's name and that Land's
name can stop all evil. Second, that Happy Land exceeds the

---

[1] These are parricide, matricide, murder of an arhant, introduction
of disharmony into the monastic community, and striking a Buddha so as to cause him to bleed.

paths of the three worlds. If a man is born in that Land, he automatically puts an end to the evils of body, mouth, and mind. Third, Amitābha Buddha's power of enlightenment and persistent tenacity can naturally arrest the mind that seeks after lower stages of the Vehicle. These three kinds of *chih* arise from Buddha's real merit. Therefore it is said that "one wishes truly to practice *śamatha* (concentration).

How does one observe? With wisdom one observes. With right mindfulness one observes Him, because one wishes truly to practice *vipaśyanā* (insight). . . .

Vipaśvanā is translated *kuan* (insight) in two senses. First, while yet in this world, one conceives a thought and views the merit of the above-mentioned three kinds of adornments. This merit is real, hence the practitioner also gains real merit. "Real merit" is the ability to be reborn with certainty in that Land. Second, once one has achieved rebirth in that Pure Land one immediately sees Amitābha Buddha. The pure-hearted bodhisattva who has not yet fully perceived is now able to perceive fully the Law Body that is above differences and, together with the pure-hearted bodhisattvas and the bodhisattvas of the uppermost station, to attain fully to the same quiescent equality. Therefore it is said that "one wishes truly to practice *vipaśyanā*." . . .

How does one apply [one's own merit] to and not reject all suffering beings? By ever making the vow to put such application first, in order to obtain a perfect heart of great compassion.

"Application" has two aspects. The first is the going aspect, the second is the returning aspect. What is the "going aspect"? One takes one's own merit and diverts it to all the beings, praying that all together may go to be reborn in Amitābha Buddha's Happy Land. What is the "returning aspect"? When one has already been reborn in that Land and attained to the perfection of concentration and insight, and the power of saving others through convenient means, one returns and enters the withered forest of life and death, and teaches all beings to turn together to the Path of the Buddha.

[From *Wang-sheng lun chu*, in *Taishō daizōkyō*, XL, 827–36]

The Orthodoxy of the Pure Land Faith

*The Compendium on the Happy Land from which these extracts
are taken was compiled by Tao-ch'o (d. 645), a T'ien-t'ai monk
who was particularly devoted to the recitation of the Buddha's
name and became one of the great patriarchs of Pure Land Buddhism. Here he answers questions which arise over apparent inconsistencies between Pure Land teachings and traditional doctrines of
Buddhism.*

Question: According to the holy doctrine of the Great Vehicle, if the bodhisattva evinces toward the beings a loving
view or great compassion, he should immediately resist it.
Now the bodhisattva encourages all beings to be reborn in
the Pure Land. Is this not a combining with love, a grasping
at character? Or does he escape defiling attachments [in spite
of this]?

Answer: The efficacy of the dharmas practiced by the bodhisattva is of two kinds. Which are they? One is perception
of the understanding of Emptiness and Perfect Wisdom.
The second is full possession of great compassion. In the
case of the former, by virtue of his practice of the understanding of Emptiness and Perfect Wisdom, though he may
enter into the cycles of birth and death of the six stages of
existence, he is not fettered by their grime or contamination.
In the case of the latter, by virtue of his compassionate
mindfulness of the beings, he does not dwell in Nirvāna.
The bodhisattva, though he dwells in the midst of the Twofold Truth, is ever able subtly to reject existence and nonexistence, to strike the mean in his acceptances and rejec-
tions and not to run counter to the principles of the Great
Way. . . .

Question: There are some who say: "The realm of purity
which one contemplates is restricted to the inner mind. The
Pure Land is all-pervasive; the mind, if pure, is identical with
it. Outside of the Mind there are no dharmas. What need
is there to enter the West[ern Paradise]?"

Answer: Only the Pure Land of the dharma-nature dwells in
principle in empty all-pervasion and is in substance unre-
stricted. This is the birth of no-birth, into which the superior

gentlemen[1] may enter. . . . There are the middle and lower classes [of bodhisattvas], who are not yet able to overcome the world of characters, and who must rely on the circumstance of faith in the Buddha to seek rebirth in the Pure Land. Though they reach that Land, they still dwell in a land of characters. It is also said: "If one envelops conditions and follows the origin,[2] this is what is meant by 'no dharmas outside the Mind.' But if one distinguishes the Twofold Truth to clarify the doctrine, then the Pure Land does not conflict with the existence of dharmas outside the Mind." Now let us interpret through question and answer.

Question: There are some who say that one vows to be reborn in this filthy land in order to convert the beings by one's teaching, and that one does not vow to go to the Pure Land to be reborn. How is this?

Answer: Of such persons also there is a certain group. Why? If the body resides in [an estate from which there is] no backsliding, or beyond, in order to convert the sundry evil beings it may dwell in contamination without becoming contaminated or encounter evil without being transformed, just as the swan and the duck may enter the water but the water cannot wet them. Such persons as these can dwell in filth and extricate the beings from their suffering. But if the person is in truth an ordinary man, I only fear that his own conduct is not yet established, and that if he encounters suffering he will immediately change. He who wishes to save him will perish together with him. For example, if one forces a chicken into the water, how can one not get wet? . . .

Question: There are some who say: "Within the Pure Land there are only enjoyable things. Much pleasure in clinging to enjoyment hinders and destroys the practice of the Way. Why should one vow to go thither and be reborn?"

Answer: Since it is called "Pure Land," it means that there are no impurities in it. If one speaks of "clinging to enjoyment," this refers to lust and the afflictions. If so, why call it pure?

Question: The *Scripture of the Buddha of Limitless Life* says: "If the beings of the ten directions shall with intense

---

[1] That is, the bodhisattvas of the upper stages.
[2] Rising above conditioned things to seek the Absolute.

belief and desire for as much as ten moments wish to be reborn in my Land, and if then they should not be reborn there, may I never attain enlightenment." Now there are men in the world who hear this holy teaching and who in their present life never arouse their minds to it, but wait until the end approaches and then wish to practice such contemplation. What do you say of such cases?

Answer: Such cases are not true. Why? The scriptures say: "Ten continuous moments may seem not to be difficult. However, the minds of ordinary men are like a zephyr, their consciousness is more capricious than a monkey's. It runs through the six objects of sensual perception without rest." Everyone should arouse his faith and first conquer his own thoughts, so that through the accumulated practice it will become his nature and the roots of goodness become firm. As the Buddha proclaimed to the great king, if men accumulate good conduct, at death they will have no evil thoughts, just as, when a tree is first bent in a certain direction, when it falls it will follow that bent. Once the sword and the wind arrive, and a hundred woes concentrate upon the body, if the practice is not there to begin with, how can contemplation be consummated? Everyone should form a bond with three or five comrades to enlighten one another. When life's end faces them, they should enlighten one another, recite Amitā-bha Buddha's name to one another, and pray for rebirth in Paradise in such a way that voice succeeds upon voice until the ten moments of thought are completed. It is as, when a wax seal has been impressed in clay, after the wax has been destroyed, the imprint remains. When this life is cut off, one is reborn immediately in the Comfortable and Pleasant Land. At the time one enters completely into the cluster of right contemplation. What more is there to worry about? Everyone should weigh this great blessing. Why should one not conquer one's own thoughts ahead of time?

[From *An-lo chi,* in *Taishō daizōkyō,* XLVII, 8–11]

THE PARABLE OF THE WHITE PATH

Shan-tao (613–681), a disciple of Tao-ch'o, is another of the great patriarchs of the Pure Land faith. He is known especially for his

Kuan-ching shu, a commentary on the Amitāyur-dhyāna Sūtra, in which appears this famous parable vividly delineating the existential crisis of man and his need for faith.

And to all those who wish to be reborn in the Pure Land, I now tell a parable for the sake of those who would practice the True Way, as a protection for their faith and a defense against the danger of heretical views. What is it? It is like a man who desires to travel a hundred thousand *li* to the West. Suddenly in the midst of his route he sees two rivers. One is a river of fire stretching South. The other is a river of water stretching North. Each of the two rivers is a hundred steps across and unfathomably deep. They stretch without end to the North and South. Right between the fire and water, however, is a white path barely four or five inches wide. Spanning the East and West banks, it is one hundred steps long. The waves of water surge and splash against the path on one side, while the flames of fire scorch it on the other. Ceaselessly, the fire and water come and go.

The man is out in the middle of a wasteland and none of his kind are to be seen. A horde of vicious ruffians and wild beasts see him there alone, and vie with one another in rushing to kill him. Fearing death he runs straightway to the West, and then sees these great rivers. Praying, he says to himself: "To the North and South I see no end to these rivers. Between them I see a white path, which is extremely narrow. Although the two banks are not far apart, how am I to traverse from one to the other? Doubtless today I shall surely die. If I seek to turn back, the horde of vicious ruffians and wild beasts will come at me. If I run to the North or South, evil beasts and poisonous vermin will race toward me. If I seek to make my way to the West, I fear that I may fall into these rivers."

Thereupon he is seized with an inexpressible terror. He thinks to himself: "Turn back now and I die. Stay and I die. Go forward and I die. Since death must be faced in any case, I would rather follow this path before me and go ahead. With this path I can surely make it across." Just as he thinks this, he hears someone from the east bank call out and encourage him: "Friend, just follow this path resolutely and there will be no danger of death. To stay here is to die."

And on the west bank there is someone calling out, "Come straight ahead, single-mindedly and with fixed purpose. I can protect you. Never fear falling into the fire or water!"

At the urging of the one and the calling of the other, the man straightens himself up in body and mind and resolves to go forward on this path, without any lingering doubts or hesitations. Hardly has he gone a step or two when from the east bank the horde of vicious ruffians calls out to him: "Friend, come back! That way is perilous and you will never get across. Without a doubt you are bound to die. None of us means to harm you." Though he hears them calling, the man still does not look back but single-mindedly and straightway proceeds on the path. In no time he is at the west bank, far from all troubles forever. He is greeted by his good friend and there is no end of joy.

That is the parable and this is the meaning of it: what we speak of as the "east bank" is comparable to this world, a house in flames. What we speak of as the "west bank" is symbolic of the precious land of highest bliss. The ruffians, wild beasts, and seeming friends are comparable to the Six Sense Organs, Six Consciousnesses, Six Dusts, Five Components, and Four Elements [that constitute the "self"]. The lonely wasteland is the following of bad companions and not meeting with those who are truly good and wise. The two rivers of fire and water are comparable to human greed and affection, like water, and anger and hatred, like fire. The white path in the center, four or five inches wide, is comparable to the pure aspiration for rebirth in the Pure Land which arises in the midst of the passions of greed and anger. Greed and anger are powerful, and thus are likened to fire and water; the good mind is infinitesimal, and thus is likened to a white path [of a few inches in width]. The waves inundating the path are comparable to the constant arising of affectionate thoughts in the mind which stain and pollute the good mind. And the flames which scorch the path are comparable to thoughts of anger and hatred which burn up the treasures of dharma and virtue. The man proceeding on the path toward the West is comparable to one who directs all of his actions and practices toward the West[ern Paradise]. The hearing of voices from the East bank encouraging and exhorting him to pursue the path straight to the West, is like Shākyamuni Buddha, who has already disappeared from the sight of men but whose teachings may still be pursued and are therefore likened to "voices." The calling out of the ruffians after he has taken a few steps is comparable to those of different teachings and practices and of evil views who wantonly spread their ideas to lead people astray and create disturbances, thus falling themselves into sin and losing their way. To speak of someone calling from the West bank is comparable to the vow of Amitābha. Reaching the West bank, being greeted by the good friend and rejoicing there, is comparable to all those beings sunk long in the sea of birth and death, floundering and caught in their own delusions, without any means of deliverance, who accept Shākyamuni's testament directing them to the West and Amitābha's compassionate call, and obeying trustfully the will of the two Buddhas while paying no heed to the rivers of fire and water, with devout concentration mount the road of Amitābha's promised power and when life is o'er attain the other Land, where they meet the Buddha and know unending bliss.

[From *Taishō daizōkyō*, XXXVII, 272–3]

THE MEDITATION SCHOOL

Introduction

The Meditation school, called *Ch'an* in Chinese from the Sanskrit *dhyāna*, is best known in the West by the Japanese pronunciation *Zen*. As a religious practice, of course, meditation was not peculiar to Ch'an; it had been a standard fixture in all forms of Buddhism, whether Indian or Chinese, from earliest times. Indian texts on yoga practice and *dhyāna* were among the first Buddhist works translated into Chinese, and they found an enthusiastic audience amongst the intelligentsia, many of whom were ardent followers of Taoism. Yet these Indian texts were obscure and at times almost unintelligible; thus the concept of *dhyāna* gradually went through a process of sinicization, whereby it was greatly simplified and altered. Before the emergence of Ch'an as an independent

sect, early Buddhist monks had arrived at a variety of interpretations, some highly scholastic and close to the Indian
original, and others quite near to the later Ch'an version.

Ch'an is unique, however, in the great emphasis it placed
on meditation, using it, particularly in the early period of
training, as a means of attaining an intuitive awareness of
the Ultimate Truth or First Principle. In order to achieve
this intuitive recognition, all conceptual thinking was to be
set aside and all external influences to be rejected. Therefore,
scriptural writings and learned discussions were dispensed
with (at least in the earlier stages of study) and emphasis
was placed chiefly on the ability to meditate properly and
profitably. In fact, achievement in meditation was equated
with intuitive wisdom.

Ch'an likes to style itself as "a separate transmission outside the scriptures, not dependent on words and phrases,"
and to describe its teachings as "transmitted from mind to
mind." Here the Master plays a dominant role: all practice
and study is done under his direction. The monk is completely subservient to his will, and it is the Master who
verifies the degree of progress a monk has made; and it is
the Master again who acknowledges the understanding of
his disciple and who, in the end, transmits his teaching to
him.

"To see into one's own nature and become Buddha" is the
objective of all Ch'an practitioners and it is to this end that
all their study is directed. Different Masters developed various techniques to bring the student to realization and awakening. In addition to meditation over a period of months
and years, physical work, initially instituted for the purpose
of supporting the community of monks, was stressed and
eventually became an integral part of the Ch'an training
program. Going on pilgrimage from one Master to another
in order to test and mature one's understanding became
standard practice in the sect. But the most commonly used
method was that of the *kung-an* (*kōan* in Japanese). Originally a legal term meaning "public case," it came to refer
to the brief stories, primarily questions and answers of an
enigmatic or paradoxical nature, with which Ch'an literature
abounds. In most likelihood the first kōans were used in
public meetings before the assemblage of monks. A monk

would step forward, pose his question, hear his answer, and retire to meditate upon its purport. Gradually these kōans came to be written down, collected, and to gain wide circulation. Instead of making kōans of their own, the stories of famous old priests were used by later Masters in teaching their own disciples, until eventually a system evolved in which a series of kōans formed what might almost be called a planned program of instruction, in which the student would meditate until he had satisfied his Master that he had come to an intuitive understanding of each kōan. Frequently these kōans could not be answered verbally, which in part accounts for the beatings, shouts, and gestures so often described in the stories. Often a Master would find his disciple's mind so sensitized and receptive that a scream, a blow of the stick, or a blasphemous word would be the cause of his awakening to the Truth.

Traditionally Ch'an traces its origins to the Buddha who, holding a flower before the assembly, saw Kāshyapa smile and realized that he alone had understood. Thus the True Law was entrusted to Kāshyapa and from him it passed through twenty-eight generations in India until it came to Bodhidharma, a prince of southern India, who arrived in China in 520 A.D. and became the First Patriarch there. From Bodhidharma the Law was passed to succeeding generations until Hui-neng (d. 713), the Sixth Patriarch, inherited the teachings. This is the traditional version of early Ch'an, but it is so encrusted with legendary accretions that it is almost impossible to know what the true historical facts are. Recent research, particularly by Dr. Hu Shih, has shown that a person known as Bodhidharma was indeed in China, but during the years 420–479. An ascetic, his teachings were based on the Lankāvatāra Sūtra, and he practiced an exceedingly simplified form of meditation. His disciples continued his teachings and attracted a considerable body of followers, until by the start of the eighth century a school of meditation, of sufficient significance to have had a history[1] of its own, had

---

[1] The Leng-chia shih-tzu chi, a work found in the Tun-huang caves, details the history of the Lanka sect from Bodhidharma through Shen-hsiu. Hui-neng is mentioned in passing as one of several disciples of the Fifth Patriarch. This book belongs to the Northern

been formed. By the third decade of the same century Ch'an had gained enormous popularity and had split into two schools, the Northern which stressed gradual enlightenment, and the Southern, which advocated sudden awakening. Shen-hsiu (605?–706) and Hui-neng, both disciples of the Fifth Patriarch, are traditionally given as the respective leaders of these two schools. Hu Shih, however, has demonstrated rather convincingly that Shen-hui (670–762) was the real founder of Southern Ch'an. In 734 he attacked the Northern school which, under Imperial patronage, enjoyed unrivalled prestige. Claiming his teacher Hui-neng to be the true heir of the Fifth Patriarch, he condemned the meditation concepts of the Northern school, maintaining that the Southern enlightenment doctrine which emphasized "absence of thought" and the "identity of meditation (*samādhi*) and intuitive wisdom (*prajñā*)" was the true teaching. His eloquence won the day; Southern Ch'an was accepted as the official teaching, and its popularity increased, not only in the cities but in outlying areas as well. During the eighth century numerous Ch'an teachers, all tracing themselves to Hui-neng, spread their versions of the meditation doctrines, and many Ch'an works were composed: histories, treatises, biographies, all of which added to the legends and stories, until by the ninth century the traditions concerning the early masters assumed very nearly the form in which they are found today.

During the T'ang dynasty all sects of Buddhism enjoyed the lavish patronage of the court and the elite, vast temples were erected, and great fortunes amassed by the church. Ch'an alone remained aloof, to a great extent, from these excesses; indeed in its early period its temples served more as educational institutions than as places of worship. Thus when the inevitable reaction came with the persecution of 845, Ch'an was left relatively untouched. Furthermore, while the anti-Buddhist measures wreaked great havoc in the capital cities, they were felt to a much lesser degree in the provinces. This was particularly so in northern China where the

---

school of Ch'an. Histories celebrating the Southern school quickly made their appearance, and one of them, the *Pao-lin chuan* (801), which today survives only in part, set the pattern for the great Ch'an histories of later centuries.

military commanders, who were "barbarians," with little interest and fewer prospects in the Confucian environment of the cities, continued their enthusiastic support of Ch'an. It was in the north that one of its greatest leaders, I-hsüan (d. 867) of Lin-chi propagated his iconoclastic doctrines and individualistic teachings with great success. The Lin-chi school, established by his followers, came to dominate Chinese Buddhism in the succeeding centuries. During the T'ang and Five Dynasties periods a variety of Ch'an sects developed, the so-called "Five Schools and Seven Houses," but by the eleventh century the most significant were the Lin-Chi and the Ts'ao-tung, which claimed Liang-chieh (807–869) of Tung-shan as its founder, and had been further developed by Pen-chi (840–901) of Ts'ao-shan and other Masters. By this time Ch'an had abandoned its aloofness to mundane affairs and had become an organized church, which took over the functions and ceremonies previously associated with other sects, and exercised a considerable influence among intellectual circles at the capital.

The selections given below include excerpts from a basic Ch'an work attributed to Hui-neng and examples of two methods of Ch'an teaching, the sermon and the question-and-answer.

The Platform Scripture of the Sixth Patriarch

This short work is said to represent a collection of a number of sermons and the autobiography of Hui-neng (d. 713), as transcribed by his disciple Fa-hai. Hu Shih, however, believes it to be the work of an eighth-century follower of Shen-hui, another pupil of Hui-neng. Our text, which was discovered in the Tun-huang caves, is corrupt and contains numerous errors, and from the standpoint of both content and style, can best be described as primitive. Its continued popularity in China, however, is attested to by the great number of versions that have appeared over the centuries. The traditional version, current today, which was printed some five hundred years after the present text, is greatly revised and expanded and is almost twice the size of the original. Translated here are the autobiography and several passages which reflect the thought which was afterward developed and expanded by later Ch'an masters. The section numbers follow those established by D. T. Suzuki in his edition of the text.

2. The Master Hui-neng said: "Good friends, purify your minds and concentrate on the Dharma of the Great Perfection of Wisdom."

The Master stopped speaking and quieted his own mind. Then after a good while he said: "Good friends, listen quietly. Although my father was originally an official at Fan-yang, he was dismissed from his post and banished as a commoner to Hsin-chou in Ling-nan. While I was still a child my father died and my mother and I, a solitary child, moved to Nan-hai. We suffered extreme poverty and here I sold firewood in the market place. By chance a certain man bought some firewood and then took me with him to the lodging house for officials. He took the firewood and left. Having received my money and turning towards the front gate, I happened to see another man who was reciting the *Diamond Scripture*.

"I asked him: 'Where do you come from that you have brought this sūtra with you?'

"He answered: 'I have made obeisance to the Fifth Patriarch Hung-jen at the East Mountain, Feng-mu shan, in Huang-mei hsien in Ch'i-chou. At present there are over a thousand disciples there. While I was there I heard the Master encourage the lay followers, saying that if they recited just the one volume, the *Diamond Scripture*, they could see into their own natures and with direct apprehension become buddhas.'

"Hearing what he said, I realized that I was predestined to have heard him. Then I took leave of my mother and went to Feng-mu shan in Huang-mei and made obeisance to the Fifth Patriarch, the priest Hung-jen.

3. "The priest Hung-jen asked me: 'Where are you from that you come to this mountain to make obeisance to me? Just what is it that you are looking for from me?'

"I replied: 'I am from Ling-nan, a commoner from Hsin-chou. I have come this long distance only to make obeisance to you. I am seeking no particular thing, but only the Buddhadharma.'

"The Master then reproved me, saying: 'If you're from Ling-nan then you're a barbarian. How can you become a buddha?'

"I replied: 'Although people from the south and people from the north differ, there is no north and south in Buddha nature. Although my barbarian's body and your body are not the same, what difference is there in our Buddha nature?'

"The Master wished to continue the discussion with me; however, seeing that there were other people nearby, he said no more. Then he sent me to work together with the assembly. Later a lay disciple had me go to the threshing room where I spent over eight months treading the pestle.

4. "Unexpectedly one day the Fifth Patriarch called all his disciples to come, and when they had assembled, he said: 'Let me preach to you. For people in this world birth and death are vital matters. You disciples make offerings all day long and seek only the field of blessings, but you do not seek to escape from the bitter sea of birth and death. Your own self-nature obscures the gateway to blessings; how can you be saved? All of you return to your rooms and look into yourselves. Men of wisdom will of themselves grasp the original nature of their prajñā intuition. Each of you write a verse and bring it to me. I will read your verses and if there is one who has awakened to the cardinal meaning, I will give him the robe and the Dharma and make him the Sixth Patriarch. Hurry, hurry!'

5. "The disciples received his instructions and returned each to his own room. They talked it over among themselves, saying: 'There's no point in our purifying our minds and making efforts to compose a verse to present to the priest. Shen-hsiu, the head monk, is our teacher. After he obtains the Dharma we can rely on him, so let's not compose verses.' They all then gave up trying and did not have the courage to present a verse.

"At that time there was a three-sectioned corridor in front of the Master's hall. On the walls were to be painted pictures of stories from the Laṅkāvatāra Sūtra, together with a picture in commemoration of the Fifth Patriarch transmitting the robe and Dharma in order to disseminate them to later generations. The artist, Lu Chen, had examined the walls and was to start work the next day.

6. "The head monk Shen-hsiu thought: 'The others won't present mind-verses because I am their teacher. If I don't offer a mind-verse, how can the Fifth Patriarch estimate the degree of understanding within my mind? If I offer my mind-verse to the Fifth Patriarch with the intention of gaining the Dharma, it is justifiable; however, if I am seeking the patriarchship, then it cannot be justified. Then it would be like a common man usurping the saintly position. But if I don't offer my mind then I cannot learn the Dharma. For a long time he thought about it and was very much perplexed.

"At midnight, without letting anyone see him, he went to write his mind-verse on the central section of the south corridor wall, hoping to gain the Dharma. 'If the Fifth Patriarch sees my verse [tomorrow and is pleased with it, then I shall come forward and say that I wrote it. If he tells me that it is not worthwhile then I will know that] [1] there is a weighty obstacle in my past karma, that I cannot gain the Dharma and shall have to give up. The honorable patriarch's intention is difficult to fathom.'

"Then the head monk, Shen-hsiu, at midnight, holding a candle, wrote a verse on the wall of the central section of the south corridor, without anyone else knowing about it. The verse read:

The body is the bodhi tree,
The mind is like a clear mirror.
At all times we must strive to polish it,
And must not let the dust collect.

7. "After he had finished writing this verse, the head monk Shen-hsiu returned to his room and lay down. No one had seen him.

"At dawn the Fifth Patriarch called the painter Lu to draw illustrations from the *Laṅkāvatāra Sūtra* on the south corridor. The Fifth Patriarch suddenly saw this verse, and having read it, said to the painter: 'I will give you thirty

---

[1] There is a lacuna in the Tun-huang text at this point. The missing passage has been supplied from the Northern Sung version (*Kōshōji* text).

thousand cash. You have come a long distance to do this arduous work, but I have decided not to have the pictures painted after all. It is said in the *Diamond Scripture:* "All forms everywhere are unreal and false." It would be best to leave this verse here and to have the deluded ones recite it. If they practice in accordance with it they will not fall into the three evil ways. Those who practice by it will gain great benefit.'

"The Master then called all his disciples to come, and burned incense before the verse. The disciples came in to see and were all filled with admiration.

"[The Fifth Patriarch said]: 'You should all recite this verse so that you will be able to see into your own natures.[2] With this practice you will not fall [into the three evil ways].'

"The disciples all recited it, and feeling great admiration, cried out: 'How excellent!'

"The Fifth Patriarch then called the head monk Shen-hsiu inside the hall and asked: 'Did you write this verse or not? If you wrote it you are qualified to attain my Dharma.'[3]

"The head monk Shen-hsiu said: 'I am ashamed to say that I actually did write the verse, but I do not dare to seek the patriarchship. I beg you to be so compassionate as to tell me whether I have even a small amount of wisdom and discernment of the cardinal meaning or not.'

"The Fifth Patriarch said: 'This verse you wrote shows that you still have not reached true understanding. You have merely reached the front of the gate but have yet to be able to enter it. If common people practice according to your verse they will not fall. But in seeking the ultimate enlightenment (bodhi) one will not succeed with such an understanding. You must enter the gate and see your own original nature. Go and think about it for a day or two and then make another verse and present it to me. If you have been able to enter the gate and see your own original nature, then I will give you the robe and the Dharma.' The head monk Shen-hsiu left, but after several days he was still unable to write a verse.

---

[2] This statement contradicts the story as it later develops. It represents, probably, an interpolation in the text.
[3] A further contradiction; the text is corrupt here.

8. "One day an acolyte passed by the threshing room reciting
this verse. As soon as I heard it I knew that the person who
had written it had yet to know his own nature and to discern
the cardinal meaning. I asked the boy: 'What's the name of
the verse you were reciting just now?'

"The boy answered me saying: 'Don't you know! The
Master said that birth and death are vital matters, and he
told his disciples each to write a verse if they wanted to in-
herit the robe and the Dharma, and to bring it for him to
see. He who was awakened to the cardinal meaning would
be given the robe and the Dharma and be made the Sixth
Patriarch. There is a head monk by the name of Shen-hsiu
who happened to write a verse on formlessness on the wall
of the south corridor. The Fifth Patriarch had all the disciples recite the verse, [saying] that those who awakened to it
would see into their own self-natures, and that those who
practiced according to it would attain emancipation.'

"I said: 'I've been treading the pestle for more than eight
months, but haven't been to the hall yet. I beg you to take
me to the south corridor so that I can see the verse and make
obeisance to it. I also want to recite it so that I can establish
causation for my next birth and be born in a Buddhaland.'

"The boy took me to the south corridor and I made obeisance before the verse. Because I was uneducated I asked
someone to read it to me. As soon as I had heard it I understood the cardinal meaning. I made a verse and asked someone who was able to write to put it on the wall of the west
corridor, so that I might offer my own original mind. If you
do not know the original mind, studying the Dharma is to
no avail. If you know the mind and see its true nature, you
then awaken to the cardinal meaning.[4] My verse said:

The Bodhi tree is originally not a tree,
The mirror also has no stand.
Buddha nature is always clean and pure;
Where is there room for dust?

Another verse said:

[4] These two sentences are out of context and represent a later interpolation.

The mind is the Bodhi tree,
The body is the mirror stand.
The mirror is originally clean and pure;
Where can it be stained by dust?

"The followers in the temple were all amazed when they saw my verse. Then I returned to the threshing room. The Fifth Patriarch realized that I had a splendid understanding of the cardinal meaning. Being afraid lest the assembly know this, he said to them: 'This is still not complete attainment.'

9. "At midnight the Fifth Patriarch called me into the hall and expounded the *Diamond Scripture* to me. Hearing it but once, I was immediately awakened, and that night I received the Dharma. None of the others knew anything about it. Then he transmitted to me the Dharma of Sudden Enlightenment and the robe, saying: 'I make you the Sixth Patriarch. The robe is the proof and is to be handed down from generation to generation. My Dharma must be transmitted from mind to mind. You must make people awaken to themselves.'

"The Fifth Patriarch told me: 'From ancient time the transmission of the Dharma has been as tenuous as a dangling thread. If you stay here there are people who will kill you. You must leave at once.'

10. "I set out at midnight with the robe and the Dharma. The Fifth Patriarch saw me off as far as Chiu-chiang Station. I was instantly enlightened. The Fifth Patriarch instructed me: 'Leave, work hard, take the Dharma with you to the south. For three years do not spread the teaching or else calamity will befall the Dharma. Later work to convert people; you must guide deluded persons well. If you are able to awaken another's mind, he will be no different from me.[5] After completing my leave-taking I set out for the south.

11. "After about two months I reached Ta-yü ling. Unknown to me, several hundred men were following behind, wishing to try to kill me and to steal my robe and Dharma. By the

[5] Following the Northern Sung text.

time I had gone halfway up the mountain they had all turned back. But there was one monk of the family name of Chen, whose personal name was Hui-ming. Formerly he had been a general of the third rank and he was by nature and conduct coarse and evil. Reaching the top of the mountain he caught up with me and threatened me. I handed over the dharma-robe, but he did not dare to take it.

"[He said]: 'I have come this long distance just to seek the Dharma. I have no need for the robe.' Then, on top of the mountain, I transmitted the Dharma to Hui-ming, who when he heard it, was at once enlightened. I then ordered him to return to the north and to convert people there.

13. "Good friends, my teaching of the Dharma takes meditation and wisdom as its basis. Never under any circumstances say that meditation and wisdom are different; they are one unity, not two things. Meditation itself is the substance of wisdom; wisdom itself is the function of meditation. Just when there is wisdom, then meditation exists in wisdom; just when there is meditation, then wisdom exists in meditation. Good friends, this means that meditation and wisdom are alike. Students, be careful not to say that meditation first gives rise to wisdom, or that wisdom first gives rise to meditation, or that meditation and wisdom are different from each other. To hold this view implies that things have duality, and if good is spoken while the mind is not good, meditation and wisdom will not be alike. If mind and speech are both good, then the internal and the external are the same and meditation and wisdom are identical. The practice of self-awakening does not lie in verbal arguments. If you argue which comes first, meditation or wisdom, you are deluded people. You won't be able to settle the argument and instead will attach to objective things and will never escape from the four states of phenomena.[6]

14. "The samādhi of oneness is direct mind at all times, walking, staying, sitting, and lying. The Vimalakīrti Sūtra says: 'Direct mind is the place of practice; direct mind is the Pure Land.' Do not with a dishonest mind speak of the

[6] Birth, being, change, and death.

directness of the Dharma. If while speaking of the samādhi of oneness, you fail to practice direct mind, you will not be disciples of the Buddha. Just practicing direct mind only, and in all things having no attachments whatsoever, is called the samādhi of oneness. The deluded man clings to the characteristics of things, adheres to the samādhi of oneness, [thinks] that direct mind is sitting without moving and casting aside delusions without letting things arise in the mind. This he considers to be the samādhi of oneness. This kind of practice is the same as insentiency and is the cause of an obstruction to the Tao. Tao must be something that circulates freely; why should he impede it? If the mind does not abide in things the Tao circulates freely; if the mind abides in things, it becomes entangled. If sitting in meditation without moving is good, why did Vimalakīrti scold Shāriputra for sitting in meditation in the forest? [7]

"Good friends, some people[8] teach men to sit viewing the mind and viewing purity, not moving and not activating [the mind], and to this they devote their efforts. Deluded people do not realize that this is wrong, attach to this doctrine and become confused. There are many such people. Those who instruct in this way are from the outset greatly mistaken.

17. "Good friends, in this teaching of mine, from ancient times up to the present, all have set up no-thought as the main doctrine, non-form as the substance, and non-abiding as the basis. Non-form is to be separated from form even when associated with form. No thought is not to think even when involved in thought. Non-abiding is the original nature of man.

"Successive thoughts do not stop; prior thoughts, present thoughts, and future thoughts follow one after the other without cessation. If one instant of thought is cut off, the Dharma body separates from the physical body, and in the midst of successive thoughts there will be no place for attachment to anything. If one instant of thought attaches, then successive thoughts attach; this is known as being fettered. If in all things successive thoughts do not attach, then

---

[7] Reference is to a passage in the Vimalakīrti Sūtra.
[8] Practitioners of Northern Zen.

you are unfettered. Therefore, non-abiding is made the basis.

"Good friends, being outwardly separated from all forms, this is non-form. When you are separated from form, the substance of your nature is pure. Therefore, non-form is made the substance.

"To be unstained in all environments is called no-thought. If on the basis of your own thoughts you separate from environment, then in regard to things thoughts are not produced. If you stop thinking of the myriad things and cast aside all thoughts, as soon as one instant of thought is cut off you will be reborn in another realm. Students, take care! If you do not stop notions of the Dharma, it will be bad enough that you yourselves are in error, but how much worse if you encourage others in these mistakes. The deluded man, however, does not himself see and slanders the teachings of the sūtras. Therefore, no-thought is established as a doctrine. Because man in his delusion has thoughts in relation to his environment, heterodox ideas stemming from these thoughts arise, and passions and false views are produced from them. Therefore, this teaching has established no-thought as a doctrine.

"Men of the world, separate yourselves from views; do not activate thoughts. If there were no thinking, then no-thought would have no place to exist. 'No' is the 'no' of what? 'Thought' means 'thinking' of what? 'No' is the separation from the dualism which produces the passions. 'Thought' means thinking of the original nature of True Reality. True Reality is the substance of thoughts; thoughts are the function of True Reality. If you give rise to thoughts from your self-nature then, although you see, hear, perceive, and know, you are not stained by the manifold environments, and are always free. The *Vimalakīrti Sūtra* says: 'Externally, while distinguishing well all the forms of the various dharmas; internally, he stands firm within the First Principle.'

18. "Good friends, in this teaching from the outset sitting in meditation does not concern the mind nor does it concern purity; we do not talk of constancy. If someone speaks of 'viewing the mind,' [then I would say] that the 'mind' is of itself delusion, and as delusions are just like fantasies, there

is nothing to be seen. If someone speaks of 'viewing purity,' [then I would say] that man's nature is of itself pure, but because of false thoughts, True Reality is obscured. If you exclude delusions then the original nature reveals its purity. If you activate your mind to view purity without realizing that your own nature is originally pure, delusions of purity will be produced. Since this delusion has no place to exist, then you know that whatever you see is nothing but delusion. Purity has no form, but nonetheless, some people try to postulate the form of purity and consider this to be Ch'an practice. People who hold this view obstruct their own original natures and end up by being bound by purity. One who practices constancy does not see the faults of people everywhere. This is the constancy of self-nature. The deluded man, however, even if he doesn't move his own body, will talk of the good and bad of others the moment he opens his mouth, and thus behave in opposition to the Tao. Therefore, both 'viewing the mind' and 'viewing purity' will cause an obstruction to Tao."

35. The Prefect [9] bowed deeply and asked: "I notice that some monks and laymen always invoke the Buddha Amitābha and desire to be reborn in the West. I beg of you to explain whether one can be born there or not, and thus resolve my doubts."

The Master said: "Prefect, listen and I shall explain things for you. At Shrāvastī the World-honored one preached of the Western Land in order to convert people, and it is clearly stated in the sūtra, '[The Western Land] is not far.' [10] It was only for the sake of people of inferior capacity that the Buddha spoke of nearness; to speak of farness is only for those of superior attainments. Although in man there are naturally two types, in the Dharma there is no inequality. In delusion and awakening there is a difference, as may be seen in slowness and fastness of understanding. The deluded person concentrates on Buddha and wishes to be born in the

[9] Wei Ch'u, a government official, of whom little is known.
[10] Quotation from the Scripture of the Contemplation of the Buddha of Limitless Life.

other land; the awakened person makes pure his own mind. Therefore the Buddha said: 'In accordance with the purity of the mind the Buddha land is pure.' [11]

"Prefect, people of the East [China], just by making the mind pure, are without crime; people of the West [The Pure Land of the West], if their minds are not pure, are guilty of a crime. The deluded person wishes to be born in the East or West, [for the enlightened person] any land is just the same. If only the mind has no impurity, the Western Land is not far. If the mind gives rise to impurities, even though you invoke the Buddha and seek to be reborn [in the West], it will be difficult to reach there. If you eliminate the ten evils,[12] you will proceed ten thousand *li*; if you do away with the eight improper practices,[13] you will pass across eight thousand *li*. But if you practice direct mind, you will arrive there in an instant.

"Prefect, practice only the ten virtues.[14] Why should you seek rebirth [in the Western Land]? If you do not cut off the ten evils, what Buddha can you ask to come welcome you? If you awaken to the sudden Dharma of birthlessness, you will see the Western Land in an instant. If you do not awaken to the Sudden Teaching of Mahāyāna, even if you concentrate on the Buddha and seek to be reborn, the road will be long. How can you hope to reach there?"

The Sixth Patriarch said: "I will move the Western Land in an instant and present it to you right before your eyes. Does the Prefect wish to see it or not?"

The Prefect bowed deeply: "If I can see it here, why should I be reborn there? I ask you in your compassion to make the Western Land appear for my sake. It would be most wonderful."

The Master said: "There is no doubt that the Western Land can be seen here in China. Now let us disperse." The assembly was amazed and did not know what to do. . . .

[11] Quotation from the *Vimalakīrti Sūtra*.

[12] Killing, stealing, adultery, lying, double-tonguedness, coarse language, filthy language, covetousness, anger, perverted views.

[13] The eight delusions and attachments which arise in opposition to the true form of the various dharmas: birth, destruction, oneness, differentiation, past, future, permanence, and cessation.

[14] The opposite of the ten evils, above.

42. There was another priest by the name of Fa-ta, who had been reciting the *Lotus Sūtra* continuously for seven years, but his mind was still deluded and he did not know where the True Dharma lay. [Going to Mt. Ts'ao-ch'i, he bowed and asked]:[15] "I have doubts about the *Sūtra*, and because the Master's wisdom is great, I beg of him to resolve my doubts."

The Master said: "Fa-ta, you are very proficient in the Dharma but your mind is not proficient. You may have no doubts insofar as the sūtras are concerned [but your mind itself doubts].[16] You are searching for the True Dharma with falsehood in your mind. If your own mind were correct and fixed, you would be a man who has taken the *Sūtra* to himself. All my life I have not known written words, but if you bring me a copy of the *Lotus Sūtra* and read a section of it to me, upon hearing it, I shall understand it at once."

Fa-ta brought the *Lotus Sūtra* and read a section to the Master. Hearing it, the Sixth Patriarch understood the Buddha's meaning, and then discoursed on the *Lotus Sūtra* for the sake of Fa-ta.

The Sixth Patriarch said: "Fa-ta, the *Lotus Sūtra* does not say anything more than is needed. Throughout all its seven volumes it gives parables and tales about causation. The Tathāgata's preaching of the Three Vehicles was only because of the dullness of people in the world. The words of the *Sūtra* clearly state that there is only one vehicle of Buddhism, and that there is no other vehicle."

The Master said: "Fa-ta, listen to the one Buddha vehicle, and do not seek two vehicles, or your nature will be deluded. Where in the sūtras do we find this one Buddha vehicle? Let me explain to you. The *Sūtra* says:[17] 'The various Buddhas and the World-honored One appeared in this world because of the one great causal event.' How do you understand this Dharma? How do you practice this Dharma? Listen and I shall explain to you.

"The mind has nothing to do with thinking because its fundamental source is empty. To discard false views, this is

---

[15] Lacuna in text. Supplied from Northern Sung edition.
[16] A further lacuna.
[17] The *Lotus Sūtra*.

the great causal event. If within and without you are not deluded then you are apart from duality. If on the outside you are deluded you attach to form; if on the inside you are deluded you attach to emptiness. If within form you are apart from form and within emptiness you are separated from emptiness, then within and without you are not deluded. If you awaken to this Dharma, in one instant of thought your mind will open and you will go forth in the world. What is it that the mind opens? It opens Buddha's wisdom, and the Buddha means enlightenment. Divided there are four gates: the opening of the wisdom of enlightenment, the instruction of the wisdom of enlightenment, the awakening of the wisdom of enlightenment, and then entering into the wisdom of enlightenment. This is called opening, instructing, awakening, and entering.[18] Entering from one place,[19] this is the wisdom of enlightenment, and [with this] you see into your own nature, then you succeed in transcending the world."

The Master said: "Fa-ta, it is my constant wish that all people in the world will always of themselves open the wisdom of the Buddha in their own mind-grounds. Do not cultivate the 'wisdom' of sentient beings. The people of the world have error in their minds, create evil with stupidity and delusion, and thus cultivate the 'wisdom' of sentient beings. If people in the world are correct in their minds, they will give rise to wisdom and illuminate it, and open up for themselves the wisdom of the Buddha. Do not open up the 'wisdom' of sentient beings! Open the wisdom of the Buddha and then transcend the world."

The Master said: "Fa-ta, this is the one-vehicle Dharma of the *Lotus Sūtra*. Later on in the *Sūtra* the Buddha's teaching is divided into three [vehicles] in order to benefit the deluded. Depend only on the one Buddha vehicle."

The Master said: "If you practice with the mind you turn the *Lotus*; if you do not practice with the mind, you are turned by the *Lotus*. If your mind is correct you will turn the *Lotus*; if your mind is incorrect you will be turned by the *Lotus*. If the wisdom of the Buddha is opened it will turn

[18] Paraphrase of a passage in the *Lotus Sūtra*.
[19] Unclear, but reference may be to the place of the True Dharma, mentioned at the beginning of this section.

the *Lotus*; if the 'wisdom' of sentient beings is opened, it will be turned by the *Lotus*."

The Master said: "If you practice the Dharma with great effort, this then is turning the *Sūtra*."

Fa-ta, upon hearing this, at once gained great enlightenment and broke into tears. "Master," he said, "indeed up to now I have not turned the *Lotus*, but for seven years I have been turned by it. From now on I shall turn the *Lotus*, and in consecutive thoughts practice the practice of the Buddha."

The Master said: "The very practice of Buddha, this is Buddha."

Among the audience at that time there was none who was not enlightened.

[From photographic reproductions of the Tun-huang manuscript, housed in the Stein Collection (S5475) at the British Museum]

Seeing into One's Own Nature

This sermon by I-hsüan (?–867), known more commonly as Lin-chi, the name of the small temple in which he served, is contained in his Recorded Sayings. It represents a portion of a much longer address, delivered before an assembly of monks and laymen, and is one of the most famous sermons in the Lin-chi school of Ch'an. Nowhere, perhaps, do we find a more forceful expression of the doctrine of seeing into one's own nature and awakening to the Buddha within each person.

The Master addressed the assembly: "Followers of the Way, the Law of the Buddha has no room for elaborate activity; it is only everyday life with nothing to do. Evacuate, pass your water, put on your clothes, eat your food; if you are tired lie down. The fool will laugh but the wise man will understand. A man of old has said: 'Those who practice meditation seeking things on the outside are all imbeciles.' If you make yourself master in all circumstances, any place you stand will be the true one. In whatever environment you find yourself you cannot be changed. You encounter evil influences; yet even the five crimes[1] which lead to the neth-

[1] Killing father, mother or arhant; doing harm to the body of the Buddha; disturbing the peace of the community of monks.

ermost hell will of themselves form the great sea of deliverance. Students today do not know the Law; they are like half-blind sheep who gobble up anything that comes close to their noses. They cannot distinguish between slave and master, guest and host. People such as these enter the Way with deluded minds and become involved in confused and crowded places. One cannot call them true monks who have left their homes; they are really nothing but laymen.

"Monks who have left their homes must be aware of what true understanding is. They must distinguish buddha and demon, true and false, sacred and profane. If they are aware in this way, then they can be called true monks who have left their homes. If they cannot distinguish buddha and demon, it is as if they had left one ordinary home only to enter another. Such people are called common karma-creating beings; they cannot yet be called true monks who have left their homes. Suppose one had a single buddha-demon, indistinguishable in one body, like milk and water mixed together. It is only the King of Geese who can drink the milk and leave the water. Followers of the Way, with a clear eye destroy both buddha and demon. If you love the sacred and hate the profane you will continue floating and sinking in the sea of birth and death."

Someone asked: "What is this buddha-demon?"

The Master said: "A single moment of doubt on your part is the buddha-demon. Once you realize that all things are not produced, the mind, too, is like an illusion and, without a single speck of dust, is at all times pure. This is the Buddha. Moreover, buddha and demon are the two states, purity and impurity. In my view there is no Buddha, no sentient being, no past, no present; whatever you gain you gain, and there is no need to spend time. There is nothing to practice, nothing to prove, nothing to obtain, nothing to lose; at all times there is no other thing. And even if there were something else, I say that it would be nothing but a dream and an illusion. Everything I've been talking about just comes to this.

"Followers of the Way, that person [you] who is standing before me, resolute and clear, listening to my sermon, gets bogged down nowhere. He penetrates in all directions and throughout the three worlds is everywhere free. Although he enters into the differentiations of all things, he cannot be changed. Within one moment he penetrates the Dharma world. When he meets a Buddha he preaches to that Buddha, when he meets a patriarch he preaches to that patriarch, when he meets an arhant he preaches to that arhant, when he meets a hungry ghost he preaches to that ghost. In any land he travels, although he devotes himself to the conversion of sentient beings, he never for a moment is apart [from his understanding]. All places are pure and his light penetrates in all directions, and all things are the One.

"Followers of the Way, the resolute man must know right now that from the outset there is nothing to do. But because your faith is insufficient, from moment to moment you rush about seeking; you throw away your heads and then go looking for them[2] and are yourselves unable to stop. Even the Perfect Immediate Bodhisattva,[3] when he makes his appearance in the Dharma world, looks to the Pure Land, despises the profane and seeks the sacred. Those such as he have yet to forget both taking and throwing away; their minds are still involved with uncleanliness and purity. This is not the view of the Ch'an sect. At once everything is the present; indeed there is no time. Even what I have been preaching to you is no more than medicine used temporarily to cure a disease. There is no such thing as a fixed principle. If you understand this you are a true monk who has left his home, able to enjoy ten thousand gold coins a day.

"Followers of the Way, do not go about haphazardly accepting the sanction of any old master, saying: 'I understand Ch'an, I understand the Way!' Even though your eloquence be like a rushing torrent, it will be nothing but hell-producing karma. If you are a true student of the Way you will not look to the faults of the world, but will single-mindedly seek true understanding. Once you have achieved this true understanding and made it clear, then for the first time everything will have been completed."

Someone asked: "What is true understanding?"

The Master said: "You enter the profane, enter the sacred,

---

[2] Reference is to Yajñadatta, who seeing his head in a mirror, thought he had lost it.
[3] The highest bodhisattva rank.

enter impurity, enter purity, enter the various Buddha worlds,
enter the palace of Maitreya, enter the world of Vairochana,
and everywhere all these worlds appear they are established,
exist, decay, and perish into nothingness. The Buddha appeared in this world, turned the Wheel of the Law and later
entered Nirvāna, but his past and future cannot be seen.
Thus, seeking his birth and death is to no avail. Therefore,
entering the world of no birth and no destruction and traveling about it everywhere, you enter the world of the Lotus-
treasury, see the emptiness of all things, and know that all
things are unreal. It is only the man who listens to the Law
and is not conditioned by anything who is the mother of all
the Buddhas. Therefore, the Buddha was produced from the
non-conditioned. If you awaken to this non-conditioned,
Buddha is then something that need not be attained. Once
you are aware of this, this is then true understanding.

"Students do not understand, attach to words and phrases,
and because they are blocked by terms such as sacred and
profane, their eye of wisdom is obscured and they cannot
gain awakening. Things like the twelve divisions of the teachings are but obvious explanations. Students do not know this
and thus base their understanding on such things. Because
they depend on them they fall into cause and effect and are
unable to escape birth and death in the three worlds. If you
wish to attain freedom in moving through the world of birth
and death, then know the man who right now is listening
to the Law. He is without shape, without characteristics,
without root, without basis, yet always brisk and lively.
There is no trace of the activity of all his many devices. If
you try to find him he is far away; if you seek him he goes
against you. Given a name, this is the mystery.

"Followers of the Way, do not acknowledge this dream-
like illusory world, for sooner or later death will come. Just
what is it that you are seeking in this world that you think
will give you emancipation? Go out into the world, and seeking only the barest minimum of food, make do with it; spend
your time in the shabbiest of garments and go to visit a good
teacher. Do not heedlessly seek after pleasure. Time is precious and things change with each moment. In their grosser
aspects they are subject to the four elements, earth, water,
fire and wind; in their more detailed aspects they are subject

to the incessant oppression of the four states, birth, existence, change, and death. Followers of the Way, come to know the states of the four kinds of non-form and keep yourselves from being swayed by environment."

Someone asked: "What are the states of the four kinds of non-form?"

The Master said: "With a single instant of doubt in your mind, the element earth comes and impedes you; with a single instant of love in your mind, water comes and drowns you; with a single instant of anger in your mind, fire comes and burns you; with a single instant of joy in your mind, wind comes and shakes you. If you understand this well, you will not be swayed by the things around you, and everywhere you will be able to take advantage of your environment. You may rise in the east and set in the west, rise in the south and set in the north, rise in the center and set on the borders, rise on the borders and set in the center.[4] You may walk on water as if it were land and walk on land as if it were water. Why is this so? It is because you have realized that the four elements are nothing but a dream and an illusion.

"Followers of the Way, you who are listening to the Law right now, it is not the four elements that govern you, but you who can make use of these elements. If you understand this well, then whether you go or you stay you will be free. To my way of thinking there is nothing to be despised. You may say you love the sacred, but sacred is nothing but a name. Students turn to Mt. Wu-t'ai and seek Manjushrī there. They are mistaken from the start. There is no Manjushrī on Mt. Wu-t'ai. Do you want to know Manjushrī? He is your own activity right now, at all times unchanging, constant without a single moment of doubt—this is the living Manjushrī. The brilliance of one instant of non-differentiation on your part—this on all occasions and in all places is the true Samantabhadra. The one instant of thought in which you of yourself unfetter your bonds and are emancipated wherever you go—this is becoming one with Avalokiteshvara. Together these three are both hosts and compan-

[4] An allusion to the six different kinds of shakings of the universe when the Buddha entered into the samādhi of "joyful wandering."

ions, and when they appear they appear together and at the same time. The one is at once the three and the three at once the one. If you understand this, then for the first time you will be qualified to read the sūtras."

The Master addressed the assembly: "Students today must have faith in themselves and must not seek things on the outside. Don't take what someone else has said and on the basis of it make judgments on what is false and what is true. Even if they be [the sayings of] patriarchs and Buddhas, they are no more than written traces. Some people fasten on to some phrase of the past, or fixing on something with both an obvious and a hidden meaning, allow doubts to arise and then, staggering in surprise, rush madly about asking questions, and end up completely confused.

"Resolute fellows, do not spend your days in idle talk, arguing with a one-track mind about landowner and thief, good and bad, sensual pleasures and alms-giving. Here I make no distinction between monk and layman. Just let anyone at all come and I will discern him at once. No matter from where he comes, any words he may have to say will be nothing but a dream and an illusion.

"On the other hand, when I see a person who has reached a state of understanding, I see the mysterious principle of the many Buddhas. The state of the Buddhas cannot of itself proclaim: 'I am the state of the Buddhas.' The follower of the Way, dependent on nothing, comes forth himself, resplendent in the state of his understanding. If someone comes forward and asks me about seeking the Buddha, I meet him on the basis of the state of purity. If someone comes forward and asks me about the bodhisattva, I meet him on the basis of the state of compassion. If someone comes forward and asks me about bodhi, I meet him on the basis of the state of purity and mystery. If someone comes forward and asks me about Nirvāna, I meet him on the basis of the state of calmness and quiet. Although there are countless differentiations in the states, men themselves are not different. Therefore it is said: 'The form appears in accordance with the thing, just as the moon in the water.' [5]

"Followers of the Way, if you wish to attain what is truly

---

[5] Quotation from the *Sūtra of the Golden Light*.

so you must be resolute, and then for the first time you can attain it. If you vacillate you will gain nothing. A cracked jar won't do for storing ghee. A person of great capacity is not deluded by other men. If he makes himself master in all circumstances, then any place he stands will be the true one. No matter who comes along, do not accept anything [that he says]. An instant of doubt on your part and a demon will steal into your mind, just as doubt on the part of even a bodhisattva will give an opening to the demon of birth and death. Just stop your thoughts and do not seek things on the outside! Penetrate whatever comes before you! Have faith in your own activity right now; there is no other thing. An instant of thought in your mind produces the three worlds, and circumstances serve to obscure the environment and turn into the six dusts.[6] What are you lacking in your immediate functioning at this very moment? In one instant you enter into purity, enter into defilement, enter the palace of Maitreya, enter the three-faceted world,[7] and everywhere you travel you see that all things are nothing but empty names."

[From Lin-chi Hui-chao ch'an-shih yü-lu, in Taishō daizōkyō, XLVII, 498a–499a]

Anecdotes of the Master Ts'ao-shan

Pen-chi (840–901), more commonly known as Ts'ao-shan, the name of the mountain on which he lived, was one of the many T'ang Ch'an Masters whose sayings and stories were recorded by his disciples and preserved over the years in manuscript or in printed books. Stories of these Masters were gathered together in the great compilation Ching-te ch'uan-teng lu, or Records of the Transmission of the Lamp (1004). Ts'ao-shan is generally associated with the Ts'ao-tung sect (Sōtō in Japanese), and one theory holds that the name of the sect is derived from a combination of the names of the mountains on which he and his teacher Tung-shan lived. It is more likely, however, that the "Ts'ao" of Ts'ao-tung stems from Ts'ao-ch'i, the name of the temple at which Hui-neng, the Sixth Patriarch, served. Ts'ao-shan's line became extinct in the eleventh century, and it was not until the Ming period that his Recorded Sayings appeared in a collection of works by famous monks, and not until 1741 that they first were published as an independent work,

---

[6] Sight, sound, smell, taste, touch, and idea.
[7] Reference is to a passage in the Flower Garland Sūtra.

and this in Japan. The text, other than the brief biographical information, contains short paradoxical stories concerning the Master, which indicate to the initiate the depth of his understanding of Ch'an. In later centuries stories such as these came to be used as "public cases" (kōan), subjects for meditation by Ch'an students. Unsolvable by ordinary rational thinking, they require that the practicer abandon his usual thought processes in order to arrive at a solution acceptable to his mentor.

BIOGRAPHY OF TS'AO-SHAN

The Master Pen-chi of Mt. Ts'ao in Fu-chou was a native of P'u-t'ien in Ch'üan-chou. His family name was Huang. While young he was interested in Confucianism, but at nineteen he left his home to become a monk, entering the temple at Mt. Ling-shih in Fu-t'ang hsien in Fu-chou, where at twenty-five he took the precepts. In the early years of the Hsien-t'ung era (860–872) the Ch'an sect flourished greatly and just at this time the Master [Liang]-chieh (807–869) was in charge of the monastery at Tung-shan. Pen-chi went there to request instruction of him.

Tung shan asked: "What's your name, monk?"

"Pen-chi."

Tung-shan said: "Say something more."

"I won't."

"Why not?"

"My name is not Pen-chi."

Tung-shan was much impressed with his potential, allowed him entry to his quarters and in secret gave sanction to his understanding. After staying there for several years he took his leave of Tung-shan.

Tung-shan asked: "Where are you going?"

Pen-chi answered: "I'm going to a changeless place."

Tung-shan said: "If there's a changeless place you won't be going there."

Pen-chi replied: "Going is also changeless."

Then he said goodbye and left, wandering about and doing as he pleased. At first he was asked to stay at Mt. Ts'ao in Fu-chou and later he lived at Mt. Ho-yü. At both places students flocked to him in great numbers.

Someone asked: "What sort of person is he who is not a companion to the ten thousand dharmas?"

The Master said: "You tell me! Where have all the people in Hung-chou gone?"

Someone asked: "Do the eye and the eyebrow know each other?"

The Master said: "No, they don't."

"Why not?" he asked.

The Master said: "Because they are in the same place."

"In that case they can't be told apart," he said.

The Master replied: "Yet the eyebrow is not the eye."

"What about the eye?" he asked.

The Master said: "It goes straight to the point."

"What about the eyebrow?" he asked.

The Master said: "I have my doubts."

"Why do you have doubts?" he asked.

The Master said: "If I didn't have doubts then it would go straight to the point."

Someone asked: "In phenomena what is true?"

The Master said: "The very phenomena are themselves truth."

"Then how should it be revealed?" he asked.

The Master lifted the tea tray.

Someone asked: "In illusion what is true?"

The Master said: "Illusion is from the outset true."

"In illusion what is manifested?" he asked.

The Master said: "The very illusion is itself manifestation."

"If this is so then one can never be apart from illusion," he said.

The Master replied: "No matter how you seek illusion you won't find it."

Someone asked: "What about a person who is always present?"

The Master said: "He met me just now and has gone out."

"What about a person who is never present?" he asked.

The Master said: "It is difficult to find such a person."

A monk called Ch'ing-jui said: "I am alone and poor; I beg of you to help me."

The Master said: "Monk Jui, come close." When he approached the Master added: "You've had three cups of wine at Po's house in Ch'üan-chou and yet you say that your lips are still dry."

Someone asked: "If you form an idea [about It], it's only a mere resemblance, isn't it?"

The Master said: "Even if you don't form an idea, it's still a mere resemblance."

"How do these differ?" he asked.

The Master said: "You're a man who doesn't feel pain and itching, aren't you?"

Ching-ch'ing asked: "What is the principle of pure emptiness when the time comes that the body no longer exists?"

The Master said: "The principle is just like this. What about things then?"

Ching-ch'ing said: "Like principle as it is; also like things as they are."

The Master said: "It's all right to trick me, but what are you going to do about the eyes of all the sages?"

Ching-ch'ing said: "If the eyes of the sages don't exist, how is it possible to tell that it's not like this?"

The Master said: "Officially a needle is not allowed through, but horses and carriages enter by the back door."

Yün-wen asked: "If a person who doesn't change himself should come would you receive him?"

The Master said: "I haven't got time to waste with such business."

Someone asked: "A man of old has said: 'Men all have it,' but I'm covered with the dusts of the world and wonder whether I do or not."

The Master said: "Show me your hand." Then he pointed to the man's fingers: "One, two, three, four, five. Enough!"

Someone asked: "The patriarch Lu sat facing the wall. What was he trying to show?"

The Master covered his ears with his hands.

Someone asked: "I have heard that there is an old saying: 'It has never happened that someone falling to the ground doesn't rise up from the ground.' What is 'falling?' "

The Master said: "If you know [that you've fallen], it's all right."

"What is rising?" he asked.

The Master said: "You've risen."

Someone asked: "I've heard that the teachings (*Nirvāna Sūtra*) say: 'The great sea does not harbor a corpse.' What is the 'sea?' "

The Master said: "It includes the whole universe."

He asked: "Then why doesn't it harbor a corpse?"

The Master said: "It doesn't let one whose breath has been cut off stay."

The man asked: "Since it includes the whole universe, why doesn't it let one whose breath has been cut off stay?"

The Master said: "In the whole universe there is no virtue; if the breath is cut off there is virtue."

He asked: "Is there anything more?"

The Master said: "You can say there is or there isn't, but what are you going to do about the dragon king who holds the sword?"

Someone asked: "With what sort of understanding should one be equipped to satisfactorily cope with the cross-examinations of others?"

The Master said: "Don't use words and phrases."

"Then what are you going to cross-examine about?"

The Master said: "Even the sword and ax cannot pierce it through!"

He said: "What a fine cross-examination! But aren't there people who don't agree?"

The Master said: "There are."

"Who?" he asked.

The Master said: "Me."

Someone asked: "Without words how can things be expressed?"

The Master said: "Don't express them here."

"Where can they be expressed?" he asked.

The Master said: "Last night at midnight I lost three coins by my bed."

Someone asked: "What about when the sun has yet to rise?"

The Master said: "I've also been like that."

"What about when the sun has risen?" he asked.

The Master said: "The sun is about half a month behind me."

The Master asked a monk: "What are you doing?"

"I'm sweeping," he replied.

The Master asked: "Are you sweeping in front of the Buddha image or behind it?"

"Both at the same time," the monk answered.

The Master said: "Bring me my sandals."

The Master asked the head monk Ch'iang-te: "In what sūtra do we find the story about the bodhisattva who, while in samādhi, heard Gandhahastī crossing the river?"

The monk said: "The *Nirvāna Sūtra.*"

The Master asked: "Did he hear him before entering samādhi or after?"

The monk said: "You are carried away by the stream."

The Master said: "You're very eloquent, but you've only been able to say half of it."

The monk asked: "How about you?"

The Master said: "I'll go to meet him (Gandhahastī) at the river shoal."

Someone asked: "How should I take charge [of It] all day long?"

The Master said: "When passing through a village where there's an epidemic, don't let even a single drop of water touch you."

Someone asked: "What is the master of the Body of Essence?"

The Master said: "They say: 'There are no people in Ch'in.' " [1]

The monk said: "You're talking about the Master of the Body of Essence, aren't you?"

The Master said: "Kill!"

Someone asked: "With what sort of person should one associate in order always to hear the unheard?"

The Master said: "Sleep under the same canopy."

He said: "But that way it's still you who can hear it. How can I always hear the unheard?"

The Master said: "By not being the same as trees and rocks."

"Which comes before and which afterwards?" he asked.

The Master said: "Haven't you ever heard the saying: 'Always to hear the unheard?' "

Someone asked: "Who is he in this nation who is putting his hand to the hilt of his sword?"

"Me!" said the Master.

"Whom are you trying to kill?" he asked.

The Master said: "Everyone in the world."

He asked: "What would you do if you met your original father and mother?"

The Master said: "What is there to choose?"

He said: "What are you going to do about yourself?"

The Master said: "Who can do anything about me?"

"Why don't you kill yourself?" he asked.

"No place to lay hold of," the Master said.

Someone asked: "What about: 'When the ox drinks water and the five horses do not neigh?' " [2]

The Master said: "I can abstain from harmful foods." On another occasion he answered the same question with: "I've just come out of mourning."

Someone asked: "What sort of people are those who are always sinking in the sea of birth and death?"

[1] Reference is to a passage in a story in the *Tso chuan*, Wen 13.
[2] The ox is the mind; the horses the five sense organs.

The Master said: "The second month."

He asked: "Do they try to escape?"

The Master said: "Even if they try to escape there is still no way out."

He asked: "If they do escape, what sort of people would receive them?"

The Master said: "Prisoners in cangues."

A monk brought up the story: "Yüeh-shan (751–834) asked a monk: 'How old are you?' The monk said: 'Seventy-two.' Yüeh-shan asked: 'Is this seventy-two years?' When the monk said 'Yes,' Yüeh-shan hit him. What does this story mean?"

The Master said: "The first arrow may not be so bad, but the second one pierced the man deeply."

The monk asked: "Was there any way to escape the stick?"

The Master said: "When the king's edict is in force all the feudal lords yield the way."

Someone asked: "What is the essential meaning of Buddhism?"

The Master said: "[Countless dead bodies] fill all the chasms and valleys." [3]

Someone asked: "What is the lion?"

The Master said: "The other animals cannot come near him."

He asked: "What is the lion cub?"

The Master said: "It devours its father and mother."

He asked: "Since other animals can't come near, how is it that they are eaten by the lion cub?"

The Master said: "When the cub roars the father and mother[4] are both destroyed."

He asked: "How about the grandfather and grandmother? Are they destroyed too?"

"They too," the Master said.

He asked: "What about after they are destroyed?"

[3] The extinction of mankind.

[4] The text reads: "Grandfather and grandmother," but it is probable that the "grand" is an extraneous character.

The Master said: "The whole body returns to the father."

He said: "Why did you say just now that the grandfather and grandmother are also destroyed?"

The Master said: "Haven't you ever heard that even a prince can govern a country well and that one can pick some flowers even from a withered tree?"

Someone asked: "What do you think about: 'The moment discrimination arises, one becomes confused and loses one's mind?' " [5]

The Master said: "Kill, kill!"

A monk brought up the story: "Someone asked Hsiang-yen: 'What is the Way?' and Hsiang-yen answered: 'A dragon's song from a withered tree.' This person then said: 'I don't understand,' and Hsiang-yen replied: 'An eye in the skull.' The same person later asked Shih-shuang: 'What is a dragon's song from a withered tree?' and Shih-shuang replied: 'There's still some joy remaining.' Then he asked: 'What is an eye in the skull?' and Shih-shuang replied, 'There's still some consciousness remaining.' "

The Master then responded with a verse:

A dragon's song from a withered tree—this is truly seeing the Way.

No consciousness in the skull—now for the first time the eye is clear.

Yet when joy and consciousness are exhausted, they still do not completely disappear;

How can that person distinguish purity amidst the turbid?

The monk then asked the Master: "What about 'a dragon's song from a withered tree?' "

The Master said: "The blood vessel is not cut off."

The monk asked: "What about 'an eye in the skull?' "

The Master said: "It can't be completely dried up."

The monk said: "I don't know whether there is somebody who can hear?"

[5] Quotation from the *Hsin-hsin ming*.

The Master said: "In the great earth there is not a single person who has not heard."

The monk said: "Then what kind of a phrase is 'a dragon's song from a withered tree?' "

The Master said: "I don't know what phrase this is, but [I do know that] all who hear are doomed."

Although the Master furthered the development of those of superior capacity, he did not leave any pattern by which he could be traced. After he was examined by Tung-shan's Five Ranks[6] [and passed it], he was esteemed as an authority throughout the Ch'an world. At one time Mr. Chung of Hung-chou repeatedly urged him [to preach in public], but he declined. In return he copied a verse on the secluded life in the mountains composed by the Master Ta-mei (752– 839) and sent it to him. One night in late summer of the first year of Tien-fu (901) he asked a senior monk: "What's the date today?"

The monk answered: "The fifteenth day of the sixth month."

The Master said: "I've spent my whole life going on pilgrimages [from one Ch'an temple to another], but every place I came to I limited my meditation sessions to the ninety days." Next day at the hour of the dragon he passed away.

He was sixty-two years of age and had been a monk for thirty-seven years. His disciples erected a pagoda for him and installed his bones within it. The Imperial Court bestowed on him the posthumous title Yüan-cheng ta-shih and on his pagoda the name Fu-yüan.

[From Ching-te ch'uan-teng lu, in Taishō daizōkyō, LI, 336–337]

CONCLUSION: THE FATE OF BUDDHISM

In the preceding chapters we have seen how Buddhism underwent a significant development in China, adapting itself

---

[6] A dialectic doctrine, devised by Tung-shan and perfected by Ts'ao-shan, in explanation of the identity of the relative and the Absolute. It is greatly influenced by the Book of Changes.

to native attitudes so as to emphasize those aspects of the two traditions most congenial to each other. Perhaps the most striking evidence of this comes in the tendency to accentuate the positive, to reassert the fundamental affirmation of life and acceptance of this world which, as we noted earlier, was so characteristic of the Chinese tradition. Thus in the philosophical schools most influential in China we found the absolute negation of reality balanced by its absolute affirmation, as in the T'ien-t'ai and Hua-yen philosophies. In the more devotional Buddhism we found Amitābha worshiped as the personification of limitless life and light, presiding over a Pure Land paradise in the west vividly pictured as the "land of peace and happiness," in concrete terms that appealed to the realistic religious imagination of the ordinary Chinese. Where "birth" and "rebirth" in original Buddhism had connoted only suffering through endless cycles of transmigration, in Pure Land Buddhism the painful associations were gone when "rebirth" meant, for the faithful believer in Amitābha, to be reborn in his "happy land." Finally, in Ch'an Buddhism we find a simple acceptance of man and of life just as they are. The instantaneous realization of Buddhahood as identical with one's actual nature reflects the Chinese confidence in life and man's innate potentialities for good. In these respects, then, Buddhism acquired a characteristic flavor and coloration in China.

We may ask the further question, however: to what extent did this adaptation to Chinese traditions make Buddhism itself acceptably Chinese? To what extent was Buddhism itself assimilated or absorbed into the Chinese tradition? Only partial and tentative answers to these broad questions may be offered here.

One relevant fact is that Buddhism survived in China without completely surrendering its identity, without being so totally absorbed that it became indistinguishable from the mass of Chinese popular religions. Buddhist elements did indeed diffuse into this heterogeneous mass and thus became virtually lost in a mixture more recognizably Chinese than Buddhist. But Buddhism itself maintained an independent existence down to modern times in the form given to it by the Ch'an school, which in the Sung period and after became predominant over all the other schools. It may be difficult to judge how far the temples and monasteries which identified themselves with Ch'an Buddhism lived up to the standards set in the earlier period; no doubt the tendency toward syncretism prevailed to greater or lesser degree in many of these establishments, and discipline may often have been lax. Nevertheless certain Buddhist traditions sharply at variance with deep-rooted Chinese attitudes persisted, among them vegetarianism, abstinence from liquor, and monastic celibacy.

In Japan, although organizationally and culturally speaking Buddhism remained a more significant part of national life, orthodoxy in such matters was more loosely adhered to or else totally abandoned. The persistence of celibacy in China is especially striking. Long after it had yielded to the family system in Japan, through the adoption of a married clergy and hereditary succession of religious authority, celibacy continued to be the rule for the Chinese clergy. Significantly, Chinese monks adopted the first syllable of the Buddha's name, Shākyamuni, as their "family" name, thus revealing their powerful instinct for some kind of family association, but it was the name they changed rather than the form.

Another relevant fact is that, although sustaining an independent life, Buddhism went into serious and steady decline from the late T'ang dynasty (tenth century A.D.) onwards. In the succeeding Sung dynasty Ch'an Buddhism was still a vital cultural force, particularly in literature and the arts, and this influence dwindled only gradually in later centuries. Nevertheless, from the Sung onward a Confucian revival wrested the intellectual initiative from Buddhism, strengthened its hold on the political establishment, and became the dominant ideological factor in Chinese society and culture. Buddhism was relegated to a less conspicuous place in the national life—a refuge for the dissenter and the disillusioned, a service for the deceased and bereaved.

Just why Buddhism should have fallen to this low estate is less clear than the fact that it did. What was it about Buddhism that, in spite of the adaptations already made to Chinese tradition, eventually disqualified it from the allegiance of most educated Chinese? What prevented Buddhism from finding a secure place within the dominant thought tradition of China? Can we discern here not so much alleged weaknesses of Buddhism as characteristic differences or even limitations in both Buddhism and Chinese tradition? These are large questions, and any adequate treatment of them would cover the whole spectrum of Chinese social and cultural life in the later dynasties. Our discussion here must be confined to the narrower ground of the reactions to Buddhism in Neo-Confucianism, the ideology of the educated elite.

The debt of Neo-Confucianism to Buddhism is already well recognized, not only by modern scholars judging from a greater distance and with greater detachment, but even by later Confucianists of the seventeenth and eighteenth century who deplored the unconscious but—as they saw it—insidious influence of Buddhism on their Neo-Confucian predecessors. This debt is of two types: first, the concepts and terminology appropriated from earlier philosophic discussions of the Chinese Buddhists; and second, the benefit deriving from the response Neo-Confucianists were forced to make to the challenge of Buddhist metaphysics, which extended them well beyond the limits of classical philosophical discussion and compelled them to seek higher ground from which to defend tradition.

To defend tradition, however, was their conscious aim, not to synthesize Confucianism with Buddhism and Taoism. The basic tendencies and impulses of the Neo-Confucian revival in the Sung reflected a belief in certain fundamental ideas: the ethical precepts founded on the primary human relationships and obligations; the world-view which saw these precepts as integral with an immutable cosmic order, both rational and moral in character; the possibility of reforming human society in accordance with this rational and moral order; and the conviction that the study of history, both for its moral lessons and for what it reveals of the development of human institutions, could serve as a guide to the conduct of life and government.

With all of these values most Neo-Confucianists considered Buddhism incompatible. There was a small, but not insignificant, minority in the period of Neo-Confucian ascendancy who expressed a belief in the compatibility, the "oneness" of the "Three Teachings" (Confucianism, Taoism, and Buddhism). The idea that these several teachings all lead to one ultimate Truth is a commonplace also in Chinese popular religion. But such eclecticism never succeeded in formulating a view of the complementarity of these teachings in which each was recognizable to itself. Those flexible enough in their interpretation of Confucianism to find in it much convergence with Buddhism soon lost their credentials as orthodox Confucianists.

On the other side, Neo-Confucianists outspoken in condemning Buddhism rarely showed a comprehensive or profound knowledge of Buddhist teachings. Their new metaphysics may have served as an answer to the challenge of Buddhism, but it is not the product of a direct philosophical dialogue between the two. Much less does it provide a philosophical synthesis based on a genuine desire to assimilate Buddhism. Although many Neo-Confucians had some exposure to Buddhism and some actually studied it, few were sufficiently well versed in the doctrine and its literature to discuss key points with any precision. Probably the typical Neo-Confucian attitude is expressed by the Sung philosopher Ch'eng Yi, who advised his followers: "You must simply put it [Buddhism] aside without discussing it; do not say 'We must see what it is like,' for if you see what it is like you will yourselves be changed into Buddhists. The essential thing is decisively to reject its arts." Or again: "If you make a complete investigation of Buddhist doctrines sorting out the good from the bad, before you have finished you will certainly have changed into a Buddhist. Only judge them by their practice; their practical teaching being what it is, what can their idea be worth?" [1]

The Neo-Confucian rejection of Buddhism, then, starts from a practical judgment that Buddhism is incompatible with the Chinese way of life and proceeds to a defense of what it considers most essential to that way of life. Of the two major criticisms which it makes of Buddhism, one, that Buddhism is life-denying while the Chinese Way is life-affirming, bespeaks not merely a Confucian but more broadly a Chinese attitude. To cite Ch'eng Yi again, "Man is a living thing;

[1] *Cf.* A. C. Graham, *Two Chinese Philosophers*, London 1958, pp. 84, 88.

the Buddhists speak not of life but of death. Human affairs are all visible; the Buddhists speak not of the manifest but of the hidden. After a man dies he is called a ghost; the Buddhists speak not of men but of ghosts. What man cannot avoid is the ordinary Way; the Buddhists speak not of the ordinary but of the marvelous. That by which the ordinary is as it is is principle; the Buddhists speak not of principle but of illusion. It is to what follows birth and precedes death that we should devote our minds; the Buddhists speak not of this life but of past and future lives. Seeing and hearing, thought and discussion are real evidence; the Buddhists do not treat them as real, but speak of what the ear and eye cannot attain, thought and discussion cannot reach." [2]

These charges, which are echoed by later Neo-Confucianists, reaffirm the centrality of "this" life and "this" world in the sense we have understood them in earlier Chinese tradition, while Buddhism is considered to deprecate life in this world especially through its attack on the senses and sense experience. The Buddhists do not "speak of what is manifest" to the senses; they do not regard "seeing, hearing and thought as real"; they seek what is "beyond the ordinary life" and faculties of man. One may question whether this characterization is as true of the more developed forms of Buddhism, particularly Ch'an Buddhism, in which the Chinese feeling for life has been assimilated. How for instance do we reconcile such a charge with the statement of the Ch'an master Lin-chi (I-hsüan, d. 867): "Followers of the Way, the Law of Buddha has no room for elaborate activity; it is only everyday life with nothing to do. Evacuate, pass your water, put on your clothes, eat your food; if you are tired lie down."

The explanation for this apparent discrepancy is to be found perhaps in the broader context of Lin-chi's statement, which suggests the acceptance of ordinary life on the simultaneous condition that one recognize its "emptiness." Thus, in the same sermon he admonishes: "Followers of the Way, do not acknowledge this dream-like, illusory world, for sooner or later death will come. Just what is it that you are seeking in this world that you think will give you emancipation? Go

[2] *Ibid.*, p. 85.

out into the world, and seeking only the barest minimum of food, make do with it; spend your time in the shabbiest of garments and go to visit a good teacher." From this we see that the significance of this world derives solely from the freedom one achieves over it. This life is real only insofar as one also recognizes it to be illusory and identifies Saṃsāra (the transmigratory world) with Nirvāna.

We are reminded in this way that Ch'an is still Buddhist and that behind every Mahāyāna affirmation stands either Mādhyamika skepticism or Hīnayāna pessimism. Similarly, the great meditation on concentration and insight in T'ien-t'ai Buddhism involves contemplation of the emptiness of things and the contamination of the senses, through the so-called Ten Objects of Contemplation. Starting with the various components of the empirical self and its environment, this contemplation rises through the cravings, passions, af-flictions, distractions, hallucinations and delusions which are hindrances to emancipation until it passes beyond the dan-gers even of the boddhisattva state to attain Buddhahood.

Finally, in the cult of Amitābha we find a stark contrast between life's perilous sea, pictured in the darkest, most ter-rifying terms, and the positive goal of peace, bliss and limit-less life beckoning from the "other shore." Here, truly, is an other-worldly refuge from "this" world seen as a flaming sea of passion, delusion and suffering. Shan-tao, explaining the human predicament in his parable of the White Path, shows man beset on all sides by evil beasts, poisonous vermin and vicious ruffians, symbolizing the sense organs, the conscious-nesses, and the various psychic and physical constituents of the ordinary human self. The white path is "comparable to the pure aspiration for rebirth in the Pure Land which arises in the midst of the passions of greed and anger."

From this we may conclude that even in the most "Chi-nese" of the Mahāyāna schools there was still enough of Buddhist pessimism regarding the human condition to ren-der plausible, though not necessarily to prove, the Neo-Con-fucian view that Buddhism held to a morbid view of life. Parenthetically, we may wonder how the Neo-Confucianists, for their part, could have been so immune to tragedy and suffering as not to feel more poignantly what the Buddhists sensed so deeply; but this fact only underscores the stubborn optimism of the native intellectual tradition.

The second charge against Buddhism, and probably the most crucial, is that it is an inherently "selfish" approach to life. Almost every generation and school of Neo-Confucianism has turned in this same indictment. Ch'eng Yi says:

> You cannot say that the teachings of the Buddhists are ignorant, for actually they are quite profound. But essentially speaking, they can finally be reduced to a pattern of selfishness. Why do we say this? In the world there cannot be birth without death or joy without sorrow. But wherever the Buddhists go, they always want to pervert this truth and preach the elimination of birth and death and the neutralization of joy and sorrow. In the final analysis this is nothing but self-interest.[3]

Lu Chiu-yüan (Lu Hsiang-shan 1139–93), whose School of the Mind is often spoken of as influenced by Buddhism, unequivocally supports the idea that the "selfishness" of Buddhism derives from its escapist view of human life. "They consider life to be extremely painful, and so inquire how to escape from it . . . Therefore they say 'Birth and death are a great matter.' And as for what you have spoken of as 'the development of the Mind of the Boddhisattva,' it is directed solely toward this one great matter [of birth and death]. The teachings of Buddhism are established in accordance with this; that is why it is spoken of as selfish and concerned with gain. Being righteous and unselfish, Confucianism deals with the world; being selfish and concerned with gain, Buddhism withdraws from the world. The Buddhists, even when they strive to ferry souls across the sea of suffering, always aim at withdrawing from the world." [4]

There is no need to proliferate examples of this point of view, which may be found equally in the writings of the

---

[3] Cf. W. T. de Bary, W. T. Ch'an and B. Watson (ed.), Sources of Chinese Tradition, New York 1960, p. 533.

[4] Cf. Hsiang-shan hsien-shen ch'üan-chi (SPTK), 2/2ab Letter to Wang Shun-po, translation adapted from Siu-chi Huang, Lu Hsiang-shan, New Haven 1944, p. 154, and Fung Yu-lan, A History of Chinese Philosophy, Princeton 1953, Vol. II, p. 578.

great Chu Hsi (1130–1200), his most important latter-day critic, Wang Yang-ming (1472–1529) and many others. It is a charge which touches at the heart of Buddhism—at the Hīnayāna, for which selflessness had been the supreme ideal of personal virtue; and at the Mahāyāna, which, having itself accused the Hīnayāna of a selfish preoccupation with individual salvation, set forth the ideal of the compassionate boddhisattva who seeks to save all beings. It is the boddhisattva that answers to Lu's description of one who "strives to ferry souls across the sea of suffering." How then is he to be considered selfish? The boddhisattva, having attained enlightenment and the right to Nirvāna, nevertheless foregoes the reward of his own meritorious efforts in order to make the "great return" to the *samsāra* world and voluntarily take upon himself the sufferings of others. How is he accused of an escapist "withdrawal from the world"?

Here the discrepancy between the Confucian and Buddhist views on the question of "selfishness" may be clarified—though probably not resolved—by considering the meaning of "self" in each. For the Confucianist "cultivation of self" (*hsiu-shen*) was a basic ideal in life. As set forth in the so-called *Four Books*, especially the *Great Learning*, it meant development of the individual's total personality, with equal emphasis on his physical growth, intellectual attainment, moral training and aesthetic refinement. The ideal of self-renunciation, so strong in Indian religions, had no place here. For according to the strongly ethical view of man in Confucianism, his nature and personality were defined very largely (though not exclusively) in terms of his natural social relationships. Fulfilling his inescapable obligations to his parents, his family, his teacher and his ruler, the individual subordinated to them his personal selfish desires—but never his personality. Rather such discipline constituted the essential and natural means of developing his "self" or "person." Selfishness only became a problem if the individual attempted to renounce these obligations and egotistically thought of his own self as independent of the familial, social and political relations that in fact sustained human life (his own as well as others).

Buddhism in China challenged this whole system of values from the outset, not out of any special disrespect for family and society but out of a primary insistence on the individual's freeing himself from any attachment to or dependence upon externals which would prevent realization of his true nature or self. However, this unconditional drive for the attainment of the unconditioned state allowed for no more definition of the "self" or "one's nature" than was discovered in the final intuition of "Enlightenment" or "Buddhahood." This was an insight that transcended all logical categories or moral judgments. It passed beyond the realm of "good and evil."

Again, we need not look further than the texts and teachers already cited for confirmation of this view and illustration of its seeming "selfishness" in Confucian terms. The aforementioned meditation text of the third century A.D., strongly Hīnayānist in flavor, speaks of the second stage of trance as no longer requiring one "to advance good in order to reduce evil. When the two thoughts of delight and good are both themselves extinguished, the ten evils vanish like smoke." Much later the Ch'an Master Lin-chi, who explains the significance of "true monks who have left their homes" (a conventional term for the Buddhist who has cut his attachments to the world in general but also more pointedly to his family) identifies his ultimate goals as follows: "If you wish to attain freedom in moving through the world of birth and death, then know the man who right now is listening to the Law. He is without shape, without characteristics, without root, without basis, yet always brisk and lively. There is no trace of the activity of all his many devices. If you try to find him he is far away; if you seek him he goes against you. Given a name this is a mystery." [5]

It is not difficult to see how such language as this would appear to corroborate the assertions of Neo-Confucianists that Buddhism was "directed solely to the one great matter of birth and death," that it spoke "not of what is manifest but of what is hidden . . . not of the ordinary but of the marvelous." And had they read Shan-tao's parable, how must they have reacted to his equation of human greed with human affection, likening these to two great rivers of fire and water which threaten to engulf man? The Confucianist, no less than the Buddhist, disdained sensuality and sought to

[5] See p. 228.

restrain lust, but affection (*ai*, love) was another thing. The natural affections constituted the basis of human relations for him, and the perfection of virtue—humanity or benevolence—which Neo-Confucianists like Ch'eng Hao and Chu Hsi raised to the level of a cosmic principle, was often defined as "love" (*ai*).

If the boddhisattva transcended good and evil, human affections, and the natural obligations of human relationships, then in the eyes of the Confucianists his compassionate activity, "his ferrying of souls to the other shore," likewise must be understood as helping them to rise above rather than to face personal and social responsibilities. His function was to enlighten the deluded and free them from attachment, not to grapple with the problems of human society. Moreover it was a condition of his reentry into the world that he feel no obligation to help and no sense of attachment to those helped. Whether he served this or that good cause (in humanitarian terms) was ultimately a matter of indifference.

For the Confucianist an impersonal, intangible ideal of this sort could never substitute for the solid ground of moral principle as the basis for personal cultivation and social welfare. Wang Yang-ming says: "The Buddhist attaches himself to a state in which neither good nor evil exist,[6] and disregards all else, so that he is unable to deal with the world. Whereas in the case of the Confucian sage the absence of good and evil means simply that he neither acts because of personal likes nor acts because of personal dislikes. . . . To say of someone that he does not act according to likes and dislikes, means simply that in his likes and dislikes he wholly conforms to Principle. . . ." And conforming to Heavenly Principle, says Wang, "he can assist in its creative activities." [7]

For Wang and his fellow-Confucians there can in reality be no state beyond good and evil, because (as we have seen)

[6] Strictly speaking this misrepresents the Buddhist view, which insists upon non-attachment even to the state beyond good and evil. So strong, however, is the Confucian sense of moral choice and life commitment that it allows no middle ground here.

[7] *Cf.* Fung Yu-lan, *History of Chinese Philosophy* II, p. 617. Adapted from the translation of Derk Bodde.

the human order and cosmic order are truly one. Conforming himself to Heavenly Principle, and thus growing in accordance with the moral order uniting Heaven and man, the Sage achieves fulfillment in a creative process that is no less mystical for being practical. As Lu Hsiang-shan explains, man has his five senses precisely because they enable him to discern right and wrong, fulfill the Way of Man, and thus unite himself to Heaven-and-Earth. Given this faith in the perfectability of man in society, partaking in a cosmic harmony of life and love, it was difficult for the Confucianist to see the value of Emptiness and easy to believe that Buddhist wisdom or compassion had no place in his universe.

If from this point of view the Way of the Boddhisattva and the Confucian ideal of the Noble Man remained mutually exclusive, still this very incompatibility may suggest to us how and in what manner Buddhism could survive in the face of such hostility. Set apart from the dominant political and social ethic, it could provide for those whose experience of life did not confirm the lofty Confucian ideal, who could not be caught up in its Utopian vision or be sustained any longer by its optimistic view of human perfectability. These may not have been the majority, and yet in every age of later Chinese history there were some who found themselves overpowered by personal misfortune, by the evil and weakness in man, by the contradictions and frustrations of life in society, or by the oppressive weight of external sanctions which constantly threatened the delicate balance Confucius had struck between the respective claims of the individual and the group. For such as these—perhaps dedicated officials thwarted by tyranny and corruption in the government, perhaps sensitive souls recoiling from the grossness of human passions and ambitions, or perhaps parents from whom death had suddenly taken the son upon whom their hopes of posterity and security in old age depended—for these Buddhism provided an alternative outside the established forms of social organization which had become inhospitable or intolerable. Within this larger context of Chinese life then, Buddhism had indeed its own role, and while at odds with the dominant tradition, at the same time complemented it.

BUDDHISM IN *Japan*

8

THE INTRODUCTION OF BUDDHISM
TO JAPAN

INTRODUCTION

Throughout history the Japanese have been remarkable for their quickness in learning from others, and just as remarkable for their tenacity in holding on to what they have learned for themselves. They can be youthful and open to new experiences, while still clinging to ancient traditions; at once progressive and conservative, volatile and stable, naïve and sophisticated. And in the reception of Buddhism this same duality appears. Compared to the Chinese, the Japanese seem to have been more eager, open and wholehearted in taking up this foreign faith, more thorough in transforming and assimilating it, and more persistent in holding to it.

But Japan, when Buddhism came in the sixth century A.D., was young in more than spirit. Not only compared to China, but by any ordinary standard, her civilization was undeveloped. It lacked a written literature, historical records, codified laws, a tradition of philosophical discussion, and many of the arts and sciences associated with the classical civilizations of China, India, and the Near East. Native Shinto, with neither written scriptures nor a formulated theology, could offer resistance only from its entrenched position in the daily lives of the people, but could not compete with Buddhism on its own terms.

The latter, by contrast, was nearly a thousand years old

at the time of its introduction. As the first world religion, it had marched triumphantly to the east and west, raising temples and monasteries, and filling grottoes and caves with an amazing profusion of art. It had become a well-organized and tested faith constituted under its Three Treasures—the Buddha, the Law (Dharma), and the Monastic Orders (Sangha). It possessed a highly developed and decorated pantheon as its object of worship, a tremendous accumulation of literature in the Tripiṭaka, and a disciplined clergy dedicated to the propagation of the teachings by oaths of celibacy, sobriety, and poverty. Moreover, it had been greatly strengthened in both theory and practice by its experience in China, an experience of adaptation which anticipated many of the problems Buddhism would encounter in Japan.

The importance of Buddhist missionary activity in Japan went far beyond the propagation of the faith alone. Chinese and Korean monks, carried across stormy seas by religious zeal, at the same time served as the carriers of superior Chinese culture. They were no doubt well aware that identification or association with this high culture lent them great prestige in the eyes of admiring Japanese, but whether they chose to capitalize on this or not, it would in any case have been impossible to disengage this new religion from its cultural embodiment in China, the land of its adoption. To establish the new faith in Japan required the transplanting of essential articles—images, vestments, books, ritual devices —as well as of ideas. The Japanese apprenticeship in the study of Chinese writing was undoubtedly served in the copying by hand of large numbers of Buddhist sūtras, distributed by imperial order to the various temples and monasteries. Furthermore, to erect temples and monasteries, carpenters and artisans had to be brought over along with missionary priests. This is illustrated by an entry in the *Nihongi* for the reign of Sujun (c. 588):

This year the land of Paekche sent envoys, and along with them the Buddhist priests, Hyejong [and others] with a present of Buddhist relics. The land of Paekche sent the Buddhist ecclesiastics Susin [and others] with tribute and also with a present of Buddhist relics, the Buddhist priest Yongjo, the ascetics Yongwi [and others], the temple carpenters, Taeryangmidae and Mungagoja, a man learned in the art of making braziers and chargers . . . men learned in pottery . . . and a painter named Poega.[1]

But it is apparent, too, that Buddhist priests were vessels for the transmission of branches of learning having no direct connection with religious doctrine or institutions, yet which they evidently regarded as being in no way incompatible with the former. Thus during the tenth year of Suiko (602) it is recorded:

A Paekche priest named Kwallŭk arrived and presented by way of tribute books of calendar-making, of astronomy, and of geomancy, and also books on the art of invisibility and magic. At this time three or four pupils were selected and made to study under Kwallŭk. Ōchin, the ancestor of the scribes of Yako, studied the art of calendar-making. Kōsō, Otomo no Suguri, studied astronomy and the art of invisibility. Hinamitatsu, the Imperial Chieftain of Yamashiro, studied magic. They all studied so far as to perfect themselves in these arts.[2]

Thus Buddhism's penetration of Japan during these early centuries was facilitated by its identification with the impressive civilization of China. In its own right, however, Buddhism must have made a deep impression on the Japanese. Until this time their religion had been strongly centered on the world of nature and the spirits. It was an optimistic faith, almost naïvely optimistic in its celebration of life and its enjoyment of the beauties and bounty of nature. Sin, sickness, and death were hardly faced. They were the subject of taboos, not of discussion. Buddhism, for its part, may have seemed deeply pessimistic in its premise that to live is to suffer. But by insisting that suffering could be dealt with, since it is the consequence of thought and action which man can control, Buddhism helped the Japanese for the first time to face the darker side of things. Age-old fears gave way to a new confidence in man's ability to deal with sin and death. A new human ideal was held up for the nature- and spirit-worshiping Japanese. With a keener sense of moral responsibility and self-restraint went a growing sense of moral

[1] Aston, *Nihongi*, II, 117.
[2] Aston, *Nihongi*, II, 126.

power. New energies were summoned up by the call to a life
of discipline, self-mastery, and high aspiration. The life of
the spirit, aiming at liberation from the world, replaced the
life of the spirits and man's helpless dependence on nature
as the basis of religious thought and practice.

Two developments in art and architecture reflect this shift.
Prior to the introduction of Buddhism the greatest structures
produced by the Japanese were the enormous tomb mounds
in which their rulers were buried. Here were concentrated
all the wealth and power at his disposal, and all the goods
of this world which he might hope to take with him into
the next. Thus the tombs, like the pyramids of Egypt, were
huge earthly monuments to death, gateways to a gloomy sub-
terranean existence in the after-life. But with the spread of
Buddhism the construction of such tomb mounds on a mam-
moth scale virtually ceased. A more spiritual view of both life
and death rendered such provision for the departed irrelevant
and valueless. In their place rose the Buddhist temple with
its winged roofs and the pagoda with its soaring tower. The
spiritual treasures of the Buddha, the Law and the Monastic
Order provided for one alike in life and death.

The second development was the appearance of the Buddha figure in sculpture and painting. In Shinto the objects
of worship were unseen spirits or their manifestation in natural phenomena. Even living beings and historical figures,
when deified, lost their human qualities and assumed a supernatural aura. The sense of the divine in Shinto always partook of a sense of mystery. In the shrine the god-body lay
hidden in its sanctuary and even in public processions it was
shrouded with elaborate secrecy. In Buddhism the objects
of worship prominently displayed in temple halls were recognizably human—idealized perhaps, or highly stylized, but
not for the most part so endowed with superhuman features
or mystical symbolism as to obscure the basic human qualities of detachment, compassion, patience, courage, sublime
peace, and joy. They were, originally at least, public figures,
exhibited where all the faithful could be inspired by the lofty
virtues and ideals the Buddhas and Bodhisattvas embodied.
And there can be little doubt that this artistic revelation of
Buddhist truth, openly proclaimed as the expression of a universal—and therefore common, realizable—way of life, had

far more impact on the aesthetically minded Japanese than did many volumes of scripture.

THE VISION OF PRINCE SHŌTOKU

The first historical figure to exemplify the new Buddhist ideal was Prince Shōtoku (574–622), regent during the reign of his aunt Empress Suiko. Shōtoku played such an important role in the political and cultural revolution which took place in this period that he soon became a legend, the object of the hero-worshiping and deifying tendency so strong in the native religious tradition. It may be forever impossible to determine which of the accomplishments credited to him were actually his. Nevertheless, the significance of the changes he sponsored in Japanese life is clearly discernible, whatever his direct contribution to them may have been.

Shōtoku's historical task was to create a unified state out of an essentially tribal or clan society, divided by strong sectionalism and regionalism. His so-called "Seventeen Article Constitution" suggests the ideological basis on which such a universal state might be achieved. Fundamentally it is a Confucian document, but as nothing quite like it has appeared elsewhere in the Confucian world, no label does justice to its unique and unprecedented character. Fundamentally Confucian it is in placing almost no emphasis on the legal structure of government but trying instead to affirm the moral responsibilities of both rulers and ruled. Sovereignty derives from Heaven, symbolizing the natural, moral order. Individual and social morality likewise derive from Heaven, as shown in man's Heaven-bestowed nature, with its moral sense, and in the natural social relationships through which this sense is given expression. On these premises it is the purpose and function of the Constitution to establish a single hierarchy of authority, which will define the responsibilities and duties of all-under-Heaven, and which culminates in the Emperor, the Son of Heaven. It is, however, a hierarchy of mutual respect, based upon the ritual order ordained by Heaven to govern political life and social intercourse. Thus articles Three and Four of the Constitution read:

"III. When you receive the imperial commands, fail not scrupulously to obey them. The lord is Heaven, the vassal is Earth. Heaven overspreads, and Earth upbears. When this is so, the four seasons follow their due course, and the powers of Nature obtain their efficacy. If the Earth attempted to overspread, Heaven would simply fall in ruin. Therefore is it that when the lord speaks, the vassal listens; when the superior acts, the inferior yields compliance. Consequently when you receive the imperial commands, fail not to carry them out scrupulously. Let there be a want of care in this matter, and ruin is the natural consequence.

"IV. The ministers and functionaries should make decorous behavior their leading principle, for the leading principle of the government of the people consists in decorum. If the superiors do not behave with decorum, the inferiors are disorderly: if inferiors are wanting in proper behavior, there must necessarily be offenses. Therefore it is that when lord and vassal behave with decorum, the distinctions of rank are not confused: when the people behave with decorum, the government of the commonwealth proceeds of itself."

It is significant that Prince Shōtoku, a devout Buddhist, should have relied so heavily here on Confucian ethical and political philosophy. Buddhism could not help him in this. Though it offered a personal discipline leading to emancipation from the world, it had never provided the basis of a political and social order. Confucianism alone, of the teachings available to Shōtoku, dealt with this problem.

At the same time however, Shōtoku insisted that Buddhism was not wholly irrelevant to the problem either. In the second article of his Constitution he exhorts his people:

"Sincerely reverence the Three Treasures. They are the final refuge of the four generated beings and the supreme objects of faith in all countries. Few men are utterly bad. They may be taught to follow [Buddhism]. But if they do not betake themselves to the Three Treasures, wherewith shall their crookedness be made straight?" [1]

On the surface these statements hardly seem more than pious platitudes, and one might easily conclude that their real purpose is only to enlist the aid of religion in upholding public morality. Nevertheless, there is significance in Shōtoku's mention of the "final refuge of all beings." He acknowledges that the individual has an end which transcends his

[1] Adapted from Aston, *Nihongi*, II, 128.

role in the human community. And in saying that "few men are utterly bad," he also recognizes that a man's condemnation by human society or the state is not final. The rhetorical question with which he concludes also implies that the heart of man cannot be touched except by religion. The state would be powerless to "straighten" a man if religion could not reach the depths of his spirit and rectify his inner motivation.

While therefore Shōtoku is unable to establish the direct relevance of Buddhism to the new political order, it is important to him that the spiritual order should be affirmed along with the secular, lest the latter be taken as absolute. And in Article Ten we find further clues as to what he has in mind:

"Let us cease from wrath and refrain from angry looks. Nor let us be resentful when others differ from us. For all men have hearts and each heart has its own leanings. Their right is our wrong and our right is their wrong. We are not unquestionably sages, nor are they unquestionably fools. Both of us are simply ordinary men. How can any man lay down a rule by which to distinguish right from wrong? For we are all, one with another, wise and foolish, like a ring which has no end . . ." [2]

Clearly here Shōtoku disavows the claim to absolute authority which Chinese rulers customarily made for themselves. And this disavowal has special meaning in relation to the theory of sovereignty which Shōtoku had adopted from China, as elaborated especially in the Han dynasty. According to this view, Heaven, as exemplified by the regular procession of the heavenly bodies, represented an unvarying order which served as the norm for life on earth. The ruler, as Son of Heaven, established this model for men through his ordering of the ritual and through regulating his own conduct. It was for him to establish clear standards and a universal pattern for his subjects; it was for them to follow and be nourished by his paternal guidance, as the world of nature followed the sun and its seasons, which gave life to all things according to their natures.

From this standpoint for the Chinese ruler to talk as

[2] Adapted from Aston, *Nihongi*, II, 131.

Shōtoku does in Article Ten is unthinkable. It would be the height of irresponsibility and moral weakness. But with Shōtoku, though he too is inspired by this vision of a natural, hierarchical order as the model for human society, there is also a consciousness of the weakness and frailty of men which Han Confucian theorists could not acknowledge, given their faith in the moral order and man's capacity for fulfilling it. Shōtoku strives like them for the ideal, yet remains skeptical of its final achievement. Utopian visions do not blind him to the workings of human pride and passion in the ruler, no less than in other men. Such skepticism undoubtedly reflects a view of truth and an awareness of illusion strongly conditioned by Buddhism.

More particularly it suggests the influence of the Mādhyamika philosophy as taught in the Three Treatises school (Jap. Sanron). Another name for this school, it will be recalled, was the Way of Emptiness, from its characteristic teaching of Emptiness as the ultimate character of all things. Things are empty of any enduring selfhood or identity, because they are transitory and subject to change. Only Emptiness endures, is final and absolute. From this emphasis on universal change we may see how directly the Mādhyamika stands in opposition to the Han Confucian view of the universe as stable and orderly. Heaven could not be taken as the unvarying model for life on earth. It too was subject to change. The Way of Emptiness insisted on the need to free oneself from anything external, including such concepts as Heaven, in order to seek the ultimate, undifferentiated reality within. Externals are so changeable that they can only deceive. They must therefore be negated exhaustively until all the distinctions and concepts which arise from incomplete knowledge are destroyed and ultimate truth is intuitively realized.

We are left to wonder how Shōtoku reconciled two such diametrically opposed views in his own mind, and perhaps all we can say is that the answer must lie on the side of intuitive truth rather than in the domain of the demonstrable.

In characters woven into a tapestry by Lady Tachibana and preserved in Shōtoku's temple, the Hōryūji, the Mādhyamika philosophy is summed up: "The world is empty and false; only the Buddha is true." This was the teaching with which the Hōryūji was identified at its founding; three Korean monks of the Three Treatises school taught there. But the original name of the temple indicated a more positive aim than the doctrine of Emptiness alone would suggest. It was *Hōryū gakumon ji* or Temple of Learning for the Prospering of the Law. In contrast to the Shinto shrine, which was purely and simply a place of worship, this monastery was to be a center of learning. Its layout included a library, a lecture hall and a place of study or meditation. One could not quite compare it to the monasteries or universities of medieval Europe in the range or character of the studies conducted there, but the Hōryūji, and other institutions like it in Japan at that time, served some of the same function by spreading a higher culture in a comparatively uncivilized country.

There is also significance in the word "law" which appears in the name of this temple, as in several other temples of the period. Just as the Seventeen Article Constitution or "Exemplary Law" of Prince Shōtoku represented the universal law of the land in a secular sense, so the Hōryūji symbolized the universal spiritual law of Buddhism. Both were essential to Shōtoku's conception of the universal state he was building.

Traditional accounts state that the Prince's own studies of the Buddhist scriptures resulted in his writing commentaries on three major Buddhist texts, the *Lotus, Vimalakīrti,* and *Śrīmālā* sūtras. Whether he actually did write these commentaries has been disputed, but that is no great concern of ours. The fact that they were influential texts in Shōtoku's time and prominently identified with him is what matters. Reflected in them are the ideals and values gaining acceptance among the ruling class.

In the title of the *Lotus Sūtra*, "The Lotus of the Wonderful Law" we find repeated again the theme of law in the spiritual sense. Moreover the central teaching of the *Lotus* is universal salvation. Everyone and everything has within it the potentiality of Buddhahood. Every teaching, text and school finds in the *Lotus* the fulfillment of their promise of liberation from the world. One need only rely on the *Lotus*, have faith in it and spread that faith, to be assured of salvation. With this a new notion of individual worth and an egalitarian conception of a spiritual community were spread abroad, which could not but have revolutionary implications for the highly differentiated society of ancient Japan.

In the *Vimalakīrti Sūtra* (*Yuima kyō*) is found the story of the layman, Vimalakīrti, who remains a householder and yet attains the wisdom of a Bodhisattva, so that his virtue and knowledge exceed that of even those who leave the world to follow a strict religious life. It is not difficult to imagine Prince Shōtoku aspiring to a similar role as the enlightened statesman who remains in the world to fulfill his secular duties and at the same time fulfills the religious role of the Bodhisattva in helping others to salvation.

Finally there is the story of Shrīmālā, the virtuous queen who led a noble life and suffered much for the Buddhist Faith to gain the assurance of ultimate salvation. It is said that Shōtoku lectured to the Empress Suiko on this text, wearing the robes of a Buddhist monk. No doubt he hoped to inspire Suiko to take Queen Shrīmālā as her model.

Thus the three texts associated with Prince Shōtoku's name exemplify three ideals fostered by his new order, relating the doctrine of universal salvation to the life in society of both men and women. From this we may discern the lineaments of his total conception of the new life Japan was embarking on. The vision he had was not simply of men subordinating their private interests and local loyalties to the good of a unified state and a more integrated secular community. In serving the new political and social order they were also achieving their own individual salvation. The new society would be also a Buddha-land, in which rulers fostered their subjects' welfare both materially and spiritually.

If we may make a distinction from modern secular totalitarianism, which subordinates the individual to society and tends to see him as having no end other than service to the party or state, Shōtoku's new order might be described as totalistic. He asks men to subordinate individual interests to the general welfare, and politically he insists on the need for a single centralized state, but recognizing the ultimacy of individual salvation, he dedicates the state to the promotion of religion and thereby redeems the individual's contribution to society in spiritual benefits. Service to the state is service to the Buddha, and through the Buddha comes salvation for all.

There may be some question as to how fully realized all this was in Shōtoku's mind or how clearly articulated to his contemporaries, but the elements were all there and Japan's development in the succeeding two hundred years followed in general along these lines, though not always in perfect synchronization of the secular and religious. There are periods in which the development of the secular state and society takes precedence over the promotion of Buddhism, and vice versa. But for the most part the two grow side by side, and the history of Buddhism during this early period is closely linked to the support of the ruling class. Although Buddhism never comes forward with its own political philosophy or ideology, it is closely identified with the state by reason of its heavy dependence on Imperial protection and noble patronage. Much of Buddhist thought during the seventh and eighth centuries is preoccupied with the benefits to church and state of their mutual association.

BUDDHISM IN THE NARA PERIOD (EIGHTH CENTURY)

The principal Buddhist sects or schools of the seventh and eighth centuries A.D. were based on some of the most advanced teachings of Chinese Buddhism in the period just preceding. We have already observed in Shōtoku's time the influence of the Three Treatises school, which continued up to the Nara period (708–781). A teaching of this subtlety could not expect to obtain wide acceptance in Japan any more than in China, and it is difficult to see, from its very nature, how it might be the subject of further philosophical development. Though by no means un-philosophical itself, the Mādhyamika school was implicitly anti-philosophical. On the other hand, one should not underestimate its importance in preparing the ground for other teachings. Most other Mahāyāna schools, especially those emphasizing faith or intuition, took the ground cleared by Mādhyamika skepticism as their starting point.

At Hōryūji the Three Treatises school was eventually superseded by the Consciousness-only (Yuishiki) or Dharma-Character (Hossō) school, which flourished in the early

Nara period. In the long run, however, this rather complex system of subjective idealism did not prove congenial to Japanese tastes. It might be admired as a great achievement of the Indians and Chinese, but it did not enjoy sustained growth or significant development in Japanese hands. This was, nevertheless, an important phase of Japan's early education in Buddhism, and its structuring of the levels of consciousness was often referred to in later meditative practice.

The Flower Garland (Kegon) school came the closest to becoming the state ideology of the Nara period. It preached a cosmic harmony presided over by Lochana Buddha, who sits on a lotus throne of a thousand petals, each of which is a universe containing thousands of worlds like ours. Within the harmony of the Flower Garland all beings are interrelated and interdependent. Religious deliverance is attained through realization of this fundamental communion of all things in the Buddha. The world is potentially a Buddha-land, providing only that the ruler and his subjects join in making it so. Thus the cosmic harmony becomes the spiritual basis of the universal state, as the state becomes the material support of Kegon Buddhism.

It is highly problematical how much of these lofty and sometimes abstruse doctrines was understood by Japanese Buddhists of the Nara period. Expressions of religious fervor generally assumed a tangible form. The patronage of Buddhism by the court led to the building of the magnificent temples and monasteries of Nara, some of which still survive. Certain court ceremonies such as the open confession of sins (keka) show how the strong desire to lead a religious life permeated ruling circles. Buddhist influence led also to the making of highways and bridges, to the use of irrigation, and to exploration of distant parts of the country by itinerant monks (who drew the earliest Japanese maps). Such features of Japanese life as the public bath and cremation also date from Buddhist inspiration of this time.

The responsibilities of a ruler, and indeed the entire question of the relationship between the state and Buddhism, were most completely discussed in the Sūtra of the Golden Light. This masterpiece of Buddhist literature is a synthesis of the creative doctrines of Mahāyāna Buddhism, presented in a form aesthetically most appealing and impressive. It played a more important role than any other in establishing Buddhism as the religion of Japan, and its influence continued undiminished for centuries. It opens with an eloquent proclamation of the eternity of Buddha's life, and declares that he exists not only as a historical figure with a human form, but in the cosmos as the ultimate Law or Truth, and in the life hereafter as the savior possessed of an all-embracing love. Since Buddha is omnipresent, everything that exists is subject to his eternal vigilance of boundless compassion. The sūtra declares further that the gates of the Paradise of the Lotus where Buddha dwells are always open to all humanity, for anyone can become a Buddha. The methods the sūtra especially recommends for bringing about this change for the better are expiation and self-sacrifice; the climax of the entire narration is the parable of Buddha giving himself up to a hungry lion.

The central theme of the entire sūtra, however, is the virtue of wisdom—*prajñā*, which distinguishes good from evil and right from wrong. Everyone, from the king to his lowliest subject, must obey the dictates of the inner light of reason. The religious life starts with an awareness of one's sins and the desire to atone for them. It is wisdom which enables us to surmount these failings, and the highest expression of the triumph of wisdom is an act of self-sacrifice. Wisdom is associated also with healing; Buddha is not only supremely possessed of wisdom but is the great healer. It was this aspect of Buddha which appealed most to Japanese of the Nara period as is witnessed by the predominant role of Yakushi, or the Healing Buddha, not only in temples specifically dedicated to him, but in all centers of worship. The *Sūtra of the Golden Light* contains a chapter entirely devoted to medicine and healing, illustrating the close connection between religious belief and medicine. (It should be noted also that Buddhist priests introduced many medicines from China during the Nara period.)

The political aspects of the sūtra are most clearly stated in the chapter on laws (*Ōbōshō-ron*). It is declared that government and religion are united by the Buddhist Law (or Dharma). The law of men must be universal but not final, always subject to change, with peace as its ultimate end. Any king who violates the Law will be punished; but as long as he is faithful to it, Buddha will see to it that he enjoys immeasurable blessings. Japanese monarchs during the Nara period held this sūtra in such reverence that they attempted to make of it an instrument of state policy. Copies of the sūtra were distributed in all the provinces in A.D. 741 by order of the Emperor Shōmu, one of the most devout rulers. At about the same time Shōmu ordered each province to build a seven-storied pagoda, and to establish a Guardian Temple of the Province and an Atonement Nunnery of the Province.

It was Shōmu also who was responsible for the building of the Great Image of Lochana Buddha, the most famous monument of the Nara period. Just as Lochana Buddha is the central figure of the cosmogony of the *Kegon Sūtra*, the Great Image and its temple were intended as the center of the provincial temples and nunneries. The *Kegon Sūtra* is said to have been the teaching delivered by Buddha immediately after attaining enlightenment, when he made no attempt to simplify the complexities of his doctrines for the benefit of the less capable. Its difficulty kept it from attaining the popularity of the *Sūtra of the Golden Light*, but its importance is evident from the efforts devoted to the completion of the Great Image (over fifty feet high). When in 749 gold was discovered in Japan for the first time, it was regarded as an auspicious sign for the completion of the monument. The Emperor Shōmu declared:

This is the Word of the Sovereign who is the Servant of the Three Treasures, that he humbly speaks before the Image of Lochana.

In this land of Yamato since the beginning of Heaven and Earth, Gold, though it has been brought as an offering from other countries, was thought not to exist. But in the East of the land which We rule . . . gold has been found.

Hearing this We were astonished and rejoiced, and feeling that this is a Gift bestowed upon Us by the love and blessing of Lochana Buddha, We have received it with reverence and humbly accepted it, and have brought with Us all Our officials to worship and give thanks.

This We say reverently, reverently, in the Great Presence of the Three Treasures whose name is to be spoken with awe.[1]

[1] Sansom, "The Imperial Edicts in the Shoku-Nihongi," *TASJ*, 2d series, I, 26.

We cannot but be struck by the humility of the terms employed by Shōmu. For him to have claimed to be a "servant" of the Three Treasures marks an astonishing departure from the previously held ideas of kingship in Japan. There seemingly remained only one further step to be taken to make Japan into a true Buddha-land: to have a sovereign who was a member of the Buddhist clergy so that the country could be governed in perfect consonance with these teachings. During the reign of Shōmu's daughter, the Empress Shōtoku, the transference of rule to a Buddhist priest all but happened.

In A.D. 764 the Empress Shōtoku, who had previously abdicated, suddenly decided to reassume the throne in spite of the Buddhist vows she had taken. In the same proclamation she declared that she was appointing Dōkyō, a Master of the Hossō sect, to be her chief minister. Dōkyō steadily rose in power. In 766 he was appointed "king of the law" (hōō), and several years later the Empress, acting on a false oracle, was on the point of abdicating the throne in his favor. However, the powerful conservative forces at the court blocked this move, and Japan never again came so close to becoming a Buddha-land. The Empress Shōtoku died in 770, Dōkyō was disgraced, and the new rulers turned away from Nara to Kyoto, where new forms of Buddhism were to dominate the scene.

BUDDHISM AND THE STATE

The full title of this work, Sūtra of the Sovereign Kings of the Golden Light Ray (Konkō myō saishō ō gyō),[1] refers to the Deva Kings who came to pay homage to the Buddha. To its inspiration is due the first temple built by the court, the Shitennō (or Four Deva Kings). When Temmu seized the throne in 672, this sūtra appears to have influenced his decision to promote Buddhism in the interest of the new regime. His predecessor, Tenchi, had been clearly associated with the Confucian political order, and, as we have seen, Tenchi's assumption of power was justified by numerous portents indicating that he had received the Mandate of Heaven. Temmu found a similar justification in the Golden Light Sūtra,

[1] Corresponds to the *Suvarṇaprabhāsottama Sūtra*. Cf. pp. 105–8.

which set forth a doctrine of kingship based on merit—merit achieved in former existences and through wholehearted support of Buddhism. It is thus strongly implied that kings rule by a kind of "divine right," which is not based on any hereditary claim but rather on the ruler's proper performance of his duties. In the latter case, not only will his realm enjoy the peace and harmony from the beneficial influence of Buddhist teachings on public morality, but even the cosmic order will respond to the ruler's virtue and bestow blessings upon him and his people. Here, then, is a Buddhist parallel to the Han Confucian view of sovereignty, without the concessions made by Han theorists to dynastic inheritance. It is no wonder that Temmu held this sūtra in particular honor, and fostered the growth of Buddhism by ordering every family to have a Buddhist shrine in its house.

Then the Four Deva Kings, their right shoulders bared from their robes in respect, arose from their seats and, with their right knees touching the ground and their palms joined in humility, thus addressed Buddha:

"Most Revered One! When, in some future time, this *Sūtra of the Golden Light* is transmitted to every part of a kingdom—to its cities, towns and villages, its mountains, forests and fields—if the king of the land listens with his whole heart to these writings, praises them, and makes offerings on their behalf, and if moreover he supplies this sūtra to the four classes of believers, protects them and keeps all harm from them, we Deva Kings, in recognition of his deeds, will protect that king and his people, give them peace and freedom from suffering, prolong their lives and fill them with glory. Most Revered One! If when the king sees that the four classes of believers receive the sūtra, he respects and protects them as he would his own parents, we Four Kings will so protect him always that whatever he wishes will come about, and all sentient beings will respect him." . . .

Then Buddha declared to the Four Deva Kings:

"Fitting is it indeed that you Four Kings should thus defend the holy writings. In the past I practiced bitter austerities of every kind for 100,000 kalpas (eons). Then, when I attained supreme enlightenment and realized in myself universal wisdom, I taught this law. If any king upholds this sūtra and makes offerings in its behalf, I will purify him of suffering and illness, and bring him peace of mind. I will protect his cities, towns and villages, and scatter his enemies. I will make all strife among the rulers of men to cease forever.

"Know ye, Deva Kings, that the 84,000 rulers of the 84,000 cities, towns and villages of the world shall each enjoy happiness of every sort in his own land; that they shall all possess freedom of action, and obtain all manner of precious things in abundance; that they shall never again invade each other's territories; that they shall receive recompense in accordance with their deeds of previous existences; that they shall no longer yield to the evil desire of taking the lands of others; that they shall learn that the smaller their desires the greater the blessing; and that they shall emancipate themselves from the suffering of warfare and bondage. The people of their lands shall be joyous, and upper and lower classes will blend as smoothly as milk and water. They shall appreciate each other's feelings, join happily in diversions together, and with all compassion and modesty increase the sources of goodness.

"In this way the nations of the world shall live in peace and prosperity, the peoples shall flourish, the earth shall be fertile, the climate temperate, and the seasons shall follow in the proper order. The sun, moon, and the constellations of stars shall continue their regular progress unhindered. The wind and rain shall come in good season. All treasures shall be abundant. No meanness shall be found in human hearts, but all shall practice almsgiving and cultivate the ten good works. When the end of life comes, many shall be born in Heaven and increase the celestial multitudes."

[From Tsuji, *Nihon Bukkyō Shi*, Jōsei-hen, 194–95]

The Ideal of the Buddhist Layman

The Vimalakīrti Sūtra (Yuima-kyō) eulogizes Buddha's lay disciple, Vimalakīrti, who lives as a householder and yet achieves a saintliness unmatched even by those following monastic discipline. At the Japanese court this ideal of the Buddhist layman found favor among men taking an active part in state affairs, and under Fujiwara auspices a date was reserved on the court calendar for the reading and expounding of this sūtra. An extant commentary on the Vimalakīrti text has been traditionally ascribed to Prince Shōtoku, but it is pos-

sible that Shōtoku only sponsored or joined in its preparation by Korean monks.

The second chapter, given here, describes the virtues of Vimala-kīrti and presents his discourse on the nature of the human body as contrasted to the body of the Buddha.

At that time, there dwelt in the great city of Vaishālī a wealthy householder named Vimalakīrti. Having done homage to the countless Buddhas of the past, doing many good works, attaining to acquiescence in the Eternal Law, he was a man of wonderful eloquence,

Exercising supernatural powers, obtaining all the magic formulas (dhāranīs), arriving at the state of fearlessness.

Repressing all evil enmities, reaching the gate of profound truth, walking in the way of wisdom,

Acquainted with the necessary means, fulfilling the Great Vows, comprehending the past and the future of the intentions of all beings, understanding also both their strength and weakness of mind,

Ever pure and excellent in the way of the Buddha, remaining loyal to the Mahāyāna,

Deliberating before action, following the conduct of Buddha, great in mind as the ocean,

Praised by all the Buddhas, revered by all the disciples and all the gods such as a Shakra and the Brahmā Sahāpati ("lord of the world"),

Residing in Vaishālī only for the sake of the necessary means for saving creatures, abundantly rich, ever careful of the poor, pure in self-discipline, obedient to all precepts,

Removing all anger by the practice of patience, removing all sloth by the practice of diligence, removing all distraction of mind by intent meditation, removing all ignorance by fullness of wisdom;

Though he is but a simple layman, yet observing the pure monastic discipline;

Though living at home, yet never desirous of anything,

Though possessing a wife and children, always exercising pure virtues;

Though surrounded by his family, holding aloof from worldly pleasures;

Though using the jeweled ornaments of the world, yet adorned with spiritual splendor;

Though eating and drinking, yet enjoying the flavor of the rapture of meditation;

Though frequenting the gambling house, yet leading the gamblers into the right path;

Though coming in contact with heresy, yet never letting his true faith be impaired;

Though having a profound knowledge of worldly learning, yet ever finding pleasure in things of the spirit as taught by Buddha;

Revered by all as the first among those who were worthy of reverence;

Governing both the old and young as a righteous judge;

Though profiting by all the professions, yet far above being absorbed by them;

Benefiting all beings, going wheresoever he pleases, protecting all beings as a judge with righteousness;

Leading all with the Doctrine of the Mahāyāna when in the seat of discussion;

Ever teaching the young and ignorant when entering the hall of learning;

Manifesting to all the error of passion when in the house of debauchery; persuading all to seek the higher things when at the shop of the wine dealer;

Preaching the Law when among wealthy people as the most honorable of their kind;

Dissuading the rich householders from covetousness when among them as the most honorable of their kind;

Teaching kshatriyas [i.e., nobles] patience when among them as the most honorable of their kind;

Removing arrogance when among brahmans as the most honorable of their kind;

Teaching justice to the great ministers when among them as the most honorable of their kind;

Teaching loyalty and filial piety to the princes when among them as the most honorable of their kind;

Teaching honesty to the ladies of the court when among them as the most honorable of their kind;

Persuading the masses to cherish the virtue of merits when among them as the most honorable of their kind;

Instructing in highest wisdom the Brahmā gods when among them as the most honorable of their kind;

Showing the transient nature of the world to the Shakra gods when among them as the most honorable of their kind;

Protecting all beings when among the guardians as the most honorable of their kind;

—Thus by such countless means Vimalakīrti, the wealthy householder, rendered benefit to all beings.

Now through those means he brought on himself sickness. And there came to inquire after him countless visitors headed by kings, great ministers, wealthy householders, lay-disciples, brahman princes and other high officials. Then Vimalakīrti, taking the opportunity of his sickness, preached to anyone who came to him, and said:

"Come, ye gentlemen, the human body is transient, weak, impotent, frail, and mortal; never trustworthy, because it suffers when attacked by disease;

Ye gentlemen, an intelligent man never places his trust in such a thing; it is like a bubble that soon bursts.

It is like a mirage which appears because of a thirsty desire.

It is like a plantain tree which is hollow inside.

It is like a phantom caused by a conjurer.

It is like a dream giving false ideas.

It is like a shadow which is produced by karma.

It is like an echo which is produced by various relations.

It is like a floating cloud which changes and vanishes.

It is like the lightning which instantly comes and goes.

It has no power as the earth has none.

It has no individuality as the fire has none.

It has no durability as the wind has none.

It has no personality as the water has none.

It is not real and the four elements are its house.

It is empty when freed from the false idea of me and mine.

It has no consciousness as there is none in grasses, trees, bricks or stones.

It is impotent as it is revolved by the power of the wind.

It is impure and full of filthiness.

It is false and will be reduced to nothingness, in spite of bathing, clothing, or nourishment.

It is a calamity and subject to a hundred and one diseases.

It is like a dry well threatened by decay.

It is transient and sure to die.

It is like a poisonous snake or a hateful enemy or a deserted village as it is composed of the (five) *skandhas*, the (twelve) *āyatanas* and the (eighteen) *dhātus*.[1]

O ye gentlemen, this body of ours is to be abhorred, and the body of Buddha is to be desired. And why?

The body of Buddha is the body of the law.

It is born of immeasurable virtues and wisdom.

It is born of discipline, meditation, wisdom, emancipation, wisdom of emancipation.

It is born of mercy, compassion, joy, and impartiality.

It is born of charity, discipline, patience, diligence, meditation, emancipation, samādhi, learning, meekness, strength, wisdom, and all the Pāramitās.

It is born of the necessary means.

It is born of the six supernatural powers.

It is born of the threefold intelligence.

It is born of the thirty-seven requisites of enlightenment.

It is born of the concentration and contemplation of mind.

It is born of the ten powers, threefold fearlessness, and the eighteen special faculties.

It is born by uprooting all wicked deeds and by accumulating all good deeds.

It is born of truth.

It is born of temperance.

Of these immeasurable pure virtues is born the body of Tathāgata. "Ye gentlemen, if one wishes to obtain the body of Buddha and exterminate the diseases of all beings he should cherish the thought of supreme enlightenment."

Thus Vimalakīrti, the wealthy householder, rightly preached for the profit of those who came to visit him on

[1] Components of the human being, the five *skandhas* are form (body), sensation, perception, psychic construction, and consciousness. The twelve *āyatanas* are the six senses and six sense organs. The eighteen *dhātus* are the six sense organs, six sense objects, and six senses.

his bed of sickness and made all these countless thousand people cherish the thought of supreme enlightenment.

[Adapted from Hokei Idzumi, "Vimalakīrti's Discourse," *The Eastern Buddhist*, III, No. 2, 138–41]

9

SAICHŌ AND THE LOTUS TEACHING

INTRODUCTION

One day in the seventh moon of 788 a young monk made his
way up the side of Mt. Hiei repeating this song of prayer he
had composed:

O Buddhas
Of unexcelled complete enlightenment
Bestow your invisible aid
Upon this hut I open
On the mountain top.[1]

The monk was Saichō (767–822) and the little temple he
founded was to develop into the center of learning and culture of the entire nation; such it remained until, by order of
an impetuous military leader, the complex of 3,000 temple
buildings on Mt. Hiei was razed in 1571. Saichō's temple
would almost certainly never have attained so remarkable a
growth had it not been for the decision of the Emperor
Kammu to move the capital away from Nara, the stronghold
of the Six Sects of Buddhism. Kammu was a Confucian by
training and as such was opposed to the encroachment of

[1] *Dengyō Daishi zenshū*, IV, 756.

political power by the Buddhist clergy. The attempt to establish Dōkyō as ruler of Japan represented the closest the
monks came to success in creating a "Buddha-land," but even
when this failed they were by no means reduced to a purely
religious status. It was in order to restore to the sovereign
his full prerogatives that Kammu determined to move the
seat of the government. In this decision he had the support
of the Fujiwara and certain other important families traditionally opposed to Buddhism, as well as such immigrants
from China and Korea as the Hata, who are credited with
having introduced sericulture to Japan. Saichō himself was
of Chinese descent, as was another outstanding figure of
the period, the General Sakanoue Tamuramaro, who extended the imperial domains to the northern end of the main
island of Japan.

Although Kammu's dislike of the secular ambitions of the
monks and his impatience at their interminable wrangling
had made him generally anti-Buddhist, he realized that he
needed Buddhist support for the reforms he intended to
effect. Saichō met ideally Kammu's needs. He had originally
left Nara because of his dissatisfaction with the worldliness
and, as he considered, the decadence of the monasteries
there. He became convinced that only in an entirely different
environment could a true moral purge and ethical awakening
take place. When he first established his little temple, the
area around Mt. Hiei was mainly uncultivated marshland,
but six years later, in 794, it was chosen as the site of the
capital. Saichō may have been instrumental in the adoption
of this site; in any case, once the removal there had been
effected he enjoyed the patronage of the Emperor Kammu.
Saichō was sent to China in 804, chiefly to gain spiritual
sanction for the new Buddhist foundation on Mt. Hiei.
China was considered to be the "fatherland" of Japanese
Buddhism, and without Chinese approval Saichō's monastery
had no standing alongside those of the powerful sects in
Nara.

Saichō does not appear originally to have desired to found
a new sect. When his first temple was opened, the Healing
Buddha was enshrined there, just as in so many of the Nara
temples. While he was in China, however, he studied the
Tendai (T'ien-t'ai) teachings, and he brought back this doc-

trine to Japan after a year abroad. The Tendai sect, as founded by Saichō, was essentially the same as its parent sect in China, and was based like it on the teachings of the *Lotus Sūtra*. The Nara sects, with the exception of the Kegon, had derived authority for their doctrines from secondary sources —the commentaries—instead of from the sūtras. Saichō denounced this feature of Nara Buddhism in pointing out the superiority of the Tendai teachings based on Buddha's own words.

Saichō referred often to the "Two Vehicles" of Nara Buddhism. By this he meant Hīnayāna and what may be called Quasi-Mahāyāna, the latter referring to such schools as the Hossō and Sanron. Against these doctrines Saichō upheld the "One Vehicle" of the true Mahāyāna. The emphasis on "oneness" took various forms. It meant, most importantly, universality, in contrast, say, to the Hossō sect, which had evolved as an aristocratic and hierarchic religion, with certain persons excluded by their inborn shortcomings from Buddhist perfection; Tendai Buddhism preached enlightenment for all. Saichō declared that all men had innate in them the possibility of gaining enlightenment:

In the lotus-flower is implicit its emergence from the water. If it does not emerge, its blossoms will not open; in the emergence is implicit the blossoming. If the water is three feet deep, the stalk of the flower will be four or five feet; if the water is seven or eight feet deep, the stalk will be over ten feet tall. That is what is implied by the emergence from the water. The greater the amount of water, the taller the stalk will grow; the potential growth is limitless. Now, all human beings have the lotus of Buddhahood within them. It will rise above the mire and foul water of the Hīnayāna and Quasi-Mahāyāna, and then through the stage of the bodhisattvas to open, leaves and blossoms together, in full glory.[2]

Another aspect of oneness as found in Tendai Buddhism was the insistence on the basic unity of Buddha and all other beings. In every person is the Buddha-nature which must be realized. No matter how wicked a man may be, he is potentially a Buddha. The way that one may attain Buddhist perfection is to follow the way of Buddha by leading a life of

[2] *Dengyō Daishi zenshū*, I, 436.

moral purity and contemplation. Indeed, it was his emphasis on moral perfection rather than any more metaphysical aspect of the Tendai philosophy which most conspicuously appeared in Saichō's teachings.

In contrast, again, with the Nara Buddhists who lived in the old capital, Saichō required Tendai monks to remain in the seclusion of the monastery on Mt. Hiei for twelve years. There they received the "training of a bodhisattva," including a study of the Mahāyāna sūtras (especially the *Lotus*), and the Chinese T'ien t'ai meditation known as "Concentration and Insight" (*Shikan*). The discipline on Mt. Hiei was severe, necessarily so if, as Saichō hoped, the monastery was to supply the nation with its teachers and leaders.

There was a close connection between Mt. Hiei and the court, but it was a relationship quite unlike that which existed between the sovereigns and the great temples when the court was in Nara. The Emperor Shōmu had proclaimed himself to be the slave of the Three Treasures, and his daughter was willing to yield the throne to a monk, but the new Buddhism was in the service of the court and not its master. Saichō's monastery was declared to be the "Center for the Protection of the Nation," and Saichō constantly reiterated his belief that Mahāyāna Buddhism was the great benefactor and protector of Japan. He distinguished three classes of monks among those who would "graduate" from Mt. Hiei. The first class was those gifted both in their actions and words; they were the "treasure of the nation" and more precious than the richest jewels. Such monks were to remain on Mt. Hiei and serve their country by their religious practices. Monks who were not so gifted either in actions or in words would leave the mountain and become servants of the state. Some would teach; others would engage in agricultural and engineering projects for the nation's benefit.

Saichō's writings sometimes appear to be tinged with nationalism, probably because of his strong feelings for the prestige of the court. Many of the important Buddhist monks of the Nara period had been Chinese or Koreans and showed little specific attachment for the Japanese court or Japan itself. Saichō, on the other hand, in spite of his Chinese ancestry was thoroughly Japanese in his love of what he called "the country of Great Japan" (*Dai-Nippon-Koku*) and in his reverence for the sovereign. In the oath which the Tendai monks were required to swear, Saichō included a moving acknowledgment of the sect's debt to the Emperor Kammu. The fortunes of Tendai Buddhism were in fact so closely linked at first to Kammu that when he died in 806 Tendai's supremacy was immediately threatened. The Nara priests were bitterly opposed to Saichō because of his part in the removal of the capital, and because of their jealousy over the honors that Kammu had later bestowed on the Tendai monk. One of the charges against Saichō was that he was not properly qualified to pose as a "monk who sought the Buddhist Law in China" (the title Saichō often used) because he had failed to visit Ch'ang-an, the Chinese capital. The accusations exchanged between Nara and Mt. Hiei became increasingly acrimonious.

Another threat to the prosperity of Tendai came in the same year as Kammu's death—the return to Japan of Kūkai, who was to become the great religious leader of the period. Kūkai quickly ingratiated himself with Kammu's successor by presenting him with many treasures from China. Before long Kūkai's Shingon Buddhism, with its emphasis on aestheticism, was in higher favor with the court than the severely moral Tendai school.

The relations between Saichō and Kūkai were at first very friendly. Saichō eagerly sought to learn the teachings which Kūkai brought back from China. This was one of the most appealing sides of Saichō's character—his genuine desire to improve his knowledge and understanding of Buddha's Law regardless of whether or not the material he studied formed part of the Tendai teachings. He stated as his principle:

A devout believer in Buddha's Law who is also a wise man is truly obliged to point out to his students any false doctrines, even though they are principles of his own sect. He must not lead the students astray. If, on the other hand, he finds a correct doctrine, even though it is a principle of another sect he should adopt and transmit it. This is the duty of a wise person. If a man maintains his partisan spirit even when his teachings are false; conceals his own errors and seeks to expose those of other people; persists in his own false views and destroys the right views of others—what could be more stupid than that? From this time forward, monks in charge of instruction in the Law must desist from such practices.[3]

Saichō was much impressed by the esoteric teachings. He was baptized by Kūkai at the latter's first initiation rites, and frequently borrowed works on esotericism from him. Saichō even sent Taihan, one of his favorite disciples, to study with Kūkai. The happy relations between Saichō and Kūkai came to an abrupt end, however, when Kūkai, writing on Taihan's behalf, refused Saichō's request that he return to Mt. Hiei. When Saichō asked to borrow a certain esoteric sūtra, Kūkai this time replied that if he wished to study the Truth it was everywhere apparent in the cosmos, but if he wished to learn about Esoteric Buddhism he would have to become a regular student. The tone of Kūkai's letter was extremely unpleasant, and we cannot be surprised that Saichō was embittered by it. Saichō's last years were unhappily spent. His most ardent wish, that a Mahāyāna ordination center be established on Mt. Hiei, so that Tendai Buddhists might be completely free from the Nara ordination hall with its Hīnayāna practices, was successfully opposed by the Nara Buddhists. Only after Saichō's death in 822 was permission finally granted.

Saichō's lasting contributions to Buddhism were probably more in the field of organization than of doctrine. His writings are in an undistinguished and even tedious style, often repetitious, seldom engrossing. They possess, however, an earnestness and sincerity which tell us much about the man. Saichō may not dazzle us by the brilliance of his achievements the way Kūkai does, but the student of Buddhism may well turn to him for an example of the highest ideals of the Buddhist priesthood.

Vow of Uninterrupted Study of the Lotus Sūtra

[Composed by Saichō and taken by the monks of Mt. Hiei]

The disciple of Buddha and student of the One Vehicle [name and court rank to be filled in] this day respectfully affirms before the Three Treasures that the saintly Emperor

[3] *Dengyō Daishi zenshū*, I, 447.

Kammu, on behalf of Japan and as a manifestation of his unconditional compassion, established the Lotus sect and had the *Lotus Sūtra*, its commentary, and the essays on "Concentration and Insight," copied and bound, together with hundreds of other volumes, and installed them in the seven great temples. Constantly did he promote the Single and Only Vehicle, and he united all the people so that they might ride together in the ox-cart of Mahāyāna[1] to the ultimate destination, enlightenment. Every year festivals[2] of the *Golden Light Sūtra* were held to protect the state. He selected twelve students, and established a seminary on top of Mt. Hiei, where the Tripiṭaka, the ritual implements, and the sacred images were enshrined. These treasures he considered the guardian of the Law and its champion during the great night of ignorance.

It was for this reason that on the fifteenth day of the second moon of 809 Saichō with a few members of the same faith, established the uninterrupted study of the *Sūtra of the Lotus of the Wonderful Law*.

I vow that, as long as heaven endures and earth lasts, to the most distant term of the future, this study will continue without the intermission of a single day, at the rate of one volume every two days. Thus the doctrine of universal enlightenment will be preserved forever, and spread throughout Japan, to the farthest confines. May all attain to Buddhahood!

[From *Dengyō Daishi zenshū*, IV, 749]

Regulations for Students of the Mountain School

Saichō's importance as a religious organizer is apparent in these regulations for the students who were annually appointed by the government to study Tendai Buddhism. The ideal he held up for the

[1] Three vehicles are described in the *Lotus Sūtra*; of them the ox-cart stands for Mahāyāna.
[2] These festivals, often called *gosaie* ("imperial vegetarian entertainments" of priests), were held during the first moon in the Imperial Palace from 802, when Kammu founded them, until 1467. (See De Visser, *Ancient Buddhism in Japan*, pp. 471–79.) The text studied was that of the *Golden Light Sūtra*.

monks was a lofty and demanding one: that they should combine the religious dedication of the bodhisattva with the Confucian virtues of service to the state and society.

The stylistic failings of Saichō's writings are also apparent in this work, but his repetition of such words as "treasure of the nation" has a certain cumulative power.

The original version of these regulations is in three sections of which the first two are translated here.

What is the treasure of the nation? The religious nature is a treasure, and he who possesses this nature is the treasure of the nation. That is why it was said of old that ten pearls big as pigeon's eggs do not constitute the treasure of a nation, but only when a person casts his light over a part of the country can one speak of a treasure of the nation. A philosopher of old [1] once said that he who is capable in speech but not in action should be a teacher of the nation; he who is capable in action but not in speech should be a functionary of the nation; but he who is capable both in action and speech is the treasure of the nation. Apart from these three groups, there are those who are capable neither of speech nor action: these are the betrayers[2] of the nation.

Buddhists who possess the religious nature are called in the west bodhisattvas; in the east they are known as superior men.[3] They hold themselves responsible for all bad things, while they credit others with all good things. Forgetful of themselves, they benefit others: this represents the summit of compassion.

Among Buddha's followers there are two kinds of monks, Hīnayāna and Mahāyāna; Buddhists possessing a religious nature belong to the latter persuasion. However, in our eastern land only Hīnayāna images are worshiped,[4] and not the Mahāyāna ones. The Great Teaching is not yet spread; the

[1] Saichō quotes from Mou Tzu, p. 13b, Ping-chin-kuan ts'ung-shu edition.

[2] This word seems far too strong for the offense. There may be a corruption in the text: Mou Tzu calls these people "mean" (or "lowly").

[3] Or "gentlemen"—the name given by Confucius to the people who followed his code.

[4] Even though Nara Buddhism was predominantly Mahāyāna, for the most part the images worshiped were Hīnayāna.

great men have not been able to rise. I fervently pray that, in accordance with the wishes of the late Emperor,[5] all Tendai students annually appointed will be trained in the Mahāyāna doctrines and become bodhisattva monks.[6]

REGULATIONS FOR THE TWO STUDENTS
ANNUALLY APPOINTED BY THE COURT

1. All annually appointed Tendai Lotus students, from this year 818 to all eternity, shall be of the Mahāyāna persuasion. They shall be granted Buddhist names, without however losing their own family names. They shall be initiated into the Ten Precepts of Tendai before they become novices, and when they are ordained government seals will be requested for their papers.

2. All Mahāyāna students, immediately after their ordination, shall be administered the oaths of Sons of Buddha, and then become bodhisattva monks. A government seal will be requested for the certificates of oaths. Those who take the Vow will be required to remain on Mt. Hiei for twelve years without ever leaving the monastery. They shall study both disciplines.

3. All monks who study the Concentration and Insight (*Shikan*) discipline shall be required every day of the year to engage in constant study and discussion of the *Lotus, Golden Light, Benevolent Kings, Protector* and other Mahāyāna sūtras for safeguarding the nation.[7]

4. All monks who study the Vairochana discipline shall be required every day of the year to recite the True Words (*mantra*) of the Vairochana, the Peacock, the Eternal, the Crown and other sūtras for safeguarding the nation.[8]

5. Students of both disciplines shall be appointed to positions in keeping with their achievements after twelve years'

[5] Emperor Kammu (reigned 781–806) shortly before his death issued this order.
[6] That is, Mahāyāna monks, for the bodhisattva was held up by Mahāyāna Buddhism as the ideal to be followed.
[7] Japanese names for the sūtras: Hokke-kyō, Konkō-kyō, Ninnō kyō, and Shugo-kyo.
[8] Japanese names for the sūtras: Dainichi-kyō, Kujaku-kyō, Fukū Kensaku Kannon-gyō, Ichiji Chōrinnō-gyō. These represent the esoteric discipline.

training and study. Those who are capable in both action and speech shall remain permanently on the mountain as leaders of the order: these are the treasure of the nation. Those who are capable in speech but not in action shall be teachers of the nation, and those capable in action but not in speech shall be the functionaries of the nation.

6. Teachers and functionaries of the nation shall be appointed with official licenses as Transmitters of Doctrine and National Lecturers. The national lecturers shall be paid during their tenure of office the expenses of the annual summer retreat and provided with their robes. Funds for these expenses shall be deposited in the provincial offices, where they will be supervised jointly by provincial and district governors.

They shall also serve in such undertakings which benefit the nation and the people as the repair of ponds and canals, the reclamation of uncultivated land, the reparation of landslides, the construction of bridges and ships, the planting of trees and ramie[9] bushes, the sowing of hemp and grasses, and the digging of wells and irrigation ditches. They shall also study the sūtras and cultivate their minds, but shall not engage in private agriculture or trading.

If these provisions are followed, men possessing the religious nature will spring up one after another throughout the country, and the Way of the Superior Man shall never die.

The above six articles are based on the teachings of mercy and will lead all sentient beings to the Great Teaching. The Law of Buddha is eternal; because the nation will always remain strong, the seeds of Buddhism will not die.

Overcome by profound awe, I offer these articles of Tendai and respectfully request the imperial assent.

Saichō, the Monk who Formerly Sought the Law in China. [19 June 818]

[From *Dengyō Daishi zenshū*, I, 5–10]

[9] A plant whose fibers are similar to those of hemp in their properties and uses.

10

KŪKAI AND ESOTERIC BUDDHISM

INTRODUCTION

Outstanding among the Buddhist leaders of the Heian period was Kūkai (774–835), a man whose genius has well been described, "His memory lives all over the country, his name is a household word in the remotest places, not only as a saint, but as a preacher, a scholar, a poet, a sculptor, a painter, an inventor, an explorer, and—sure passport to fame —a great calligrapher." [1]

Kūkai came from one of the great aristocratic families. At the time of the decision to move the capital from Nara, Kūkai's family was closely associated with the group opposed to the move, and was even implicated in the murder of the leader of the opposing faction. The subsequent disgrace of his family may have been a factor in Kūkai's eventual decision to become a Buddhist monk rather than to win the high place in the government that his talents and birth should have guaranteed him. Even as a small boy he showed exceptional ability in his studies, and was taken under the protection of his maternal uncle, a Confucian scholar. In 791 Kūkai entered the Confucian college in the capital. According to some sources, it was in the same year that he completed the

[1] G. B. Sansom, *Japan, a Short Cultural History*, London 1946, p. 230.

first version of his *Indications to the Three Teachings*, a work
which treats the doctrines of Confucianism, Taoism, and
Buddhism more or less novelistically. In its early form the
book may actually have been intended more as a literary
exercise than as an interpretation of the three religions.
If it was in fact composed in 791, it was an amazing achievement for a youth of seventeen, but, as often in the case of
the great men of former ages, it may be that Kūkai's admirers
have sought to make him appear even more of a prodigy than
he was.

The 797 version of the *Indications* was Kūkai's first major
work. In it he proclaimed the superiority of Buddhism over
the other two religions discussed because it went beyond
them in its concern for man's future existence. Kūkai did not
deny the validity of Confucian and Taoist beliefs as such, but
pointed out how inadequate they were. For Kūkai Buddhism
was not only superior, but actually contained all that was
worthwhile in the other two beliefs. We can thus find even
in this early work signs of the syncretism which marked his
mature philosophy. Although Kūkai clearly reveals himself
as Buddhist in the *Indications*, we know that he was not
satisfied with the forms of the religion known to him in
Japan. In later years he recalled that period of his life:
"Three vehicles, five vehicles, a dozen sūtras—there were so
many ways for me to seek the essence of Buddhism, but still
my mind had doubts which could not be resolved. I be-
seeched all the Buddhas of the three worlds and the ten
directions to show me not the disparity but the unity of the
teachings." [2]

In the hope of finding the unifying Buddhism he sought,
Kūkai sailed to China in 804 with the same embassy that
Saichō also accompanied, although on a different ship. At
this early date a voyage to China was extremely hazardous;
ships which arrived safely were the exception and not the
rule. When Kūkai's ship was about to sail, apprehension of
the dangers was so great that the ambassadors' "tears fell like
rain and everybody present also wept." [3] The crossing took

[2] From Kūkai's so-called *Testament*, written by another hand.
Quoted in Moriyama (ed.), *Kōbō Daishi Den*, p. 85.
[3] Kuwabara Jitsuzō, "Daishi no nittō" in *Kōbō Daishi to Nihon
Bunka*, p. 479.

thirty-four days, and instead of arriving at the mouth of the Yangtze, the probable goal, the ship reached the coast of Fukien, where the authorities were at first unwilling to let the Japanese ashore. Kūkai's mastery of written Chinese here served the embassy in good stead; the governor was so impressed that he created no further obstacles.

Kūkai proceeded with the embassy to the capital at Ch'ang-an. There he met his great master Hui-kuo (746–805) who was immediately struck by the young Japanese and treated him as his chosen disciple. After Hui-kuo's death in the following year Kūkai was selected to write the funeral inscription, a signal honor for a foreigner. He returned to Japan late in 806. The Emperor Kammu, who had strongly favored the removal of the capital from Nara, and who was thus presumably not so well disposed towards Kūkai, had died in the spring of that year. After Kūkai had been granted many honors, he asked in 816 for permission to build a monastery on Mt. Kōya, which later became the center of the Shingon sect. In 822 Saichō, Kūkai's rival, died, and in the following year Kūkai was appointed Abbot of the Tōji, the great Buddhist temple which commanded the main entrance to the capital. He died in 835 on Mt. Kōya.

The Buddhism which Kūkai learned in China and brought back to Japan was known as the True Words (*Mantrayāna* in Sanskrit, *Shingon* in Japanese). The name itself indicates the importance accorded to speech as one of the Three Mysteries—body, speech, and mind. These three faculties are possessed by every human being, but in them resides all secrets, and through them one can attain to Buddhahood. The mysteries of the body include the various ways of holding the hands (known as mudrā) in accordance with the Buddha or bodhisattva invoked, the postures of meditation, and the handling of such ritual instruments as the symbolic thunderbolt (*vajra*) and lotus flowers. The mysteries of speech included the "true words" and other secret formulas. The mysteries of the mind referred mainly to the "five wisdoms," methods of perceiving truth. In Shingon Buddhism these mysteries are transmitted orally from master to disciple and not written in books where anyone might read of them. This constitutes one of the main differences between esoteric (for the initiated) and exoteric (for the public) Buddhism.

The reason given for keeping these teachings secret is that, unlike the doctrines of Shākyamuni, the historical Buddha, which were expounded with the limitations of his audience in mind, the esoteric teachings were voiced for his own enjoyment by Vairochana, the cosmic Buddha. The truths of the esoteric teachings were considered to be absolute, independent of place or time, and uniting in them the truths of all schools of thought. Only the initiated could hope to understand fully doctrines of such magnitude.

In the Esoteric school of Buddhism the relation between a master and his disciples was extremely close. Often the master would divulge all of his knowledge of the secret teachings only to one pupil of outstanding ability. Kūkai related how his master, Hui-kuo, waited almost until his death before he found in the Japanese an adequate receptacle for his knowledge. The personal nature of the transmission of the teachings was such that no independent Shingon sect was formed in China. It was left to Kūkai to present the Shingon teachings as a systematized doctrine and thus establish a sect. The immediate occasion for Kūkai's *Ten Stages of Religious Consciousness*, in which Shingon is treated as a separate philosophy, was a decree issued in 830 by the Emperor Junna ordering the six existing Buddhist sects to submit in written form the essentials of their beliefs. Of the works submitted at this time, Kūkai's *Ten Stages* was by far the most important, both in quality and magnitude. It consisted of ten chapters, each one presenting a successive stage upward of religious consciousness. The work was written entirely in Chinese, not merely good Chinese for a Japanese writer, but with an ornate poetical style which may remind one somewhat of Pope's attempt in the *Essay on Man* to present philosophical ideas in rhymed couplets. Kūkai's use of this cumbersome medium of expression was dictated largely by the fashion of his time. We may regret this today, for in spite of Kūkai's remarkable mastery of the techniques of Chinese composition, his statement of the doctrines of Shingon Buddhism was inevitably hampered by the necessity of casting his words into a rigid and unsuitable mold. His writings are today difficult to understand, and his attempts at parallel constructions made him at times prolix, but in spite of such handicaps Kūkai remains the towering intellectual figure of Japanese Buddhism.

The *Ten Stages* was the first attempt made by a Japanese to appraise existing Buddhist literature of every variety preliminary to his elucidation of the doctrines of a new sect. Kūkai even went beyond the field of Buddhism in his discussion of the stages of the religious life: Confucianism and Taoism were considered as two stages of the ten. At the bottom of the ten stages Kūkai placed the animal life of uncontrolled passions, the life without religious guidance. Only one step upwards was Confucianism, where the mind is as yet ignorant of the true religion, but is led by teaching to the practice of secular virtues. The third stage was Taoism (and, according to some authorities, Brāhmanism), where the believers hope for heaven but ignore its nature. Two Hīnayāna stages follow; here there is a partial understanding only, and the highest aspiration is that of personal extinction in Nirvāna. This is in contrast to the Mahāyāna belief that even those who have attained Heaven must descend to the lower stages of existence to help save others. The sixth stage is the first of Mahāyāna belief sometimes identified as Quasi- or Pseudo-Mahāyāna. It includes Hossō Buddhism which "aims at discovering the ultimate entity of cosmic existence in contemplation, through investigation into the specific characteristics of all existence, and through the realization of the fundamental nature of the soul in mystic illumination." [4] Because it is Mahāyāna, it is also characterized by its compassion for those who still wallow in ignorance. The seventh stage is the Sanron, which follows Nāgārjuna in the "Eightfold Negations" as a means of eliminating all false conceptions which hinder the mind in its search for the truth. The eighth stage is that of the universality of Tendai, where one moment contains eternity and a sesame seed may hold a mountain. The Kegon teaching with its insistence on interdependence and convertibility, form the ninth stage. At the summit are the esoteric teachings of Shingon.

Although Kūkai insisted on the difference between the exoteric teachings of other schools of Buddhism and the esoteric Shingon teachings, an examination of doctrine would

[4] M. Anesaki, *History of Japanese Religion*, p. 95.

seem to show that the concept of Vairochana, the cosmic
Buddha, had been anticipated by the Tendai concept of the
eternal Buddha or the Kegon interpretation of Lochana Buddha. The essential difference was that the latter two concepts
of Buddhahood were purported to have been visions revealed
to the historical Buddha, while the Vairochana Buddha discussed by Kūkai was not merely an ideal, but the cosmos
itself, limitless, without beginning or end. The cosmos was
held to consist of six elements: earth, water, fire, air, space,
and consciousness. Unlike certain other Buddhist schools,
Shingon did not consider the world to be consciousness only;
matter and mind are inseparable, "two but not two." In the
Shingon insistence on consciousness as an element it differed
from the Chinese Five Elements which were physical forces.
Esoteric Buddhism was able to synthesize both the previous
Buddhist concepts of the universe and the yin-yang theory
of five elements. It was later also to coalesce with Shinto.

The great appeal of Esoteric Buddhism for Heian Japan
lay in its aesthetic qualities. Kūkai himself excelled in the
arts, and this fact may partially explain the important role
which art played in his teachings. Kūkai's master, Hui-kuo,
had told him that only through art could the profound meaning of the esoteric scriptures be conveyed, and when Kūkai
returned to Japan he elaborated this theory:

The law (dharma) has no speech, but without speech it cannot
be expressed. Eternal truth (*tathatā*) transcends form, but only by
means of form can it be understood. Mistakes will be made in the
effort to point at the truth, for there is no clearly defined method
of teaching, but even when art does not excite admiration by its
unusual quality, it is a treasure which protects the country and
benefits the people.

In truth, the esoteric doctrines are so profound as to defy their
enunciation in writing. With the help of painting, however, their
obscurities may be understood. The various attitudes and mudrās
of the holy images all have their source in Buddha's love, and one
may attain Buddhahood at sight of them. Thus the secrets of the
sūtras and commentaries can be depicted in art, and the essential
truths of the esoteric teaching are all set forth therein. Neither
teachers nor students can dispense with it. Art is what reveals to
us the state of perfection.[5]

[5] From Kūkai's *Memorial on the Presentation of the List of Newly*

The arts were generally considered by Kūkai's school under four aspects: 1) painting and sculpture, 2) music and literature, 3) gestures and acts, and 4) the implements of civilization and religion. Ability in any or all of the arts may be achieved by a mastery of the Three Mysteries, and can result in the creation of flowers of civilization which are Buddhas in their own right. For Kūkai whatever was beautiful partook of the nature of Buddha. Nature, art and religion were one. It is not difficult, then, to see why so aesthetic a religion found favor at a time when Japanese civilization was at the height of its flowering.

Probably the most important use of painting made by the Shingon school was in the two Mandalas, representations of the cosmos under the two aspects of potential entity and dynamic manifestations. The indestructible potential aspect of the cosmos is depicted in the Diamond (Vajra) Mandala. In the center Vairochana Buddha is shown in contemplation, seated on a white lotus and encircled by a white halo. Around him are various Buddhas and the sacred implements. The dynamic aspect of the cosmos is depicted in the Womb (Garbha) Mandala, "wherein the manifold groups of deities and other beings are arrayed according to the kinds of the powers and intentions they embody. In the center there is a red lotus flower, with its seed-pod and eight petals, which symbolizes the heart of the universe. . . ." [6] Vairochana Buddha is seated on the seed-pod of the lotus and the petals are occupied by other Buddhas.

The Mandalas were used to represent the life and being of Vairochana Buddha, and also served to evoke mysterious powers, much in the way that the mudrās were performed. One important ceremony where the Mandalas figured was that in which an acolyte was required to throw a flower on the Mandalas. The Buddha on which his flower alighted was the one he was particularly to worship and emulate. It is recorded that Kūkai's flower fell on Vairochana Buddha both in the Diamond and Womb Mandalas. His master was

---

Imported Sūtras, quoted in Moriyama (ed.), Kōbō Daishi Den, p. 249.
[6] Anesaki, History of Japanese Religion, pp. 126–27.

amazed at this divine indication of the great destiny in store for the young Japanese.

An unusual feature of Kūkai's teachings was the emphasis placed on a knowledge of Sanskrit. It is not certain what degree of proficiency Kūkai himself was able to attain in Sanskrit after his relatively brief study of the language in China, but with his unusual gifts he may well have gained a considerable command. He described the importance of Sanskrit:

Buddhism had its inception in India. The lands of the West and those of the East are culturally and geographically far removed, and both in language and writing India differs from China. Thus we have had to rely on translations in order to study the Buddhist texts. However, the True Words in the original language are exceedingly abstruse, each word possessing a profound meaning. This meaning is changed when its sound is altered, and can easily be falsified by different punctuation. One may get a rough impression of the meaning, but no clear understanding. Unless one reads the Sanskrit original it is impossible to distinguish the qualities of the vowels. That is why we must go back to the source.[7]

According to traditional accounts at least, Kūkai put his Sanskrit to excellent use in the invention of the Japanese syllabary (kana), a contribution which made possible the glorious literature of the Heian Period. Regardless of Kūkai's part, it is certain that the syllabary was evolved in imitation of Sanskrit use.

Esoteric Buddhism became the most important religion of Heian Japan. Although its profound secrets could be transmitted only from masters to their disciples, the main features of the doctrines could be grasped quite easily. Life was conceived of in terms of constant change, upwards to Buddhahood, or downwards to hell, when Mahāyāna compassion led the enlightened ones to seek the salvation of those still living as "butting goats." However, the esoteric teachings did not deny the importance of this world and of happiness in this life. By correct performance of the mysteries, material benefits could immediately be obtained. This belief led at first towards a spirit of intellectual curiosity in the things of this

[7] Moriyama, Kōbō Daishi Den, p. 246.

world which distinguishes Shingon from most other forms of Buddhism. Later, however, the hope of securing practical advantages through the intermediary of an adept in magical formulae led to many superstitious excesses. It was partly in protest against this latter development of Shingon Buddhism that dissident sects and reforming movements arose in the medieval period.

Indications to the Three Teachings (Sangō shīki)

In the Indications, the earliest of his writings, Kūkai evaluates Confucianism, Taoism, and Buddhism, and concludes that Buddhism is the most profound of the three religions. He thereby justifies his entrance into its priesthood, which followed soon afterward.

The work consists of four parts: the preface, which gives his reason for writing, namely, his intention to become a Buddhist monk; the speeches of Tortoise Hair (Kimō), who represents Confucianism; of Nihil (Kyobuinji), who speaks for Taoism; and of Mendicant X (Kameikotsuji), who upholds Buddhism and whose identity with Kūkai is suggested at one point. A concluding poem summarizes the essence of the three teachings and indicates Kūkai's determination to abandon his effort to become a state official.

The dialogue is developed by Kūkai in a dramatic way. At the home of their host, Hare's Horn (Tokaku), the Confucianist Tortoise Hair is asked to admonish a delinquent youth known as Leech's Tusk (Shitsugakōshi). After the Confucianist reproves the young man and lectures him about the excellence of the Confucian virtues of filial piety and loyalty, the Taoist scoffs at his teaching, and explains the superiority of the Taoist Way which leads to the attainment of longevity. Next the Buddhist mendicant, who has joined the group, criticizes Taoism and advocates the teaching of Buddha. Tortoise Hair, Nihil, and the others are so deeply impressed that they are converted to Buddhism.

The following translation is an excerpt from the Speech of Mendicant X.

"Towering Mt. Meru [the center of the universe], which reaches almost to the Milky Way, will be reduced to ashes by the fires of the last day of earth. The oceans which reach as far as the distant skyline will also disappear when exposed to the seven suns at the end of this epoch. The infinite Heavens and Earth will be liquidated and the round firmament will likewise be burned and destroyed. Existence even in Heaven is as transient as lightning, and the period on earth of a Taoist "immortal," even with his extended life span, is as short as a clap of thunder. How much shorter, then, for human beings who are not endowed with diamond-like bodies but whose flesh is as insubstantial as tiles or pebbles! The five skhandas which constitute our physical being are illusions like the image of the moon reflected on water; the four great elements (earth, water, fire, and air) that constitute the natural world are as transitory as vapors of hot air. Man runs about within the circle of the twelve links of the chain of causation,[1] which characterizes this life of ignorance, like a monkey leaping from branch to branch. The eight unavoidable sufferings[2] bring forth anxiety and give pain to the innermost heart. The flames of greed, hatred, and stupidity burn day and night, and the thicket of the 108 defilements[3] flourishes throughout the four seasons.

"Our fragile body is easily dispersed, like particles of dust in the wind or the flower petals in spring. When the time comes our temporal life passes away like leaves carried off by the winds of autumn. . . .

"The storm of impermanence does not overlook even the Taoist 'immortal.' The demon which deprives men of their lives does not discriminate between noble or base. One cannot buy eternal life with wealth or be kept alive by secular power. No matter how much of the elixir of life one may drink, nor how deeply one may inhale the exquisite incense that recalls the departed soul, one cannot prolong one's life even for a second. Who can escape from going to that land that lies deep underground?

"Once a corpse rots in the grass, it can no longer be restored to its original state. The departed spirit cannot escape

---

[1] Ignorance, will, consciousness, name and form, six sense organs, contact, sensation, craning, attachment, becoming, birth, old age and death.

[2] Suffering derived from birth, old age, disease, death, separation from loved ones, meeting with hated ones, not being able to obtain what one wants, and passion.

[3] In Buddhism, it is thought that a man has a hundred and eight defilements. To remind man of these defilements and to encourage him to eliminate these defilements, the standard Buddhist rosary consists of a hundred and eight beads.

from being boiled in an iron pot. Once in Hell, the departed one may at times be thrown on a steep mountain of swords and shed much blood; at times he may suffer from the excruciating pain of a high mountain of spears piercing his breast. Sometimes he is run over by a flaming wagon wheel which bears the weight of many thousands of stones; and at other times he is made to sink into a bottomless river of ice. Sometimes he is forced to drink boiling water, or to swallow molten iron, or he is roasted in roaring flames. In these circumstances he can obtain nothing to drink, let alone even hear drink mentioned. He has no way of getting even the tiniest morsel of food. Lions, tigers, wolves open wide their mouths and leap at him with watering lips; the horse-headed devils, eyes wide in anticipation, come seeking him out. Though he may raise desperate cries for help from Heaven, he finds no response and his chances for pardon decrease each night. An appeal to the king of Hell is useless; he has no sympathy at all. . . . Once you fall into Hell, repentance is of no value. No matter how long you wait, even till the end of time, you will repeat your cries in vain. Alas! If you do not make an effort to emancipate yourself now, and if you once fall into the hell of mass suffering, however much you may lament and be tormented, there will be no one to help you. Exert yourselves; do your best while you are on this earth."

Tortoise Hair and the others were filled with anguish and their hearts were about to burst with terror. Their stomachs burned, although they had swallowed no fire, and their breasts felt as if pierced, although no swords had been thrust through them. They beat their breasts, and cried, and rolled on the ground. Looking up, they appealed to Heaven in their sorrow. They acted as if bereft of their parents or wives. One fainted out of dread, the other out of grief. Thereupon, Mendicant X took up a jar and sprinkled water on their faces after purifying it with a sacred formula. In a little while they recovered consciousness, but, as though drugged, they spoke no words. . . .

Some while later, they knelt on the ground with tears in their eyes, twice bowed in reverence, and said:

". . . Because of your compassionate instruction, we now realize that our ways have been shallow and worthless. We deeply regret our past and shall try to do our best to enter the right path. O merciful and venerable one, please show us the right way!"

Mendicant X replied: "Indeed it is fortunate that you have repented before you went too far. Now I will tell you of the origins of suffering in this life of transmigration and of the bliss of Nirvāna. On these points the Duke of Chou and Confucius did not speak, nor did Lao Tzu and Chuang Tzu preach. Even the followers of Hīnayāna do not know about the attainment of bliss. Only the bodhisattvas who are destined to be Buddhas in the next stage can obtain and enjoy it. . . .

". . . Unless a man seeks the superior in the evening and enlightenment in the morning, he cannot approach the Body of Essence (Dharmakāya) and break through the vast ocean of transmigration. Borne on the raft of the six perfections,[4] he should cross to the other side. He should cross the waves of passion on the ship of the noble eightfold path, using the mast of effort and the sail of meditation, with the armor of patience for protection from thieves, and the sword of wisdom to defend against enemies. Whipping the horse of the seven means[5] to attain enlightenment, he should gallop away from the ocean of transmigration and transcend the clamorous dust-filled world. Then as a token of a predicted future enlightenment, he will receive the gem hidden in the headdress of the Universal Monarch, as did Shāriputra and the Nāga (serpent) girl, who offered her necklace to the Buddha.[6] Soon he will pass through the ten stages of attaining enlightenment. The stages may be many, but the required disciplines are not difficult to fulfill. Meanwhile, he will overcome all obstacles and attain Suchness, and upon reaching enlightenment may be called the Lord, the Buddha. Then he will live in unity, transcending diversities and discriminations; by virtue of a wisdom shining like a clear mir-

[4] Offerings, morality, patience, effort, meditation, wisdom.
[5] Contemplation, choosing a correct doctrine, effort, joy, freshness, meditation, and indifference.
[6] Predictions that Shāriputra and the Nāga girl would be future Buddhas appear in the Lotus Sūtra. After the Nāga girl had offered the Buddha a priceless necklace, she was transformed into a man and later attained Buddhahood.

ror, he will be detached from both the abuse and the praise of the world. He will attain the state which transcends generation and destruction, which knows neither increase nor decrease, and which is tranquil and serene, rising above the three divisions of time (past, present, and future). How magnificent and splendid will he be! Not even the Yellow Emperor, the Sage King Yao, and Fu Hsi [of ancient China] will be worthy of tending his footgear, nor will the Universal Monarch (Chakravartin), Indra, Brahmā, and the rest be worthy to serve as his footmen. No matter how much abuse the devils and heretics heap on him, it will be in vain, and no matter how much praise the disciples of the Buddha and those who have attained enlightenment may offer him, it will still be inadequate. . . .

". . . Manifesting himself in numberless forms in countless places, he reveals himself as a man [Shākyamuni] who follows the path to Enlightenment and leads people to Nirvāna. Showing his majestic dignity, appearing on the paths which people frequent, and exhibiting countless miracles, he sends his message all over the world.

"Then he waits for all beings to come to him. Riding on the wind of the clouds they come, as numerous as the raindrops from heaven or the particles of spray from a fountain on earth. . . .

"Then the Buddha, preaching in a language which can be understood by all, crushes their illusions. He turns the entire world into a different one and reduces Mt. Meru to a poppy seed. Pouring a rain of nectar, he admonishes and guides them; he gives them the food of joy, the doctrine which contains wisdom, and the method of moral discipline. They celebrate peace on earth, saying that the Emperor of Truth will come and all will be awakened. They enjoy themselves so much that they even forget what they owe to the Emperor [the Buddha]. This is the place where all sentient beings from innumerable worlds gather in reverence. This is the noblest and the best capital, the source of ultimate value. Who can match the Buddha, the grandest and the loftiest of all!"

[From *Kōbō Daishi zenshū*, III, 347–355]

Kūkai and His Master

This passage and the one following are taken from the Memorial Presenting a List of Newly Imported Sūtras which Kūkai wrote to the emperor upon his return from studying in China. In addition to listing the many religious articles which he brought back with him, Kūkai reported on the results of his studies and extols the doctrines into which he was initiated. Among the points which he especially emphasizes are 1) his personal success in gaining acceptance by the greatest Buddhist teacher of the day in China; 2) the authenticity of this teaching in direct line of succession from the Buddha; 3) the great favor in which this teaching was held by the recent emperors of the T'ang dynasty, to the extent that it represented the best and most influential doctrine current in the Chinese capital; and 4) the fact that this teaching offers the easiest and quickest means of obtaining Buddhahood, probably an important recommendation for it in the eyes of a busy monarch.

During the sixth moon of 804, I, Kūkai, sailed for China aboard the Number One Ship, in the party of Lord Fujiwara, ambassador to the T'ang court. We reached the coast of Fukien by the eighth moon, and four months later arrived at Ch'ang-an, the capital, where we were lodged at the official guest residence. The ambassadorial delegation started home for Japan on March 11, 805, but in obedience to an imperial edict, I alone remained behind in the Hsi-ming Temple where the abbot Eichū had formerly resided.

One day, in the course of my calls on eminent Buddhist teachers of the capital, I happened by chance to meet the abbot of the East Pagoda Hall of the Green Dragon Temple. This great priest, whose Buddhist name was Hui-kuo, was the chosen disciple of the master Amoghavajra. His virtue aroused the reverence of his age; his teachings were lofty enough to guide emperors. Three sovereigns revered him as their master and were ordained by him. The four classes of believers looked up to him for instruction in the esoteric teachings.

I called on the abbot in the company of five or six monks from the Hsi-ming Temple. As soon as he saw me he smiled with pleasure, and he joyfully said, "I knew that you would come! I have been waiting for such a long time. What pleas-

ure it gives me to look on you today at last! My life is drawing to an end, and until you came there was no one to whom
I could transmit the teachings. Go without delay to the ordination altar with incense and a flower." I returned to the
temple where I had been staying and got the things which
were necessary for the ceremony. It was early in the sixth
moon, then, that I entered the ordination chamber. I stood
in front of the Womb Mandala and cast my flower in the
prescribed manner. By chance it fell on the body of the Buddha Vairochana in the center. The master exclaimed in delight, "How amazing! How perfectly amazing!" He repeated
this three or four times in joy and wonder. I was then given
the fivefold baptism and received the instruction in the
Three Mysteries that bring divine intercession. Next I was
taught the Sanskrit formulas for the Womb Mandala, and
learned the yoga contemplation on all the Honored Ones.

Early in the seventh moon I entered the ordination chamber of the Diamond Mandala for a second baptism. When
I cast my flower it fell on Vairochana again, and the abbot
marveled as he had before. I also received ordination as an
āchārya early in the following month. On the day of my
ordination I provided a feast for five hundred of the monks.
The dignitaries of the Green Dragon Temple all attended
the feast, and everyone enjoyed himself.

I later studied the Diamond Crown Yoga and the five
divisions of the True Words teachings, and spent some time
learning Sanskrit and the Sanskrit hymns. The abbot in-
formed me that the Esoteric scriptures are so abstruse that
their meaning cannot be conveyed except through art. For
this reason he ordered the court artist Li Chen and about
a dozen other painters to execute ten scrolls of the Womb
and Diamond Mandalas, and assembled more than twenty
scribes to make copies of the Diamond and other important
Esoteric scriptures. He also ordered the bronzesmith Chao
Wu to cast fifteen ritual implements. These orders for the
painting of religious images and the copying of the sūtras
were issued at various times.

One day the abbot told me, "Long ago, when I was still
young, I met the great master Amoghavajra. From the first
moment he saw me he treated me like a son, and on his
visit to the court and his return to the temple I was as in-

separable from him as his shadow. He confided to me, 'You will be the receptacle of the esoteric teachings. Do your best! Do your best!' I was then initiated into the teachings of both the Womb and Diamond, and into the secret mudrās as well. The rest of his disciples, monks and laity alike, studied just one of the Mandalas or one Honored One or one ritual, but not all of them as I did. How deeply I am indebted to him I shall never be able to express.

"Now my existence on earth approaches its term, and I cannot long remain. I urge you, therefore, to take the two Mandalas and the hundred volumes of the Esoteric teachings, together with the ritual implements and these gifts which were left to me by my master. Return to your country and propagate the teachings there.

"When you first arrived I feared I did not have time enough left to teach you everything, but now my teaching is completed, and the work of copying the sūtras and making the images is also finished. Hasten back to your country, offer these things to the court, and spread the teachings throughout your country to increase the happiness of the people. Then the land will know peace and everyone will be content. In that way you will return thanks to Buddha and to your teacher. That is also the way to show your devotion to your country and to your family. My disciple I-ming will carry on the teachings here. Your task is to transmit them to the Eastern Land. Do your best! Do your best!" These were his final instructions to me, kindly and patient as always. On the night of the last full moon of the year he purified himself with a ritual bath and, lying on his right side and making the mudrā of Vairochana, he breathed his last.

That night, while I sat in meditation in the Hall, the abbot appeared to me in his usual form and said, "You and I have long been pledged to propagate the esoteric teachings. If I am reborn in Japan, this time I will be your disciple"

I have not gone into the details of all he said, but the general import of the Master's instructions I have given. [Dated 5th December 806.]

[From *Kōbō Daishi zenshū*, I, 98–101]

The Transmission of the Law

The ocean of the Law is one, but sometimes it is shallow and sometimes deep, according to the capacity of the believer. Five vehicles have been distinguished, sudden or gradual according to the vessel. Even among the teachings of sudden enlightenment, some are exoteric and some esoteric. In Esotericism itself, some doctrines represent the source while others are tributary. The masters of the Law of former times swam in the tributary waters and plucked at leaves, but the teachings I now bring back reach down to the sources and pull at the roots.

You may wonder why this is so. In ancient times Vajrasattva personally received the teaching from Vairochana. After many centuries it was transmitted to the Bodhisattva Nāgārjuna, who later transmitted it to the Āchārya Nāgabodhi. He in turn transmitted it to the Āchārya Vajrabodhi, the master of Indian and Chinese learning, who first taught the esoteric doctrines in China during the K'ai-yüan era (713–42). Although the emperor himself reverenced his teachings, Vajrabodhi could not spread them very widely. Only with our spiritual grandfather Amoghavajra, the great master of broad wisdom, did the teachings thrive. After he had been initiated by Vajrabodhi, Amoghavajra visited the place in southern India where Nāgabodhi had taught, and silently mastered the eighteen forms of yoga. After attaining a complete understanding of the Womb Mandala and other parts of the esoteric canon, he returned to China during the T'ien-pao era (742–65). At this time the Emperor Hsüan-tsung was baptized; he revered Amoghavajra as his teacher.

In later years both the Emperors Su-tsung and Tai-tsung in turn received the Law. Within the imperial palace the Monastery of the Divine Dragon[1] was established, and in the capital ordination platforms were erected everywhere. The emperor and the government officials went to these

---

[1] "Divine dragon" was an era (705–6) during the reign of the Emperor Chung-tsung.

platforms to be formally baptized. This was the period when the Esoteric sect began to flourish as never before; its methods of baptism were widely adopted from this time on.

According to exoteric doctrines, enlightenment occurs only after three aeons; the esoteric doctrines declare that there are sixteen chances to live as a bodhisattva in this life. In speed and in excellence the two doctrines differ as much as Buddha with his supernatural powers and a lame donkey. You who reverence the good, let this fact be clear in your minds! The superiority of the doctrines and the origins of the Law are explained at length in the five esoteric formulas of Vajrasattva and in the memorials and answers written by Amoghavajra.

[From *Kōbō Daishi zenshū*, I, 83–84]

The Ten Stages of Religious Consciousness

In his master work, The Ten Stages of Religious Consciousness, Kūkai presented a systematic evaluation of the principal schools of Buddhist teaching, as well as of Confucianism, Taoism and Brāhmanism. When it was shown to the reigning emperor, the latter praised it highly but requested that Kūkai compose a simplified and condensed version which would make less formidable reading. His Precious Key to the Secret Treasury was written in response to this request.

In the opening lines of his Introduction, Kūkai acknowledges how difficult it is to make a comprehensive study of the numerous scriptures and texts representing the development of Buddhist doctrine, yet he insists that only by referring to them (as he does in the body of this work) can the manifold aspects of religious truth be made known. As a result the condensation itself is an imposing monument of scriptural scholarship. In the Introduction, however, Kūkai gives a concise résumé of his views, presented in verse, prose, and tabular form. His language is highly rhetorical and at times so obscure or allusive that a variety of interpretations or translations may be derived from a few words of text.

INTRODUCTION

From the deep, dim, most distant past,
A thousand thousand tomes we hold
Of sacred texts and learned lore.

Profound, abstruse, obscure and dark,
Teachings diverse and manifold—
Who can encompass such a store?

Yet, had no one ever written such,
And if no one read what they have told,
What should we know, what should we know?
However hard they strove in thought,
The saint today, the sage of old
Would still be lost, have naught to show.

The ancient god with herb and balm[1]
Took pity on the stricken host
Of suffering, sore humanity.
And he who made the compass-cart[2]
Showed them the way whose way was lost,
A guide in their perplexity.

Yet senseless dawdlers in this world,
The threefold realm of fantasy,
Mad, their madness do not perceive;
And all the fourfold living things
Are blinded so they cannot see
How blind they are, the self-deceived.

Born, reborn, reborn and reborn
Whence they have come they do not know.
Dying, dying, ever dying
They see not where it is they go.

How could the Great Enlightened One, feeling a fatherly
compassion for all sentient beings and seeing the misery of
their existence, silently let it pass? It was for this reason indeed that He provided many sorts of remedies to guide them

[1] Shen-nung, the early Chinese God of Agriculture.
[2] The Duke of Chou, statesman instrumental in founding the Chou
dynasty of Ancient China, was said to have provided a "south-
pointing chariot" for some foreign emissaries who could not find
their way back home.

in their perplexities. To this end he established the following teachings:

1. [The first stage of religious consciousness is the brutish existence described above.]

2. That which, through personal cultivation of the Five Cardinal Virtues and Three Human Relationships, promotes social order by enabling prince and minister, father and son each to fulfill his proper mission in life. [Confucianism.]

3. That which, through practice of the six disciplines and the four methods of mental concentration, produces contempt for the world below and desire for that above, from which one may proceed to the attainment of happiness in heaven. [Brāhmanism and popular Taoism.]

4. That which, recognizing that the self is unreal and represents only a temporary combination of the Five Components[3] strives to achieve the eight forms of disentanglement and six supernatural powers that come from concentrated meditation. [The Shrāvaka vehicle of Hīnayāna Buddhism practiced by the direct disciples of the Buddha.]

5. That which, through personal practice of the meditation on the Twelve Links of Causation,[4] makes one aware of the impermanence and ego-lessness of all things, and thus uproots the seeds of karma. [The pratyeka-buddha vehicle of Hīnayāna Buddhism, practiced by those seeking enlightenment for themselves.]

6. That which, from a sense of unlimited compassion for others, and following the highest inner knowledge which transcends all external circumstances, overcomes all impediments within the mind to transform the eight consciousnesses into the Fourfold Wisdom of the Buddha.[5] [Hossō school of Quasi-Mahāyāna.]

7. That which, by understanding one's nature through

---

[3] Form (body), sensation, perception, psychic construction, and consciousness.

[4] See p. 296, n. 1.

[5] According to the psychological doctrines of the Hossō school the eight consciousnesses are transformed into the wisdom of accomplishing works, awareness of diversity, awareness of equality, and the wisdom of mirror-like objectivity.

the method of eightfold negation[6] and by transcending ordinary forms of argument through realization that Truth is void of name or character, brings the mind to a state of tranquility, absolute and indescribable. [Sanron school of Quasi-Mahāyāna.]

8. That which, by realizing the absolute and universal way in one's primal nature, causes the Bodhisattva of Mercy, Kannon,[7] to smile with delight. [Tendai school of Mahāyāna.]

9. That which, by embracing cosmic existence in the first awakening of religious consciousness, causes the Bodhisattva Fugen[8] to beam with satisfaction. [Kegon school of Mahāyāna.]

10. By these teachings the dust and stains of the world are cleansed away, revealing the splendor and solemnity of the world of the Mandalas. As the performer of the Mantra meditates on the syllables *Ma* and *Ta*, the Buddha's nature shines forth and dispels the darkness of ignorance. In the lasting light of sun and moon appear the Bodhisattvas of Wisdom, while the Five Buddhas[9] reign supreme, each making his characteristic sign of the hand. The universe is filled with the radiance of the Four Mandala Circles[10] representing the Buddha-world.

Achala, the God of Fire, with his left eye closed and right wide open, glares out over the realm of sentient beings and stills the stormy winds of worldly desire. The King of Tri-

[6] Negation of all predication: no production, no extinction; no annihilation, no permanence; no unity, no diversity; no coming, no going.

[7] Avalokiteshvara—here a symbol of the Tendai doctrine of the One in the Many, the identity of noumenon and phenomenon.

[8] Samantabhadra—here a symbol of the Kegon doctrine of the interdependence of all things, all-embracing love.

[9] The Cosmic Buddha, the Buddhas of the four quarters and the Bodhisattvas of the four corners make up the central figures of the Mandalas.

[10] The Great Circle, consisting of graphic Buddha figures, the Symbol Circle, consisting of the articles carried by each; the Law Circle, consisting of letters representing saintly beings; and the Circle of Works, represented by sculptured figures.

umph, Trailokyavijaya, three times roars forth his mighty
"*Hūm*," evaporating the unruly waves of lust. The Eight
Angelic Maidens[11] [at the corners of the Diamond Mandala]
float through the clouds and over the seas to make their exquisite offerings, while the Four Queens of Wisdom[12] are
enraptured by the bliss of the Law.

Such is this state that even those most advanced in the
various stages of ordinary Buddhism are unable even to
glimpse it, and those who have diligently cultivated the
Three Divisions of the Eightfold Path[13] cannot approach it.
It is the secret of all secrets, the enlightenment of all en-
lightenments. [Esoteric Buddhism.]

Alas, men are ignorant of the treasures they possess, and
in their confusion consider themselves enlightened. What
is it but utter foolishness! The Buddha's compassion is indeed profound, but without his teaching how can they be
saved? The remedies have been provided, yet if men refuse
to take them, how can they be cured? If we do naught but
spend our time in vain discussion and vain recitation, the
King of Healing will surely scold us for it.

Now there are nine kinds of medicine[14] for the diseases
of the mind, but the most they can do is sweep away the
surface dust and dispel the mind's confusion. Only in the
Diamond Palace[15] do we find the secret treasury opened
wide to dispense its precious truths. To enjoy them or reject
them—this is for everyone to decide in his own mind. No
one else can do it for you; you must realize it for yourself.

Those who seek Buddha's wisdom must know the difference between a true jewel and an ordinary stone, between
cow's milk and the milk of an ass. They must not fail to

[11] Those of the first division, serving inside, representing the smile,
hair tresses, song and dance; those of the second division, serving
outside, representing incense, flowers, lanterns and ointment.
[12] Representing the Diamond (*Vajra*), Jewel (*Cintāmani*), Law
(Dharma) and Action (Karma).
[13] Right Views, Thought, Speech and Action are the elements of
human character or self-control; Right Mindfulness, Endeavor and
and Livelihood are the elements of human life or self-purification;
Right Concentration is the element of self-development.
[14] The first nine teachings or stages of religious consciousness.
[15] Esoteric Buddhism.

distinguish them; they must not fail to distinguish them.

The ten stages of religious experience, as revealed in the scriptures and their commentaries, are clearly and systematically presented in what follows.

[From *Kōbō Daishi zenshū*, I, 417–19]

A School of Arts and Sciences

Kūkai's proposal for the establishment of a "School of Arts and Sciences (Shugei shuchi-in)" reveals two important tendencies in his thought. First is the universalistic and egalitarian character of Mahāyāna Buddhism. Citing the teachings of the Lotus Sūtra which stresses the essential oneness of all being, Kūkai asks support for a school to be open to all, regardless of social status or economic means. The second reflects Kūkai's catholic outlook, affirming the value of both religious and secular studies, and of combining the Three Teachings (Confucianism, Taoism, and Buddhism) in the curriculum of the school.

Generally, in Japan as in China, religious and secular studies represented two separate ways of life. Saichō, it will be recalled, wished his monks to combine a religious and secular vocation, but classical Confucian studies had a very subordinate role in the training of monks on Mt. Hiei, for whom social action and public service were conceived by him in very practical terms.

In Kūkai's time secular education was closely linked to official recruitment and training, and largely restricted to the ruling classes. Though ostensibly Confucian, it failed to measure up to Confucius' own ideals of brotherhood, as Kūkai points out. The aristocratic character of Japanese society, indeed, proved strongly resistant to the potentially democratic elements in Buddhism and Confucianism. In this case, though a Fujiwara nobleman donated an attractive site for the school, Kūkai had difficulty obtaining continuing support for his work, and it was forced to close ten years after his death, in 845.

. . . Having dedicated myself to the salvation of all beings, and hoping to establish a school for the study of the Three Teachings [Buddhism, Confucianism, and Taoism], I asked Lord Fujiwara for the donation of his residence. Without even exchanging a formal document of agreement, he immediately offered me the house, which may well be worth one thousand gold pieces, for the sake of accumulating merit toward his enlightenment.

Thus, I obtained this superb site, as lovely as the park of Jeta,[1] without having to spend any money. My long cherished desire was at once fulfilled. I have given it the name of School of Arts and Sciences and made up a tentative program as follows:

The Nine Schools[2] and Six Arts[3] are the boats and bridges that save the world; the Ten Baskets[4] and the Five Sciences[5] are the treasures that benefit people. The Tathāgatas of the past have studied them, those of the present are now studying them, and those of the future will also, thereby attaining great enlightenment. Bodhisattvas of the ten directions have studied them all and realized the all-pervading wisdom. Unless one resorts to these studies, one cannot gain the essentials of how to establish oneself in the world, cannot learn the principles of governing the country, and cannot attain Nirvāna on the other shore, terminating the transmigratory life on this shore.

Emperors have built state temples; their subjects have constructed private temples; in this way they have made efforts to spread the Way [Buddhism]. But those who wear robes in the temples study Buddhist scriptures; while scholars and students at the government college study non-Buddhist texts. Thus they are all stuck when it comes to books representing the Three Teachings and Five Sciences [as a whole]. Now I shall build a school of arts and sciences, offering instruction in the Three Teachings, and invite capable persons to join. With the aid of these teachings, which can be compared to the sun [Buddhism], the moon [Taoism], and the stars [Confucianism], my sincere desire is to enlighten those who

[1] The park where Shākya Buddha had his monastery and taught. It is said that the rich man Anāthapiṇḍika bought the park from Prince Jeta, paying him the sum of gold pieces needed to cover the surface of the land, and offered the park to the Buddha.

[2] The nine schools of philosophy: Confucian, Taoist, Yin-yang, Legalist, Logic ("Names"), Mo-ist, Horizontal and Vertical Alliances, Unclassified Teachings, and Agriculture.

[3] Rites, music, archery, charioteering, writing and mathematics.

[4] The classification of all teachings into ten categories in Buddhism. "Basket" signifies a container of the scriptures.

[5] The five subjects of study in Buddhism: grammar, logic, medicine, arts and Buddhism.

are wandering in the dark down the wrong path, and lead them to the garden of enlightenment mounted on the Five Vehicles. . . .

It may be objected, however: "The government maintains a state college where the arts and sciences are encouraged and taught. What good is a mosquito's cry [a private school] compared to rumbling thunder [a government school]?"

My reply is: "In the capital of China, a school is set up in each ward to teach the young boys. In each prefecture a school is maintained in order widely to educate promising young students. Because of this, the capital is filled with talented young men and the nation is crowded with masters of the arts. In the capital of our country, however, there is only one government college and no local schools. As a result, sons of the poor have no opportunity to seek knowledge. Those who like to study, but live a great distance from the college, encounter great difficulty traveling to and fro. Would it not be good, then, to establish this school to assist the uneducated?" . . .

Although I am not of much ability, I am determined to pursue the plan under way; I will not give up this task, no matter how difficult it may be. Thus I may requite my vast obligations to the emperors, my parents, the people, and the Three Treasures, and also make this a means of realizing Ultimate Truth, achieving the Highest Wisdom and winning final deliverance.

REGULATIONS FOR INVITING THE INSTRUCTORS

Confucius said in the *Analects*: "It is best to live in a community where the spirit of benevolence prevails. Unless one dwells in its midst, how can he attain true knowledge?" [IV,1] He also said: "One should study the [six] arts." It is stated in the [*Mahāvairocana*] *Sūtra*: "By the time one has become an authentic master, one should have studied the various arts and sciences." A commentary [to the *Daśabhūmika*] also says: "In order to attain enlightenment, a bodhisattva studies the five sciences." Therefore, Sudhana visited a hundred and ten cities to seek the teachings of fifty-[three] teachers,[6] the Bodhisattva "Always Crying" went crying

[6] This story appears in the *Gandavyūha Sūtra*.

throughout the city in his search for wisdom; both sought seriously for the profound Dharma. . . .

Even if one finds a suitable place, there will be no way of getting an understanding without teachers. Therefore, first of all, teachers should be invited. Of these there should be two kinds: those who teach the Way and those who teach secular subjects. The teachers of the Way must teach the Buddhist scriptures, and the secular teachers must set forth the non-Buddhist texts. That religious and secular teachings should not be separated is the noble saying of my teacher.

(A) INSTRUCTION BY TEACHERS OF THE WAY

To teach both exoteric and esoteric Buddhism is the pleasure of the clergy. Should there be students who want to study non-Buddhist texts alongside Buddhism, let the secular teachers take care of them. For those who want to study Buddhist scriptures and commentaries, the clergy should spare no efforts, abiding by the Four States of Mind [7] and the Four All-Embracing Virtues.[8] Without discriminating between noble and low-born, the clergy should offer instruction in Buddhism as appropriate to all students.

(B) INSTRUCTION BY SECULAR DOCTORS

The secular doctors should be well versed in one part of each of the following subjects: The Nine Classics,[9] the Nine Schools,[10] the three Profound texts,[11] the three Histories,[12] the Seven Outlines,[13] and the Histories of the Seven Dynas-

---

[7] The Four Brahma Vihāras—positive loving kindness, compassion, joy, and indifference.

[8] In order to lead others to love and receive the truth of Buddhism one must: 1) give them what they like; 2) speak affectionate words to them; 3) practice conduct profitable to them; and 4) cooperate with and adapt oneself to them.

[9] The Book of Changes, the Book of Odes, the Book of History, the Record of Rites, the Book of Ritual, the Rites of Chou, the Tso Chuan, the Kung-yang Chuan, the Ku-liang Chuan.

[10] Cf. note No. 2.

[11] The Book of Changes, Tao-te ching, and Chuang Tzu.

[12] Historical Records of Ssu-ma Ch'ien, the History of Former Han, and the History of Later Han.

[13] Outlines of compilations made of the six arts; the schools of phi-

ties.[14] Through one text in each of these subjects they should be able to instruct the students in poetry, metrical prose, pronunciation, reading, punctuation, and interpretation. . . .

Should there be religious who desire to study non-Buddhist subjects, the secular doctors should teach them according to their needs. If young, uneducated children wish to learn how to read and write, genuine teachers should instruct them in a spirit of deep compassion, filial piety, and loyalty. Whether the students are high-born or low, rich or poor, they should receive appropriate instruction and their teachers should be unremitting in admonishing them. "The beings in the three worlds are my children" roars the Buddha [in the *Lotus Sūtra*]. And there is the beautiful saying of Confucius: [in *Analects*, VII, 5] "All within the four seas are brothers." Do honor to them!

(c) MEALS FOR BOTH TEACHERS AND STUDENTS:

"Man is not a hanging gourd [fed by the vine]" said Confucius. That man lives on food is what Shākya Buddha taught. If one wants to propagate the Way, one must necessarily feed those who follow it. Whether they be religious or laymen, teacher or student, any who want to study should be provided with free meals. I am a poor monk however, and am unable to bear the expenses of the school. For the time being, I shall somehow provide the means, but should there be anyone who cares to render a service to the nation or who wishes to escape from illusions and realize enlightenment, let him give a donation, no matter how small the amount may be, to help me fulfill my aspirations. May we, then, ride together on the vehicle of Buddhism to benefit the people of later generations.

> *Written by Kūkai*
> *On the Fifteenth Day of the Twelfth Month,*
> *the Fifth Year of Tenchō* (828)
>> [From *Kōbō daishi zenshū*, III, 535–539]

losophy; poetry and metrical prose; military science; divination; technical, medical, and agricultural subjects.
[14] The Histories of Sung, Ch'i (Southern), Liang, Ch'en, Wei, Ch'i (Northern), and Chou.

11 ❀

AMIDA AND THE PURE LAND

INTRODUCTION

"There is only one Way," the *Lotus Sūtra* says again and again, "not two or three." All human beings are to achieve Buddhahood through the same Great Vehicle, Mahāyāna. No class or group is to be disqualified; there are to be no separate categories, such as the Hīnayāna and pseudo-Mahāyāna sects distinguish, for those of different social status or individual capability. No matter what means men avail themselves of, all find their ultimate fulfillment in the single, universal Way of Mahāyāna.

This was the central truth of the Buddhist faith which reigned supreme in the Heian period. The two leading sects, Tendai and Shingon, both acknowledged such an idealistic and egalitarian view of man's potentialities for enlightenment. But, as we have seen, in the practice of this Mahāyāna faith compromises were made which reflected the more aristocratic character of Japanese society in this period, especially the strong consciousness of rank and status which pervaded the life of the Heian court. There was an established hierarchy in almost every sphere of activity: there were three grades of royal princes, called *hon*, and there were eight ranks for government officials, each subdivided into Senior and Junior. Even court gossip gave voice to the passion for making distinctions of grade and quality, as evidenced by the sharp judgments of a Lady Shōnagon, in her *Pillow Book*, or by the second chapter of *The Tale of Genji*, in which young men of the court assess the beauty and talents of women they have known in terms of *shina*, "grade."

In a sense, too, Kūkai's *Ten Stages of Religious Consciousness* exemplifies the same tendency, for in assigning each type of belief its proper place in the total scheme of salvation, Kūkai also assigned it a certain relative value and made clear its peculiar limitations. This quality perhaps in Kūkai's Esoteric Buddhism, as well as its emphasis on art and ritual, accounts for the high favor which his new faith won in the citadels of Heian culture. For the Esoteric doctrine, which entrenched itself not only at court but at Nara, the old center of Buddhism, and at Mt. Hiei, the Tendai center, put far less stress in practice on the universal hope of attaining Buddhahood than it did on the special means to be employed by each individual. The Buddha and all creatures were made of the same stuff, the same six elements. But in the diverse manifestations of the Mandala might be seen the different aspects and functions of the Three Mysteries: Body, Speech, and Mind. Through their proper functioning alone could Buddhahood be attained, and the secret knowledge of these functions was possessed by the Shingon priesthood alone. Inasmuch as Shingon Buddhism was esoteric, it also tended to be exclusive.

In the twelfth century, with the sudden collapse of the Kyoto court and the onset of the feudal era, among the swift and bewildering changes that ensued was a sweeping redirection of the religious life of Japan. It is not surprising that the established sects of Buddhism should have declined with the waning fortunes of their aristocratic patrons, but in an age often seen as dominated by hardened warriors and held in the tight grip of military government, it may seem paradoxical that Japanese Buddhism should for the first time have become a mass movement, a democracy of faith, offering to everyone tangible hope for salvation in this life. Yet this is the most evident and significant feature of medieval Buddhism; that it was not preserved as a mere heirloom of the *ancien régime*, but elbowed its way out among the people and made itself at home in the households of humble folk.

In this popularization of Buddhism no doctrine or sect

was more influential than that associated with the Buddha Amida,[1] whose Western Paradise or "Pure Land" offered a haven to weary souls in that strife-torn age. It was Amida, the Buddha of Boundless Light, who aeons ago vowed that all should be saved who called on his name, a pledge which became known as the "Original Vow." It was to the Pure Land, a special place prepared by Amida, that the Buddha welcomed those who had won eternal bliss by calling on his name, *Namu Amida Butsu*, with single-minded and whole-hearted devotion. This was the invocation which became known as the *Nembutsu*, a term which originally signified meditation on the name of Amida, but later meant simply the fervent repetition of his name. The scriptural authority for this teaching came from a sūtra in which Shākyamuni describes his former existence as a Buddha-to-be (bodhisattva), who accepts Buddhahood only on condition that he can establish a land of bliss for all who invoke his name (as Amida) in perfect trust. In another sūtra Shākyamuni offers a devout queen her choice of many Buddha-lands and, after she has chosen that of Amida, he instructs her in the meditation which will lead to her admission there.

This faith was not by any means the creation of medieval Japan. It derived from the Mahāyāna Buddhism of Northern India and Central Asia, and for centuries the worship of Amida had been tremendously popular in China. Nevertheless the spread of Pure Land doctrines in medieval times represented a striking change in outlook for the Japanese, and in the process of establishing itself, the doctrine too underwent profound changes. For one thing, the earlier forms of Japanese Buddhism had all stressed the attainment of Buddhahood, the achieving of enlightenment, whereas this faith aimed at rebirth in a land of bliss. At the same time there was a shift in emphasis away from the individual's efforts to achieve enlightenment toward an exclusive reliance on the saving power of the Buddha. This meant a strong monotheistic tendency—all honor and devotion to Amida alone—in contrast to the strong polytheistic tendency of Esoteric Buddhism, with its multitude of icons directing worship to a vast pantheon of Buddhas and bodhisattvas.

[1] Skt: Amitābha.

From the social as well as the religious standpoint two far-reaching changes wrought by the spread of Amidism were the transformation of the Buddhist clergy and the recognition of women's right to equal opportunities for salvation along with men. The champions of Amida-worship started a trend away from the traditional concept of the Buddhist clergy, who had left the world as celibate followers of a monastic discipline, toward a new role as religious leaders living in society a life which differed little from the layman's. One of the reasons which led them out of the isolation of the monasteries was a desire to bring religion directly to those outside, including women. When the great monastic centers of Hiei and Kōya were established, their founders ordained that these sacred precincts should never be visited by women. An incidental advantage of this ban was no doubt to insure against violations of the vows of celibacy, but what primarily dictated it was the view that women were a source of defilement (probably because they were subject to menstruation, long regarded as a form of pollution). Women were thus effectively excluded from participation in some of the more important religious observances. But the new religious leaders were determined that women should enjoy every opportunity for salvation open to men.

PIONEERS OF PURE LAND BUDDHISM

The rise of Pure Land Buddhism was not merely an outgrowth of the new feudal society, translating into religious terms the profound social changes which then took place. Already in the late Heian period we find individual monks who sensed the need for bringing Buddhist faith within the reach of the ordinary man, and thus anticipated the mass religious movements of medieval times. Kūya (903–972), a monk on Mt. Hiei, was one of these. The meditation on the Buddha Amida, which had long been accepted as an aid to the religious life, he promoted as a pedestrian devotion. Dancing through the city streets with a tinkling bell hanging from around his neck, Kūya called out the name of Amida and sang simple ditties of his own composition, such as:

Hito tabi mo	He never fails
Namu Amida bu to	To reach the Lotus Land of Bliss
Yū hito no	Who calls,
Hasu no utena ni	If only once,
Noboranu wa nashi.	The name of Amida.

And—

Gokuraku wa	A far, far distant land
Harukeki hodo to	Is Paradise,
Kikishi kado	I've heard them say;
Tsutomete itaru	But it can be reached
Tokoro narikeri.	By those who want to go.

In the market places all kinds of people joined him in his dance and sang out the invocation to Amida, "Namu Amida Butsu." When a great epidemic struck the capital, he proposed that these same people join him in building an image of Amida in a public square, saying that common folk could equal the achievement of their rulers, who had built the Great Buddha of Nara, if they cared to try. In country districts he built bridges and dug wells for the people where these were needed, and to show that no one was to be excluded from the blessings of Paradise, he traveled into regions inhabited by the Ainu and for the first time brought to many of them the evangel of Buddhism.

As Kūya became known as "the saint of the streets" for his dancing, so another Tendai monk, Ryōnin (1072–1132), later became known especially for his propagation of the *Nembutsu* through popular songs. Ryōnin's great success in this medium reflected his own vocal talents and his mastery of traditional liturgical music. At the same time his advocacy of the *Nembutsu* chant reflected the influence upon him of Tendai and Kegon doctrine. From the former philosophy he drew the idea that "one act is all acts, and all acts are one act." From the *Flower Garland (Kegon) Sūtra* he took the doctrine of the interrelation and interdependence of all things: "one man is all men and all men are one man." Joining these to faith in Amida, he produced the "circulating *Nembutsu*" or "Nembutsu in communion" (*Yūzū nembutsu*). If one man calls the name of Amida, it will benefit all men; one man may share in the invocations of all others. Spreading this simple but all-embracing idea in a musical form, Ryōnin became an evangelist on a vast scale. Among his early converts were court ladies, and the Emperor Toba was so deeply impressed that he gave Ryōnin a bell made from one of his own mirrors. With this he traveled the length and breadth of the land, inviting everyone to join him in the "circulating *Nembutsu*" and asking them to sign their names in a roster of participants. According to tradition the entries accumulated during a lifetime of evangelizing added up to the modest figure of 3,282.

In the thirteenth century these same methods were employed by the evangelist Ippen (1239–1289), who believed that the grace of Amida was present everywhere, in Shinto shrines as well as Buddhist temples of all denominations. For him the important thing was not to build new places of worship, but for the faithful to dance and sing together in praise of Amida, anywhere, any time. In the roster he kept of persons joining in his movement the names were said to have reached the incredible total of 2,300,001,724.

A man who did as much as Kūya and Ryōnin to popularize faith in Amida, without ever leaving the monastic life, was Genshin (942–1017). He too was from Mt. Hiei, to which the great Ennin had first brought the practice of meditation on the name of Amida. From his early study of the *Lotus Sūtra* and his great devotion to his aged mother, Genshin became convinced that there must be some means of obtaining salvation which was open to all, laymen as well as monks, women as well as men. And the method he espoused after years of pious study—loving trust in the saving power of Amida—he wished to bring to all in a vivid and forceful manner. This he did in his *Essentials of Salvation*, which brought together in one book passages from the great body of Buddhist scriptures describing various aspects of the religious life. For Genshin, as for all Tendai schoolmen, there are ten realms of existence with the world of the Buddha at one end and Hell at the other, human existence standing in between. Man's religious life starts with an aversion for Hell, the perpetual battleground of human greed, lust, and desire for power. As he shrinks from those actions which result in the miseries of Hell, man is drawn to the land made blissful by the light, life, and love of Amida. This is the essence of religion: disgust for Hell and desire for the Pure Land. Genshin's work was to inspire all men with these sentiments by depicting in lucid and graphic terms the horrors of Hell and attractions of the Western Paradise. So effectively did he convey in popular form the fruits of his scriptural studies that his book, *The Essentials of Salvation*, not only won the acclaim of Chinese authorities to whom he sent a copy, but it became a sort of "best-seller" in medieval times, going through several printed editions. With so learned a monk as its champion, the popularization of Amidism gained added impetus.

But Genshin was not content to express himself in literary form alone and turned to painting and sculpture as well. The written word could only be appreciated by those able to read, and since Genshin wrote in a modified form of Chinese, his work was not accessible to many. Painting and sculpture, on the other hand, had the advantage of direct and instantaneous appeal to all. Unfortunately we do not possess much reliable evidence of Genshin's work in these media, but there can be no doubt that he was the originator of a new religious art. Liberating Buddhist painting from the stiff and stereotyped forms of Shingon iconography, he introduced new subjects such as the torments of Hell, the glories of Paradise, and the compassionate Amida with his attendant bodhisattvas welcoming the blessed to the Pure Land. These scenes he represented with a freshness of imagination and devotional atmosphere reflecting his own deep piety. The diary of a court lady of that time testifies to the effectiveness of his painting, for when one of his screens was brought into the palace the ladies-in-waiting had nightmares over the realistic treatment of hell-fire and its screaming victims. There is an enormous painting attributed to him, now in the Mt. Kōya Museum, which shows Amida and his retinue coming out to receive the souls of the redeemed. It is recognized as probably the greatest of Japanese religious paintings. Another famous painting believed to be his is called "Amida Beyond the Hill." It shows Buddha rising like the moon over Genshin's mountain-home and bathing Lake Biwa in the resplendent light of his benign countenance.

Thus the pioneers of Pure Land Buddhism developed new

means of communication—dancing, music, painting, sculpture, and popular religious tracts—in order to bring the Buddha-land within sight of all. With these available, Buddhism was ready to take a wider and deeper hold on the life of the people than ever before.

The Essentials of Salvation

This famous work by Genshin, describing the torments of Hell, the Pure Land, and the advantages of the Nembutsu, is in ten divisions as listed below by the author. The following excerpts are the initial chapters in the first two divisions, dealing with Hell and the Pure Land. Scriptural authorities cited by Genshin are deleted from the text.

The teaching and practice which leads to birth in Paradise is the most important thing in this impure world during these degenerate times.[1] Monks and laymen, men of high or low station, who will not turn to it? But the literature of the exoteric and the esoteric teachings of Buddha are not one in text, and the practices of one's work in this life in its ritualistic and philosophical aspects are many. These are not difficult for men of keen wisdom and great diligence, but how can a stupid person such as I achieve this knowledge? Because of this I have chosen the one gate to salvation of the *nembutsu*. I have made selections from the important sūtras and shāstras and have set them forth so that they may be readily understood and their disciplines easily practiced. In all there are ten divisions, divided into three volumes. The first is the corrupt life which one must shun, the second is the pure land for which one should seek, the third is the proof of the existence of the pure land, the fourth is the correct practice of Nembutsu, the fifth is the helpful means of practicing the Nembutsu, the sixth is the practice of Nembutsu on special occasions, the seventh is the benefit resulting from Nembutsu, the eighth is the proof of the bene-

---

[1] Reference is to *mappō*, the last of the three periods of Buddhist law, that of degeneration and destruction of the law which extends for countless years. The first period, *shōbō*, the period of the true law, lasted 500 years. The second period, *zōbō*, the period of the simulated doctrine, endured 1,000 years.

fit accruing from Nembutsu alone, the ninth is the conduct leading to birth in Paradise, and the tenth comprises questions and answers to selected problems. These I place to the right of where I sit lest I forget them.

The first division, the corrupt land which one must shun, comprises the three realms[2] in which there is no peace. Now, in order to make clear the external appearances of this land, this division has seven parts: 1) hell; 2) hungry demons; 3) beasts; 4) fighting demons; 5) man; 6) Deva; and 7) a conclusion.

The first of these, hell, is furthermore divided into eight parts: 1) The hell of repeated misery; 2) The hell of the black chains; 3) The hell of mass suffering; 4) The hell of wailing; 5) The hell of great wailing; 6) The hell of searing heat; 7) The hell of great searing heat, and 8) The hell of incessant suffering.

The hell of repeated misery is one thousand yojanas[3] beneath the Southern Continent[4] and is ten thousand yojanas in length and breadth. Sinners here are always possessed of the desire to do each other harm. Should they by chance see each other, they behave as does the hunter when he encounters a deer. With iron claws they slash each other's bodies until blood and flesh are dissipated and the bones alone remain. Or else the hell-wardens, taking in their hands iron sticks and poles, beat the sinners' bodies from head to foot until they are pulverized like grains of sand. Or else, with a sword of awful sharpness, they cut their victims' bodies in regular pieces as the kitchen worker slices the flesh of fish. And then a cool wind arises, and blowing, returns the sinners to the same state in which they were at the outset. Thereupon they immediately arise and undergo torment identical to that which they had previously suffered. Elsewhere it is said that a voice from the sky above calls to the sentient beings to revive and return to their original state. And again, it is said that the hell-wardens beat upon the ground with iron pitchforks calling upon the sinners to

[2] Past, present, and future.
[3] The distance an army can march in one day.
[4] India and adjoining regions.

revive. I cannot tell in detail of the other sufferings similar to those already told. . . .

Fifty years of human life is equivalent to one day and night in the realm of the Four Deva Kings,[5] and there life lasts five hundred years. The life in the realm of the Four Deva Kings is the equivalent of one day and night in this hell, and here life lasts five hundred years. People who have taken the life of a living creature fall into this hell. . . .

Outside the four gates of this hell are sixteen separate places which are associated with this hell. The first is called the place of excrement. Here, it is said, there is intensely hot dung of the bitterest of taste, filled with maggots with snouts of indestructible hardness. The sinner here eats of the dung and all the assembled maggots swarm at once for food. They destroy the sinner's skin, devour his flesh and suck the marrow from his bones. People who at one time in the past killed birds or deer fall into this hell. Second is the place of the turning sword. It is said that iron walls ten yojanas in height surround it and that a terrible and intense fire constantly burns within. The fire possessed by man is like snow when compared to this. With the least of physical contact, the body is broken into pieces the size of mustard-seeds. Hot iron pours from above like a heavy rainfall, and in addition, there is a forest of swords, with blades of exceptional keenness, and these swords, too, fall like rain. The multitude of agonies is in such variety that it cannot be borne. Into this place fall those who have killed a living being with concupiscence. Third is the place of the burning vat. It is said that the sinner is seized and placed in an iron vat, and boiled as one would cook beans. Those who in the past have taken the life of a living creature, cooked it, and eaten of it, fall into this hell. Fourth is the place of many agonies. In this hell there are a trillion different numberless tortures which cannot be explained in detail. Those who at some time in the past bound men with rope, beat men with sticks, drove men and forced them to make long journeys, threw men down steep places, tortured men with smoke, frightened small children, and in many other ways brought suffering to

[5] The lowest of the six heavens in the world of desire.

their fellow man, fall into this hell. Fifth is the place of darkness. It is said that here is pitch blackness that burns constantly with a dark flame. A powerful and intense wind blows against the adamantine mountains causing them to grind against each other and to destroy each other, so that the bodies of the sinners in between are broken into fragments like grains of sand. Then a hot wind arises which cuts like a sharply honed sword. To this place fall those who have covered the mouths and noses of sheep or who have placed turtles between two tiles and crushed them to death. Sixth is the place of joylessness. Here, it is said, is a great fire which burns intensely night and day. Birds, dogs, and foxes with flaming beaks whose intensely evil cries cause the sinner to feel the greatest of fear, come constantly to eat of the sinner, whose bones and flesh lie in great confusion. Hard-snouted maggots course about inside the bone and eat of the marrow. Those who once blew on shells, beat drums, made frightening sounds, or killed birds and animals fall to this hell. Seventh is the place of extreme agony. It is located beneath a precipitous cliff where a fire of iron burns continuously. People who once killed living creatures in a fit of debauchery descend to this hell. . . .

The second division is the Pure Land towards which one must aspire. The rewards of Paradise are of endless merit. Should one speak of them for a hundred kalpas or even for a thousand kalpas, one would not finish describing them; should one count them or give examples of them, there would still be no way to know of them. At present, ten pleasures in praise of the Pure Land will be explained, and they are as but a single hair floating upon the great sea.

First is the pleasure of being welcomed by many saints. Second is the pleasure of the first opening of the lotus.[6] Third is the pleasure of obtaining in one's own body the ubiquitous supernatural powers of a Buddha. Fourth is the pleasure of the realm of the five wonders. Fifth is the pleasure of everlasting enjoyment. Sixth is the pleasure of influencing others and introducing them to Buddhism. Seventh is the pleasure of assembling with the holy family. Eighth is the pleasure of beholding the Buddha and hearing

[6] The pleasure of being first born into this land.

the Law. Ninth is the pleasure of serving the Buddha according to the dictates of one's own heart. Tenth is the pleasure of progressing in the way of Buddhahood. . . .

First is the pleasure of being welcomed by many saints. Generally when an evil man's life comes to an end, the elements of wind and fire leave first, and as they control movement and heat, great suffering is felt. When a good man dies, earth and water depart first, and as they leave gently, they cause no pain. How much less painful then must be the death of a man who has accumulated merit through *nembutsu!* The man who carries this teaching firmly in his mind for a long time feels a great rejoicing arise within him at the approach of death. Because of his great vow, Amida Nyorai,[7] accompanied by many bodhisattvas and hundreds of thousands of monks, appears before the dying man's eyes, exuding a great light of radiant brilliance. And at this time the great compassionate Kanzeon[8] extending hands adorned with the hundred blessings and offering a jeweled lotus throne, appears before the faithful. The Bodhisattva Seishi[9] and his retinue of numberless saints chant hymns and at the same time extend their hands and accept him among them. At this time the faithful one, seeing these wonders before his eyes, feels rejoicing within his heart and feels at peace as though he were entering upon meditation. Let us know then, that at the moment that death comes, though it be in a hut of grass, the faithful one finds himself seated upon a lotus throne. Following behind Amida Buddha amid the throng of bodhisattvas, in a moment's time he achieves birth in the Western Paradise. . . .

The pleasures in the Thirty-threefold heaven[10] which last a billion years, the pleasures of deep meditation in the palace of the Great Brahmā heaven,[11] are not pleasures at all, for the cycle of transmigration is not at an end, and one cannot escape the evils of the three worlds. But once one is in the embrace of Kannon and is seated upon the treasure lotus throne, one has crossed the sea of suffering and is born for

---

[7] Amitābha Tathāgata.
[8] More commonly Kannon.
[9] Mahāsthāmaprāpta.
[10] Tōri-ten.
[11] Daibon.

the first time in the Pure Land. The pleasure felt in the
heart at this time cannot be put into words.

A *gāthā* by Nāgārjuna says, "If upon death a man attains
birth in this land, the virtue he attains is endless. That is
why I devote my life to Amida." . . .

Second is the pleasure of the first opening of the Lotus.
After the believer is born into this land and when he experiences the pleasures of the first opening of the lotus, his
joy becomes a hundred times greater than before. It is comparable to a blind man gaining sight for the first time, or to
entering a royal palace directly after leaving some rural region. Looking at his own body, it becomes purplish gold in
color. He is gowned naturally in jeweled garments. Rings,
bracelets, a crown of jewels, and other ornaments in countless profusion adorn his body. And when he looks upon the
light radiating from the Buddha, he obtains pure vision, and
because of his experiences in former lives, he hears the
sounds of all things. And no matter what color he may see
or what sound he may hear, it is a thing of marvel. Such is
the ornamentation of space above that the eye becomes lost
in the traces of clouds. The melody of the wheel of the
wonderful Law as its turns, flows throughout this land of
jeweled sound. Palaces, halls, forests, and ponds shine and
glitter everywhere. Flocks of wild ducks, geese, and mandarin
ducks fly about in the distance and near at hand. One may
see multitudes from all the worlds being born into this land
like sudden showers of rain. And one may see a throng of
saints, numerous as the grains of sand in the Ganges, arriving
from the many Buddha-lands. There are some who climb
within the palaces and look about in all directions. There
are those who, mounted upon temples, dwell in space. Then
again there are some who, living in the sky, recite the sūtra
and explain the Law. And again there are some who, dwelling in space, sit in meditation. Upon the ground and amid
the forests there are others engaged in the same activities.
And all about there are those who cross and bathe in the
streams and those who walk among the palaces singing and
scattering flowers and chanting the praises of the Tathāgata.
In this way the numberless celestial beings and saints pursue
their own pleasures as they themselves desire. How indeed
can one tell in detail of the throng of incarnate Buddhas

and bodhisattvas which fills this land like clouds of incense and flowers!

> [From Yampolsky, *The Essentials of Salvation*, pp. 10–16, 90–94]

HŌNEN

What we have so far referred to as Pure Land Buddhism or Amidism was not a separate sect or school. Images of Amida and his two attendant bodhisattvas, Seishi and Kannon (known to the West as the Goddess of Mercy), were to be found in the temples of every sect, and recitation of the Nembutsu was a common adjunct to meditative practices that aimed at a state of enlightenment or ecstasy. The popularization of this formula did not, therefore, break down the walls of sectarian allegiance or seriously undercut existing religious observances. It was only with the appearance of Hōnen (1133–1212) that such a sharp break with other forms of Buddhism occurred.

In his epoch-making work *Senchakushū*, which translated in full means "Collection of Passages on the Original Vow of Amida, in Which the Nembutsu Is Chosen Above All Other Ways of Achieving Rebirth," Hōnen made it unmistakably clear that the Invocation to Amida was superior to all other religious practices. Traditional methods he characterized as the Path of Holiness, which involved the practice of severe disciplines leading to enlightenment, and which relied for their efficacy upon the personal merits and effort of the aspirant. The other Path was that of the Pure Land, involving only the recitation of the Nembutsu and complete reliance on the grace of Amida, not upon oneself. Since it was widely accepted that the world was passing through a stage of utter religious degeneration, as foretold by the Buddha, Hōnen believed that the Path of Holiness was beyond the capability of most men to pursue successfully. Their only sure hope of salvation in such times was to follow the second Path, since its success was dependent only on the unfailing mercy and power of Amida. In Hōnen's terms the former way was the "difficult path," relying on "one's own power," whereas the Nembutsu offered an "easy path," relying on the "power of another." The Nembutsu was therefore the greatest and most excellent of all disciplines, and enjoyed the protection of all other Buddhas as well as of Amida.

When this book, originally written for the edification of the premier, Fujiwara Kanezane, was eventually published, monks from Mt. Hiei seized all available copies, together with the blocks from which they were printed, and consigned them to the flames. Hōnen had already exposed himself to attack on personal grounds. Being a man of deep charity and believing that all men were equally immersed in sin, on one occasion he gave shelter in his mountain hermitage to a young court lady, about to deliver a child by a secret union. Some people insinuated that Hōnen was the real father of the expected baby, but in spite of such calumny Hōnen continued to treat the lady with the deepest solicitude and tender care. Later the father was proven to be a young Taira warrior who had died in battle.

At the age of seventy-four Hōnen's success in winning converts to the new Pure Land Sect, which he had founded, resulted in his condemnation and exile. His biography tells us that in "the first year of Ken'ei (1206) . . . on the ninth day of the twelfth month, the retired Emperor Go-Toba happened to make a visit to the shrines at Kumano. It so happened that at this time Jūren and Anraku and some other disciples of Hōnen were holding a special service for the practice of the Nembutsu at Shishigatani in Kyoto, in which they were chanting the hymns appointed for each of the six hours of the day and night. The chanting was so impressive and awe-inspiring, with its peculiar irregular intonation, that those who heard it were strangely swayed by mingled feelings of sorrow and joy, so that many were led into the life of faith. Among them there were two maids of honor to the ex-emperor, who in his absence had gone to the service. On the emperor's return from Kumano, it would appear as if someone told him about these ladies having become nuns, suggesting that there was something wrong about their relations with these priests, so that the emperor was very angry with them, and on the ninth of the second month in the second year of Ken'ei (1207), he summoned them to the court and imposed on them quite a severe penalty." [1]

[1] Coates and Ishizuka, *Honen*, p. 598.

On his way into exile in a remote region of Shikoku, from which he returned by Imperial pardon only a year before his death, Hōnen fashioned a papier-mâché image of himself while passing away the hours aboard ship. It shows him with an enormous head having two unusual protuberances. One of these is said by his followers to represent his great scriptural erudition, which gained him the soubriquet *Chie Daiichi* (Foremost in Wisdom). The other, even more prominent, is considered a sign of his compassionate nature.

Invocation of Amida

Written in answer to questions raised by the wife of the ex-Regent, Kanezane Tsukinowa, who had already been converted to Hōnen's faith, this letter defends the exclusive practice of the Nembutsu, which the lady was thereby persuaded to take up.

I have the honor of addressing you regarding your inquiry about the Nembutsu. I am delighted to know that you are invoking the sacred name. Indeed the practice of the Nembutsu is the best of all for bringing us to Ōjō,[1] because it is the discipline prescribed in Amida's Original Vow. The discipline required in the Shingon, and the meditation of the Tendai, are indeed excellent, but they are not in the Vow. This Nembutsu is the very thing that Shākya himself entrusted to his disciple Ānanda. As to all other forms of religious practice belonging to either the meditative or non-meditative classes, however excellent they may be in themselves, the great Master did not specially entrust them to Ānanda to be handed down to posterity. Moreover the Nembutsu has the endorsation of all the Buddhas of the six quarters; and, while the discipline of the exoteric and esoteric schools, whether in relation to the phenomenal or noumenal worlds, are indeed most excellent, the Buddhas do not give them their final approval. And so, although there are many kinds of religious exercise, the Nembutsu far excels them all in its way of attaining Ōjō. Now there are some people who are unacquainted with the way of birth into the Pure Land, who say, that because the Nembutsu is so easy, it is all right

[1] Rebirth in the Pure Land.

for those who are incapable of keeping up the practices required in the Shingon, and the meditation of the Tendai sects,
but such a cavil is absurd. What I mean is, that I throw aside
those practices not included in Amida's Vow, nor prescribed
by Shākyamuni, nor having the endorsement of the Buddhas
of all quarters of the universe, and now only throw myself
upon the Original Vow of Amida, according to the authoritative teaching of Shākyamuni, and in harmony with what
the many Buddhas of the six quarters have definitely ap-
proved. I give up my own foolish plans of salvation, and
devote myself exclusively to the practice of that mightily
effective discipline of the *Nembutsu*, with earnest prayer for
birth into the Pure Land. This is the reason why the abbot
of the Eshin-in Temple in his work *Essentials of Salvation*
makes the Nembutsu the most fundamental of all. And so
you should now cease from all other religious practices, apply
yourself to the Nembutsu alone, and in this it is all-important
to do it with undivided attention. Zendō,[2] who himself attained to that perfect insight (samādhi) which apprehends
the truth, clearly expounds the full meaning of this in his
Commentary on the *Meditation Sūtra*, and in the *Two-
Volumed Sūtra* the Buddha (Shākya) says, "Give yourself
with undivided mind to the repetition of the name of the
Buddha who is in Himself endless life." And by "undivided
mind" he means to present a contrast to a mind which is
broken up into two or three sections, each pursuing its own
separate object, and to exhort to the laying aside of everything but this one thing only. In the prayers which you offer
for your loved ones, you will find that the Nembutsu is the
one most conducive to happiness. In the *Essentials of Salvation*, it says that the Nembutsu is superior to all other works.
Also Dengyō Daishi,[3] when telling how to put an end to the
misfortunes which result from the seven evils, exhorts to the
practice of the Nembutsu. Is there indeed anything anywhere
that is superior to it for bringing happiness in the present or
the future life? You ought by all means to give yourself up
to it alone.

[From Coates and Ishizuka, *Honen*, pp. 371–73]

[2] Shan-tao, Chinese patriarch of Pure Land Sect.
[3] Saichō.

The One-Page Testament

Written by Hōnen two days before he died for a disciple who asked that he "write me something with your own hand that you think will be good for me, so that I may keep it as a memento." After Hōnen's death this note was honored as his final testament and as a complete credo for the faithful.

The method of final salvation that I have propounded is neither a sort of meditation, such as has been practiced by many scholars in China and Japan, nor is it a repetition of the Buddha's name by those who have studied and understood the deep meaning of it. It is nothing but the mere repetition of the *"Namu Amida Butsu,"* without a doubt of His mercy, whereby one may be born into the Land of Perfect Bliss. The mere repetition with firm faith includes all the practical details, such as the threefold preparation of mind and the four practical rules. If I as an individual had any doctrine more profound than this, I should miss the mercy of the two Honorable Ones, Amida and Shākya, and be left out of the Vow of the Amida Buddha. Those who believe this, though they clearly understand all the teachings Shākya taught throughout his whole life, should behave themselves like simple-minded folk, who know not a single letter, or like ignorant nuns or monks whose faith is implicitly simple. Thus without pedantic airs, they should fervently practice the repetition of the name of Amida, and that alone.

[From Coates and Ishizuka, *Honen,* pp. 728–29]

SHINRAN AND THE TRUE PURE LAND SECT

Among those banished from Kyoto at the same time as Hōnen was Shinran (1173–1262), who later claimed to be Hōnen's true disciple and is regarded as the founder of the most important of all Pure Land sects. Shinran's crime, for which he was exiled to the northern province of Echigo, was that he had taken a wife in violation of the clerical vow of celibacy. His followers later alleged that Shinran had married this woman, identified by them as a daughter of the Fujiwara regent, Kanezane, at the express request of Hōnen in order to demonstrate that monastic discipline was not essential to salvation and that the family rather than the monastery should be the center of the religious life.

Letters (recently found in Echigo) written by Shinran's wife cast doubt on her Fujiwara origin, but there can be no doubt that these traditions accurately reflect Shinran's own view of his relationship to Hōnen. He saw himself as merely following out in practice the full implications of his master's teaching. The more conservative of Hōnen's followers, who made their headquarters at the former site of his hermitage, held to the traditional monastic discipline of Buddhism, including the vows of celibacy and sobriety. But Shinran believed that if salvation truly depended on nothing but the grace of Amida, it was needless and perhaps dangerous to act as if one's conduct, or one's state in life, could have any bearing on ultimate redemption.

Shinran's experience in exile convinced him that propagation of the faith among all classes of people required its apostles to identify themselves as closely as possible with the ordinary man. During the remaining years of his life he was in fact compelled to live among the people, not as an outspoken preacher boldly proclaiming his mission, but as one condemned, a social outcast, whose faith had been proscribed and was allowed, like him, only a fugitive existence. Yet Shinran never sought to justify himself before the world, to make virtues of the vices for which others condemned him. He was, he admitted, a lost soul, unsure of himself and of all else in this life except the abiding grace of Amida. His only aim was to bring this faith in Amida to those like himself who needed it most, to those ignorant and illiterate souls who could not distinguish good from bad, to "bad people" rather than "good people." Shinran even went so far as to say that wicked men might be more acceptable to Amida than good men, since the former threw themselves entirely on the mercy of the Buddha, while the latter might be tempted to think that their chances of salvation were improved by their own meritorious conduct. "If even good people can be reborn in the Pure Land, how much more the wicked man!"

Shinran's utter reliance on the power of Amida is also emphasized by his attitude toward the recitation of the Nembutsu. The conservative followers of Hōnen believed that one's devotion to Amida was deepened by continual invocation of his name, a practice Hōnen is said to have encouraged and exemplified throughout his life. But to Shinran this too seemed to imply that there was something the individual could do to win salvation; it was another manifestation of the tendency to rely on "one's own power." A single, sincere invocation is enough, said Shinran, and any additional recitation of the Name should merely be an expression of thanksgiving to Amida. Indeed on certain occasions Shinran indicated that even one audible invocation was unnecessary, providing one had inward faith in Amida's saving grace.

Another way in which Shinran stressed exclusive reliance on Amida was by discouraging the worship of any other Buddhas. The historical Buddha himself, Shākyamuni, was merely an agent for the transmission of the true faith, a teacher and messenger but not someone to be worshiped. As might be expected, Shinran was also ready to dispense with all the sūtras except that which revealed Amida's Original Vow, even setting aside two other texts relating to Amida and the Pure Land which Hōnen had prized. Finally, of three vows attributed to Amida in this sūtra and recognized by Hōnen, Shinran discarded two. These promised a welcome to the Pure Land for all who performed meritorious deeds or repeated Amida's name. Shinran did not actually revoke them, but asserted that anyone who relied on the performance of meritorious deeds or the recitation of Buddha's name would have to endure a sort of purgatory before achieving rebirth in the Pure Land. The eighteenth or Original Vow of Amida, which placed sole trust in the Buddha, alone assured direct rebirth in the Land of Bliss.

Though Shinran reduced Buddhism to the simplest of faiths, it must not be thought that this resulted from any ignorance on his part of the depth or complexity of Buddhist doctrine. On the contrary he, like Hōnen and Genshin, had made a thorough study of traditional teachings, as his writings on doctrinal questions testify. Nevertheless it is plain that Shinran grounded himself in tradition only to overturn it. The Buddhism he so unobtrusively but persistently propagated bore little resemblance to the original creed. The Three Treasures had been transformed into one: Amida's Original (or Fundamental) Vow. Virtually nothing remained of the Buddha as manifested by Shākyamuni, of the Law as embodied in scripture, or of the religious community as represented by a celibate clergy following monastic discipline. Gone too was the traditional emphasis on ethical and intellectual excellence, on the search for enlightenment through strenuous personal effort. All of these were now but particles of dust dancing in the radiant light of Amida.

In his own lifetime Shinran made no attempt to organize a new sect around his own creed, but he did leave numerous religious communities, consisting mostly of townspeople, bound together by loyalty to him and his teachings. Eventually they were organized into the True Pure Land Sect by Shinran's lineal descendants. The most famous of these was Rennyo (1415–1499), an able organizer as well as religious leader. In an age torn by conflicting feudal loyalties, Rennyo welded his adherents together into a disciplined band, ready to fight for their faith and their independence of other feudal powers. The bond of devotion between teacher and disciple became a personal bond of militant loyalty. Shinran had urged his followers to make every act an act of thanksgiving to Amida. Now this sense of obligation was redirected to Shinran's heir, identified as the official representative of Amida in this life. "The mercy of Buddha should be recompensed even by pounding flesh to pieces. One's obligation to the Teacher should be recompensed even by smashing bones to bits!" This was the battle cry of those who defended the Temple of the Original Vow in Osaka, withstanding for ten years the attacks of Nobunaga in the late sixteenth century. By such fanatic devotion they had won for themselves the name "Single-Minded" (Ikkō), and had maintained their independence in defensive strongholds throughout the country, taking a leading part in the century of warfare which ended with Nobunaga's rise to power.

Though the True Pure Land sect ceased to be a feudal power after the unification of Japan, it has retained one important vestige of feudalism. This is the hereditary succession of its leadership, to which Shinran's abandonment of celibacy had opened the way. Generation after generation the abbots of both the Western and Eastern branches of the Temple of the Original Vow in Kyoto, primates of what is now one of the most numerous and affluent sects in Japan, have been descendants of Shinran. For those who recognize only the supreme value of Amida's love and never the claims of individual merit, such an arrangement no doubt involves the least danger of self-assertion. Moreover the discarding of the vow of celibacy has had its effect on other sects as well, which have belatedly followed Shinran's lead. Today, although a few monasteries and individuals elect to follow this rule, in none of the important sects is its observance a strict requirement.

Hymn to the True Faith in the Nembutsu (Shōshin nembutsu ge)

In this hymn, part of the daily devotions of Shinran's followers, he sums up the basic tenets of the Pure Land faith and its transmission from India through China to Japan.

I put my trust in the great Tathāgata of Infinite Life and Boundless Light!

Hōzō[1] the Bodhisattva, in the days of his humiliation, being in the presence of the Tathāgata Lord of the World, examining the degree of excellence of the Paradises of all the Buddhas, the causes of their formation, and the angels and men in them, made his great Vow and proclaimed his mighty Oath, which he meditated and selected for the space of five long kalpas; and he repeated the Vow of announcing his Holy Name "Amida" in all the Ten Quarters.

Universally doth he send forth his endless, boundless, all-pervading, unrivaled, supreme Light, his Light of Purity, of Joy, of Wisdom, His changeless, unconceivable, unexplainable Light, brighter than the brightness of Sun or Moon. His Light illuminates worlds more numerous than dust, and all sentient creatures enjoy it and are illuminated thereby.

His Holy Name which was revealed by his Vow of Salvation, is the fundamental Power that justly determines us to enter his Pure Land. His Vow to make us put our sincere

---

[1] Japanese form of the name given to Amida during his earthly existence. [Ed.]

trust in it is the effective cause which produces perfect
Enlightenment. His Vow to lead us without fail into Nirvāna
has been fulfilled; in consequence of it, we can acquire the
same rank as the bodhisattva in this life, and Nirvāna[2] in the
next.

The reason why the Tathāgata Shākyamuni was revealed
to the world was solely that he might proclaim the Boundless Ocean of Amida's Fundamental Vow. Men, numerous
as the Ocean Waves, who are subject to the Five Obstacles
and entangled in Evil, should certainly listen to the Tathāgata's true words.

If once there be aroused in us but one thought of joy and
love [in consequence of the Vow], we turn just as we are with
our sins and lusts upon us, towards Nirvāna. Laymen and
saints alike, even those who have committed the five deadly
sins, and slandered the Holy Laws of Buddha, will yet, by
faith in the power of the Tathāgata, enter into the enjoyment
and taste of his mercy, as surely as the water in the mountain
stream ultimately reaches the Ocean and becomes salt.

The Light of the Buddha's Heart which has taken hold
of us, illuminates and protects us continually, and dispels
the darkness of Ignorance. It is true that the dark mist of
covetousness and passion constantly overhangs the sky that
is above the believing heart. Yet, though the sky above may
be constantly overcast, beneath the cloud it is light, there is
no darkness.

When we have made Faith our own, and have received
a sight of the great mercy and a thought of pious joy, we
pass away sideways[3] from the five evil spheres of life. If any
layman, whether good or bad, hears and believes the all-
embracing Vow of Amida Buddha, him will the Tathāgata
Shākyamuni praise for his wisdom, and will call him a lotus-
flower among men.

For sentient creatures, who are heretical, evil, and proud,
to believe and accept the practice of Amida's Fundamental
Vow, is indeed a hard matter; there is nothing harder than
this.

[2] Which is to be obtained in the Pure Land. [Ed.]
[3] Not by a steep ascent, but passing directly over to the Pure Land.
[Ed.]

Abhidharma Doctors of Western India, noble priests of China and Japan, have declared to us that the true meaning of the Great Saint's (Shākyamuni's) appearance was to point to the true Vow of Amida, and the Vow is just the way for us.

Shākyamuni the Tathāgata, on the mountain peak in Lankā (Ceylon), prophesied for the people assembled to hear him that there should appear in South India, a great teacher, Nāgārjuna by name, who should destroy the conflicting views of Entity and Non-Entity, who should clearly teach the excellent law of the Mahāyāna, who should reach the Class of Joy and be born in Paradise.

He (Nāgārjuna) taught that the way of Salvation by one's own efforts is like a toilsome journey by land, that the Way of Faith in the Merits of Another is as an easy voyage in a fair ship over smooth waters, that if a man put his trust in the Fundamental Vow of Amida, he will enter at once, by Buddha's power, into the class of those destined to be born in the Pure Land. Only let him ever call upon the Name of the Tathāgata, and gratefully commemorate the great all-embracing Vow.

Vasubandhu, also, the Bodhisattva, composed his praise of the Pure Land, put his whole trust and confidence in the Tathāgata of Boundless Light, established the truth by the sūtras, and made clear the way of "crosswise going-out" through the merits of the great Fundamental Vow.

[Vasubandhu taught], with a view to the Salvation of Men through the Faith in Another's merits which Amida bestows upon us, the mystery of the One Heart. If a man enter into this Faith, he will acquire the merit of the Great Ocean of Divine Treasures, and will certainly be admitted to the Great Company of the Saints, in the present life. In the future life, he will go to the Pure Land which shines with the Light of Wisdom like the lotus, and having acquired the Holy Existence with divine power he will return to the forest of human passions, and there, in the garden of life and death, [for the salvation of his fellow creatures], will manifest himself in various transformations.

Take Donran[4] our teacher, whom the king [Wu-ti] of the

[4] T'an-luan, regarded in Japan as first Chinese patriarch of the Pure Land sect. [Ed.]

Liang Dynasty reverenced as a bodhisattva. From Bodhiruchi, the Master of the *Tripiṭaka*, he received the teaching of the Pure Land, and burning the ascetic books [in which he had hitherto put his trust], put his faith in the Paradise of Bliss. He followed the teachings of Vasubandhu [which he learned from Bodhiruchi] and clearly taught that Amida's Great Vow was the effective cause of Birth in Paradise.

[Donran taught] that the Grace of new birth into Paradise, as well as that whereby we can return to Earth to aid our fellow-beings, is a gift which we receive through the Buddha's power, and that the effective cause whereby we are justly determined to be born in the Pure Land, is only the believing heart. Wherefore, if we, blind and sinful persons, arouse this believing heart, we can perceive Nirvāna in this life. Afterwards, without fail, we reach the Pure Land of Boundless Light, and teaching all sentient creatures that are involved in misery of Earth, lead them to salvation.

Dōshaku[5] taught that the innumerable practices for perfecting righteousness by one's own efforts are of no value, and the invocation of the Name which comprises all virtues, he praised as beneficial. He spoke much of the three marks of Non-Faith and Faith, and showed that in all three Ages it is the principle of Mercy that alone rules and draws men. Though a man had done evil all his life, yet, if he were once brought near to the Great Vow, he would reach the Land of Bliss and enjoy the fruits of Salvation.

Zendō[6] was the first that understood the true will of Buddha Shākyamuni in his age, and that had pity, alike for those who practiced meditation or moral good, as for those who lived in wickedness.

Zendō taught that the Effect of Salvation is given by the Holy Light and the Sacred Name of Amida, and expounded the Great Ocean of Wisdom contained in the Fundamental Vow. The believer, having rightly received the adamantine heart of firm faith, and having answered to the calling of the Tathāgata with a joyful heart, like Vaidehī[7] receives the

---

[5] Tao-ch'o, Chinese patriarch of the seventh century. See p. 202.
[6] Shan-tao. See pp. 204–5.
[7] Queen to whom Shākyamuni was said to have taught the meditation on Amida and the Pure Land. [Ed.]

threefold assurance and immediately enters into the happiness of the Eternal Life.

Genshin studied all the teachings of Shākyamuni, and earnestly aspired to go to the Buddha's Land. He exhorted all men to go there too.

Genshin established a difference between a pure and an impure Faith, the one deep and the other shallow. Also, he taught that there are two forms of Paradise, as places of rest for those of deep and shallow faith respectively. O deadly sinner! Invoke but once Amida Buddha! He is taking hold of us. Though our eyes of flesh can not clearly see him owing to our sins, yet is his mercy constantly present to illuminate our minds.

My teacher Genkū [Hōnen] threw light on Buddhism, and had deep compassion for the laity, good or bad. It was he who originated the True Sect's teachings in this country, and propagated in this wicked world the doctrine of Amida's Selected Vow.

Genkū taught that the reason why men keep constantly returning to the Home of Error [bodily life], is entirely due to our being fast bound with doubt. In order that we may enter straight into the peaceful and eternal abode of Nirvāna, it is necessary for us to receive the believing heart.

Thus prophets and teachers, propagating the teachings of the sūtras, have saved countless men from countless evils. Monks and laymen in the present age! We must put our hearts together, and believe the words that these exalted monks have spoken.

[Adapted from Lloyd, *Shinran and His Works*, pp. 46–56]

Shinran's Humble Faith

This excerpt is from a collection of Shinran's sayings said to have been made by his disciple Yuiembō, who was concerned over heresies and schisms developing among Shinran's followers and wished to compile a definitive statement of his master's beliefs. The title Tannishō means "Collection Inspired by Concern over Heresy." There words attributed to Shinran reveal above all his utter self-abasement and glorification of Amida.

Your aim in coming here, traveling at the risk of your lives through more than ten provinces, was simply to learn the way of rebirth in the Pure Land. Yet you would be mistaken if you thought I knew of some way to obtain rebirth other than by saying the Nembutsu, or if you thought I had some special knowledge of religious texts not open to others. Should this be your belief, it is better for you to go to Nara or Mt. Hiei, for there you will find many scholars learned in Buddhism and from them you can get detailed instruction in the essential means of obtaining rebirth in the Pure Land. As far as I, Shinran, am concerned, it is only because the worthy Hōnen taught me so that I believe salvation comes from Amida by saying the Nembutsu. Whether the Nembutsu brings rebirth in the Pure Land or leads one to Hell, I myself have no way of knowing. But even if I had been misled by Hōnen and went to Hell for saying the Nembutsu, I would have no regrets. If I were capable of attaining Buddhahood on my own through the practice of some other discipline, and yet went down to Hell for saying the Nembutsu, then I might regret having been misled. But since I am incapable of practicing such disciplines, there can be no doubt that I would be doomed to Hell anyway.

If the Original Vow of Amida is true, the teaching of Shākyamuni cannot be false. If the teaching of the Buddha is true, Zendō's commentary on the *Meditation Sūtra* cannot be wrong. And if Zendō is right, what Hōnen says cannot be wrong. So if Hōnen is right, what I, Shinran, have to say may not be empty talk.

Such, in short, is my humble faith. Beyond this I can only say that, whether you are to accept this faith in the Nembutsu or reject it, the choice is for each of you to make. . . .

"If even a good man can be reborn in the Pure Land, how much more so a wicked man!"

People generally think, however, that if even a wicked man can be reborn in the Pure Land, how much more so a good man! This latter view may at first sight seem reasonable, but it is not in accord with the purpose of the Original Vow, with faith in the Power of Another. The reason for this is that he who, relying on his own power, undertakes to perform meritorious deeds, has no intention of relying on the Power of Another and is not the object of the Original Vow of Amida. Should he, however, abandon his reliance on his own power and put his trust in the Power of Another, he can be born in the True Land of Recompense. We who are caught in the net of our own passions cannot free ourselves from bondage to birth and death, no matter what kind of austerities or good deeds we try to perform. Seeing this and pitying our condition, Amida made his Vow with the intention of bringing wicked men to Buddhahood. Therefore the wicked man who depends on the Power of Another is the prime object of salvation. This is the reason why Shinran said, "If even a good man can be reborn in the Pure Land, how much more so a wicked man!" . . .

It is regrettable that among the followers of the Nembutsu there are some who quarrel, saying "These are my disciples, those are not." There is no one whom I, Shinran, can call my own disciple. The reason is that, if a man by his own efforts persuaded others to say the Nembutsu, he might call them his disciples, but it is most presumptuous to call those "my disciples" who say the Nembutsu because they have been moved by the grace of Amida. If it is his karma to follow a teacher, a man will follow him; if it is his karma to forsake a teacher, a man will forsake him. It is quite wrong to say that the man who leaves one teacher to join another will not be saved by saying the Nembutsu. To claim as one's own and attempt to take back that faith which is truly the gift of Amida—such a view is wholly mistaken. In the normal course of things a person will spontaneously recognize both what he owes to the grace of Amida and what he owes to his teacher [without the latter having to assert any claims]. . . .

The Master was wont to say, "When I ponder over the Vow which Amida made after meditating for five kalpas, it seems as if the Vow were made for my salvation alone. How grateful I am to Amida, who thought to provide for the salvation of one so helplessly lost in sin!"

When I now reflect upon this saying of the Master, I find that it is fully in accordance with the golden words of Zendō. "We must realize that each of us is an ordinary mortal, immersed in sin and crime, subject to birth and death, ceaselessly migrating from all eternity and ever sinking deeper into Hell, without any means of delivering ourselves from it."

It was on this account that Shinran most graciously used himself as an example, in order to make us realize how lost every single one of us is and how we fail to appreciate our personal indebtedness to the grace of Amida. In truth, none of us mentions the great love of Amida, but we continually talk about what is good and what is bad. Shinran said, however, "Of good and evil I am totally ignorant. If I understood good as Buddha understands it, then I could say I knew what was good. If I understood evil as Buddha understands it, then I could say I knew what was bad. But I am an ordinary mortal, full of passion and desire, living in this transient world like the dweller in a house on fire. Every judgment of mine, whatever I say, is nonsense and gibberish. The Nembutsu alone is true."

[From *Shinshū seiten*, pp. 1203–5, 1207, 1224–25]

RENNYO

All Gods and Buddhas Are Worshipped in Amida

FROM THE EPISTLES OF RENNYO

Rennyo, the eighth abbot of the True Pure Land sect, left many letters to his followers scattered in remote provinces. His grandson, Ennyo (1491–1521), selected eighty of these and compiled them into a book of five chapters. This collection of letters, called Ofumi by the Eastern Branch of the True Pure Land sect and Gobunshō by its Western Branch, is regarded as the most fundamental statement of their faith next to the writings of Shinran, and is used constantly in their services today.

Rennyo made an important contribution to the organization and promotion of his sect. He taught his humble followers the essence of Shinran's faith in understandable terms, and advised them to avoid conflicts by compromising with existing religions and temporal powers, while still holding fast to their faith. Worthy of special note is Rennyo's injunction against sectarian self-advertisement. Considering that his was to become the most numerous of Buddhist sects, it is significant that Rennyo set definite limits on overt proselytization. In another epistle (IV, 7), he says: "If by chance anyone asks to which sect you belong, you should not reply that you are a follower of the Nembutsu of our sect. Without mentioning the name of the sect, simply say that you are a follower of the practice of Nembutsu. This is the attitude which our Saint [Shinran] taught us to adopt. Do not show off to others that you are a Buddhist."

EPISTLE II-3

Among the followers of the teaching of our founder [Shinran], there have been discrepancies in what we preached. Nothing can be done now about what is past, but henceforth those who belong to our sect, from the clergy of this temple on down to those who have read but one holy scripture and also to the laymen who frequent the temple, should remember the following three articles upon which to base their judgments of approval or disapproval.

1. Do not speak ill of other teachings and sects.
2. Do not hold in light esteem the various gods, Buddhas, and bodhisattvas.
3. Obtain the faith and be born in the Pure Land.

Those who fail to observe these three articles, and do not in all earnestness regard them as essentials, should be prohibited from associating with this temple. . . .

1. The [Shinto] gods are those who have appeared temporarily in the form of deities in order to save by some means those who do not believe in the Buddha's teaching and would otherwise helplessly fall into hell; they are adaptive forms (hōben), appearing in the form of gods, whereby nonbelievers are encouraged eventually to accept Buddhism. Therefore, if the people of the present age trust in Amida Buddha, establish their faith, practice the Nembutsu, and become determined to go to the Pure Land, all the gods will be delighted that their real purpose has been fulfilled and will protect the followers of the Nembutsu. It is unnecessary especially to worship the gods, as all [acts of worshiping gods] are included in reliance upon the One Buddha, Amida. Here lies the reason for believing the gods even if you do not ask [for anything] of them.

2. The followers of our sect should not speak ill of other doctrines and sects. They are all teachings preached by Shākya Buddha during his life. When the teachings are practiced as they are preached, they should be effectivo. We, however, who live a secular way of life in this degenerate age are incapable of practicing the teachings of other schools of Buddhism; therefore, we neither rely on them nor believe in them.

3. The various Buddhas and bodhisattvas are divisions

of the body of Amida Buddha, and since Amida Buddha is the Original Teacher and the Original Buddha, to put our faith in Amida is to put our faith in the various Buddhas and bodhisattvas—in Amida Buddha all others are included.

4. What is called the true faith in the Other-Power of Tathāgata Amida as advocated by the founder Saint Shinran has its foundation in the faith in the Original Vow, casting off all heterodox practices [i.e., not directed to Amida Buddha], and trusting Amida with a singleness of heart. Following the teaching of the Founders of our sect, you must understand that the true faith in the Tathāgata Amida is faith given by the Power of Amida; consider that one moment of wholehearted trust in Amida is the moment that determines your going to the Pure Land; continue to practice the Nembutsu spontaneously for the rest of your life. It has been taught that by wholehearted trust our going to the Pure Land is determined here in our daily life, and that the Nembutsu which we recite [after the determination of faith] is to express our gratitude to the Buddha. The essential teaching of our sect, transmitted by the Founder, Saint [Shinran], lies only in this faith. Those who do not know this are regarded as outsiders and those who know this are considered followers of the True [Pure Land] Sect.

Finally, you should not show to others anything which indicates that you are numbered among the followers of the Nembutsu of our Sect. This should be defined as the ideal attitude for followers who have obtained the faith of the True Sect.

Eleventh Day of the First Month, Bummei 6 (1474)
[From Ofumi 18, *Shinshū seiten*, 1270–1273]

12 ✤

NICHIREN'S FAITH IN THE LOTUS

INTRODUCTION

The story of Nichiren (1222–1282) is one, to use his own words, of "a son of the shūdras (lowest caste)" on the sea-coast of Japan, who was destined to become "the pillar of Japan, the eye of the nation and the vessel of the country." Like most of the great religious leaders of that age, this son of a humble fisherman spent years in study and training at the great monastic center of Mt. Hiei. Unlike many others, however, he found new faith, not by turning away from the teachings of its Tendai founder, Saichō, but by turning back to them. In doing so he was forced to depart from Mt. Hiei itself, which had long since become a stronghold of Esoteric Buddhism, and to embark upon a preaching career of unceasing hardship, conflict, and persecution. But through it all he became ever more convinced of his mission to save his country and Buddhism.

For Nichiren the *Lotus Sūtra*, upon which the Tendai teaching had been based, is the key to everything. It is the final and supreme teaching of the Buddha Shākyamuni, revealing the one and only way of salvation. So it is the name of the *Lotus Sūtra*, not the name of Amida Buddha, which should be on the lips of every Buddhist. "Namu myōhō rengekyō" is the Buddha's pledge of salvation, which Nichiren often called out to the beat of a drum—"dondon

dondoko dondon." Like Shinran, Nichiren was a man of no
slight intelligence, and in his years of exile or enforced seclusion he devoted himself to an intensive study of scripture
and doctrine; but this erudition only served to adorn a simple
conviction, arrived at early in life and held to with single-
minded devotion throughout his stormy career, that faith in
the *Lotus of the Wonderful Law* was all one needed for
salvation.

Unlike Shinran, Nichiren stressed the importance of one's
own efforts and became ever more deeply convinced that he
himself was destined to fulfill a unique mission in the world.
A man of active temperament, who commanded attention
because of his forceful and magnetic personality, Nichiren
thought the *Lotus Sūtra* should be "read by the body" and
not just with the eyes. To him among its most significant
passages were those describing the saints destined to uphold
and spread abroad the truths of the Lotus. One of these was
the Bodhisattva of Superb Action,[1] who was to be a stalwart
pioneer in propagating the Perfect Truth. Another was the
Bodhisattva Ever-Abused,[2] who suffered continual insults
from others because he insisted on saluting everyone as a
Buddha-to-be, convinced that every man was ultimately destined to be such. The Lotus' account of these two saints he
regarded as prefiguring his own mission, and often he referred to himself as a reincarnation of them, especially of
the Bodhisattva Superb Action. Nichiren also found special
meaning in the vows taken by Buddha's disciples when His
eternal aspect was revealed to them at the climax of the
Lotus Sūtra. In these vows they took upon themselves to
proclaim the Supreme Scripture in evil times, and promised
to endure all the injury and abuse which was certain to descend on them. In this too Nichiren saw a prophecy of his
own sufferings.

The immediate cause of his sufferings was Nichiren's un-
relenting attack on the established sects and his outspoken
criticism of Japan's rulers for patronizing these heretics. The
repeated calamities suffered by the country at large and the
threat of foreign invasion, which he hinted at ten years be-

[1] Viśiṣṭacāritra.
[2] Sadāparibhūta.

fore the Mongol fleet appeared in Japanese waters, he regarded as the inevitable retribution for the false faith of the nation's leaders, ecclesiastical and political. Contrasted to this sad state of affairs was Nichiren's vision of Japan as the land in which the true teaching of the Buddha was to be revived and from which it was to spread throughout the world. The name Nichiren, which he adopted, symbolizes this exalted mission and his own key role in its fulfillment, for *nichi*, "the sun," represents both the Light of Truth and the Land of the Rising Sun, while *ren* stands for the Lotus.

To accomplish this aim Nichiren urged all his followers to imitate the bodhisattva ideal of perseverance and self-sacrifice. In an age of utter decadence, everyone must be a man of Superb Action, ready to give his life if necessary for the cause. Nichiren himself was sentenced to death for his bold censure of the Hōjō regency in Kamakura, and was saved only by miraculous intervention, according to his followers, when lightning struck the executioner's blade. Banished then to a lonely island in the Sea of Japan, Nichiren wrote, "Birds cry but shed no tears. Nichiren does not cry, but his tears are never dry." Ever after his narrow escape at the execution ground, Nichiren regarded himself as one who had risen from the dead, who had been reborn in the faith. "Tatsunokuchi is the place where Nichiren renounced his life. The place is therefore comparable to a paradise; because all has taken place for the sake of the Lotus of Truth. . . . Indeed every place where Nichiren encounters perils is Buddha's land." [3] In this way Nichiren made of suffering a glorious thing, and set an example for his disciples which did more to confirm their faith in the Lotus than volumes of scripture.

At least three of Nichiren's adherents followed in his footsteps as Bodhisattvas of Superb Action. One was Nichiji (1250–?), who undertook foreign missionary work at the age of forty-six, going first to Ainuland in Hokkaido and thence it is said to Siberia, from which he never returned. A stone monument he erected in northern Japan testifies to his indefatigable zeal for spreading faith in the Lotus among the heathen of unknown lands. In his youth he had accompanied

[3] M. Anesaki, *Nichiren, the Buddhist Prophet*, pp. 58–59.

his master into exile off the Sea of Japan coast, opposite
Siberia. Known as a master of prose and poetry, who wrote
for Nichiren in the latter's old age, Nichiji might have settled down to a quiet life of study and writing, but chose
instead a strenuous life exploring the unknown, with only
his faith to sustain him.

A later follower of Nichiren, named Nisshin (1407–1488),
went to Kyushu at the other end of Japan and was made
superintendent of the mission there. But he too was a Bodhisattva of Superb Action, and, dissatisfied with the easy life
of a successful missionary, returned alone to Kyoto. In this
stronghold of tradition and conservatism, Nisshin started out
as a street-corner evangelist, calling out the name of the
Lotus Sūtra to the beat of a drum, "dondon dondoko dondon." Openly he challenged the ruling shogun to suppress
all other Buddhist sects and recognize the Lotus alone.
When the shogun, who had quit monastic life to become
military dictator, was persuaded by his former clerical associates to command Nisshin to keep silent, the evangelist only
beat his drum louder. Thrown into jail and tortured, he still
would not yield to the shogun's order. Finally a brass pot
was jammed down over his head so as to keep him from talking, and thus he became known as the "pot-wearer (nabe-
kaburi)." Among the converts which he made through his
almost superhuman endurance under such suffering were the
Prime Minister Konoe, the master craftsman Hon-ami, and
also the head of the eminent Kano school of painting.

Lastly there is Nichiō (1565–1630), who led a group of
the Nichiren sect known as the Fuju-fuse—from their slo-
gan: "Accept nothing [from nonbelievers] and give nothing."
So uncompromising was he in regard to all other schools of
Buddhism that when Hideyoshi, upon unifying the country,
invited all sects to send delegates for a festival of celebration, Nichiō refused on the ground that the conqueror was
not a follower of Nichiren. A repetition of this incident
occurred when the next shogun, Ieyasu, had unified the
country, but this time Nichiō's refusal of such an invitation
led to his banishment for more than ten years. Thereafter
the Fuju-fuse school was subjected to repeated persecutions
by the Tokugawa Shogunate, and yet somehow it has man-

aged to survive into the present, though limited in numbers.

More recently some of the same uncompromising faith and militant zeal has been shown in the Sōka gakkai organization, probably the fastest growing of the post-war "new religions." This movement combines the religious dynamism and intense nationalism of Nichiren's Lotus teaching with modern political and social theories generally critical of Western liberalism. Another widely popular movement stemming from Nichirenism is the Risshō kōseikai, which is less political. It emphasizes faith healing and social action (group dynamics and therapy). Thus Nichiren's stress on moral commitment and group discipline has proven a more potent force in modern Japan than the type of detached contemplation which has often attracted Westerners to Buddhism.

Dedication to the Lotus

If you desire to attain Buddhahood immediately, lay down the banner of pride, cast away the club of resentment, and trust yourselves to the unique Truth. Fame and profit are nothing more than vanity of this life; pride and obstinacy are simply fetters to the coming life. . . . When you fall into an abyss and someone has lowered a rope to pull you out, should you hesitate to grasp the rope because you doubt the power of the helper? Has not Buddha declared, "I alone am the protector and savior"? There is the power! Is it not taught that faith is the only entrance [to salvation]? There is the rope! One who hesitates to seize it, and will not utter the Sacred Truth, will never be able to climb the precipice of Bodhi (Enlightenment). . . . Our hearts ache and our sleeves are wet [with tears], until we see face to face the tender figure of the One, who says to us, "I am thy Father." At this thought our hearts beat, even as when we behold the brilliant clouds in the evening sky or the pale moonlight of the fast-falling night. . . . Should any season be passed without thinking of the compassionate promise, "Constantly I am thinking of you"? Should any month or day be spent without revering the teaching that there is none who cannot attain Buddahood? . . . Devote yourself wholeheartedly to the "Adoration to the Lotus of the Perfect Truth," and utter

it yourself as well as admonish others to do the same. Such
is your task in this human life.

[From Anesaki, Nichiren, pp. 46–47]

Condemnation of Hōnen

Nichiren's famous tract, "The Establishment of the Legitimate
Teaching for the Security of the Country (Risshō ankoku ron)"
brought his banishment from Kamakura after he had boldly presented
it to the authorities. Writing in dialogue form, Nichiren denounced
Japan's rulers for countenancing false teachings and prophesied
grievous calamities for the nation, including foreign invasion, unless
all other Buddhist sects were suppressed in favor of the Lotus. His
sharpest attacks were directed at the worshipers of Amida, among
whose number was a high official of the regime.

In the reign of Go-Toba (1183–1198) there was a monk of
the name of Hōnen, who wrote a book called the *Senchakushū*, in which he abused the holy teachings of the age, and
misled men by the thousands. Now this man, basing his
arguments on a mistaken interpretation of Nāgārjuna's writings, in which he follows Dōshaku, Donran, and Zendō, his
predecessors in heresy, divides Buddhism into two gates, the
gate of Holiness, and the gate of Faith in the Pure Land,
and advises all men, in this age of decay, to embrace the
latter. As to the other forms of Buddhism, and as to the
other sūtras, including even the *Lotus* and the sūtras of the
Shingon tradition, he uses four words to describe what should
be our attitude towards them. "Give them up," he says,
"close the books, lay them aside, fling them away." By means
of this doctrine he has misled thousands of his followers,
both lay and clerical. . . .

As a consequence of his preaching, men refused to make
contributions to temples that were not dedicated to Amida,
and forgot to pay their tithes to priests who were not of the
Nembutsu. Thus temples and halls have fallen into ruin,
so that for a long time they have been uninhabitable, and
many cloisters have fallen into disrepair, and are covered with
rank vegetation on which the dew lies thick and undisturbed.
But none heeded the ruin of the temples, none would repair
or give support; and therefore the priests who lived there,

and the deities who protected the people, have left the temples and refuse to return. For all this who is to blame but Hōnen and his *Senchaku?*

Woe, woe! During the last thirty or forty years, thousands of people have been enchanted and led astray, so that they wander in Buddhism as men without a guide. Is it not to be expected that the good deities should be angry when men depart from the truth? Is it not natural that evil spirits should make the most of their opportunities, when they see men forsake justice and love unrighteous deeds? It is better far to exert ourselves to stay an impending calamity than to repeat the vain Nembutsu.

[From Lloyd, *The Creed of Half Japan*, pp. 315–18]

Nichiren As a Prophet

The Lord Shākya proclaimed to all celestial beings that when, in the fifth five hundred years after his death, all the truths of Buddhism should be shrouded in darkness, the Bodhisattva of Superb Action (Vishishtachāritra) should be commissioned to save the most wicked of men who were degrading the truth, curing the hopeless lepers by the mysterious medicine of the Adoration of the Lotus of the Perfect Truth. Can this proclamation be a falsehood? If this promise be not vain, how can the rulers of the people of Japan remain in safety, who, being plunged in the whirlpool of strife and malice, have rebuked, reviled, struck, and banished the messenger of the Tathāgata and his followers commissioned by Buddha to propagate the Lotus of Truth?

When they hear me say this, people will say that it is a curse; yet, those who propagate the Lotus of Truth are indeed the parents of all men living in Japan. . . . I, Nichiren, am the master and lord of the sovereign, as well as of all the Buddhists of other schools. Notwithstanding this, the rulers and the people treat us thus maliciously. How should the sun and the moon bless them by giving them light? Why should the earth not refuse to let them abide upon it? . . . Therefore, also, the Mongols are coming to chastise them. Even if all the soldiers from the five parts of India were called together, and the mountain of the Iron Wheel (Chakravāla) were fortified, how could they succeed in repelling

the invasion? It is decreed that all the inhabitants of Japan
shall suffer from the invaders. Whether this comes to pass
or not will prove whether or not Nichiren is the real propa-
gator of the Lotus of Truth.

[From Anesaki, Nichiren, p. 115]

The Value of Suffering

That Nichiren suffers so much is not without remote causes.
As is explained in the chapter on the Bodhisattva Ever-
Abused (Sadāparibhūta), all abuses and persecutions heaped
upon the bodhisattva were the results of his previous karma.
How much more, then, should this be the case with Nichiren, a man born in the family of an outcast fisherman, so
lowly and degraded and poor! Although in his soul he cherishes something of the faith in the Lotus of Truth, the body
is nothing but a common human body, sharing beastlike life,
nothing but a combination of the two fluids, pink and
white, the products of flesh and fish. Therein the soul finds
its abode, something like the moon reflected in a muddy
pool, like gold wrapped up in a dirty bag. Since the soul
cherishes faith in the Lotus of Truth, there is no fear even
before [the highest deities, such as] Brahmā and Indra; yet
the body is an animal body. Not without reason others show
contempt for this man, because there is a great contrast between the soul and the body. And even this soul is full of
stains, being the pure moonlight only in contrast to the
muddy water; gold, in contrast to the dirty bag.

Who, indeed, fully knows the sins accumulated in his previous lives? . . . The accumulated karma is unfathomable.
Is it not by forging and refining that the rough iron bar is
tempered into a sharp sword? Are not rebukes and persecutions really the process of refining and tempering? I am now
in exile, without any assignable fault; yet this may mean the
process of refining, in this life, the accumulated sins [of
former lives], and being thus delivered from the three woe-
ful resorts. . . .

The world is full of men who degrade the Lotus of Truth,
and such rule this country now. But have I, Nichiren, not
also been one of them? Is that not due to the sins accumulated by deserting the Truth? Now, when the intoxication

is over, I stand here something like a drunken man who having, while intoxicated, struck his parents, after coming to himself, repents of the offense. The sin is hardly to be expiated at once. . . . Had not the rulers and the people persecuted men, how could I have expiated the sins accumulated by degrading the Truth?

[From Anesaki, Nichiren, p. 74]

Nichiren As the Bodhisattva of Superb Action

I, Nichiren, a man born in the ages of the Latter Law, have nearly achieved the task of pioneership in propagating the Perfect Truth, the task assigned to the Bodhisattva of Superb Action (Vishishtachāritra). The eternal Buddhahood of Shākyamuni, as he revealed himself in the chapter on Life-duration, in accordance with his primeval entity; the Buddha Prabhūtaratna, who appeared in the Heavenly Shrine, in the chapter on its appearance, and who represents Buddhahood in the manifestation of its efficacy; the Saints [bodhisattvas] who sprang out of the earth, as made known in the chapter on the Issuing out of Earth—in revealing all these three, I have done the work of the pioneer [among those who perpetuate the Truth]; too high an honor, indeed, for me, a common mortal! . . .

I, Nichiren, am the one who takes the lead of the Saints-out-of-Earth. Then may I not be one of them? If I, Nichiren, am one of them, why may not all my disciples and followers be their kinsmen? The Scripture says, "If one preaches to anybody the Lotus of Truth, even just one clause of it, he is, know ye, the messenger of the Tathāgata, the one commissioned by the Tathāgata, and the one who does the work of the Tathāgata." How, then, can I be anybody else than this one? . . .

When the Buddha Prabhūtaratna sat in the Heavenly Shrine side by side with the Tathāgata Shākyamuni, the two Buddhas lifted up the banner of the Lotus of the Perfect Truth, and declared themselves to be the Commanders [in the coming fight against vice and illusion]. How can this be a deception? Indeed, they have thereby agreed to raise us mortal beings to the rank of Buddha. I, Nichiren, was not present there in the congregation, and yet there is no reason to doubt the statements of the Scripture. Or, is it possible that I was there? Common mortal that I am, I am not well aware of the past, yet in the present I am unmistakably the one who is realizing the Lotus of Truth. Then in the future I am surely destined to participate in the communion of the Holy Place. Inferring the past from the present and the future, I should think that I must have been present at the Communion in the Sky. [The present assures the future destiny, and the future destiny is inconceivable without its cause in the past.] The present, future, and past cannot be isolated from one another. . . .

[From Anesaki, *Nichiren*, pp. 83–85]

Japan As the Center of Buddhism's Regeneration

When, at a certain future time, the union of the state law and the Buddhist Truth shall be established, and the harmony between the two completed, both sovereign and subjects will faithfully adhere to the Great Mysteries. Then the golden age, such as were the ages under the reign of the sage kings of old, will be realized in these days of degeneration and corruption, in the time of the Latter Law. Then the establishment of the Holy See will be completed, by imperial grant and the edict of the Dictator, at a spot comparable in its excellence with the Paradise of Vulture Peak. We have only to wait for the coming of the time. Then the moral law (*kaihō*) will be achieved in the actual life of mankind. The Holy See will then be the seat where all men of the three countries [India, China, and Japan] and the whole Jambud-vīpa [world] will be initiated into the mysteries of confession and expiation; and even the great deities, Brahmā and Indra, will come down into the sanctuary and participate in the initiation.

[From Anesaki, *Nichiren*, p. 110]

13 ✿

ZEN

INTRODUCTION

To bring salvation within the reach of ordinary men—this was the common aim of the Buddhist sects which spread abroad in medieval Japan. Yet to achieve this same end, and to guide men through the uncertainties, turmoil and suffering of that difficult age, these new movements sometimes employed quite different means. The Pure Land and Nichiren sects, as we know, stressed the need for complete faith in something beyond oneself: the saving power of Amida or of the *Lotus Sūtra*. To find rest and security, they said, man had to turn from himself and this world to the Other World. By contrast Zen Buddhism, which first rose to prominence in these same times, firmly opposed the idea that Buddhahood is something to be sought outside oneself or in another world. Every man has a Buddha-nature, and to realize it he need only look within. Self-understanding and self-reliance are the keynote of Zen.

The means by which this inner realization may be achieved is indicated by the term Zen, meaning "meditation" or "concentration," which corresponds to the Chinese *Ch'an* (see Chapter VII). By the Sung dynasty (960–1279), Ch'an was virtually all that remained of Buddhism in China and it had a very deep influence on many aspects of the brilliant Sung culture, especially in art, poetry, and philosophy. The

Sung is also known as a period of remarkable activity in overseas trade, which at least for a time was conducted largely
under private auspices, rather than as a government mo-
nopoly. Here too Ch'an played an important role, for its
resourceful and adventurous adherents took part in commercial enterprises, and their temples along the southeast coast
of China served as hostels for merchants and distribution
centers for foreign goods. Ch'an missionaries often accompanied trading missions to Japan. It is understandable, then,
why Ch'an Buddhism should have deeply implanted itself
on Japanese soil at this time, during the twelfth and thirteenth centuries.

Actually Ch'an, or Zen, had been introduced to Japan
several times in earlier centuries with court sponsorship, both
as a special meditative discipline adopted by men of other
sects (Saichō was one of these) and as a separate, exclusive
teaching. None of these earlier attempts was lasting, however, and it remained for two great Japanese pioneers of Zen
to establish this teaching firmly on native ground. These
pioneers were Eisai (1141–1215) and Dōgen (1200–1253).
We have already seen that the history of Zen centers upon
the personality of its great masters, and that anecdotes from
the lives of these masters were a favorite means of conveying
the essential teachings of Zen. In the case of Chinese Zen
the anecdotes preserved to us deal mostly with the experience
of achieving enlightenment and the act of transmission from
one patriarch to another. But Zen is much more than a single
"enlightenment-experience"; it is a whole way of life. And
we are fortunate that in the biographies of these two Zen
pioneers we have a much fuller account of their activities,
providing us with the important links between Zen as they
saw it, Zen as they lived it, and Zen as it had an impact on
many aspects of Japanese life and culture.

ZEN PIONEERS IN JAPAN

The first pioneer, Eisai, started his religious life in the
center of Esoteric Buddhism, Mt. Hiei, but became determined that he should pursue his studies further in China
and if possible make the long journey to India, homeland

of Buddhism. He never achieved the latter ambition, but did visit China twice at a time when regular communication with the mainland had long since ceased and when only the most enterprising embarked on such a venture. In twelfth-century China Eisai found Zen to be the only form of Buddhism still flourishing, and after studying at the Zen center of T'ien-t'ung shan, returned to Japan in 1191 as a full-fledged Zen master of the Rinzai (in Chinese, *Lin-chi*) school. On his return Eisai brought with him something else which had newly won favor among the Chinese: tea. Back in Kyoto he set about urging the adoption of both Zen and tea by the Japanese, but soon encountered opposition to his new teaching from the traditional strongholds of Esoteric Buddhism in and around the capital. Resourceful and adaptable, in keeping with the spirit of Zen itself, Eisai escaped from the hostile atmosphere of Kyoto and moved on to the new center of political power in the northeast, Kamakura. Here in the seat of military government Eisai's teachings won great favor among the hardy and adventurous warriors who found Zen particularly congenial to their way of life. With support from the Hōjō regents, and with the patronage of the third ruling shogun as well as of the widow of the first, Eisai established a new center for the study of Zen and inaugurated what was to become a historic *rapprochement* between this sect and the military warlords of Japan. Nevertheless, when Eisai returned to preach in Kyoto during his last years, he was forced to compromise with the established order. He was free to propagate Zen only on condition that other Buddhist disciplines, as represented by Tendai and Shingon practices, be accorded a place in his teaching. Thus it is characteristic of Eisai's pioneer work that, by allying himself with the new political order and compromising with the established religions, he did much to legitimize Zen in Japan.

If Eisai was in this way a personification of the virtue of adaptability, which is a notable feature of Zen, Dōgen equally personified the opposite virtue in Zen: rugged determination and uncompromising independence. High born, with an emperor as an ancestor on his father's side and a Fujiwara prime minister on his mother's, Dōgen had the advantage of an excellent education in Chinese studies and showed such promise as a youth that the Fujiwara regents wished to adopt him into their own family and groom him for the prime ministership. Dōgen, however, rejected this opportunity for worldly advancement in order to take up a religious life, which was to prove for him far more difficult. At the historic centers of Buddhist monasticism, Mt. Hiei and Miidera near Lake Biwa, Dōgen was disappointed to find no true refuge from worldly life and only an academic or ritualistic interest in the Buddhist ideal. "It is taught that 'we are all born Buddhas,' but I have been unable to find among the inmates [of Mt. Hiei] a single person who looks like a Buddha," he complained. "It seems that a collection of Scriptures is worth nothing unless someone puts it to real use."

From Mt. Hiei Dōgen went to see Eisai, who died soon thereafter. Even when he undertook to follow in Eisai's footsteps to China, his quest seemed doomed to failure. At T'ien-t'ung monastery, where Eisai had studied, Dōgen's hunger for the truth was still unsatisfied after a stay of two years. He went on from one monastery to another, not drifting aimlessly but pursuing a relentless search for a true Master, a living Buddha. His disappointment was only heightened by the ease with which he himself won acceptance from some so-called "masters" who indicated their readiness to confer master's papers upon him in return for a gift of money. Worldliness and commercialism had infiltrated even the sanctuaries of the Buddha.

At last, when Dōgen was about to return home in despair, a new master, Ju-ching, came to preside over the T'ien-t'ung monastery. One night Ju-ching was explaining to the monks that the practice of Zen meant "dropping off both body and mind [transcending the dualism of matter and spirit]," and Dōgen was suddenly enlightened. Afterward he went to the master's room and started to burn incense, a sign that one has achieved enlightenment and acknowledges the Buddhahood of his master. "What has happened," Ju-ching asked, "that you should be burning incense?" Dōgen replied, "Both body and mind are dropped." "Both body and mind are dropped," Ju-ching repeated. "You have really dropped both body and mind!" Dōgen was not exactly pleased that his own claim should be accepted so readily, however. "That is rather a little thing to achieve," he countered. "Please don't set your seal on me so easily." "No, I am not setting my seal

on you so easily," his teacher assured him. But Dōgen pressed
on, almost as if he were the examiner and Ju-ching the disciple. "What do you mean by not setting your seal so easily?"
"I mean that you really have dropped both body and mind,"
reaffirmed Ju-ching. At this Dōgen finally bowed in homage,
acknowledging Ju-ching's acceptance of him. "That's dropping off the dropping," said Ju-ching.

Dōgen continued to show his independence after returning
to Japan. In Kyoto and nearby Fukakusa he refused to teach
anything but Zen, and when put under pressure to change
his ways, preferred to move on to the remote province of
Echizen rather than give in to the established order. There
is a legend, without historical basis but suggestive of Dōgen's
reputation for independence, which tells of his visiting
Kamakura to urge the Hōjō regent, Tokiyori, to restore ruling
power to the emperor in Kyoto. Obtaining no satisfaction
from Tokiyori, Dōgen quit Kamakura in disgust rather than
serve in Eisai's role as adviser to an illegitimate ruler. Nevertheless, Tokiyori was much impressed by Dōgen's strength
of character, and sent one of the latter's pupils to him bearing a grant of land for his temple. At this Dōgen was so
incensed that he not only sent his pupil away, but, in a
manner reminiscent of Taoist sages in China who refused the
throne, ordered that the chair the monk had sat in be destroyed, the ground under the chair dug three feet deep and
the earth thrown away.

Still, for all of his independence and intransigeance,
Dōgen's attitude toward traditional Buddhism was notably
softer than most of his Zen predecessors in China. The danger of intellectualism and of reliance upon the written word
had stirred up controversy among Zen schools on the continent, with some taking the extreme view that the patri-
archal man-to-man transmission alone was authentic and that
the scriptural transmission was not true Buddhism. Dōgen
sided with those who upheld the essential unity of the two
forms of teaching. The study of scripture was not to be condemned, except where it led to the sūtras' gaining mastery
over the student rather than the student gaining mastery over
the sūtras. "Stay on top of the Lotus; don't let it get on top
of you." Far from being a passive receptacle for the written
word, Dōgen himself devoted much of his life to writing and

achieved a remarkable literary output. Believing in the fundamental unity of the various schools, in his writings he sought less to establish the correctness of Zen than to assert the fundamental truths of Buddhism. The "Zen" label he had little use for; it was the teaching of the Buddha, "Buddhism," with which he identified himself. Accordingly he was drawn more and more to the Indian, especially the Hīnayāna sources, of this teaching than to the Chinese. In the personal example of the Founder he found the simplest and best method of achieving enlightenment. Shākyamuni's way of sitting in meditation under the Tree of Enlightenment was the "proven" or "tested" method of realizing the Truth. Yet sitting in meditation with the object of achieving enlightenment is too selfish an approach; Buddhahood cannot be sought after or obtained for oneself, but only for its own sake. Dōgen quoted an earlier master of his school who said, "If you want to obtain a certain thing, you must first be a certain man. Once you have become a certain man, obtaining that certain thing won't be a concern of yours any more."

In this respect Dōgen took issue with the Rinzai school of Zen, which Eisai had introduced to Japan. Rinzai had developed a special technique and discipline, the *kōan*, leading to the sudden attainment of enlightenment. The *kōan* was a theme upon which the student might focus his mind, consisting of a problem or dilemma together with the resolution of it worked out by some earlier master. Since the solution was beyond the reach of ordinary logical processes, few students could comprehend it without spending months and years in intent absorption with the *kōan*. Then all at once realization took place, induced perhaps by some accidental occurrence—a sound or sight—impinging upon the consciousness of the individual, or else by some deliberate act of the master—a shout or blow on the head—intended to startle and awaken the mind of the disciple. This sudden intuition or realization is what D. T. Suzuki, the best-known interpreter of Zen to the West in recent times, has called "Enlightenment-experience."

From the point of view of Dōgen, and of the Sōtō (Chinese *Ts'ao-tung*) school of Zen which he introduced to

Japan,[1] this preoccupation with the momentary experience of enlightenment and the deliberate use of the *kōan* formula to achieve it, was directed too much toward "obtaining a certain thing" and might be too self-assertive. It also placed too great stress on mental perception, realization through the mind alone rather than through all of the faculties and activities of the "whole man." Therefore Dōgen minimized the value of the *kōan* and stressed instead the importance of "sitting in meditation" (*zazen*) without any thought of acquisition or attainment, without any specific problem in mind. Through such a discipline, bodily as well as mental, moral as well as intellectual, a gradual and life-long realization took place rather than a sudden awakening.

From the Rinzai point of view the defect of this method was its emphasis upon stillness in meditation, which led to empty passivity on the part of the individual rather than to the active, dynamic self-introspection stimulated by the *kōan*. Yet on Dōgen's part, at least, there was no lack of dynamism, the difference being that for him it was applied to the conduct of life rather than to the achievement of a particular experience. In this again he reflected the strongly ethical character of the Sōtō school in China. Just as the practice of sitting is not just a means to an end, but the realization of Buddhahood itself, so Buddhahood is realized constantly in life by selfless action and strenuous effort, with no thought of achieving an end apart from the means. Man's only possession is time, and this is his only insofar as he uses it creatively, because Buddhahood is not a static thing to be achieved once but something that grows with each effort. Thus life is a work of art and Zen is the flowering of life— the discipline of creative labor.

In another section we shall discuss the ways in which the creative powers of Zen were brought to bear upon some of the humblest activities of men and the lowliest objects of nature to raise them to the level of great art, and thereby to

[1] Dōgen himself emphatically repudiated any sectarian allegiance, but his later followers identified him with this school because he was most sympathetic to and influenced by the teachings of Sōtō masters. As a school Sōtō became far more influential in Japan than it ever was in China.

permeate the Japanese way of life to its core. Among the Zen masters responsible for this, however, was one who also had such outstanding success in the political sphere as to be worthy of mention here. He is Musō Soseki (1275–1351), who came to be known as Musō Kokushi, or "Musō the National Master." In his time there were already several full-fledged Zen masters in Japan, both native and Chinese domiciled in Japan. Yet, like Dōgen, Musō found his way to Zen with difficulty. Leaving his teachers, he wandered all over Japan to seek a revelation of Truth in its mountain fastnesses and forests, by its lakesides and seashores. Finally, spending the night deep in a lonely wood, he found his answer in the sight of embers catching fire again. Thereafter Musō served as an adviser to several rulers in succession at a time when political power was changing hands with startling rapidity. First the Hōjō regents invited him to preside over a monastery in Kamakura. Then Go-Daigo, attempting to reassert imperial rule in Kyoto, enlisted Musō's services and at his suggestion in 1325 sent the first official mission to China in almost five centuries, opening a new era in foreign commerce and diplomacy. Finally the new shogun, Ashikaga Takauji, after disposing of Go-Daigo, asked Musō to serve as his spiritual mentor and seems to have experienced a deep religious conversion under Musō's influence. Takauji built for him the famous monastery of Tenryū-ji, and when in 1339 the shogun also sent a mission to China, almost certainly at Musō's urging, it sailed in a ship bearing the name of this temple. Musō also inspired Takauji to erect a temple and pagoda in each province, reviving the idea of a state-established Buddhist church first instituted by the Emperor Shōmu in the seventh century, as a means both of propagating Buddhist teaching and of creating good will among the people toward the Ashikaga regime.

Thus, as the recognized "National Master of Seven Reigns," a title awarded him three times during his life and four after death, Musō did much to gain for Zen a favored position at court and to solidify the alliance initiated by Eisai between it and Japan's military rulers. With such advantages, even though it failed to win converts in such great numbers as the Pure Land and Nichiren sects did among the more humble folk, Zen was nevertheless able to make its influence felt among the political, intellectual, and artistic leaders of medieval times and thus to shape to a remarkable extent the cultural traditions deriving from this period.

Propagation of Zen for the Protection of the Country

(Preface to Kōzen gokoku ron)

In this tract Eisai attempted to win for Zen a legitimate place in the religious life of the nation, arguing that this teaching was conducive to the general welfare and national security, and defending it against the charge of the established sects that it was negativistic and obscurantist. The title indicates that political and nationalistic considerations loomed large in Eisai's mind, just as they had with Saichō centuries before when winning for Tendai the patronage of the imperial house against opposition from the older Nara sects. Ironically Eisai's chief adversaries at the Kyoto court were the monks of Mt. Hiei monastery, which Saichō had founded. For this reason Eisai stresses Saichō's reputed part in the introduction of Zen meditative practices earlier, as well as the legitimate succession of Zen patriarchs from Shākyamuni Buddha, scriptural authorities for the teaching, the endorsement of it by leading Buddhists of the past—in short, all the necessary points for rendering it socially acceptable in the orthodox world. Eisai's preface gives a brief summary of his position.

Great is Mind. Heaven's height is immeasurable, but Mind goes beyond heaven; the earth's depth is also unfathomable, but Mind reaches below the earth. The light of the sun and moon cannot be outdistanced, yet Mind passes beyond the light of sun and moon. The macrocosm is limitless, yet Mind travels outside the macrocosm. How great is Space! How great the Primal Energy! Still Mind encompasses Space and generates the Primal Energy. Because of it heaven covers and earth upbears. Because of it the sun and moon move on, the four seasons pass in succession, and all things are generated. Great indeed is Mind! Of necessity we give such a name to it, yet there are many others. the Highest Vehicle, the First Principle, the Truth of Inner Wisdom, the One Reality, the Peerless Bodhi, the Way to Enlightenment as taught in the Laṅkāvatāra Sūtra, the Treasury of the Vision of Truth, and Insight of Nirvāna. All texts in the Three Vehicles of Bud-

dhism[1] and in the eight treasuries of Scripture, as well as all
the doctrines of the four schools and five denominations of
Zen are contained in it. Shākya, the greatest of all teachers,
transmitted this truth of the Mind to the golden-haired monk
[Kāshyapa], calling it a special transmission not contained in
the scriptures. From the Vulture Peak it moved to Cockleg
Cave, where it was greeted with a smile.[2] Thus with the mere
twist of a flower a thousand trees were made to bloom; from
one fountainhead sprang ten thousand streams of Truth.

As in India, so in China this teaching has attracted followers and disciples in great numbers. It propagates the Truth
as the ancient Buddha did, with the robe of authentic transmission passing from one man to the next. In the matter of
religious discipline, it practices the genuine method of the
sages of old. Thus the Truth it teaches, both in substance
and appearance, perfects the relationship of master and disciple. In its rules of action and discipline, there is no confusion of right and wrong.

After the Great Master [Bodhidharma] sailed by way of
the South Seas and planted his staff of Truth on the banks
of East River in China, the vision of the Law soon made its
appearance in Korea and the Oxhead school of Zen from
North China made its way to Japan. Studying it, one dis-
covers the key to all forms of Buddhism; practicing it, one's
life is brought to fulfillment in the attainment of enlightenment. Outwardly it favors discipline over doctrine, inwardly
it brings the Highest Inner Wisdom. This is what the Zen
sect stands for.

In our country the Divine Sovereign shines in splendor
and the influence of his virtuous wisdom spreads far and
wide. Emissaries from the distant lands of South and Central
Asia pay their respects to his court. Lay ministers conduct

[1] Hīnayāna, Quasi-Mahāyāna, and True Mahāyāna.
[2] When the Hindu god Brahmā came to Shākyamuni Buddha at the
Vulture Peak offering him a flower and requesting him to teach
the Law, Buddha took the flower and turned it in his fingers without saying a word. Everyone in the assemblage was mystified, but
at the nearby Cockleg Cave the disciple Kāshyapa smiled in joyful recognition. Buddha thereupon entrusted to Kāshyapa the secret
transmission of the Law, which was later passed on to others by
similar "mind-signs."

the affairs of government; priests and monks spread abroad religious truth. Even the truths of the Four Hindu Vedas are not neglected. Why then reject the five schools of Zen Buddhism?

There are, however, some persons who malign this teaching, calling it "the Zen of dark enlightenment." There are also those who question it on the ground that it is "utter Nihilism." Still others consider it ill-suited to these degenerate times, or say that it is not what our country needs. Or else they may express contempt for our mendicant ways and our alleged lack of documentary support for our views. Finally there are some who have such a low opinion of their own capabilities that they look upon Zen as far beyond their power to promote. Out of their zeal for upholding the Law, these people are actually suppressing the treasures of the Law. They denounce us without knowing what we have in mind. Not only are they thus blocking the way to the gate of Zen, but they are also ruining the work of our great forebear at Mt. Hiei [Saichō]. Alas, alas, how sad, how distressing!

It is for this reason that I venture to make a general survey of the Three Vehicles for consideration of philosophers today, and to record the essential teachings of our sect for the benefit of posterity. The work is in three chapters consisting of ten sections, and is entitled *The Propagation of Zen for the Protection of the Country.*

[From *Taishō daizōkyō*, Vol. 80, Zoku shoshūbu, p. 2]

Drink Tea and Nourish Life

(From the *Kissa yōjō ki*)

Though Zen is a meditative school of Buddhism, far from encouraging passivity it attaches the highest value to action. There is nothing incongruous, therefore, in the fact that its leading exponents led a very active life and devoted themselves to practical enterprises such as commerce and diplomacy. One of the most enduring of Eisai's contributions to Japanese life was his advocacy of tea-drinking, which did much to make it the national beverage. Typically too, Zen monks in later years went on to make the preparation and imbibing of this common drink one of the most highly refined of household arts: the Tea Ceremony.

Tea is the most wonderful medicine for nourishing one's health; it is the secret of long life. On the hillsides it grows up as the spirit of the soil. Those who pick and use it are certain to attain a great age. India and China both value it highly, and in the past our country too once showed a great liking for tea. Now as then it possesses the same rare qualities, and we should make wider use of it.

In the past, it is said, man was coeval with Heaven, but in recent times man has gradually declined and grown weaker, so that his four bodily components and five organs have degenerated. For this reason even when acupuncture and moxa cautery are resorted to the results are often fatal, and treatment at hot springs fails to have any effect. So those who are given to these methods of treatment will become steadily weaker until death overtakes them, a prospect which can only be dreaded. If these traditional methods of healing are employed without any modification on patients today, scarcely any relief can be expected.

Of all the things which Heaven has created, man is the most noble. To preserve one's life so as to make the most of one's allotted span is prudent and proper [considering the high value of human life]. The basis of preserving life is the cultivation of health, and the secret of health lies in the well-being of the five organs. Among these five the heart is sovereign, and to build up the heart the drinking of tea is the finest method. When the heart is weak, the other organs all suffer.

According to the Esoteric scripture known as the Conquest of Hell, the liver likes acid foods, the lungs pungent foods, the heart bitter, the spleen sweet, and the kidney salty. . . . Thus the five organs have their own taste preferences. If one of these preferences is favored too much, the corresponding organ will get too strong and oppress the others, resulting in illness. Now acid, pungent, sweet, and salty foods are eaten in great quantity, but not bitter foods. Yet when the heart becomes sick, all organs and tastes are affected. Then, eat as one may, one will have to vomit and stop eating. But if one drinks tea, the heart will be strengthened and freed from illness. It is well to know that when the heart is ailing, the skin has a poor color, a sign that life is ebbing away. I wonder why the Japanese do not care for bitter things. In the great country of China they drink tea, as a result of which there is no heart trouble and people live long lives. Our country is full of sickly-looking, skinny persons, and this is simply because we do not drink tea. Whenever one is in poor spirits, one should drink tea. . . .

[From *Gunsho ruijū*, XV, 899–901]

Conversations of Dōgen

The following excerpts from the conversations of Dōgen as recorded by his disciple Ejō have an air of intimacy and a simple directness not usually found in the formal writings of the master. The first selections reveal the radical faith of this Zen pioneer, and incidentally provide a valuable commentary on the life and character of Dōgen's predecessor, Eisai.

Spoken during an evening conversation:

The late Abbot [Eisai] once said: "The food and clothing which each of you monks uses should not be thought of as something I have given you. They are all gifts from Heaven, and I am nothing but an intermediary. Everyone receives what is needed to sustain his allotted life and there is no sense in making a fuss over it. Don't think you are under any obligation to me for these things," he always used to tell us. In my opinion no finer words could be spoken.

When the T'ien-t'ung monastery [in China] was presided over by the Zen Master Hung-chih, provision was made for one thousand students, seven hundred of them inmates and three hundred transients. With such a fine master presiding, however, monks flocked there from all over the country. The number of inmates mounted to one thousand, while the transients increased to five hundred. So the steward appealed to Hung-chih: "We have provisions for only one thousand. With this great crowd there will never be enough to go round. Please send some away." Hung-chih replied, "Every man has a mouth to feed, but that is not your fault, so stop complaining!"

When I think about this now, it seems to me that everyone is born with his share of clothing and food. Seeking for food does not make it appear; abandoning the search does not make it disappear. Remember that even laymen leave such matters in the hands of Providence, while they strive for the virtues of loyalty and piety. How much less should monks who have left the world be concerned over such external matters! The Buddha prescribes their fortunes and the heavens provide their food and clothing. Moreover, everyone has his own share of life; without seeking for it or thinking about it, this allotted share comes from the natural course of things. Suppose you run after more and pile up great treasures —what will you do with them when Evanescence pays you a visit? Therefore the student should drive all thought of such external matters from his mind, and devote himself single-mindedly to the pursuit of Truth.

Yet some say that the propagation of Buddhism in these latter degenerate days, on this remote island, would be facilitated if a secure and peaceful abode were prepared where monks could practice the teachings of Buddha without any worries over food, clothing, and the like. To me this seems wrong. Such a place would only attract men who are selfish and worldly, and among them could be found no one at all with a sincere religious intention. If we give ourselves over to the comforts of life and the enjoyment of material pleasures, then even though hundreds of thousands were induced to come here, it would be worse than having no one here at all. We would acquire only a propensity for evil, not a disposition for the practice of Buddha's Law.

If on the contrary you live in spotless poverty and destitution, or go begging for your food, or live on the fruits of the field, pursuing your study of the Truth while suffering real deprivation, then if even one man hears of your example and comes to study with you out of genuine devotion to the Truth, it will be a real gain for Buddhism. If, however, you feel that spotless poverty and destitution will discourage people, and consequently provide an abundance of food and clothing, a great many may come but they will have no real interest in Buddhism. In the former case you will obtain eight ounces of gold, and in the latter a half-pound of tinsel.

[From the *Shōbō genzō zuimonki*, pp. 35–36]

Exertion

The great Way of the Buddha and the Patriarchs involves the highest form of exertion, which goes on unceasingly in cycles from the first dawning of religious truth, through the test of discipline and practice, to enlightenment and Nirvāna. It is sustained exertion, proceeding without lapse from cycle to cycle. Accordingly it is exertion which is neither self-imposed nor imposed by others, but free and uncoerced. The merit of this exertion upholds me and upholds others. The truth is that the benefits of one's own sustained exertion are shared by all beings in the ten quarters of the world. Others may not be aware of this, and we may not realize it, but it is so. It is through the sustained exertions of the Buddhas and Patriarchs that our own exertions are made possible, that we are able to reach the high road of Truth. In exactly the same way it is through our own exertions that the exertions of the Buddhas are made possible, that the Buddhas attain the high road of Truth. Thus it is through our exertions that these benefits circulate in cycles to others, and it is due only to this that the Buddhas and Patriarchs come and go, affirming Buddha and negating Buddha, attaining the Buddha-mind and achieving Buddhahood, ceaselessly and without end. This exertion too sustains the sun, the moon, and the stars; it sustains the earth and sky, body and mind, object and subject, the four elements, and five compounds.

This sustained exertion is not something which men of the world naturally love or desire, yet it is the last refuge of all. Only through the exertions of all Buddhas in the past, present, and future do the Buddhas of past, present, and future become a reality. The merits of these exertions are sometimes disclosed, and thus arises the dawn of religious consciousness which is then tested in practice. Sometimes, however, these merits lie hidden and are neither seen, nor heard, nor realized. Yet hidden though they may be, they are still available because they suffer no diminution or restriction whether they are visible or invisible, tangible or intangible. . . .

The exertion that brings the exertion of others into realization is our exertion right at this moment. This exertion of the moment is not innate or inherent in us, nor does it come and go, visiting or departing. What we call the "moment" does not precede exertion. The "moment" is when exertion is actually being performed. That is to say, the exertion of a day is the seed of all Buddhas, it is the exertion of all Buddhas.[1] By this exertion Buddhahood is realized, and those who do not make an exertion when exertion is possible are those who hate Buddha, hate serving the Buddha, and hate exertion; they do not want to live and die with Buddha, they do not want him as their teacher and companion.

At this moment a flower blossoms, a leaf falls—it is a manifestation of sustained exertion. A mirror is brightened, a mirror is broken—it is a manifestation of sustained exertion. Everything is exertion. To attempt to avoid exertion is an impossible evasion, for the attempt itself is exertion. And to belabor oneself, because it is impossible to be otherwise than one is, is to be like the rich man's son who left home to seek his fortune, only to endure poverty in a foreign land.[2] Though in his wanderings the son may be fortunate enough not to lose his life altogether, it would still have been better had he not abandoned his father's treasures in the first place. Nor should we risk losing the treasures of the Law, which never allows of any abandonment of exertion. Our benevolent father and great master, Shākyamuni Buddha, began his exertions deep in the mountains at the age of nineteen. At the age of thirty he labored to achieve the Enlightenment which embraced all sentient beings. Until the age of eighty he labored in the forests and in monasteries, without any thought of returning to his royal palace or of sharing in the wealth of his kingdom. Not once did he put on a new robe; not once did he exchange his bowl for another. Not for one

[1] The sense of this passage seems to be: "Exertion is not inherent in our nature in the sense that it operates automatically and can be taken for granted; nor on the other hand is it extraneous to our nature in the sense that it must be acquired. Our nature is only realized insofar as we exert our efforts. Similarly time does not exist apart from exertion, and all exertion is one in time, the reality of the moment. Thus our exertions today contribute to the realization of Buddhahood in the past, and the Buddha's exertions contribute to our realization."

[2] The parable of a prodigal son in the *Lotus Sūtra*.

day, not for an hour, did he seek to take care of himself, but lived on the offerings of others and endured the ridicule of heretics. His whole life was one long exertion of begging food and clothing, a life that knew nothing but sustained exertion.

[From Zenshū seiten, zokuhen, Shōbō genzō gyōji, pp. 676–78]

Realizing the Solution (Genjō Kōan)

[Against the notion that enlightenment is a single, momentary experience]

To study the way of the Buddha is to study your own self. To study your own self is to forget yourself. To forget yourself is to have the objective world prevail in you. To have the objective world prevail in you, is to let go of your "own" body and mind as well as the body and mind of "others." The enlightenment thus attained may seem to come to an end, but though it appears to have stopped this momentary enlightenment should be prolonged and prolonged.

[From Hashida, Shōbō genzō shakui, I, 142–69]

Sitting and the Kōan

In the pursuit of the Way [Buddhism] the prime essential is sitting (zazen). . . . By reflecting upon various "public-cases" (kōan) and dialogues of the patriarchs, one may perhaps get the sense of them but it will only result in one's being led astray from the way of the Buddha and the patriarchs. Just to pass the time in sitting straight, without any thought of acquisition, without any sense of achieving enlightenment—this is the way of the patriarchs. It is true that our predecessors recommended both the kōan and sitting, but it was the sitting that they particularly insisted upon. There have been some who attained enlightenment through the test of the kōan, but the true cause of their enlightenment was the merit and effectiveness of sitting. Truly the merit lies in the sitting.

[From the Shōbō genzō zuimonki, pp. 98–99]

The Importance of Sitting

When I stayed at T'ien-t'ung monastery [in China], the venerable Ching used to stay up sitting until the small hours of the morning and then after only a little rest would rise early to start sitting again. In the meditation hall he went on sitting with the other elders, without letting up for even a single night. Meanwhile many of the monks went off to sleep. The elder would go around among them and hit the sleepers with his fist or a slipper, yelling at them to wake up. If their sleepiness persisted, he would go out to the hallway and ring the bell to summon the monks to a room apart, where he would lecture to them by the light of a candle.

"What use is there in your assembling together in the hall only to go to sleep? Is this all that you left the world and joined holy orders for? Even among laymen, whether they be emperors, princes, or officials, are there any who live a life of ease? The ruler must fulfill the duties of the sovereign, his ministers must serve with loyalty and devotion, and commoners must work to reclaim land and till the soil—no one lives a life of ease. To escape from such burdens and idly while away the time in a monastery—what does this accomplish? Great is the problem of birth and death; fleeting indeed is our transitory existence. Upon these truths both the scriptural and meditation schools agree. What sort of illness awaits us tonight, what sort of death tomorrow? While we have life, not to practice Buddha's Law but to spend the time in sleep is the height of foolishness. Because of such foolishness Buddhism today is in a state of decline. When it was at its zenith monks devoted themselves to the practice of sitting in meditation (*zazen*), but nowadays sitting is not generally insisted upon and consequently Buddhism is losing ground." . . .

Upon another occasion his attendants said to him, "The monks are getting overtired or falling ill, and some are thinking of leaving the monastery, all because they are required to sit too long in meditation. Shouldn't the length of the sitting period be shortened?" The master became highly indignant. "That would be quite wrong. A monk who is not really devoted to the religious life may very well fall asleep in a half hour or an hour. But one truly devoted to it who has resolved to persevere in his religious discipline will eventually come to enjoy the practice of sitting, no matter how long it lasts. When I was young I used to visit the heads of various monasteries, and one of them explained to me, 'Formerly I used to hit sleeping monks so hard that my fist just about broke. Now I am old and weak, so I can't hit them hard enough. Therefore it is difficult to produce good monks. In many monasteries today the superiors do not emphasize sitting strongly enough, and so Buddhism is declining. The more you hit them the better,' he advised me."

[From the Shōbō genzō zuimonki, pp. 50–52]

Body and Mind

Is the Way [of liberation] achieved through the mind or through the body? The doctrinal schools speak of the identity of mind and body, and so when they speak of attaining the Way through the body,[1] they explain it in terms of this identity. Nevertheless this leaves one uncertain as to what "attainment by the body" truly means. From the point of view of our school, attainment of the Way is indeed achieved through the body as well as the mind. So long as one hopes to grasp the Truth only through the mind, one will not attain it even in a thousand existences or in aeons of time. Only when one lets go of the mind and ceases to seek an intellectual apprehension of the Truth is liberation attainable. Enlightenment of the mind through the sense of sight and comprehension of the Truth through the sense of hearing are truly bodily attainments. To do away with mental deliberation and cognition, and simply to go on sitting, is the method by which the Way is made an intimate part of our lives. Thus attainment of the Way becomes truly attainment through the body. That is why I put exclusive emphasis upon sitting.

[From the Shōbō genzō zuimonki, p. 52]

[1] E.g. Kūkai, who asserted the identity of mind and body and the possibility of achieving liberation "in the body" (i.e., in this life).

Sermon of Musō Kokushi at the Opening of Tenryū Monastery

The following sermon was delivered at the original opening of the Tenryū monastery, dedicated to the memory of Go-Daigo, when Musō Kokushi became its founding abbot. In it he reminds his audience that even among the patriarchs of Zen the transmission of the Buddhist Law involved some form of preaching to proclaim its Truth to the world, and accordingly he proceeds to explain or suggest the fundamentals of Zen teaching.

In the tenth month of the second year of the Rekiō period (1339) an imperial decree ordered the conversion of the detached palace of the ex-Emperor Kameyama into a monastery dedicated to the memory of the ex-Emperor Go-Daigo, and also nominated the Master to be its founding prior. In the fourth year of Kōei (1345), 4th month, 8th day, the Meditation Hall was opened for the first time [with their lordships General Takauji and Vice-General Tadayoshi in attendance]. At the Hall the Master first performed the ceremony in commemoration of the Buddha's birth and then proceeded to say:

"The appearance in this world of all Buddhas, past, present, and future, is solely for the purpose of preaching the Law and helping all creatures to cross over to the shore of Liberation. The arts of oratory and types of intonation employed by Shākya were all meant to serve as a guide to the preaching of the Law, while the Deer Park and Vulture Peak served as places of spiritual instruction. The school of the Patriarch Bodhidharma stressed the method of individual instruction directed toward the essential nature, thus setting themselves off from the schools which stressed the teaching of doctrine. But closer examination of their aims reveals that Bodhidharma's followers likewise sought to transmit the Law and rescue men from the confusions of this world. Thus all of the patriarchs, forty-seven in India and twenty-three in China, each signalized his succession to the partriarchate by making a statement on the transmission of the Law. The Great Master Bodhidharma said, 'I came here primarily to transmit the Law and save men from their blinding passions.'

So it is clear that Hui-k'o's cutting off his arm in the snow[1] and the conferring of the robe at midnight upon Hui-neng[2] were both meant to signify transmission of the true Law from one patriarch to another. In all circumstances, whether under a tree, upon a rock, in the darkness of a cave or deep in a glen, the Law has been set forth and transmitted by such signs to whoever possessed the right qualifications. . . .

"What is that which we call the 'Law'? It is the Truth inherent in all its perfection in every living creature. The sage possesses it in no greater measure than does the ordinary man. Enlarge it and it will fill the universe; restrict it and it can be contained in a fraction of an inch. Yesterday or to-day, it undergoes no change or variation. All that the Buddhas have taught, whether as the Mahāyāna, the Hīnayāna, the pseudo or the authentic, the partial or the complete—all are embraced in it. This is the meaning of the 'Law.'

"Everything the world contains—grass and trees, bricks and tile, all creatures, all actions and activities—are nothing but manifestations of this Law. Therefore is it said that all phenomena in the universe bear the mark of this Law. If the significance of this were only grasped, then even without the appearance in this world of a Tathāgata (Buddha), the enlightenment of man would be complete, and even without the construction of this Hall the propagation of the Law would have achieved realization.

"As for myself, appearing before you today on this platform, I have nothing special to offer as my own interpretation of the Law. I merely join myself with all others—from the founder Shākya Tathāgata, the other Buddhas, bodhisattvas, saints and arhants, to all those here present, including patrons and officials, the very eaves and columns of this hall, lanterns and posts, as well as all the men, animals, plants and seeds in the boundless ocean of existence—to keep the Wheel of the Law in motion.

"On such an occasion as this, you may say, 'What can we

[1] Hui-k'o, the second Chinese patriarch, cut off his arm to show that he would stop at nothing in his determination to pursue Zen, and thereupon was accepted by Bodhidharma as his student.
[2] The ceremony of transmission was performed secretly at night to shield Hui-neng, the sixth Chinese patriarch, from the recriminations of a disappointed contender for that honor.

do?' " Holding out his cane, he exclaimed, "Look here, Look here! Don't you see Shākyamuni here right now walking around on the top of my cane? He points to heaven and then to earth, announcing to the entire audience, 'Today I am born again here with the completion of this new hall. All saints and sages are assembling here to bring man and heaven together. Every single person here is precious in himself, and everything here—plaques, paintings, square eaves and round pillars—every single thing is preaching the Law. Wonderful, wonderful it is, that the true Law lives on and never dies. At Vulture Peak, indeed, this Law was passed on to the right man!'

"It is thus that Shākya, the most venerable, instructs us here. It is the teaching which comes down to men in response to the needs of their situation. But perhaps, gentlemen, you wish to know the state of things before Shākya ever appeared in his mother's womb?" [He tapped his cane on the floor] "Listen, Listen!"

[From the *Taishō daizōkyō*, Vol. 80, pp. 460c–61a]

Letter of Takuan to the Shōgun's Fencing Master

Takuan Sōho (1573–1645) was a commanding figure in Rinzai Zen at the beginning of the Tokugawa period. In 1628 Takuan, representing a radical group at Daitokuji in Kyoto, where he had received his training, protested against Bakufu regulations and the government's intervention in temple affairs in order to increase its administrative power. As a result, in the following year, he was exiled to the province of Dewa in the northern part of Japan. In 1632 he was released, but was not permitted to leave Edo to return to Daitokuji until two years later. While he was in Kyoto, some of his admirers who were influential in the Bakufu asked him repeatedly to meet the third Shōgun, Iemitsu. Takuan could no longer refuse their urgent requests and reluctantly went to Edo in 1635, taking residence with Yagyū Tajima no Kami, a great fencing master of the day.

The story has it that Iemitsu once asked Yagyū the secret of his knowledge of swordsmanship. Yagyū replied that he had mastered the art through the practice of Zen under Takuan. At their first meeting the Shōgun was very much attracted by Takuan, and thereafter would not release him from Edo. The Zen Master, however, had no ambition to associate with the Shōgun and other dignitaries of high rank. He complained to his students about his unfortunate circumstances, for his cherished desire was to be free to live out his life, unnoticed by the world, in a quiet mountain spot. In order to keep Takuan near him, therefore, the Shōgun built the Tōkaiji in Edo and installed him as its head.

With an unassuming attitude, Takuan taught the Shōgun, daimyō, and the commonfolk. He was a man of wide learning and left thousands of letters written to his followers and other writings in simple Japanese which were readily accessible even to the humble people. The following translation is a part of a letter written for Yagyū Tajima no Kami at the latter's request, in which he explains the secrets of the mastery of swordsmanship by means of Zen and includes cautionary words in a Confucian vein concerning his student's conduct.

Where should a swordsman fix his mind? If he puts his mind on the physical movement of his opponent, it will be seized by the movement; if he places it on the sword of his opponent, it will be arrested by the sword; if he focuses his mind on the thought of striking his opponent, it will be carried away by the very thought; if the mind stays on his own sword, it will be captured by his sword; if he centers it on the thought of not being killed by his opponent, his mind will be overtaken by this very thought; if he keeps his mind firmly on his own or on his opponent's posture, likewise, it will be blocked by them. Thus the mind should not be fixed anywhere.

Should someone say: "If the mind is fixed somewhere external to the body, it will be seized by the point on which the mind is fixed, and as a result [the swordsman] will be slain; the best thing to do is to bear the mind firmly in the abdomen and to move freely according to the movements of his opponent." Fine, but when considered from the highest viewpoint of Buddhist Dharma, a practice such as focusing the mind in the abdomen is vulgar and far from being perfect; it belongs to the stage of the monk just beginning his Zen training. . . . If he tries to center his mind in the abdomen, the mind will be made to stop by the very thought that one must not let it go; he can be neither free nor spontaneous in his activities.

Should someone ask: "In that case where on our body should the mind be fixed?" I would answer: If your mind is fixed on the right hand, it will be seized by the right hand

and the movements of the other parts of your body will be imperfect; if your mind is focused on the eyes or on the legs, it will be the same. Where should your mind be kept? If your mind is not fixed anywhere, it will pervade throughout the body; then should the hands be in action, they will function to their fullest capacity. If your mind is fixed on a certain spot, it will be seized by that spot and no activities can be performed efficiently. . . . In short, not to fix your mind anywhere is essential. Not fixed anywhere, the mind is everywhere. If the mind is fixed at any particular external point, the other points are left unguarded. When the mind is made so that it is not fixed at any point, it is able to pervade throughout the whole.

A distinction should be made between the Original Mind and the deluded mind. The Original Mind is the mind that pervades throughout the body without being attached to any particular point. The deluded mind is that which is firmly fixed on a particular spot. When fixed on a spot, the Original Mind turns into the deluded mind. When the Original Mind is lost, the performance of the bodily activities is hindered. Do not let the Original Mind be lost. The Original Mind is like water which flows freely without staying at one spot, whereas the deluded mind is like ice, with which you cannot even wash your face. . . .

There is a passage [in the *Vajracchedikā Sūtra*] that says: "The mind should operate without abiding anywhere." When an intention to do something arises, your mind stops at that intention. It means that without stopping at anything the mind should work. An expert in the arts is someone whose mind works fully, yet whose mind is bound to no particular [thought or object]. Out of bondage attachment grows, and transmigration takes place; the stopping of the mind is the bondage which causes birth and death [i.e., transmigration]. . . . It is important not to fix your mind on what you see or hear. The concentration of the mind is not the ultimate in Buddhism; it belongs to the stage of apprenticeship, when you are trying not to lose the mind or not to be disturbed. If you practice concentration for years, you will reach the stage where you will be free [from attachment] to whatever object you direct your mind. The ultimate stage is that in which "the mind should operate without abiding anywhere." The concentration of mind belongs to the stage wherein you make an effort to guard your mind from functioning freely, in the belief that once the mind is left free it will become disturbed. The concentration of the mind is a temporary discipline; to assume this attitude at all times would not be to advantage. It is like tying a cat with a rope to prevent it from catching a baby sparrow which is tied up nearby. If your mind is tied down by a rope as is the cat, your mind cannot function properly. It is better to train the cat not to harm the sparrow when they are together, so that it can be free to move anywhere rather than be tied. This is the meaning of the passage, "The mind should operate without abiding anywhere." Set your mind free as you would set the cat free; then your mind will work freely, unfixed, wherever it may go. Apply this to the mastery of swordsmanship: Do not let your mind stop, trying to figure out how to strike; forget how; strike without fixing your mind on the opponent. The man who opposes you is empty, and you yourself are empty; regard your striking hands and the sword as empty, yet do not be seized by [the concept of] emptiness. . . . The same can be said of dancing. Merely hold your fan and take steps. As long as your thoughts are on how to improve the gestures of your hands and the movement of your legs and how to dance well, your dance cannot be called first-rate. When your mind is still captured by your hands and legs, your performance is not yet perfected. Performances done without having abandoned the mind are dull. . . .

You are an unrivaled master of the sword among people today and compare favorably with the expert swordsmen of the past; you are now a renowned man with a high official title and a fief. Do not forget, day or night, your grave obligations [to your lord, Shōgun Iemitsu]; think only of how you can repay these obligations and fulfill your duty of loyalty. . . . A moment of thought may develop into good or evil; consider well the inception of good and evil. When you abstain from evil and practice good, your mind will naturally be sincere. . . . I have heard that, in choosing your pupils, you have a tendency [to select or reject them on the basis of your likes and dislikes and not of their intrinsic goodness]; I do not like this practice of yours. . . .

As to the bad behavior of your son, it is wrong to blame him for his evil acts while you yourself are acting improperly. You must correct yourself first before you give him any advice; then he will be guided towards the right path. . . .

To adopt or to reject anything should be done on the basis of propriety. Never accept bribes from daimyō, taking advantage of your present position of being the favorite of the lord; do not forget your sense of propriety because of greed. Your liking for wild dancing, your conceit in your own Nō performances, and your forcing of other daimyō to join in these performances, are simply the results of a disease of the mind. I have heard also that you strongly recommend to your lord those who are good at making flattering remarks. You must seriously reflect upon these points again and again. It brings to mind the poem [composed by Hōjō Tokiyori]:

Kokoro koso kokoro   Mind deludes mind:
           mayowasu   Such is mind;
        kokoro nare   Let not the mind be
Kokoro ni kokoro   Unmindful toward the
        kokoro yurusuna   mind.

[From *Takuan Oshō zenshū*, Vol. V, Fudōchi shim-myōroku, pp. 12–27]

Night Thoughts of Takuan

"Birth and death (*saṃsāra*) are no other than Nirvāna"; "defilement (*kleśa*) is no other than enlightenment (*bodhi*)"; "delusion and enlightenment are non-dual"—such expressions teach us that beings are essentially in an empty and serene state in which there is no birth or death. The essential nature of defilement is no other than perfect enlightenment; what we think of as delusion is no other than enlightenment. All phenomena are like phantoms or dreams; when one perceives that they are essentially non-existent, one sees no particular marks of individuation in them and thus is free from attachment to them. In order to preclude attachment this view of the non-existence of everything is taught. When this view is thoroughly realized, attachments will be severed. Having achieved this, upon returning to the world

one finds that there are no particular marks to be destroyed
and no attachments to be severed.

The present followers of Zen, however, attach themselves
to the particular marks and cling to them. They seize upon
the expressions accomplished masters have uttered out of a
profound experience and flash them about as if they themselves had shared the same experience. The language employed is the same, but there exists as great a gap in the
understanding of present-day Zen followers and the understanding of their masters as there is between heaven and
earth. They talk about Zen as though they were describing
colors with their eyes closed.

Everything should be done spontaneously. It should not
be done as a result of premeditation. What is premeditated
in the mind does not correspond to reality. There is nothing
to which emptiness cannot accommodate, be it long, short,
square, or round; only the mind, kept empty, can tackle
anything that confronts it.

When the mind is preoccupied, one cannot judge matters
objectively because the preoccupation blocks the mind. The
mind that is occupied leaves no room to accept anything
else. A guest room can be used to receive guests only when
it is empty. If occupied, where is there room for guests?
Everything which appeals to the mind is like the guests, and
our mind is like the guest room. When the guest room is
cleared, only then can the guests be received and entertained
in a desired manner. . . . When the clouds do not appear,
the sky is clear of objects and remains serene. The clouds
come and float in the sky, but the space the clouds occupy
is not prepared in advance. After the clouds move away,
there remains no trace in the sky. . . .

> [From *Takuan Oshō zenshū*, Vol. V, *Tōkai yawa*,
> p. 19; pp. 84–85]

The Autobiography of Hakuin

*Hakuin (1686–1769) is the father of modern Rinzai Zen; all
present-day masters of this sect claim descent from him. He was an
extraordinary man, indomitable in his search for the truth of Zen.
A sincere and heroic personality, he gave all his efforts to the revival*

of Zen Buddhism. He rejected formalistic and intellectual Zen, as well as the syncretism with the Nembutsu practice which was popular in China at the time. Denouncing all secular ambitions among the clergy, he dedicated himself to the promotion of what he considered true Zen. Among his followers were all classes of people—farmers, samurai, daimyō, both men and women. Like Takuan he taught those who seriously sought after Zen for its own sake, regardless of their social background.

Hakuin is unusual among Zen masters in that he left many writings in colloquial Japanese, as well as in the literary language and in Kambun. These are often in the form of letters or essays written to his followers. He was a versatile master who excelled not only in writing but also in painting, calligraphy, and sculpture. We find in Hakuin's writings a most detailed account of his Zen experience; similar descriptions are seldom to be found in other Zen literature. Translated here are excerpts from a collection of long letters known as Orategama. These include his autobiography, his approach to Zen, and his personal experience of it.

When I was seven or eight years old, I went with my mother to a temple and heard a sermon on the description of the hells found in the *Maha shikan*.[1] The monk eloquently recounted the states of suffering in the various hells where beings moan aloud in pain, where they are continuously tormented, suffer from extreme heat, or where their bodies are dismembered like the petals of the red lotus. The monk described things so vividly that he terrified both clergy and laymen alike and made their hair stand on end. Returning home, I counted the number of killings I had committed as far as I could recall; I became horrified and did not know what to do. I was goose flesh all over. In secret I took up the chapter on Avalokiteshvara (*Lotus Sūtra* XXV) and the *dhāranī* (magic spells) on great compassion and recited them day and night.

One day when my mother and I were taking a bath together, my mother asked the maid to add more firewood as she wanted the water warmer. Gradually my skin became sensitive to the heat. The [iron] bathtub started to rumble. Imagining what happened in the hells, I let out an anguished scream, so loud that it was heard by our neighbors.

[1] *Mo-ho chih-kuan*, by the T'ien-t'ai master, Chih-k'ai.

After this incident, the wish to become a Buddhist monk constantly crept into my mind, but my parents would not consent. Meanwhile, I commuted to the temple regularly to recite the sūtras and to learn the Chinese classics. At fifteen I left home to live in a monastery. At that time I made a vow: unless I could gain the power by which fire could not burn my body nor water drown me, I would not take rest even should I die. I spent days and nights reciting sūtras and practicing prostration single-heartedly [in front of the image of Buddha]. I tested my body by touching my thigh with a glowing iron rod, but I felt pain as I would ordinarily. Disappointed, I said to myself: "I took the monastic vows against my parents' will but I have seen no sign of progress."

I had heard that the *Lotus Sūtra* was the king of all sūtras, respected even by the ghosts and the gods. They say that when those who are suffering in the other world, still in search of salvation, make contact with people in this world, they never fail to specify [that] the *Lotus Sūtra* [should be recited for their salvation]. I then thought that if recitation by someone else removes the sufferings of another, how much more effective it would be if it were read by oneself. It also seemed to me that the *Sūtra* must contain profound mystical doctrines. Thereupon, I picked up the *Lotus Sūtra* and in secret started reading it, only to discover that it was filled with parables, with the exception of the sections on the doctrines which state that there is only One Vehicle [the final and perfect Mahāyāna] and that all dharmas (phenomena) are in [the state of] Nirvāna. If this sūtra had any influence, I thought, the Chinese classics and the books of all the other schools must be equally effective; there was no particular reason why this sūtra should be esteemed so highly. The great hopes I had had were completely dashed. This disappointment occurred when I was sixteen years old.

At nineteen I had a chance to read the *Shōjūsan*[2] which

---

[2] Ch. *Cheng-tsung-tsan*, a work in four chüan (1254) by Hsi-sou Shao-t'an, giving biographical information, stories and verses of seventy famous Ch'an priests of the T'ang and Five Dynasties periods.

tells how the master Gantō was killed by bandits. His voice is said to have resounded three *li*.[3] I wondered why so thoroughly accomplished a master as Gantō, who was like a unicorn or phoenix among monks or like a dragon in the ocean of Buddhism, could not escape the swords of the bandits. [If such a man was unable to escape from danger] how could I avoid the sticks of the demons in hell? What good was it to practice Zen in search of the truth? What a fraud Buddhism was! I regretted that I had thrown myself into this group of weird and wicked men. I was tormented, wondering what to do next, and did not eat for three days. For a long time afterward I felt disappointment in Buddhism. Staring at Buddhist images and sūtras was like staring at mud. To lessen my grief, I concentrated on non-Buddhistic books and took pleasure in poetry and prose.

At twenty-two I went to the province of Wakasa. While attending a gathering in honor of Kidō[4] I suddenly found myself with a glimmer of awakening. Later, in the province of Iyo, I read and was stimulated by the *Busso Sankyō*,[5] and again found myself meditating intensely. Without a single moment of rest, I concentrated on "*Mu*," [6] but was grieved at being unable to achieve the state of perfect unity, whether asleep or awake.

In the spring of my twenty-fourth year, I was painfully struggling at the Eiganji in the province of Echigo. I slept neither day nor night, forgetting either to eat or sleep. A great doubt suddenly possessed me, and I felt as if frozen to death in the midst of an icy field extending thousands of *li*. A sense of an extraordinary purity permeated my bosom. I could not move. I was virtually senseless. What remained was only "*Mu*." Although I heard the master's lectures in the Lecture Hall, it was as though I were listening to his dis-

[3] The Chinese master Yen-t'ou, who had promised his disciples that he would give a shout on his deathbed; therefore, when surrounded by the bandits, he cried out aloud, unafraid and triumphant.

[4] Hsü-t'ang Chih-yü (1185–1269). Famed Sung master.

[5] Fo-tsu san-ching, a Ming dynasty collection including two sūtras used in Ch'an (Zen) and a work of the T'ang master, Wei-shan (771–853).

[6] Reference is to the first kōan in *Mumonkan* (*Wu-men-kuan*), usually the kōan on which the student begins his Zen study.

course from some sixty or seventy steps outside the Hall,
or as if I were floating in the air. This condition lasted for
several days until one night I heard the striking of a temple
bell. All at once a transformation came over me, as though
a layer of ice were smashed or a tower of jade pulled down.
Instantly I came to my senses. I felt like the master (Gantō);
[I realized that although he was slain] he had lost nothing
throughout the three divisions of time. Former doubts were
completely dissolved, like ice which had melted away. "How
marvelous! How marvelous!" I cried out aloud. There was no
cycle of birth and death from which I had to escape, no
enlightenment for which I had to seek. There was no point
even in devoting time to the seventeen hundred kōan which
have been handed down. My pride soared like a mountain,
and my arrogance surged like the high tide. In my own secret
thoughts I felt that there had never been anyone in the past
two or three hundred years who had experienced so intense
and joyous a breakthrough as I had. Shouldering this experience, I immediately set out on the road to the province
of Shinano.

I interviewed Master Shōju[7] and presented in verse my
insight on enlightenment. The master took the verse in his
left hand, saying, "This is what you have understood through
your brain." Holding out his right hand, he said, "Now show
me your intuitive insight."

"If there is anything at all to present to the master, it
should be vomited away," I said, and made a vomiting sound.

The master asked, "What is your understanding of
Jōshū's[8] 'Mu'?"

I replied, "How can 'Mu' be attached to the hands and
legs?"

The master twisted my nose and said, "It is still attached
to your hands and legs." I was about to ask what he meant,
when the master burst out laughing and said, "This is a
poor devil attached to the scriptures." I ignored him. He
continued, "Do you think you understand enough?"

"What do you think is missing?" I asked.

[7] Shōju Etan (1642–1721), Hakuin's teacher.
[8] Chao-chou Ts'ung-shen (778–897). One of the most famous
T'ang masters, mentioned in numerous kōan.

The master began to tell me the story of the death of Master Nansen.[9] I covered my ears and started to leave. The master called me back, "Senior monk!" I turned toward him. "You poor devil attached to the scriptures!" he added. From that time on whenever the master saw me he called me "a poor devil attached to the scriptures."

One evening the master sat cooling himself on the veranda. I again presented him with my verse on enlightenment. The master said, "Delusions and fancies!" I shot back, "Delusions and fancies!" Grabbing me, the master showered me with twenty or thirty blows of his fists and finally threw me off the veranda. It was the evening of the fourth day of the fifth month, after a long spell of rain. I lay in the mud as if dead, unconscious, breathless and unable to move. The master was on the veranda laughing aloud. After a little while I regained my senses. I rose and bowed to him. Perspiration ran down my entire body. The master shouted, "Here is a poor devil attached to the scriptures!" From then on I took up serious study of the kōan on the death of Nansen, not stopping to eat or sleep.

One day I experienced some sort of enlightenment. I entered the master's room and expressed my views on the kōan. They were wrong. The master only repeated, "a poor devil attached to the scriptures." I thought to myself that I had better leave and try elsewhere.

One day I went to beg food in the town. A madman seized a broom and was about to hit me; unexpectedly I experienced a sudden breakthrough of the kōan on the death of Nansen that I had hitherto been unable to penetrate. Furthermore, it seemed to me that one after the other the kōans of the Masters Sōzan[10] and Daie[11] were spontaneously solved. I returned [to the temple] and presented my insights on them. The master said neither "yes" nor "no," but merely smiled. But from that time on he stopped calling me "a poor devil attached to the scriptures." After this happened, I experienced enlightenment two or three times, accompanied

---

[9] Nan-ch'üan P'u-yüan (748–834). A well-known T'ang Master.

[10] T'ang Master. Biography unknown.

[11] Ta-hui Ts'ung-k'ao (1089–1163). Ch'an Master of Sung, famed advocate of the use of kōan.

by an intense ecstasy. Some experiences can be expressed, but others, to my regret, cannot be put into words. I wandered about as if I were in a daze.

I returned [to Daishōji in Numazu] and took care of my sick old master. One day I read a verse sent by Sokkō[12] to his disciple Nampo:[13] "At the gate, when I saw you off, there was a bamboo bush; its leaves, stirred by the pure breeze, also waved to you." I felt a great joy as though I had found light in a dark night and unconsciously cried out aloud: "Today for the first time I am the complete master of words." I stood up and then bowed down.

After that I went to the province of Ise. One day I was walking during a heavy rainfall and the water reached as high as my knees. All of a sudden I understood even more clearly the deep meaning of the kōan of Master Daie. I was so happy that I could not remain standing; I fell into the water, and forgot completely about getting up again. My clothes and packages were soaked. A startled passer-by offered to help me up. As he did, I let out a hearty laugh. The man thought I was mad.

In the winter of the same year, while I was practicing Zen at the Shinoda monastery (Inryōji) in the province of Izumi, I experienced a state of enlightenment on hearing the snow fall. Next year at the Reishō monastery in the province of Mino, while I was doing the walking meditation, I had a great ecstatic delight which surpassed any I had experienced before.

At the age of thirty-two I settled in this dilapidated temple [Shōinji]. In a dream one night my mother handed me a purple silk robe. When I lifted it I felt great weights in both sleeves. Examining it, I found in each sleeve an old mirror about five or six inches in diameter. The reflection of the right-hand mirror penetrated deep into my heart. My own mind, as well as mountains and rivers, the entire earth, became serene and bottomless. The left-hand mirror had no luster on its entire surface. Its face was like that of a new iron pan not yet touched by fire. Suddenly I became aware

---

[12] Pseudonym for Hsü-t'ang Chih-yü, see n. 4, p. 384.
[13] Nampo Jōmyō (1235–1309). Also known as Daiō Kokushi, the founder of the line of Rinzai Zen to which Hakuin belonged.

that the luster on the left-hand mirror surpassed that of the right by a million times. After this incident, the vision of all things was like looking at my own face. For the first time I realized the meaning of the words, "The eyes of the Tathāgata behold the Buddha-nature."

After this experience I read the *Hekigan roku* (*Pi-yen lu*) and found that my comprehension of it differed greatly from what my previous understanding had been. Then later one night I took up the *Lotus Sūtra*, and read it again. Immediately I perceived the perfect, true, and ultimate significance of the *Lotus* and all my initial doubts cleared away. I recognized the many errors I had made in some of my earlier understandings of enlightenment. I found myself in tears. The practice of Zen, one must realize, is by no means simple. . . .

[From *ORategama*, in *Zemmon hōgoshū*, II, 81–85]

The Dynamic Practice of Zen

FROM A LETTER OF HAKUIN TO A RETAINER
OF LORD NABESHIMA

Your letter was delivered to me by messenger yesterday. I imagine you must feel greatly relieved at having satisfactorily completed your duty of entertaining the Koreans. I appreciate your inquiry about my health; I am fine as always. It is excellent that you have been making efforts in the practice of Zen in both its active and quiescent aspects. I agree with all of the opinions you expressed in your letter and am very much pleased with your accomplishments.

Virtually all Zen students, if they get started in the wrong direction with their practice, tend toward the extremes of either the quiescent aspect or the active aspect of Zen practice, and so fall into a state of either depression or distraction, which results in crushing pains in the lungs and loss of vitality, and may even lead to their becoming incurably ill. . . .

When I was young I entertained an incorrect understanding of Zen practice and put my efforts in the wrong direction. I believed that the goal of Buddhism was to achieve a perfect tranquility of mind; therefore, I eschewed activity, always sought after quietude in some gloomy corner, and practiced a dead Zen. I was obsessed by trivial matters and easily upset. Being unable to practice active Zen single-mindedly, I could not restrain my emotions and was often unsettled and despondent. I was weak in both mind and body; sweat poured from beneath my arms and my eyes were dim with tears; being depressed all the time I lacked the urge to take up the challenge to gain the truth of Buddhism.

A bit later, fortunately, I was guided by an excellent master[1] and received from him secret instructions on the introspective method [of hygiene]. While I practiced this method faithfully for three years, my chronic ailment gradually disappeared, as frost or snow melts in the rays of the morning sun. Up to then the kōan seemed implausible, impenetrable, incomprehensible, and impossible to solve—had seemed indeed like blocks of ice filled with poison. With the recovery from my illness this difficulty disappeared. Now I am seventy years old, but my vitality is ten times as great as when I was thirty or forty. I am robust in spirit and mind; I need not even lie down to sleep. Sometimes I spend two, three, or as many as seven days without lying down at all, but my mental power never declines. Surrounded by three to five hundred bellicose disciples, I have given lectures on the scriptures or on the collections of Zen masters' sayings for thirty or fifty days at a time, never feeling fatigue. I am convinced that this is due to the power derived from the practice of the introspective method.

If you pay attention to the soundness of your body and exert yourself in the practice of introspective Zen, you will experience enlightenment frequently without consciously seeking it. Do not discriminate between active and quiescent Zen; just keep practicing assiduously. This attitude is of primary importance. Often you may think that you are making quite a bit of progress in the practice of quiescent Zen but not in the practice of active Zen. A man who clings to quiescent Zen can never succeed in active Zen. If by chance he steps into the hustle and bustle of the world, the vitality which he thought he had obtained will be completely lost; he will find himself so lacking in vigor as to be inferior to the man who has had no Zen practice at all. A trifle will

---

[1] Hakuyū, semilegendary hermit, said to have lived in a cave in the hills of Shirakawa, near Kyoto.

upset him, make him nervous, and cause him to act like a coward. If this is the result of practicing Zen, then where is the vitality one is supposed to obtain through this practice? The Master Daie said: "Zen practiced in a state of activity is superior a millionfold to that practiced in quietude." The Master Hakuzan[2] has also said that unless Zen is practiced in a state of activity, there is no way of perfecting one's effort; it is like trying to cross a steep mountain ridge as narrow as a sheep's forehead, with a hundred and twenty pound load on one's back. By writing this I am not particularly trying to turn you against practice in quietude and thus consciously to promote practice in a state of activity. What is essential is to practice Zen wholeheartedly, to such an extent that you are unaware of either the active or quiescent states. It is said, therefore, that a true student of Zen is unaware of the act of moving while he is in motion and of sitting while he sits. In order to plumb the very depths of your true Nature and to gain a genuine power which you can use freely in any circumstances, nothing surpasses the practice of Zen in a state of activity.

Suppose we have in our possession so many gold coins that we must ask someone to guard them. The man appointed shuts up the room, bars the door with an iron chain, sits near the gold and guards it. The gold therefore cannot be stolen by an outsider. Yet we cannot say that the safety of the gold is the result of this man's merit. It is like the self-centered practice of the Hīnayānists who seek enlightenment only for themselves. Now supposing this man were asked to deliver those gold coins to a certain place, and to do so must make his way past nests of thieves and outlaws swarming like bees and ants. If the man is courageous enough, he will wear a great sword at his waist, tuck up his skirts above the knees, fasten the gold to the end of a pole and take it fearlessly to that certain place, without once having to fight the thieves. Then certainly he should be praised as a hero of great merit and courage. This is like the perfect bodhisattva who seeks his own enlightenment and at the same time endeavors to lead people to salvation. The "gold coins" refer

[2] Po-shan Yüan-lai (1575–1650). Ming dynasty master of the Sōtō sect.

to the indomitable will in the practice of correct Zen; "thieves and outlaws swarming like bees and ants" indicate the delusions which derive from greed, defilement, passion, and opposition to the Noble Eightfold Path; "the man" signifies a Mahāyānist who practices the true Zen; "this certain place" refers to the other shore of Nirvāna, endowed with eternity, bliss, the Great Self, and purity. For these reasons, a student of Zen who penetrates into the mystery is encouraged to practice Zen in the midst of full activity.

Frequently the Hīnayānists of old are regarded with scorn, but I wonder if present-day students of Zen can equal them in the power of their insight and in the brilliance of their wisdom and virtue. The Hīnayānists were inferior in methods of discipline and were fond of quietude; they simply had no knowledge of the noble activities of a bodhisattva. Since they lacked the aspiration to establish a kingdom of Buddha, the Tathāgata compared them to pus-discharging foxes, and Vimalakīrti scolded them for being the kind of people who would burn off buds and cause seeds to rot.

The Third Patriarch said, "If one wishes to turn to the One Vehicle, one must have no aversion to the objects of the senses and the mind." [3] This does not mean that we should be attached to these objects, but that we must incessantly keep practicing Zen with the correct view, neither being attached to the objects of the senses and mind nor discarding them, but being like the waterfowl whose wings do not get wet even when submerged in water. It also means that if we try only to avoid the objects of the senses and mind and fear the eight kinds of wind that fan our mind,[4] we will fall unconsciously into the pit of the Hīnayānists, and thus never be able to attain the truth of Buddha.

The Master Yōka[5] said: "The power of insight obtained by the practice of Zen while in the midst of the objects of the senses will, like a lotus grown in the midst of fire, never be destroyed." This was not said to encourage us to indulge

[3] Seng-t'san's Hsin-hsin ming. Taishō daizōkyō, XLVIII, 376C.
[4] Profit, sorrow, slander, good reputation, praise, criticism, pain, and pleasure.
[5] Yung-chia Hsüan-chüeh (665–713). One of the outstanding disciples of Hui-neng, the Sixth Patriarch.

in the pleasures of the objects of the senses, but to have us be masters of our environment while still remaining surrounded by these objects, like the lotus flower which rises unsoiled above the muddy waters. Even a man living in a forest or in the fields, eating only once a day at six o'clock in the morning and practicing Zen day and night, finds it difficult to concentrate wholeheartedly on his discipline. How much more difficult is it for one who lives with his wife or brothers and sisters in the busy world! Unless one opens the eye [of wisdom] that sees into one's own Nature, one cannot expect to be united with [the truth of Buddha]. Therefore, the Master Bodhidharma said, "If one seeks to attain Buddhahood, one must see into one's own Nature."

If you suddenly gain insight into the true reality of all things as only the One Vehicle reveals them, since the very objects of the senses will be Zen meditation, and the five sense objects will be the One Vehicle, words, and silence, activity and quietude will always be found in the midst of Zen meditation. If you perfect this, your power of insight will be incomparably greater than that of a man who has practiced Zen in solitude in a forest; the difference between him and yourself will be like the difference between heaven and earth. . . .

The ordinary lotus, being an aquatic plant, withers when it is brought near to fire; is not fire then a dreadful enemy of the lotus? A lotus flower [*bodhi*, enlightenment] which blossoms in the midst of fire increases its beauty and glowing luster the more it faces the blazing flame. A man who practices Zen [in quietude], detesting the pleasures of the objects of the five senses, even if he may have mastered the discipline of emptying both *ātman* and the substantiality of things, and even if he may claim to have the clearest vision of enlightenment, once he has left quietude and become involved in activity, will be like a clam or shrimp out of water, or like a monkey without trees. He will have no vitality at all, and, like the lotus in water that is faced with fire, will wither immediately.

If you keep practicing Zen spiritedly and dauntlessly in the midst of the objects of the senses and mind, plunging your entire being into your study, completely losing yourself in concentration, not making the slightest error and summoning up your entire spirit, like the man who delivered the many gold coins safely, you will surely gain a great joy as if you had crushed an iron mountain to pieces, uplifted the basis of your own mind, and, trampling the root of birth and death, had dispersed it without a trace in empty space. You will be like the lotus blooming in the midst of fire, which increases its beauty and fragrance when it encounters the flame. Why is this so? Fire is no other than the lotus; the lotus is no other than fire!

[From Orategama in Zemmon hōgoshū II, 13–19]

ZEN AND THE ARTS

At the time Eisai and Dōgen ventured forth to China, the Japanese government had long since abandoned official relations with that country and took little interest in the course of events on the mainland. But the Mongol conquests of China and Korea in the thirteenth century suddenly posed a threat for the Japanese themselves, and when the Hōjō regency had to make momentous decisions Zen monks were chosen as its advisers because they were considered to have a first-hand knowledge of China. This was the beginning of a long history of secular service by Zen monks, especially in the realm of foreign affairs, which lasted almost until the seventeenth century. Later when the third Ashikaga Shogun Yoshimitsu (1358–1408) had successfully entered into foreign trade with the Chinese Ming dynasty in the hope of restoring the finances of the shogunate, he celebrated his new prosperity by building a great Zen monastery. Yoshimitsu in effect instituted a department of foreign affairs with a Zen monk as its head, and from his time onwards every delegation sent overseas by the government was led by a Zen monk. In the sixteenth century and later, local maritime potentates who engaged in foreign trade followed the example of the central government in appointing a Zen monk as commissioner or chief delegate. The influence of Zen in medieval Japan was thus not confined to religious activities but was also highly practical.

Because of the strategic position the Zen monks occupied in the government, it was not difficult for them to extend the influence of Zen teachings to much of medieval culture. Virtually the only institutions of popular education during the period were the *tera-koya* (temple schools) run by Zen monks. All literature came under the spell of Zen, although the influence of Zen is perhaps most striking in the Nō theatre, which had got its start under the tutelage of Esoteric Buddhism. The bare simplicity of the Nō stage and scenery is a reflection of Zen aesthetic principles, and the movements of the actors themselves are based largely on those of swordsmanship, with which Zen had many intimate connections. Sometimes we find Zen teachings voiced by characters in a Nō play, but it is more in the underlying aesthetic concepts that we may detect Zen's great influence on the Nō.

In painting, no less than in literature, Zen aesthetics played a role of considerable magnitude. Shingon Buddhism had emphasized the artistic aspects of religion and had been responsible for many works of lasting beauty, most characteristic of which were the elaborate Mandala and the polychromed images of the different bodhisattvas. With Zen, however, simplicity and suggestion came to assume a dominant role in Japanese painting. In place of the brightly colored images of raging Fudō or of the thousand-armed Kannon, we find monochrome sketches of Zen masters, of sweeping landscapes, or of a single bird on a withered bough.

The great influence on literature and art of Zen Buddhism did not originate in Japan. Already in Sung China, Zen had been considered to be one in essence with both poetry and painting, but although Zen reached the height of its influence at that time in China, its overall effect on secular culture appears of strictly limited magnitude when compared with that of Taoism and Confucianism. In Japan, however, Zen had no serious rivals at court or in the intellectual and artistic circles of the Ashikaga period. And Zen monks occupied a favorable position for asserting their leadership in cultural matters, particularly in poetry and painting, because their special contacts as trade commissioners with China enabled them to introduce into their poetry and paintings the latest continental developments, which greatly enhanced their prestige.

The influence of Zen on Japanese culture was not limited to literature and art. As has been mentioned, there was a close connection between Zen and the Japanese warrior. Many samurai found Zen's stern masculinity and emphasis on intuitive action particularly congenial. For the believer in Zen swordsmanship might even be considered "an art of protecting life" rather than a means of killing others, and during the Tokugawa period under Zen influence swordsmanship tended to become a peaceful art rather than a brutal contest.

Perhaps, however, Zen's influence was nowhere more marked than in the evolution of the Japanese tea ceremony. The cult of tea was not exclusively affiliated with Zen Buddhism; during the Tokugawa shogunate when Neo-Confucianism was the state philosophy, the tea ceremony came to be considered an effective means of training young women in the concept of *ri*, "ritual," here interpreted as the etiquette of the hearth. The tea cult also had its commercial aspects from the outset. Zen priests not only introduced the new beverage to Japan but also the pottery in which it was served, and the tea ceremony thus came to be not only a social attraction but a source of mercantile enterprise. These features of the background of the tea ceremony should not be ignored; nevertheless it remains true that it was the expression of many of the ideals of Buddhism, in particular of Zen Buddhism.

Three Zen masters were largely responsible for the growth of the tea cult in Japan. First was the founder of Japanese Zen, Eisai, who brought tea seeds home with him on his return from a second visit to China in 1191, and had them planted on a hillside near Kyoto. In 1214, as we have seen, he wrote the *Kissa yōjō-ki*, "Drink Tea To Nourish Life" in the hope of saving the Shogun Sanetomo from alcoholism by extolling the virtues of "the cup that cheers but does not inebriate."

In order to popularize the use of tea it was considered desirable to improve the quality of the cups in which it was served. Accordingly, when Dōgen visited China in 1222 to study Zen, he was accompanied by an artisan who later established a thriving center of pottery production in Japan.

The next step was to create a setting for the demonstration of the methods of enjoying the new drink. It thus happened that when another Zen master, Musō Kokushi (1275–1351), had built a simple cottage in a secluded garden for the purpose of solitary meditation, it was found agreeable to have a nonintoxicating beverage as a mild stimulant. The three elements of the tea ceremony—the actual beverage, the pottery, and the setting—having thus been supplied, a cult before long developed with the active participation of Zen masters.

The tea hut was considered to consist of three elements— the exterior of the hut, the garden, and the interior. These were equated with three prime characteristics of Buddhist teaching: the evanescence of all things, the selflessness of all elements (dharmas), and the bliss of Nirvāna.

Outside the cottage three things call one's attention to the first lesson in Buddhism, that life is everlasting change. The first is a little roof by the fence which, protecting the visitor from the weather, reminds him that nature is always changeable. This part is known as the *machiai*, or waiting house (a name which later acquired quite another meaning as a rendezvous for lovers). The second thing lies to the right in a thicket or under the shade of trees—a simple privy. Some may think that a privy hardly fits in with the exquisite refinement of the tea ceremony, but in fact it symbolizes better than anything else the incessant changes through which the human body passes. The third thing is the gate of the cottage, through which visitors constantly pass in and out, bending their heads and drawing up their legs as they do so, for the gate does not permit one to enter while standing upright.

The first lesson, the incessant changes of nature, is succeeded by the second one, in which three stone objects in the garden teach us the selflessness of the elements. These are the stepping stones, the stone water-basin, and the stone lantern, each silently teaching its lesson in selflessness. The flag-stones are willing to remain below and to be stepped on. The water-basin, where every visitor washes himself before entering the hut, may awaken the thought that the cleansing of the hands is made possible only by the willingness of the water to take away the dirt, the second example of selflessness. Lastly, there is a stone lantern which sheds a pale light. A little thought may lead to the realization of the selflessness of the wick, which is willing to be consumed in flame in order to illumine, however faintly, a dark corner of the garden.

The visitor is next led inside, into the room where the tea

is to be served. After virtually doubling his body in order to pass through the low door, he suddenly finds himself in a realm of the most absolute peace. The room is small—only nine feet square and high—but everything in it is a marvel of purity and simplicity.

The first thing that greets the visitor is the scent of incense, which magically and indefinably transforms the atmosphere. Not only by its fragrance but by the faint wisp of its smoke does the incense catch the imagination. The ever-rising smoke symbolizes the constant aspiration of the terrestrial towards the celestial.

While the visitor sits motionlessly, watching in silence the course of the smoke, he is certain to hear the cries of a solitary bird flying by the hut, or the dripping of water in the fountain outside, or the rustle of the wind in the pines above the roof. Like the pealing of a distant temple bell, such sounds come from nowhere and lose themselves in timelessness, to awaken the enveloping silence from which all music comes and into which all music returns. Because these sounds are so fleeting, so transitory, the presence of silence is felt all the more profoundly. A moment has communion with eternity when sound meets silence to create music: this is the Buddhist philosophy of music expressed in the Avataṁsaka doctrines.

At the far end of the room, in the center, is an alcove in which hangs a scroll painting. Before it flowers are arranged. These two finite examples of form and color help to make visible the infinite, just as a single note can make us more aware of the eternal silence. Without forms or color the immense space surrounding us would remain forever a stupendous blank, an unnamable vacuum. When lines or colors cut through infinite space, painting, which is the meeting of the finite with the infinite, comes into being. The *Lotus Sūtra* says, "Everything finite tells of infinity."

The appeal of the infinite having thus been made to the senses of smell, hearing, and sight, the visitor is now ready for the enjoyment of the tea. He will be mistaken, however, if he expects to witness anything extraordinary in the preparation. The host is seated by a small open fire with the paraphernalia required, including bamboo implements, lacquerware, pots, kettles, and silk napkins. There is not a single thing which the average Japanese family does not possess, for, as the Zen masters were accustomed to say, "Religion is a most ordinary thing." The teacups are somewhat larger than the usual ones and may be works of art, but they are made of nothing more extraordinary than clay; to the Zen believer the transformation of clay into a lovely teacup is religion itself.

In the actual preparation of the tea, the host must pay special attention to four things—the fire, the water, the spoon, and the bamboo whisk. The first two are powerful elements which in other circumstances require all of man's efforts to control; the second two, the spoon to measure the powdered tea and the whisk to stir it, require delicacy and care in order to ensure a perfect balance. When the host has placed the proper measure of tea in the cup, he pours in boiled water and stirs the mixture with the whisk until it is exactly right. Then it is placed before the visitor, who must lift the cup in both hands, feeling its texture and warmth. He drinks the tea, not in one gulp but three sips, savoring the liquid as refreshing as some precious elixir though made of a most common, ordinary leaf. Thus also is sometimes transformed the common clay of humanity into an arhant, a bodhisattva, or a Buddha.

BIBLIOGRAPHY

Anesaki, Masaharu. *History of Japanese Religion; with Special Reference to the Social and Moral Life of the Nation.* London: Kegan Paul, Trench and Trübner, 1930.

————. *Nichiren, the Buddhist Prophet.* Cambridge, Mass.: Harvard University Press, 1916.

Āryadeva. *Cittavisuddhiprakarana.* Edited by P. B. Patel. Calcutta: Visva-Bharati, 1949.

Asanga. *Mahāyānasūtrālaṅkara.* Edited by Sylvain Levi. Paris: H. Champion, 1907–11.

Ashoka's Edicts. Translated by Jules Bloch as *Les Inscriptions d'Ashoka.* Paris: Société d'édition "Les Belles Lettres," 1950.

Ashvaghosha. *Buddhacarita.* Edited by E. H. Johnston. Calcutta: Baptist Mission Press, 1936.

Aṣṭasāhasrikā Prajñāpāramitā. Edited by R. Mitra. Calcutta: Asiatic Society of Bengal, 1888. (Bibliotheca Indica.)

Chi-tsang. *San-lun hsüan-i.* TD,* XLV: 1–11.

Chih-k'ai [Chih-i]. *Fa-hua hsüan-i.* TD, XXXII: 693.

Ching-te ch'uan-teng-lu. TD, LI: 336–37.

Coates, Harper Havelock, and Ryugaku Ishizuka. *Honen the Buddhist Saint, His Life and Teaching.* Tokyo: Kodokaku, 1930.

Conze, Edw. *Buddhist Texts Through the Ages.* Oxford: Bruno Cassirer, 1954.

Dengyō Daishi zenshū. 4 vols. Tokyo: Tendai-shū shūten kankō-kai, 1912.

* See entry for *Taishō daizōkyō* below.

Etō Sokuō. *Shūso to shite no Dōgen Zenji*. Tokyo: Iwanami shoten, 1949.

Fa-tsang. *Chin-shih-tzu chang*. TD, XLV: 663–67.

Gandavyūha Sūtra, new revised edition of Sanskrit text. Edited by D. T. Suzuki and Hokei Idzumi, Kyoto, 1949.

Hashida Kunihiko. *Shōbō genzō shakui*. 2 vols. Tokyo: Sankibō Busshorin, 1939–40.

Hsüan-chuang [Hsüan-tsang]. *Ch'eng-wei-shih lun*. TD, XXXI: 7, 10, 22, 25, 37, 38.

Idzumi, Hokei. "Vimalakirti's Discourse on Emancipation," *The Eastern Buddhist*, Vol. 3 (1924–25), No. 1, 55–59: No. 2, 138–53.

I-hsüan. *Lin-chi Hui-chao ch'an-shih yü-lu*. TD, XLVII: 497.

Kōbō Daishi to Nihon Bunka. Edited by Toganō Mitsudō. Kyoto: Rokudai shimpō-sha, 1929.

Kōbō Daishi zenshū. 5 vols. Tokyo: Yoshikawa Kōbun-kan; Kyoto: Rokudai shimpō-sha, 1910.

Lalitavistara. Edited by S. Lefmann. Halle, Buchhandlung des Waisenhauses, 1902–08.

Lankāvatāra Sūtra. Edited by Bunyiu Nanjio. Kyoto: Otani University Press, 1923.

Li-huo lun [Mou Tzu]. In *Hung-ming chi*. Compiled by Seng-yu. TD, LII: 1–7.

Lloyd, Arthur. *The Creed of Half Japan*. London: Smith, Elder, 1911.

——. *Shinran and His Works*. Studies in Shinshu Theology. Tokyo: Kyobunkwan, 1910.

Lotus of the Wonderful Law, [The Scripture of the]. *Miao-fa lien-hua ching (Saddharmapuṇḍarīka Sūtra)*. TD, IX: 8–9, 15.

Mahāprajñāpāramitā. Translated by Arthur Waley. In Conze (q.v.)

Maṇimēgalai. Edited by K. V. Settiyar. Tirunelvēli (Tinnevelly), 1946.

Moriyama, Shōshin, ed. *[Bunka shi jō yori mitaru] Kōbō Daishi den*. Tokyo: Buzan-ha Kōbō Daishi issen ippyaku-nen go-onki jimu-kyoku, 1934.

Pancaviṃsatisāhasrikā Prajñāpāramitā. Edited by N. Dutt. Calcutta: 1934.

Platform Sūtra of the Sixth Patriarch, Tun-huang ms. in Stein collection (S5475), British Museum.

Saddharmapuṇḍarīka. Edited by H. Kern and Bunyiu Nanjio. St. Petersburg: Academie imperiale des sciences, 1912.

Saraha. *Dohākosa*. Translated by D. S. Snellgrove. In Conze, q.v.

Satomi, Kishio. *Japanese Civilization, Its Significance and Realization: Nichirenism and the Japanese National Principles*. New York: E. P. Dutton, 1924.

Shan-tao, *Kuan ching shu*, TD, XXXVII: 272–73.

Shāntiveda. *Śikṣasamuccaya*. Edited by Cecil Bendall. St. Petersburg: Imperial Academy of Sciences, 1902. (Bibliotheca Buddhica)

Shinshū seiten. Kyoto: Chūgai shuppan, 1923.

Shōbō genzō zuimonki. Iwanami bunko, No. 530. Tokyo: Iwanami shoten, 1948.

Suvarṇaprabhāsa Sūtra [*Suvarṇabhāsottamasūtra*.] *Das Goldganzsūtra; ein Sanskrittext des Mahayāna buddhismus*. Edited by Johann Nobel. Leipzig: Otto Harassowitz, 1937.

Taishō [*shinshū*] *daizōkyō*. Edited by Takakusu Junjirō and Watanabe Kaigyoku. 85 vols. Tokyo: Taishō issaikyō kankō-kai, 1914–32 [abbrev. TD].

Takakusu, Junjiro. *The Essentials of Buddhist Philosophy*. Honolulu: University of Hawaii, 2d. ed., 1949.

Takuan oshō zenshū. Vol. V, Comp. by Taku'an oshō zenshū kankō kai, Tokyo: Kōgeisha, 1929.

T'an-luan .*Wang-sheng lun chu*. TD, XL: 827–36.

Tao-ch'o. *An-lo chi*. TD, XLVII: 8–11.

Tsuji, Zennosuke. *Nihon Bukkyō shi*. 10 vols. Tokyo: Iwanami shoten, 1944–55.

Tsung-mi, *Yüan jen lun*. TD, XLV: 707–10.

de Visser, M. W. *Ancient Buddhism in Japan*. Paris: P. Geuthner, 1928–35.

Yampolsky, Philip. *The Essentials of Salvation*. A Translation of the First Two Divisions of *Ōjō yōshū* by Genshin. Unpublished Master's thesis, Columbia University, 1948.

Zemmon hōgoshū. Comp. by Mori Daikyō. Tokyo: Kōyu-kan, 1921. Vol. 2.

Zenshū seiten, zokuhen. Comp. by Jimbo Nyoten. Tokyo: Muga sambō, 1916.

INDEX

WM. THEODORE DE BARY is Carpentier Professor of Oriental Studies in Columbia University, Chairman of the Committee on Oriental Studies and Chairman of the University Seminar on Oriental Thought and Religion. He is editor and co-author of the three-volume *Sources of Indian, Chinese and Japanese Tradition, Approaches to Asian Civilization, A Guide to Oriental Classics* and *Self and Society in Ming Thought.*

A. L. BASHAM is Professor in the School of Oriental Studies, Australian National University and author of *The Wonder that was India.* YOSHITO HAKEDA and PHILIP YAMPOLSKY are Associate Professors in the program of Buddhist studies at Columbia. Professor Hakeda is translator of *The Awakening of Faith,* a basic scripture of Mahayana Buddhism, and Professor Yampolsky of *The Platform Sutra of the Sixth Patriarch,* one of the most celebrated and controversial of Zen texts. LEON HURVITZ, Associate Professor of Japanese at the University of Washington, Seattle, has published a study of the T'ien-t'ai Buddhist teacher, Chih I. The late RYUSAKU TSUNODA was founding curator of the Japanese collection at Columbia, and co-author with Professor de Bary of *Sources of Japanese Tradition.*

The Best of the World's Best Books
COMPLETE LIST OF TITLES IN
THE MODERN LIBRARY

A series of handsome, cloth-bound books, formerly
available only in expensive editions.

MISCELLANEOUS